The First Epoch

PUBLICATIONS OF THE WISCONSIN CENTER
FOR PUSHKIN STUDIES

David M. Bethea
Series Editor

The First Epoch

The Eighteenth Century and the Russian Cultural Imagination

LUBA GOLBURT

THE UNIVERSITY OF WISCONSIN PRESS

Publication of this volume has been made possible, in part,
through support from the Andrew W. Mellon Foundation and from the
Wisconsin Center for Pushkin Studies in the Department of Slavic Languages of the
University of Wisconsin–Madison.

The University of Wisconsin Press
1930 Monroe Street, 3rd Floor
Madison, Wisconsin 53711-2059
uwpress.wisc.edu

3 Henrietta Street
London WC2E 8LU, England
eurospanbookstore.com

Library of Congress Cataloging-in-Publication Data

Golburt, Luba, author.
The first epoch : the eighteenth century and the Russian cultural imagination /
Luba Golburt.
pages cm. — (Publications of the Wisconsin Center for Pushkin Studies)
Includes bibliographical references and index.
ISBN 978-0-299-29814-2 (pbk. : alk. paper) — ISBN 978-0-299-29813-5 (e-book)
1. Russian literature—18th century—History and criticism.
2. Russian literature—19th century—History and criticism.
3. Russian literature—History and criticism—Theory, etc. I. Title. II. Series:
Publications of the Wisconsin Center for Pushkin Studies.
PG3007.G65 2014
891.709′002—dc23
2013027990

Contents

Illustrations

Acknowledgments

This is a book about diverse interpretations of the recent past. These interpretations emerged during an epoch when the pursuit of historicity first came to be seen as the most pressing of intellectual concerns. Even as the nineteenth century distanced itself from the age of empresses and the Enlightenment, the eighteenth century's legacies remained everywhere present: recognized and misapprehended, remembered and meaningfully forgotten. Any acknowledgment of prehistory or influence is necessarily partial and fragmented, for we are shaped by our recent pasts in a multitude of ways difficult to appreciate fully and consciously. This project, originating in a dissertation defended in the Comparative Literature Department at Stanford University, and maturing over the course of the past seven years of my tenure at UC Berkeley, has taken a decade to complete, in the process accruing temporal layers and pasts of its own and incurring many debts of guidance and friendship, most of which I hope to acknowledge here.

The thinking that went into this book, on everything from Pushkin to literary fashion to scholarly style, was shaped most lastingly by conversations with my principal dissertation advisor, Monika Greenleaf. Gregory Freidin and Hans Ulrich Gumbrecht offered invaluable guidance at the early stages of this project, revealing to me through their distinctive intellectual styles the multiple forms this book might take. Viktor Markovich Zhivov profoundly influenced my conception of the eighteenth century; his sudden passing as this book was nearing completion is a loss that will be felt continually and acutely. I have enjoyed much support and inspiration from my colleagues at UC Berkeley, all of whom are thanked here. Some debts call for individual acknowledgment. Irina Paperno set exacting standards of scholarly rigor and intellectual friendship; I am grateful for her incisive criticism of parts of this book and for her generous humanity. Harsha Ram has helped refine many of this book's arguments, sometimes by articulating their broader implications before these became visible to the author herself, sometimes simply by reciting poetry we both love in the halls of Dwinelle. Olga Matich read early drafts and reminded me every step of the way of the all-importance of scholarly "oomph." Anna Muza was always the ideal and most indulgent interlocutor for everything about, and around, this book. Anne Nesbet showed with understated certainty that the Romantic practice of thinking in and through nature is still viable. And Eric Naiman believed that Turgenev belonged in my story, and singled out the one sentence in this book that might become the kernel for the next one.

Discussions with many colleagues and friends have left traces through out this book: Polina Barskova, Elif Batuman, Paul Belasky, Boris Bernshtein, Zhenya Bershtein, David Bethea, Julie Buckler, Anne Dwyer, Victoria Frede, Nila Friedberg, Boris Gasparov, Amelia Mukamel Glaser, Stuart Goldberg, Gitta Hammarberg, Kate Holland, Hilde Hoogenboom, Robert P. Hughes, Lilya Kaganovsky, Andrew Kahn, Rita Kaushanskaya, Joachim Klein, Ilya Kliger, Konstantine Klioutchkine, Michael Kunichika, Marcus Levitt, John Malmstad, Michael Marrinan, Boris Maslov, Anne Eakin Moss, Igor Nemirovsky, Anna Nisnevich, Oleg Proskurin, Vera Proskurina, Renee Perelmutter, Irina Reyfman, Na'ama Rokem, Andreas Schönle, Tatiana Smoliarova, Victoria Somoff, Alyson Tapp, and William Mills Todd III. I am particularly grateful to Andrew Kahn and Irina Reyfman for expertly reviewing the manuscript for the University of Wisconsin Press and sharing their insights on many other occasions. This book was also immensely enriched by conversations with undergraduate and graduate students at UC Berkeley.

I have presented sections of this book at meetings of ASEEES, ACLA, and AATSEEL, as well as at colloquia at Amherst, Harvard, Stanford, UC Berkeley, UNC Chapel Hill, USC, and UW Madison, and am thankful to the audiences for their insights. Research for this project was made possible by the generous support of the UC Regents' Junior Faculty Fellowship, the Townsend Center for the Humanities Faculty Fellowship, the UC Berkeley Humanities Research Fellowship, and the COR Junior Faculty Research Grant; predoctoral work was funded by the Whiting Foundation Dissertation Fellowship, the Stanford Comparative Literature Department, and the Stanford Center for Russian and East European Studies Research Grant.

Initial versions of sections of chapters 2 and 5 first appeared in *The Slavic Review* under the titles "Derzhavin's Ruins and the Birth of Historical Elegy"

(65:4, Winter 2006) and "Catherine's Retinue: Fashion, Aging, and Historicism in the Nineteenth Century" (68:4, Winter 2009). Another section of Chapter 2, under the title "The Queen is Dead, Long Live the King: Paul's Accession and the Plasticity of Late Eighteenth-Century Panegyric," is forthcoming in a special issue of *Russian Literature*, ed. Joachim Klein.

I am grateful to Gwen Walker at the University of Wisconsin Press for supporting this project and patiently guiding me to its completion. Others from the press to whom I am grateful include Sheila Leary, Adam Mehring, Terry Emmrich, Marian Halls, Carla Marolt, Logan Middleton, Matthew Cosby, Brontë Wieland, Jonah Horwitz, and Elena Spagnolie. The book would have been much less readable without the sound and inspired editorial judgment of Avram Brown and the research assistance of Cameron Wiggins Bellm, Isobel Palmer, and Ian David. The index was prepared by Kirsten Painter.

Finally, I would like to thank my family—Yelena Zimon, Leonid Veksler, and Bela Veksler—for not asking too many questions on the content of this study, yet believing in the book's worth through all these years. I am grateful to Alexander Lusher, who stayed with this book almost through its completion. My grandmother Tusana Zimon influenced this book in a way that few grandmothers do, recording on tape numerous volumes of eighteenth- and nineteenth-century memoirs and novels, in the process becoming a veritable expert in the field. This book is dedicated to her and to my late great-grandmother, Berta Ratner, my very first (hi)storyteller.

The First Epoch

Introduction

The Eighteenth Century
as a Vanishing Point

Можно сказать, мой государь, что история нашего века будет интересна для потомков. Сколько великих перемен! Сколько странных приключений!
—Denis Fonvizin, letter to N. I. Panin, 26 January 1772[1]

Как посравнить, да посмотреть
Век нынешний и век минувший . . .
—A. S. Griboedov, *Woe from Wit* (1825)[2]

Какой теперь Вольтер; нынче дубина, а не Вольтер!
—F. M. Dostoevsky, "Bobok" (1873)[3]

И мертвым предкам непостижна
Потомков суетная речь.
—V. F. Khodasevich, "The centuries gone by over the world . . ." (1912)[4]

The Modern and Ancient Eighteenth Century

Standard literary histories date the energetic launch of Russian secular literature to the eighteenth century. In this period of rapid westernization, the modernizing state required a modernized vernacular culture, including new discourse-transmitting institutions (universities, social assemblies, the periodical press, various bodies of cultural administration, etc.) and enabling, both directly and indirectly, new literary genres (most importantly the ode, but also satire; elegy; Anacreontic verse; and various forms of drama, fiction, and critical prose). In these accounts, the eighteenth century stands as the originary moment of Russian modernity, both historically and literarily; it appears to bear directly on the nineteenth and twentieth centuries, which are seen, in turn, as perpetuating its legacy.[5] And yet the reception of this earlier era, starting already with the Pushkin generation of Russian writers in the 1820s and '30s, has also emphasized how subsequent periods overcame the eighteenth century's key political and cultural paradigms, its serfdom and patronage systems, with their concomitant gentry-centered culture and odic poetics. Throughout the history of its reception, the century's unquestioned importance as a turning point in the ongoing "civilizing process" is thus inevitably juxtaposed with its questionable relevance for each succeeding period.

This ambivalent status of the eighteenth century is one of the abiding paradoxes of Russian modernity, from the age of Pushkin to our own contemporary moment, or, I would speculate, at least until the demise of the Russian Empire in 1917. This book seeks to identify how the circumstances of the eighteenth century were transformed from a meaningful present into a seemingly meaningless past. One of my contentions will be that presents are changed into pasts not in a linear way, but inconsistently and incrementally, with parts being forgotten, remembered, and invented along the way. By focusing on the more imaginative appropriations of the eighteenth century, beginning in the late 1700s and ending at the beginning of the twentieth century, the book captures each successive epoch's reconsideration of a century that was continually being resurrected in order to be pronounced dead.

The dual status of the Russian eighteenth century as both modern/significant and archaic/superseded is reflected in the way its literature is taught, particularly in the West. Rarely, if ever, included in North American undergraduate Russian literature curricula, except perhaps in obligatory mentions of Peter and Catherine the Great, or as a specter haunting Pushkin's "The Bronze Horseman" ("Mednyi vsadnik," 1833), the eighteenth century is also becoming increasingly marginal to graduate-student training, in many programs covered no longer in coursework, but only in exam-geared tutorials. There is a sense that the eighteenth century requires specialized linguistic and cultural expertise, the sort of methodological and philological preparation whose appeal has been fading for at least the past few decades. With the possible exception of some texts by Gavrila Derzhavin, eighteenth-century literature appears not to speak to the contemporary educated reader, raised predominantly on Romantic aesthetics; it is deemed—perhaps not unduly—an acquired taste. At least in the general reader's history of Russian literature, the origins of its secular literary modernity have been transposed from the age of Peter I, Catherine II, and the empire to the age of Romanticism, Pushkin, and the nation. This is not to say that the field of Russian eighteenth-century studies has been dormant; on the contrary, the postmodern revival of academic interest in the Enlightenment and the eighteenth century in the West has fruitfully coincided with the post-Soviet sea change in styles of humanistic scholarship.[6] But insofar as this book attempts to register common perceptions and practices, the status of the Russian eighteenth century today appears as ambiguous as at any other point in its posthumous reception: it is the age that is uniquely both supremely significant and no longer capable of signifying.

In part, the period's paradoxical reception stems from the ambition of the very reforms that have made it so unique. This was the age of open experimentation and radical recharting of state and cultural policy on a historic scale, first sanctioned by Peter I. During this period, the gap between Russia and Europe was first broadcast as a problem and then forcibly, if incompletely, bridged. More broadly, it was the eighteenth century's optimistic pursuit of enlightenment and universalism that first cast culture as an international phenomenon, while also planting the seeds for its national formulations. This complex cultural import and development went hand in hand with the recognition of the need for public intellectual life, and with the establishment of the state and court at the center of Russian secular culture. These changes, and the conceptions of historical time associated with them, are crucial for this study. All-encompassing as these reforms had been (and perhaps due precisely to their ambitious reach), they did not, indeed could not, remain uncontested. The programmatic emulation of Europe was questioned both as a policy and as a practice already in the eighteenth century, most vociferously after the French Revolution and, later, in the wake of the anti-Napoleonic campaign. The court-centered cultural order came undone more gradually, losing its power throughout the first half of the nineteenth century and then definitively with the rise of the *raznochintsy* intelligentsia in the mid-1800s. Shaken by the emancipation of the serfs in 1861, the entire social ladder, so vigorously bolstered in the eighteenth century, ultimately collapsed in the October Revolution of 1917.

While one can point to specific historical events as having rendered certain forms of eighteenth-century life defunct, the eighteenth century's obsolescence was also underscored by more elusive transformations. Numerous memoirs and social commentary in the periodical press of the early 1800s attest that the men of the nineteenth century thought of themselves *as such*, that is, as living in a qualitatively different time and society than their eighteenth-century parents. These texts' persistent refrain declares the authors' wonderment before the new century's unprecedented acceleration of time, its "marvelous"—in the phrase of the Masonic leader Senator I. V. Lopukhin—"swiftness [*bystrina*] of scenes."[7] For Lopukhin, an admiring correspondent of the pietist thinker Johann Heinrich Jung-Stilling and a man shaped by a different, eighteenth-century temporality—a slower one, as it often seems from the retrospective standpoint—this acceleration presaged the imminent apocalypse. But it was also a sign of the new, uncertain world opened up by the upheaval of 1789 and the ensuing political commotion as well as by the commercial revolution that had reached Russia precisely in the early nineteenth century.[8] This quieter revolution made young Russians aware of, even if not yet wholly implicated in, the fast pace of fashion, the hasty chatter of the periodical press, and the rush of profit-making (including, by the 1830s, in the expanding literary market). Historical time in the early nineteenth century appeared to move faster. It was also, as compared with the eighteenth century, radically decentered.

The intellectual aspirations of the Russian cultural elite now notably exceeded the state's ambit, in part precisely because of the growth of educational and cultural spheres, itself initially spearheaded by the state in the eighteenth century.[9] Numerous European events now came within an educated reader's purview due to the expansion and diversification of the periodical press as well as the new political interconnectedness of Europe summoned by, and against, Napoleon.[10] One has only to browse the pages of *The Herald of Europe* (*Vestnik Evropy*) from the first decade of the nineteenth century to discover a profusion of "letters" from Europe, reprinted articles from the European (predominantly French) press, and reports on French fashions. But even as the local was superseded by the international in the early nineteenth-century historical imagination, historical meaning also came to be derived from the most local and domestic, social rather than exclusively political, evidence. Multiple texts—some in the original Russian, but many more reaching the Russian reader from Europe in their original languages or in French and Russian translations—considered historical time and experience from antiquarian, biographical, and autobiographical angles. This is another way in which historical time grew decentered: its chronology was no longer, or at least not primarily, governed by court and military calendars. As part of the expansion and decentralization of the social world, the domain of historical knowledge also grew to cover a much greater experiential and conceptual territory.[11] Already problematic for nineteenth-century intellectuals by virtue of the ambiguous legacy of its modernization, the eighteenth century thus obsolesced even more quickly due to changes in the very texture and experience of historical time.

These changes corresponded to one of the major revolutions in European intellectual history underway in this period: the rise of historicism and epochal consciousness, broadly defined by the emergence of new strategies for understanding history and for inscribing individuals and collective cultural forms into historical narratives.[12] History was already an important subject for the Enlightenment; however, its conception of historical experience was essentially universalist—that of historical knowledge, often didactic. A well-documented paradigm shift occurs in Europe at the outset of the nineteenth century, whereby not only is the academic study of history systematized, but historical consciousness generally begins to frame and explain experience on all levels.[13] In this turn to history as the dominant interpretive framework, the present is no longer conceived of as repeating the past in a cyclical pattern, but rather as essentially distinct from, though undeniably prefigured by it.[14] Reign-based chronologies are superseded by new ones, now delineating periods by distinctive "character" rather than specific dates. In the words of the Russian philosopher and critic Ivan Kireevskii, in this case describing his contemporary 1830s, "defining the dominant direction of the age has become a common goal for all thinking people."[15] This statement in fact illustrates its own claim, defining the character of its author's present as the pursuit of that character. Quickly popularized, this conceptual shift required a striking array of adjustments, affecting intergenerational relationships within and beyond families; altering the perception of personal and communal time, of lifecycles and life spans; and dictating new formulations of political, artistic, and literary genealogies.

Receiving from historicism its strongest theoretical reinforcement, Romantic conceptions of national identity tended to focus on a nostalgic reclamation of distant medieval pasts as foundations for individual nationhoods. Romantic "historicists"[16] primarily cultivated two epochs—the Middle Ages and contemporaneity—in the process downplaying the eighteenth century, the very age that most immediately shaped the early nineteenth century's political, philosophical, and indeed historicist, makeup. Newly legible and poeticized, the Middle Ages ironically became situated both as the distant "other" demanding careful scrutiny, and as the just now recognized "self," the age of that archaic purity in which the true character of the nation is revealed.[17] The contemporary moment similarly gained added legibility, once it was placed within a historical narrative, as the most recent point in its unfolding: formerly an unexamined "self," the present became an infinitely examinable and theorizable historical "other." Between the Middle Ages and nineteenth-century contemporaneity lay the Renaissance, whose absence was famously a point of perpetual embarrassment for Russian national history; and the eighteenth century, whose status in Russia, as I have suggested, was highly problematic. While what I have said so far summarizes a relatively familiar account of Romantic historicism more or less shared across Europe (including Russia), the status of the eighteenth century within this new conception of history—history as polarized between the Middle Ages and contemporaneity—is, I would argue, truly unique to Russia, and has, to the best of my knowledge, received very little attention from scholars of European historicism and Romanticism. For the early 1800s—"the age of the spirit of the age"[18]—it is the eighteenth century (and not primarily the antiquity of the Neo-Classicists or the Middle Ages of the Romantics) that emerged as the Russian nation's true *and* false start, its first, most recent, and most challenging past.

The Russian eighteenth century emphasized novelty, change, and cross-national comparison, but it was under the banner of precisely these three values that the *nineteenth* century was inaugurated all across Europe.[19] Thus, on the one hand, the Petrine era precociously posed and practiced one set of answers to the very same questions about modernity and its "comparative contemporaneities"[20] that would be offered, albeit perhaps in far more self-conscious and sophisticated ways, by early nineteenth-century historicists. On the other hand, as a consequence of its precociousness,[21] autocratic origins, and heavy-handedness, the version of Russian modernity put forward by the eighteenth century could not help but falter in the period of repeated challenges to monarchy and growing democratization of intellectual life that was the nineteenth century. Thus, we are faced with two alternative accounts of Russian modernity: one underscores its origins in Peter's reforms; the other, its maturation in the early nineteenth century when modernity, with its prerequisite social relations and intellectual culture, finally seems to take root and gain full legitimacy in Russia.

These alternatives have been particularly powerful in Russian *literary* history. Russian literary modernity has two competing origins, two "first" epochs: the rapid development of secular literature in the eighteenth century and Pushkin's Golden Age in the early nineteenth century.[22] The cult of Pushkin and the realism-driven narrative have tended to cast the literature of the eighteenth century, especially its nonmimetic conventions, as a kind of false start, or at best an experiment necessary for the literary achievements of the nineteenth century to be realized. Hence the tendency of post-Pushkin literary criticism, particularly of the nineteenth century, to narrowly define the eighteenth and limit its potential for signification.[23] This critical tendency is also the more paradoxical since Pushkin's indebtedness to the eighteenth century—along with his sense of his own period as belonging to the same historical and intellectual continuum as the recent past—is also amply recorded in scholarly literature.[24] It is not the primary aim of this book to correct this perception or argue for recovering the Russian eighteenth-century cultural production as a corpus that is as resonant or aesthetically appealing as its literature of later periods. The argument presented here aims, rather, for a certain refinement of our historical vision, its partial liberation from received periodizations. Russian literary history of the period extending, say, from 1750 to 1850 is both a continuum—unlikely though it might appear, if one considers the virtual incommensurability of the intellectual concerns and artistic forms found at the beginning and end of this hundred-year period—and an era of active reimagining of modernity's (and the eighteenth century's) content and legacy. In the process, and as a consequence of this process, the eighteenth century becomes the most significant—though often under-acknowledged— and ambiguous antecedent of the nineteenth century's imperative of historical distinction, the first epoch apprehended by the new epochal consciousness. Hence the eighteenth century's rapid antiquation, its devolvement into a *starina* ("the olden days") despite its undeniable hold on Russian history. But hence, too, every successive epoch's reconsideration of this century's spirit, consequences, and chronological limits.

When Was the Eighteenth Century in Russia?

The project of demarcating the boundaries of the eighteenth century is as fraught in Russia as anywhere in Europe. The eighteenth century poses remarkable problems of scope and content for its historians, and its implications for European political and intellectual history are too long-lasting to be delimited unambiguously or definitively. Various proposals for "short" and "long" eighteenth centuries attest to this complexity, as well as to the shift from chronological to epochal periodizations first set in motion by the Enlightenment, fully elaborated by nineteenth-century historicism, and operative to this day.[25] Thus, in France, the "short eighteenth century" begins with the death of Louis XIV in 1715 and ends in 1789 when the French Revolution arrives as both the Enlightenment's climax and the *ancien régime*'s ruin. In defiance of the French chronology's intellectual pull, the British "long eighteenth century" has been distended by some historians to stretch from the Civil War

of the 1640s to the beginning of the Victorian era in 1837, thus encompass-
ing as many as two chronological centuries and seemingly accentuating English history's noncataclysmic flow.[26] In German literature (for one cannot
speak of a unified German history in this period), the more liberal estimates
trace the beginnings of the eighteenth century to the philosopher Christian
Thomasius's (1655–1728) refashioning of the previously Latin scientific discourse in the German vernacular in the 1680s, and bring it to a close in 1832,
the year of Goethe's death.[27] Several chronologies have aligned the period
with intellectual currents, emphasizing the Enlightenment as the eighteenth
century's constitutive content and using publication dates of various Enlightenment sources as sites of periodization.[28] Yet another way to demarcate the
eighteenth century, and one that resonates particularly strongly with the concerns of my study, is as a period when new conceptions of history gradually
come into view, a period that Friedrich Meinecke, one of the last heirs and
most influential theoreticians of this great historicist tradition, sees "extending from Leibniz to the death of Goethe."[29] Finally, it has also become common to define a long Romantic period (based primarily on British literary
chronology) as occupying roughly the sixty years between 1770 and 1830, a
periodization that brings to the fore a crucial but often disregarded overlap
in the aesthetic and political concerns of the late Enlightenment and early
Romanticism.[30]

What is at stake in these periodizations—or in any periodizing project, for
that matter—is the attribution of character to a specific stretch of time, and a
corollary insistence on the given period's fundamental difference from adjacent
ones, its "otherness." Periodizing simultaneously claims to know the period
from within and distinguish its essential core from a distance, as well as, most
crucially, reassigns its place from an all-purpose chronology to a more narrowly constructed historical narrative. Thus, the Russian eighteenth century
commences as a period when chronology—the new century—is exceptionally
well-matched by Peter the Great's narrative of demiurgic modernization—the
new age. To be sure, cogent arguments have been made for the alignment of
Peter's reforms and the resulting sociopolitical and intellectual makeup of
the Russian eighteenth century with the European *seventeenth* century, and
of the Russian Enlightenment with European pre- and early Enlightenment
practices.[31] Even if qualified by the recognition of this nonsynchronous development, however, the Petrine myth of new beginnings preserves its imaginative hold over Russian periodization. This myth, moreover, serves as this

periodization's principal point of reference, for Peter's was fundamentally a self-periodizing project, one that both launched epochal thinking in Russia and fueled it continuously thereafter. The beginning of the century, then, is easily aligned with the commencement of Peter's unshared reign in 1696, his "Grand Embassy" of 1697–98, or any number of his reforms, perhaps the most symbolically resonant being the founding of Saint Petersburg in 1703. It is in dating the *end* of the Russian eighteenth century, however, that one inevitably assigns to the period a particular spirit and scale.

The end of the eighteenth century (or at least of its uninterrupted legacy) appears to be invoked at all the momentous junctures of nineteenth-century Russian history: from the deaths of Catherine II in 1796 and Paul I in 1801, to the victorious anti-Napoleonic campaign of 1812, the Decembrist Uprising of 1825, the emancipation of the serfs in 1861, and even, somewhat preposterously, the Revolution of 1905. What ends in 1796 is the century of empresses and court glamour; 1812 deals a decisive—though by no means final—blow to the rash naïveté of Francophile westernization; 1825 brings disillusionment, if not in Enlightenment liberalism per se, then certainly in its chances of taking root in Russia; 1861 abolishes, at least legally, Russia's most ingrained and pernicious social divide; and 1905 signals the doom of Russian gentry culture, which had its golden age during the eighteenth and early nineteenth centuries. This is not to say that the Russian eighteenth century extends from Peter I to 1905; nor am I suggesting that the eighteenth century remained continually central to nineteenth-century Russian cultural debates. On the contrary, when the eighteenth century happens to be invoked outside historiography, it is invariably (to return to my introduction's opening) in connection with its demise and irrelevance, albeit at each point conceived differently. The mobility of the Russian eighteenth century's end evidences not so much its lengthy span—indeed, ultimately it is not a very "long" eighteenth century— but rather its multiple applications precisely as a past. It is for this reason that, approaching the question of the eighteenth century's legacy in the Russian literary imagination, this book almost inevitably coalesced around the eighteenth century's endings as apprehended by nineteenth-century writers and thinkers, as well as around the representation of the recent past, both as living and dead, in Russian Classicism, Romanticism, and Realism.

Before turning to a description of this book's procedure, then, I would offer a vignette that ponders precisely these multiple endings, and at the same time illustrates this study's scope, sensibility, and main concerns.

Portraits of the Eighteenth Century: An Illustration

An event hardly befitting the outset of the twentieth century in Russia, yet somehow supremely emblematic of the new century, was the Historical Art Exhibit of Russian Portraits organized by the art critic, patron, and future famous Ballets-Russes impresario Sergei Diaghilev and opened on March 6, 1905, at the Tauride Palace in Saint Petersburg. The previous summer, only months before the first rumblings of the 1905 Revolution would render this project both passé and truly urgent, Diaghilev and his World of Art associates had scouted palaces and country estates of central and provincial Russia, ultimately assembling some four thousand portraits primarily of the nobility, from a period spanning the two centuries from Peter the Great to the late 1800s, but mainly focused on the eighteenth century and on Alexander I's reign (1801–1825). Insofar as the exhibit looked backward and took stock of a tradition about to be exploded by revolutions and avant-gardes, it also inevitably questioned whether it was possible to remain within this established tradition or, put another way, to inscribe the looming twentieth century in a historical continuum whose starting point lay in the eighteenth. The retrospective format of the exhibit thus contained within itself concerns over the prospective shape of Russian art and history. And the World of Art's attempts to revivify contemporary art by skipping over the preceding realist stretch (the work of "the Wanderers" [*peredvizhniki*]) and recovering the art of a more distant past—a tendency that has come to be known, especially with regard to fin-de-siècle architecture, as "retrospectivism"—ultimately also exposed the limits of that past's relevance.

Diaghilev's venture—fittingly the World of Art's last joint undertaking—brought to fruition the movement's interest in Russia's imperial past, especially the eighteenth century, the period which, it was hoped, might help restore the lost sense of cultural cohesion, but which ultimately only confirmed this ideal's irrecoverability.[32] Extracted in particularly great numbers from crumbling eighteenth-century palaces, the portraits were to expose the exhibit-goers to the richness of both Russia's artistic tradition and its gentry culture (particularly because much of the latter was never previously recognized as having any value at all). Once salvaged from the obscurity of family lore and displayed in a major public venue,[33] the portraits could be made to encapsulate the history of the moribund Russian gentry and especially the gentry estate, which in the gallery still stood for the history of the Russian state and nation, even though in reality it could no longer represent either and was in fact on the verge of radical annihilation. Perhaps against the organizers' expectations, the exhibit proved a closing statement for this epoch: it was both a restoration and a laying to rest.

In an oft-quoted speech, entitled "At the Hour of Reckoning" ("V chas itogov," 1905) and delivered at a Moscow banquet in his honor, Diaghilev calls attention to this ambivalent tonality of his exhibit, inviting his audience to question their own precarious historical situation as they cast their minds back upon the faces hanging in the Tauride Palace: "Do you not feel that the long gallery of portraits of people great and minor, with whom I have tried to populate the splendid halls of the Tauride Palace, is only a grand and convincing summing up of a brilliant but, alas, also a necrotic [*omertvevshemu*] period of our history. [. . .] We are the witnesses of the greatest historical moment of reckonings and endings in the name of a new, unknown culture which will come about through us, but will also sweep us aside."[34] Why would eighteenth-century portraits suggest to Diaghilev the idea of the death of his own culture? Needless to say, in 1905, Modernist eschatological vocabulary was readily available for framing any contemporary phenomenon, let alone an event so clearly steeped in historical reflection as was this exhibit; and here Diaghilev indeed echoes the Russian Symbolists and other intellectuals of the period. But more than that, the Russian eighteenth century, with its raw energy of loudly proclaimed new beginnings, seemed to call for ironic commentary in the age of decadence and anxiety over modernization, irony that, like Diaghilev's, was at once nostalgic and self-distancing. On the other hand, as Diaghilev realizes in his travels through the deteriorating gentry estates, his generation still inhabits, albeit no longer organically, the lands and interiors apportioned and furnished in the eighteenth century: "The end of a way of life [*byt*] is evident here. Desolate, boarded-up entailed estates, palaces horrifying in their dead splendor, strangely inhabited by today's sweet, average people, unable to bear the weight of erstwhile parades."[35] The persistence of these spaces comes to him as somewhat of a shock; yet also shocking is the extent of their disintegration, which would soon be hastened by the revolutions of 1905 and 1917, already well underway long before. The hollow finality of Chekhov's concluding stage direction to *The Cherry Orchard* (*Vishnevyi sad*, 1904) sums up the devastation of these estates with characteristic ambivalence: "Silence sets in, and one can only hear, far off in the garden, an axe pounding on wood."[36]

That the exhibit-goer was supposed not merely to commune with the portrayed sitters or admire the painters' art, but to inhabit, as fully as possible, historically framed interiors becomes clear from the emphasis placed by the organizers on furnishing the exhibit halls with objects recovered from palaces and estates together with the portraits. The artist and critic Mstislav Dobuzhin-skii, entrusted with locating these quasi-theatrical sets, recalls: "To make all the exhibition halls look even more festive and as if 'habitable,' they had to be appointed with furniture and antiques of the corresponding epoch."[37] The painter and theater designer Leon Bakst, whom Diaghilev charged with con-structing an eighteenth-century-style trellis garden in the center of the exhibit space, had to redo his initial design after Diaghilev had complained: "What kind of a cemetery have you set up here!"[38] Diaghilev's frustration points to one of the central questions underpinning the exhibit and dictating much of the language of endings and reckonings: should the eighteenth century be con-signed to the cemetery or revived as a make-believe reality? As we have seen, this same question characterizes the Russian eighteenth century's *Nachleben* in general. And portraiture—a genre that works through the juxtaposition of the ephemeral idiosyncrasies of an individual with the immutable essence of human character[39]—was particularly well-suited to pose this question.

Though most of the portraits' sitters had long since died, the material objects and lifestyles of their era, endowed with a greater staying power than the human, were only now (at the dawn of the twentieth century) ready to be discarded: "Here it is not people, but a way of life [*byt*] that is living out its days."[40] Diaghilev's generation (born sometime between Chekhov's superan-nuated heroine Liubov' Ranevskaia and her forward-looking daughter Ania) was perhaps the last to inherit its residences, if not its very livelihood, from the world of eighteenth-century gentry, a legacy this generation was at the same time outgrowing. As these structures fell into final disrepair and disrepute, the slow death of the eighteenth century itself seemed—ironically, only in the early 1900s—finally complete. Framing Diaghilev's far-reaching conclusions about the end of his own epoch, the paradox of a lifestyle (*byt*) persisting long after the end of actual life was an unsettling discovery enabled by renewed engage-ment with the eighteenth century. But of course, here too lay the paradox of the eighteenth century's reception as a whole: the extensions and reconsider-ations of its duration and end, repeated far beyond its chronological limits.

While primarily concerned with assessing his own contemporaries' limi-nal place in history, Diaghilev's speech thus tapped into something of a com-monplace in Russian discourse about the eighteenth century: the insistence on its pastness, and the strangeness and incompleteness of this pastness. Starting with Chatskii's recurring declarations of his epochal malaise in Alexander Griboedov's *Woe from Wit* (*Gore ot uma*, 1825), the assertion of irreconcilable

differences between the men of the eighteenth and nineteenth centuries resonates throughout Russian periodicals, memoirs, and the works of such canonical Russian writers as Alexander Pushkin, Alexander Herzen, Ivan Turgenev,
and Leo Tolstoy. This assertion only very rarely serves as a given work's central theme, and yet it continually frames the historical being of these authors
and their characters. The greater the nineteenth-century intellectuals' preoccupation with defining their own place in history, the more surely is the eighteenth century relegated to a past of alterity, its function, in essence, to cast
the contours of the present in sharp relief. Thus oversaturated with significance and at the same time denied continued contemporary relevance, the
eighteenth century, as this book will repeatedly observe, serves as a catalyst
for reflections upon contemporaneity (such as Diaghilev's), and these reflections, in turn, mark the eighteenth century as signifying the past and history's
progress, each time anew.

Tracing how the legacy of the eighteenth century is interwoven with Russian writers' attempts to define the contemporary will be the task of this book
in general; but here I would highlight one thread in this history: a fragmented
narrative of Russian eighteenth-century portraits' powers of signification from
the early 1800s up to Diaghilev's exhibit. Modern, individualizing portraiture
was in Russia itself a development of the eighteenth century, when European-
influenced, and more often than not European-painted, portraits came to replace the different conventions of the more static seventeenth-century Russian
parsuna portraits. By the end of the eighteenth century, many gentry homes,
particularly of the richer nobility in the capitals, boasted small galleries of family portraits, the same portraits that Diaghilev and his associates would redis-
cover a century later. For such a "rediscovery" to occur, the portraits had at
some point to have been forgotten, or at least to have lost value, even though
the tradition of Western-style portraiture continued uninterrupted.

Surprisingly, warnings of this potential oblivion were sounded as early as
the first decades of the nineteenth century, when portraiture was at the height
of its popularity across Europe. In 1811, a curious formulation of the problem was culled from a French source by *The Herald of Europe*. It is hard to say
how seriously we are meant to take the following passage, since most of the
magazine's moralizing on fashion seems exceptionally tongue-in-cheek. The
link between fashion and the acceleration of history, as we will see in chapter
5, is also fairly routine. Remarkable here, however, is the concern expressed
for the stability of portraiture's meaning, endangered, the reader is warned, by
new attitudes toward fashion and history:

David Lüders, *Count P. G. Chernyshev with His Wife Ekaterina Andreevna, Daughters Dar'ia, Natal'ia, Anna, and Son* (1750s). One of the portraits exhibited at the Tauride Palace and printed in Grand Prince Nikolai Mikhailovich's catalogue. Nikolai Mikhailovich, Grand Duke of Russia, *Russkie portrety XVIII i XIX stoletii*, 5:LXIII.

> Nowadays the hold of fashion extends even to those monuments that are sup-
> posed to outlive it. It guides a painter's brush in family portraits, and what do you
> know?—a portrait that has just been finished is already outmoded, and we are
> bound to begin discarding portraits of our relatives, friends, venerable ancestors!
> To be sure, one could still look at their faces, but their clothes and customs are
> so strange! Seeing these pictures, children imagine that these people had no taste
> or common sense, and from a very young age they begin to scoff at the olden
> days [*starina*], for which, as writers have noted, our respect is now considerably
> diminished. We are left with one of two things: either to laugh at the venerable
> depictions of strangely-dressed people of the olden days [*starinnye liudi*], or to
> forget them entirely.[41]

Much of the social commentary of this early period is concerned with drafting, refining, and superposing alternative chronologies, as well as commenting on the fast pace of historical process. Even as fashion in this passage precipitates the obsolescence of previous lifestyles, a new sense of intergenerational divisions also makes itself felt. The "we" of the article hover anxiously between the "venerable ancestors," who already appear strange to "us" but to whom "we" still dutifully pay obeisance, and the children who have no patience for the past's "otherness." The solution? Three exceptionally uncompromising options: veneration of ancestors, which appears untenable in the new fashion-driven world; laughter, which is symptomatic of this world's moral laxity critiqued in the piece; or forgetfulness, which seems precisely the historical strategy that the churn of fashions ultimately evokes.

The portraits in this passage are not yet explicitly associated with the eighteenth century; however, inasmuch as the reader is presented with a piece of topical reportage, the strange costumes of the preceding period would in the context of the French original belong to the *ancien régime*, and in Russia to the age of Catherine II. And yet, some level of chronological generalization is hardly accidental here: for all its insistent new-century up-to-dateness, this early article is equally invested in providing a universalist didactic critique in the style of the Enlightenment, from which this discourse is not yet sufficiently removed.

When some twenty years later, we are actually placed in front of just such portraits in Pushkin's "The Queen of Spades" ("Pikovaia dama," 1833), the sartorial detail, historical dating, and attribution of the portraits could not be more precise. They unmistakably belong to the last decades of the eighteenth century; in fact, their dual function in the novella is, on the one hand, precisely to reference the eighteenth century and, on the other, to provide the requisite protorealist detail, the Balzacian "reality effect."[42] The text observes as if from Hermann's standpoint, but certainly with a cold precision un-characteristic of Hermann: "Two portraits, painted in Paris by Mme. Lebrun, hung on the wall. One of them showed a man about forty years old, red-faced and portly, wearing a light green coat with a star; the other a beautiful young woman with an aquiline nose, with her hair combed back of her temples, and with a rose in her powdered locks."[43] Pushkin's description is minimal, even bare, delivered in the detached, unfocalized tone so characteristic of "The Queen of Spades"; any possibility of inquiring about the story behind these portraits—the life of their sitters beyond the one they lead as ornaments on the Countess's wall—is precluded by the passage's placement in the middle of a more extended enumeration of the Countess's other eighteenth-century bric-a-brac (right before "china shepherdesses, table clocks made by the famous Leroy, little boxes, bandalores, fans, and diverse other ladies' toys"[44]). At least in part, the prediction of *The Herald of Europe* has been fulfilled: the portraits— crisply rendered, but opaque and irrelevant—are sealed in a kind of interpretive vacuum. Neither quite forgotten nor ridiculed, they have, crucially, lost any affective connection to their observers. As I will argue more extensively in Part II, this kind of ambivalent self-distancing from the eighteenth century is characteristic of the 1830s and particularly of Pushkin. This is the period in which, and the writer for whom, the disengagement from the eighteenth century is a dynamic project: both an active process and a *fait accompli*.

Here we might contrast Pushkin's treatment of portraits with Turgenev's in his early story "Three Portraits" ("Tri portreta," 1846) just over a decade later. Explicitly focalized by the inquisitive narrator, the description here— while undoubtedly alluding to Pushkin—performs a very different function. The portraits occasion the narrative and, unlike in Pushkin, are exhaustively described and explicitly connected to the stories of their sitters, whose Lermontovian passions they are barely able to contain:

> I cannot say why my companions were silent, but I held my tongue because my eyes had suddenly come to rest on three dusty portraits in black wooden frames. The colours were rubbed and cracked in places, but one could still make out the faces. The portrait in the centre was that of a young woman in a white gown with lace ruffles, her hair done up high, in the style of the eighties of last century. On her right, upon a perfectly black background, there stood out the full, round face of a good-natured country gentleman of five-and-twenty, with a broad, low brow, a thick nose, and a good-humoured smile. The French powdered coiffure was utterly out of keeping with the expression of his Slavonic face. The artist had portrayed him wearing a long loose coat of crimson colour with large paste buttons; in his hand he was holding some unlikely-looking flower. The third portrait, which was the work of some other more skillful hand, represented a man of thirty, in the green uniform, with red facings, of the time of Catherine, in a white shirt, with a fine cambric cravat. One hand leaned on a gold-headed cane, the other lay on his shirt front. His dark, thinnish face was full of insolent haughtiness. The fine long eyebrows almost grew together over the pitch-black eyes, about the thin, scarcely discernible lips played an evil smile.[45]

Quite obviously preparing a narrative of triangulated infatuations, this description also emphasizes a peculiar disjuncture between the portraits' faded state and the vividness of the characters they depict. The contrast is further accentuated when the company's host shines candlelight upon them and delivers their story "in the tone of a showman at a wild beast show"[46]: if the host's attitude emphasizes precisely the ridiculousness of the past so eloquently bemoaned in the 1811 *Herald of Europe*, the narrator's rapt attention pulls the reader in the opposite direction, toward full absorption in the past. When the dramatic tale behind the portraits is told to the end, what continues to trouble the narrator, in fact what motivates the narrative in the first place, is the intangible gap between the dead, dusty surface of these artifacts and the plenitude of passion in their lived past, which remains largely uncorroborated by any remaining physical evidence.

This disjuncture, on the one hand, and the desire for access to the past, on the other—perhaps only exacerbated by Turgenev's long sojourns abroad, his acute withdrawal from the course of Russian history and much-critiqued alienation from Russian *byt*—become a virtual fixation in the writer's several (and largely ignored) narratives of the eighteenth century. Like "Three Portraits," these narratives document the past's encroaching illegibility. And it is precisely this illegibility from which the World of Art again reclaims the eighteenth century, rereading it for its own purposes of artistic renewal and historical divination. These portraits, and the briefly sketched history of their reappropriation, might frame my study as examples of that genre, portraiture, that occasions the examination of the past perhaps most corporeally, most unsettlingly.

The Vanishing Point

Following a roughly chronological trajectory from the late eighteenth through the nineteenth centuries to the early 1900s, my narrative presents the Russian eighteenth century as a testing ground for the new kinds of intense scrutiny of periodization, historical belonging, and representation that were enabled in large part by nineteenth-century historicism. If much in the history of Russian Romanticism, including its historicism, can be traced back to general European cultural trends, the eighteenth century in Russia was almost too extraordinary, its ambivalent status comparable perhaps only to the much-debated legacy of the French Enlightenment. In France, the only European country where the eighteenth century furnishes as lasting a frame of reference as in Russia, this unusual ambiguity is especially a consequence of the unprecedented historical upheaval that as early as 1789 transforms the period quite literally into an *ancien régime*. In Russia, however, the eighteenth century never achieves such definitive closure, remaining distinctly both "ancient" and "modern."[47] The century's paradoxical status as both omnipresent and absent or disappearing is precisely what my book will attempt to capture, presenting it as a veritable vanishing point in the historical canvas constructed by nineteenth-century Russian historicists.

Theory of perspective defines the vanishing point as that point where all orthogonals in a painting converge. This is the pivot which gives structure to a perspective-governed canvas and instantly magnetizes the viewer's eye. On the other hand, as the term suggests, this point vanishes on the horizon, captivating the viewer but never in a way that is overstated or even explicit. While a canvas can be parsed in terms of color, light, brushwork, subject matter, and the relationship of figure to ground, the vanishing point, never an actual point, evades such analysis. Nebulous and difficult to capture in words, it only orders the relationships among a painting's components and remains largely a theoretical construct.[48] My aim in this book is precisely to offer a perspectival rearrangement of key texts of Russian literature, demonstrating that the eighteenth century's specific and at times insignificant traces have a common origin in Russian Romantic culture's preoccupation with its recent past. Far from random, these traces are brought into a relationship by this underlying preoccupation, as nineteenth-century Russian culture tenaciously seeks to hide, downplay, amplify, or otherwise define the consequences of the formative period preceding it. The book preserves the elusive nature of the eighteenth century in its calculated omission of a sustained consideration of the century itself, unfiltered by the conceptual biases of the generations that immediately followed it. With the exception of the first chapter's inquiry into the rhetoric of historicity in the eighteenth-century ceremonial ode (an aside that is necessary for understanding subsequent developments in Russian literature's approaches to historical representation), this study never presents a historical analysis of what occurred, attending, instead, to what was imagined or desired.

Populated with many personages and stories, this book pivots around two principal protagonists: Gavrila Derzhavin (1743–1816) and Alexander Pushkin (1799–1837), the writers whose careers mark distinctive stages in Russian literary periodization, and thus have an especially profound impact upon the status of the eighteenth century in Russia's literary history. On the one hand, Derzhavin has come to be viewed as the epitome and high point of the Russian eighteenth century, while Pushkin's supple verse and protean image have established him as the progenitor of modern Russian letters. If Derzhavin, in this account, *is* the eighteenth century, Pushkin renders the eighteenth century irrevocably outdated. On the other hand, as the most prominent poet to revise the parameters of the ode, Derzhavin is far from the most typical representative of eighteenth-century poetics—paradoxically, he may in fact be singled out as "representative" precisely because of his singularity—and much in his work anticipates nineteenth- and twentieth-century Russian poetry in ways that Lomonosov's or Sumarokov's creative output does not. Similarly, Pushkin, as many scholars have demonstrated with recourse to a variety of textual evidence, is not the revolutionary innovator that traditional literary histories make him out to be, but rather a brilliant synthesizer of earlier and contemporary trends, a writer who creatively draws upon both the Enlightenment and its subsequent Romantic overcomings. In other words, Derzhavin, *pace* some received popular periodizations, is as inextricably connected to the literary history that follows him as Pushkin is to the eighteenth-century tradition that precedes him. It is therefore because both Derzhavin and Pushkin have come to stand for two distinct periods in Russian letters—the eighteenth and nineteenth centuries, Classicism and Romanticism, the two bookends of the Russian Golden Age—and because the poetics of each so clearly reach across this imposed divide between the two centuries, that my book is split into two overlapping and mutually informing halves: one centered on Derzhavin and the other on Pushkin. The former, titled "Derzhavin's Moment," considers the passing of the eighteenth century as a series of transitions experienced from within the period itself; the latter—"The Fictions of the Eighteenth Century"—enlists Pushkin's multiple engagements with the eighteenth century as points of departure for considering narratives of the recent past that emerge in the mid-1800s, when the eighteenth century is no longer a lived experience for most Russian writers.

Insofar as this book discovers that the legacy of the eighteenth century is ubiquitously interrogated, but never dominates the critical discussions or literary texts of the nineteenth century, the examination of this problem in nineteenth-century cultural history provides a prism through which many other contemporaneous social and literary formations achieve a sharper, or at least more original, focus. Chapter 1 links the much-discussed revisions of the Lomonosovian Classicist poetics in Derzhavin's "Felitsa" cycle to concurrent changes in Russian and European conceptions of historical process. Chapter 2 follows the erosion or hybridization of Derzhavin's and his contemporaries' odic poetics at a historical turning point, Catherine II's death, which Derzhavin depicts in the allegory of "The Ruins" ("Razvaliny," 1797), a poem establishing a dynamic combination of odic and elegiac modes of historical representation. Chapter 3 locates the supersession of epochs in the late-Enlightenment skepticism regarding ruler-centered historical narratives, and in the Romantic rejection of patronage as a social practice and as the enabling premise of Classicist lyric expression. Focusing specifically on the treatment of the recent past facilitates my reexamination, in chapter 4, of the narrative procedures developed in the Russian historical novel (the preferred genre of the 1830s) and helps illuminate new facets of its dialogue with European specimens of the genre and its dependence on the rapidly expanding Russian literary market. Chapter 5 negotiates the Romantic-Realist divide in approaching the subject of fashion, material culture and novelistic description in the paradigmatic text of the Russian nineteenth century, Pushkin's "The Queen of Spades." Finally, chapter 6, which catalogues and explicates the repeated appearances of eighteenth-century characters in the oeuvre of Ivan Turgenev, creates an opening for reconsidering this writer's career as at every point and in every genre invested in, and troubled by, historical reflection.

Thus brought together by their shared absorption in the afterlife of the eighteenth century, the readings assembled here—and others could have certainly been produced here as well or instead of these particular case studies—all pursue two related directions. On the one hand, exploring and variously configuring the complex interlocking of personal, creative, social, and financial life of the two centuries, the book puts forward a particular history of reception and experience. On the other, as these readings scrutinize the genres that have reshaped and rethought the eighteenth century throughout the nineteenth (the ode, elegy, critical prose, historical and realist fiction), the book contributes to the conversation on the history of literary forms, a conversation that boasts a particularly long and distinguished pedigree in Russian scholarship. If in the process, however, *The First Epoch* merely succeeds in registering the excitement and malaise of seeing and articulating history differently with each new decade or generation (starting with Lomonosov and ending in the stylized halls of Diaghilev's exhibit), or of critically and creatively forgetting and distorting the recent past (as in Pushkin and Turgenev), the book will have accomplished its humbler goal.

PART I

Derzhavin's Moment

Времен завеса отворилась!
Сретаю будущие дни:
Россия светом озарилась,
В ней зримы радостей огни;
Блаженство, счастие, науки,
Друг другу простирая руки,
Венцы лавровы подают;
Спокойства общего причину,
Великую Екатерину
Парнасски жители поют.

—M. M. KHERASKOV, "Ode to Her Imperial Majesty on
the Day of Her Solemn Accession to the Throne of All Russia,
28 June 1791"[1]

Но нет явления без творческой причины;
Сей благодатный век был век Екатерины.

—E. A. BARATYNSKII, "To Bogdanovich" (1824)[2]

С Державиным умолкнул голос лести—а как он льстил?

—A. S. PUSHKIN, letter to A. A. Bestuzhev (1825)[3]

Стихотворения Державина [. . .]—некрасивая куколка,
из которой должна была выпорхнуть, на очарование глаз
и умиление сердца, роскошно прекрасная бабочка . . .

—V. G. BELINSKII, "Derzhavin's Works" (1843)[4]

В Державине весь его век, и с золотом, и с мишурой, и с чем похуже.

—P. I. BARTENEV, letter to Ia. K. Grot (1862)[5]

«Ледяной» XVIII век принял, в его поэтике, вид лилейной мечты и утвердил власть света и любви над тьмою смерти и холодом рассудка.

—B. M. EIKHENBAUM, "Derzhavin" (1924)[6]

Prologue

In a pair of articles published in 1843 in *Notes of the Fatherland* (*Otechestven-nye zapiski*), Vissarion Belinskii offers a reappraisal of Gavrila Derzhavin's poetry, remembered, according to the critic, more through saccharine text-book clichés than through any real attempts at an analytical reading. Supple-menting his textual analyses with copious stanzas-long excerpts from the poems, Belinskii performs time and again the same basic task: extracting nuggets of pure and timeless poetry from what he perceives to be a charac-teristically eighteenth-century rhetorical dross.[7] The poetry, if one is to deduce Belinskii's aesthetic criterion, evinces a proto-lyrical voice, or an observant hyperrealist eye for detail, while the rhetoric entangles this poetry in con-voluted allegory. The former qualities, Belinskii asserts, ensure for Derzhavin a permanent place in Russian and even world literary history, even as the rhetorical flourishes permanently alienate him from his nineteenth-century readers.[8] Equipped with mid-nineteenth-century historicist optics, Belinskii sees Derzhavin as first and foremost a *homo historicus*, a "poetic exponent" (*poeticheskii vyrazitel'*) of the Catherine era,[9] prodigiously gifted, yet bound by the aesthetic short-sightedness of his epoch. Accordingly, Derzhavin's poetry becomes a yardstick by which Belinskii proposes to gauge the distance between pre- and post-Pushkin literary Russia. To read Derzhavin through Belinskii's eyes and in Belinskii's times is thus to become sensitive to the fast pace of Russian literary progress in the nineteenth century.

Though invariably a measure of the nineteenth century's moral and aesthetic advancement, Derzhavin's remoteness, if not inaccessibility, puzzles Belinskii, to the extent that both articles seem to emerge from the critic's opening reflec-tions on the poet's placement within, and negotiation of, fine epochal divisions:

On July 3 of this year will commence the *second century* since the birth of Derzhavin. . . . So, an *entire century* separates the young generations of our time from the bard of Catherine. . . . But hardly *a quarter of a century* has passed since Derzhavin's death—and, nonetheless, *whole centuries* seem to stretch between him and us. . . . Reading Derzhavin's poems nowadays, you can barely understand anything in them without a historical commentary on the mores of the *age* whose spokesman [*organ*] he was. . . . The language, way of thinking, sentiments, interests—everything, everything is alien to *our time*. . . . But Derzhavin has not died, just as the *age* he glorified has not: the *age* of Catherine laid the groundwork for the *age* of Alexander, which laid the groundwork for *our age*,—and between Derzhavin and the poets of *our time* there exist the same blood ties that connect these three *epochs* of Russian history . . .[10] [Emphasis mine]

This passage entraps Derzhavin in a series of dialectical contradictions—is he dead or alive, or ultimately both dead and alive?—but also turns the poet into a kind of hyperlink that connects the multiplying terms of Belinskii's historicist lexicon: century, age, time, epoch. The passage's insistent repetition of the word *vek* (denoting both the chronological "century" and the less quantifiable "age") makes Derzhavin stand for an entire historical period and thus exceed his biographical self, yet the term simultaneously detains him on the periphery of Belinskii's literary present.

In his treatment of Derzhavin, Belinskii (1811–48), himself squarely a man of the nineteenth century, is a literary historian of both the long and the short durée. The critic transports his readers to ancient India, Greece, and Rome; examines the Italian Renaissance and divergent versions of the Enlightenment in England, Germany, and France; but also pursues a more narrowly local and recent narrative of Russian literary history from Peter the Great to the 1840s. Thus do the articles urge their readers to recognize in Derzhavin both a recently deceased blood relation and a mythical and inaccessible—and yet, indispensable—forebear of contemporary literature. Typical of Belinskii's emphatic punctuation, the proliferating ellipses further mark not only spaces of unverbalized reflection, but also the interpreter's willful and unwitting shifts of focus among historical gradations that eschew precise classification and comparison. Derzhavin's image, on the verge of becoming obscure, proves particularly malleable as a subject of historicist analysis.

Belinskii cleverly extends Derzhavin's life—some seventy-three years between 1743 and 1816—to reference a time seemingly "entire centuries" past ("the second century will commence [since]"), but in fact ending only slightly over twenty-five years ("a quarter of a century has passed since") prior to Belinskii's disquisition. Like *vek*, a term both capacious and delimiting, designating at once time's quantity and quality, Derzhavin's life is made to encompass a whole range of historical phenomena that both invite and defy definition. Granted that, on some level, Derzhavin might only be a case study through which Belinskii here hones his recently formulated historicist approach to literature (his inquiry into "the law of historical development"[11]); still, is there not something in Derzhavin himself—in his image, life, and work—to qualify him as a historical container or frame: an emblem and interpreter of a specific transitional period in Russian letters and history? For even if, following Belinskii, we are to find in Derzhavin primarily a mouthpiece of the eighteenth century and its set of stable preoccupations (luxury, moderation, morality, *vanitas*[12]), do we not also see Derzhavin's poetry repeatedly recognize the inaccessibility and impermanence of the very aesthetics to which it aspires; or stage a precarious and potentially subversive coupling of the odic and satirical impulses; or question the reach of the poet's voice, the stability of his image over time? Moreover, isn't Derzhavin forever memorialized popularly as that "great and kindly elder"[13] who survived into the nineteenth century precisely to pass the literary baton to Pushkin (whom, "as he descended to the grave," he "blessed," *v grob skhodia blagoslovil*) and hence to the entirety of modern Russian poetry?[14] And can he thus not stand for a certain period— say, from the late 1700s to the first two decades of the nineteenth century— when Russian literature discovers new, modern historical modes of conceiving of change and time's flow?

Derzhavin indeed is the most complex and productive Russian poet whose biography and poetics straddle the elusive but nevertheless acutely sensed divide between the eighteenth and nineteenth centuries.[15] Starting with his much-cited realization in 1779 that his voice could not brave the heights of Lomonosov's encomiastic enthusiasm, and that therefore he needed to carve his own "alternative" way in Russian poetry ("to choose an entirely different path," *izbra[t'] sovsem drugoi put'*[16]), Derzhavin constantly attunes his lyre not only to the changing demands of politics and literary fashion, but also to the flux of personal circumstance and vision. If, as we shall see, the trans-personal viewpoint of the Lomonosovian panegyric tends to foreground unity, cyclicity, and permanence, Derzhavin relishes perspectival and tonal shifts, moving with expert, often tongue-in-cheek agility between the public and private spaces of poetic utterance. Within the Classicist canon, these movements propel him to range from the panegyric, which he in any case revises, to the Anacreontic lyric, for which he invents a distinctive set of voices, reaching even to the demotic. But poetic flexibility also allows him to embrace such early Romantic modes as the Ossianic, with which his verse becomes virtually synonymous in Russia; to briefly inhabit the elegy not only as a canonical genre, but also as a sensibility; and, in the last decade of his life, to experiment with national meters and genres—not only the epic, but lyrical songs and the Zhukovskian ballad as well. Thus, even Derzhavin's generic and tonal range is conditioned as much by the Classicist conception of genre hierarchy, which maintains a discrete place for different mutually incoherent but self-consistent poetic modes, as by the emerging tonal plasticity of the Romantics who, while perhaps equally attentive to the demands of genre, no longer felt bound by its hierarchical arrangements, and pressed toward interpretations at once idiographic and befitting the poet's biographical shape.[17]

Derzhavin is a *homo historicus* not simply because, to agree with Belinskii, he is constrained by the blind spots of his epoch, but more significantly because in *his* verse we can spot the coexistence of both archetypal and concrete visions of historical time and experience, and even trace the eventual shift from the archetypal to the concrete.[18] As the following chapters will suggest in approaching very diverse texts and issues, Derzhavin's verse can be placed at the intersection of a specific set of late-eighteenth-century developments in poetic practice and historical understanding that lay the groundwork, as in Belinskii's genealogical narrative, for the literary sensibilities of subsequent generations, yet also emphatically isolate him within this transitional period.[19] Conveniently for those who do not adhere to strict chronologies, Derzhavin's lifetime also encompasses several key events identifiable as signifying the end of the eighteenth century in Russia: the end of female rule or (using a slightly different lens) the death of Catherine II in 1796; the assassination of Paul I in March 1801 (coincident with the beginning of the new century); and, finally, the Napoleonic campaign, that last dramatic echo of the French Enlightenment and Revolution that reverberated all throughout the first two decades of the nineteenth century. Part I, "Derzhavin's Moment," thus proposes to stretch the poet's biographical timeline, in a manner not unlike Belinskii's, in order to examine in tandem an array of poetic, historical, and civic attitudes and attempts to capture epochal closure that take shape in Derzhavin's own writings as well as in those of his immediate predecessors, contemporaries, and later readers.

As a paradigm, then, "Derzhavin's moment" can be offered in answer to Belinskii's implicit quandary which, though partially resolved at the end of his own analysis, remains topical for most critics and scholars of Derzhavin to this day.[20] Is "the Bard of Felitsa" the last poet of the eighteenth century, or the first poet of the nineteenth?[21] How does epochal classification affect our understanding of his work and legacy? What interpretive categories should we use in reading him, Classicist or Romantic? And how do we preserve sensitivity to the porousness of these categories in this transitional period? Conversely, how are the eighteenth and nineteenth centuries construed by readers who choose to use Derzhavin as a yardstick? In my reading, Derzhavin focalizes an entire range of issues of periodization, tying the discussion of the "long eighteenth century" in Russia to specifically Russian political and poetic transformations. The following chapters use Derzhavin's writings and image to propose several codependent approaches to understanding the content and the outer limit of the Russian eighteenth century; chapter 1 associates the end of this period with the end of female rule and of the panegyric ascendancy; chapter 2, with the death of Catherine II and the fading of a certain vision of idyllic imperial space; chapter 3, with the gradual discrediting of ruler-centered historical vision, and with the move away from the hierarchical circuits of writing and reading linked to patronage.

All three chapters are concerned both with the contemporaneous and the retrospective construction of epochal time, examining the end of the eighteenth century both from the standpoint of those who lived and thought through it and from the distance of our own scholarly moment. Part I is further consolidated through its overarching interest in poetic rather than prose historical genres, responding to poetry's dominance as the period's principal mode of literary expression and, as I shall argue, of historical cognition. In a sense, this cluster of chapters examines and instantiates what Lev Pumpianskii suggestively posits as one of the Russian eighteenth century's defining characteristics, its "historiographical thoughtfulness" (*istoriograficheskaia zadumchivost'*), as well as the ode's central theme of "the inseparability of poetry and the state."[22] Emerging at a time when narrative modes of emplotment had not yet banished most other ways of thinking about history, Derzhavin-era poetry configured distinctive historical visions in its uneasy modulations of the oratorical, the lyrical, and the narrative. Rather than following Belinskii's tendentious (and extremely influential) lead and applauding the poetic at the expense of the rhetorical, these chapters will attempt to trace and describe these modulations.

1

The Empresses' Histories
Lomonosov and Derzhavin

> Panegyric and history are as remote from each other as the
> heavens are from the earth.
>
> —JEAN RACINE, marginalia to *Lucien* (cited in Marin, *Portrait of
> the King*, 75)

PANEGYRIC AND THE FEMALE RULE

With the passing of the eighteenth century, there died away a certain mode
of governance and a particular cast of relationships between the poet and his
ruler. The epoch had given the Russian Empire a unique place in modern European history (including, as we shall see, literary history) because women had
ruled there for a full two-thirds of the century. Female rulers both embodied the profound effects of Peter the Great's modernization and mitigated its
destructive thrust.[1] Female rule intensified the demand for discourses of legitimacy and glory, ultimately engendering a sizable panegyric corpus that was
unmatched in any other European literature of the period and quite out of step
with the Enlightenment's movement toward the decentralization of literary
practice and public life. It is no accident, then, that the empresses' legacies,
despite being even more ambiguous than that of Peter, appear permanently
and pervasively imprinted upon the nineteenth century's historical imagination of the eighteenth. This study therefore begins with the period of elusive
yet momentous shifts from the "age of empresses" to the "age of iron," and from
the ceremonial to personal forms of historical consciousness.

Even though pre-Petrine women had enjoyed a far more diverse range of
social possibilities than is commonly accepted, it was Peter's program of westernization that most visibly instated women in the public realm, and his unre-
stricted Law on Succession (1722) that enabled them to occupy the throne.[2]
Both the empresses' actual power and the modes for its representation were

products of eighteenth-century political and cultural transformations.[3] As a result of Russia's new westward orientation, the rich Western tradition of imperial iconography diversified and reinvigorated the Russian conceptual vocabulary of power—and most notably female power—offering, among its allegories of imperial dominion, the Greco-Roman pantheon of pagan goddesses for tsarinas to adopt, cultivate, and display for symbolic legitimation. These new representational forms were summoned to quell persistent anxieties over legitimacy in a period when power, ostensibly wielded by peace-loving female hands, had become an object of constant strife and usurpation. Coupled with memories of discordant yet highly ritualized court politics, female rule and images of strong and willful matriarchs became a hallmark—if not a cliché— of the eighteenth century in its subsequent reception.[4]

Finding its legitimacy in early eighteenth-century reforms, gynecocracy was rejected as unviable and even dangerous by the century's end. In 1797, Paul I's Law of Succession reversed Peter's and established, or at least strongly privileged, male primogeniture as the principle for inheriting the empire, thereby terminating the age of empresses both legally and symbolically.[5] With this law, female rule acquired clear historical boundaries, a beginning and an end, inadvertently also emerging as a tangible characteristic of what could now be perceived as an epoch: "the century of empresses" (*vek imperatrits*), also known as "the century of court coups d'état" (*vek dvortsovykh perevorotov*) or, indeed, "the eighteenth century." Defined by this particular cluster of political issues, the eighteenth century also became forever associated with a related constellation of legitimizing and glorifying literary forms: first and foremost, the ceremonial ode and its allegorical strategies.

This chapter assembles a distinctive version of the eighteenth century out of the rhetoric of history-telling occasioned by the deep involvement of eighteenth-century Russian poetry with the court and by the convergence of the queen-muse, under continual threat of dynastic complications and in continual need of validation, with her precariously positioned pre-professionalized panegyrist.[6] All of these characteristics of the Russian political and literary scene in the eighteenth century—high poetry's thematic focus on the monarch, the court, and the state; the poet's ostensible subservience to the encomiastic demands placed upon his craft; his marginal position in society and limited venues for literary circulation outside the court; and the particular vanity ascribed to female figures of authority—would become especially distasteful to nineteenth-century intellectuals. The latter prided themselves, increasingly as the century progressed, on carving out a literary space outside of—even opposed to—the values and venues imposed by the autocratic regime. Catering to the common expectations for female virtues, eighteenth-century ode-writers fashioned a language for reimagining even the most aggressive enthronements and military campaigns as feats restoring tranquility, and the tsarinas as working toward peace and embodying beauty. These sleights of poetic hand, along with the transformative ethos of the panegyric generally, would begin to be questioned in the Romantic period and would eventually be vehemently rejected in the second half of the nineteenth century. Thus, even Iakov Grot, Derzhavin's most vocal and productive nineteenth-century champion, acknowledges and engages in this historicist critique: "First and foremost we do not sympathize with the spirit and aims of the eighteenth-century ode, which is inextricably linked with the praise of persons; due to self-interest, this praise easily descends into obsequiousness and flattery. But neither are we sympathetic to the form of the eighteenth-century ode itself, the main form of those in which Derzhavin's creations were cast."[7]

Instead of exploring the specifics of this nineteenth-century critique, at times overeager in its celebration of progress, this chapter inspects the notions of history—public and private time as well as historical change—that were implicit in the eighteenth-century ode and came to be gradually modified as the century drew to an end. I make the case that examining encomiastic rhetoric of the second half of the eighteenth century can reveal an evolution in conceptions and attitudes toward historical time underpinning the ceremonial ode, a genre mistakenly held to lack interpretive dynamism and range because of its panegyric bias. For nineteenth-century analysts of eighteenth-century poetry, invariably preoccupied with judgment and self-distancing, the issues of panegyric insincerity, the awkwardness of the developing Russian secular language, and odic rigidity all became an unavoidable stumbling block. This chapter offers a partial view of the forms of eighteenth-century poetic "obsequiousness and flattery," their involvement in configuring a particular odic vision of history, and this vision's evolution. Though it is engaged with rhetorical forms that do not survive intact past the eighteenth century, becoming as they do in Grot's formulation "unsympathetic" (*nesochuvstvenny*), this analysis is nevertheless an indispensable beginning for *The First Epoch*. It conceives of the ode as a genre of historical interpretation and showcases Derzhavin in the role of an early interpreter, or even historian, of the eighteenth century. While the ode's main ambition is always undoubtedly to praise and idealize, it is also a public genre profoundly concerned with articulating a historical vision, vying for acknowledgement from its histories' principal actors and for control over a definitive official version of events and personages.[8] In this capacity, the ode in this book takes its place among such properly "historical" genres as the historical elegy or the historical novel.

The Allegorical Strategy

The ceremonial ode consolidated its unique sense of history around the figure of the ruling monarch, much as it was the monarch who became the pivot for odic models of inspiration and civic sentiment.[9] As a court servitor, the panegyrist was called upon to promptly relay numerous court affairs: military campaigns and victories, the ruling family's lifecycle events, processions and other ceremonies. And yet, read as a historical genre, the ceremonial ode appears uniquely unanchored from the real figures and events it purports to represent and absorb into its idealizing panegyric vision.[10] The ode is about both the ruling monarch and the process of re-visioning her in very general, mythologizing terms; it both tends toward its referent and, at least partially, suspends referentiality. The ode's proximity to its subject—indeed, its striving thereto—is everywhere thwarted, on the one hand by the realization of her physical and interpretive inaccessibility, and on the other, by the idealizing flattening of her specific attributes.

This tension renders the ceremonial ode an essentially allegorical genre even though, as we must admit, the Russian ceremonial ode ultimately did not generate particularly complex or extensive allegorical narratives. Confining itself almost entirely to epithetic description and apostrophe and to imaginary Olympian geographies, the Russian Classicist allegory remained "intermittent" and ornamental rather than "continuous" or narrative.[11] Russian ceremonial odes to Elizabeth (Elizaveta Petrovna) or Catherine II boast no allegory of the scale or complexity found in the extensive textual production surrounding Elizabeth I of England, for example. And yet, privileging as they did the emotional charge of "intermittent" allegory over the consistency of continuous allegorical narration, Russian odes, in their deep structure, were premised on a figurative understanding of historical reality. They assigned this reality simultaneously to two temporal planes: the topical/specific and the archetypal/mythical.

As a figure of rhetoric and an interpretive mode, allegory draws an implicit equation between its tenor and vehicle. But, in imagining these as two distinct entities, allegory also premises its stylistic and conceptual effect on the difference between the two (Gr. *allēgorein*—to speak both differently or figuratively and publicly).[12] The empress is and at the same time is not a goddess; she acts on a specific date in a specific location, and also resides in a timeless and unmappable realm.[13] As a subject of odic history, the empress is a person, with a specific biography and historical and geographical ambit, and at the same time she is a being (not entirely human) who transcends her biographical bounds.[14] The ode's act of allegorization invites the reader to entertain both possibilities. Unlike male rule, which, in addition to allegory, allows the panegyrist more immediate access to the discourse of particularized heroism, female rule is far more troubled as a direct odic referent, demanding an allegorical reimagining of power, royal genealogy, military force, and the queen's body.

While acts of reimagining comprise the central trope of all panegyric discourse, it is in eulogizing the female ruler that figural language acquires particular poignancy, as it diligently shuttles among the never wholly obscured physical body of the queen; her mythical form, whether as Minerva, Venus, Astraea, Felitsa, or simply an unidentified goddess; and her inevitably masculine virtues as an autocrat. It was only this figural mobility—a rhetorical flexing that had very little to do with insincerity or inauthenticity, *pace* the ode's nineteenth-century critics—that could accomplish the task of legitimizing a not entirely secure power, held in female hands, often seized violently, and wielded in the name of the anxiety-provoking Enlightenment. It was also this figural mobility that allowed the poet to find a creative position capable of transcending that of mere minion or suppliant, or indeed, of a rapturous man. The poetics of the eighteenth-century Russian ode developed its unique rhetorical forms not only in response to the pressures to modernize the Russian cultural sphere and expand Russian literary language, but also because, for the greater part of the century, its panegyric focus was to be female rule. Lev Pumpianskii memorably describes this fertile poetic field: "a woman is on the throne; civic loyalty (*vernopoddannost'*) merges with courtly love (*kurtuaznost'*), with a slight infatuation, with pastoral feelings."[15] Negotiated with particular intensity in the last decades of the "age of empresses," during Catherine II's reign, allegorical writing performed the impossible companionship between ruler (the main actor of pre-Romantic history) and poet (the chronicler and interpreter of her acts). Even as the ode elevated the empress to the Olympian summit, the panegyrist himself gained—whether ecstatically or apologetically—the Parnassian heights.[16] Allegory emboldened this ascent, fortifying the dual legitimacy of monarch and poet, forging their discursive link, and conveying a particular sense of ruler-centered historical process and narrative.[17]

Allegory's reconstitution of the present as myth can give a glimpse into the workings of odic historical vision. It is instructive to read the eighteenth-century Russian ode and its development in terms of its relationship both to allegory and to history. Thus Mikhail Lomonosov (1711–65) insists, as we shall observe, on the centripetal force of his image of the monarch. Fashioned as a unique focal point, this image welds poetic and historical reportage, allegory and history, and in fact favors the allegorical and the hyperbolic, leaving little, if any, room for distinction between the figurative signifier and its signified. Only occasionally do unadorned fact and hesitation regarding artistic license sneak into Lomonosov's odes on the heels of his otherwise all-transforming poetic enthusiasm. The central protagonist of this and the following chapters, Gavrila Derzhavin (1743–1816), on the other hand, no longer resists this distinction. Instead, he makes awareness of the subtle dislocations between figurative and historical representation the organizing principle of many of his texts, to the point of envisioning literary interpretation itself, particularly in his copious self-commentary, as an act of orienting the figurative back toward its presumed factual origins. This is precisely what Pumpianskii, speaking more generally of the transition in late eighteenth-century odic poetics, identifies as the "inevitable process of the objectification (*opredmechivanie*) of the sign," which, in his account, renders the ode itself no longer possible.[18]

This movement toward particularity that occurs within odic poetics coincides with the expansion and diversification of the public platforms for writing available to a panegyrist at the end of the eighteenth century. Many of Lomonosov's odes—even if we question their intended orality[19]—are written in awareness of the multi-genre and multi-media courtly celebrations, and thus inevitably become absorbed in the predominantly figurative work of pageantry. During the reign of Catherine II, courtly festivals can hardly be said to have lost their splendor or significance and in fact continued to be accompanied by panegyric verse; but new venues for poetic intervention and publication opened up as well, formed less by the celebratory procedures of the Baroque than by the Enlightenment values of reflection and moral judgment. Thus, in the 1780s Derzhavin begins to assert the private, individual origins of his texts, in the most famous of which, "Felitsa" (1782), he bypasses courtly spectacle in favor of a stylized, and in part textual, exchange between panegyrist and monarch. Even if never daring to claim any parity between the writer and his addressee, this exchange verges on the personal. Most significantly, the odes of Derzhavin are far less interested than those of Lomonosov in siding with a public situated in the same distanced, subservient position to the monarch as the panegyrist; Derzhavin thereby approaches his subject much too closely for the allegory to go entirely unexamined or untroubled.

The late 1700s can thus be read specifically as a period that accommodates the transition between these two representative odic positions: what we can roughly sum up as Lomonosov's mythologizing and Derzhavin's particulariz-ing poetic attitudes. Once we see this instability within the ode itself, within the evolving panegyric formulas of historical understanding, we can compli-cate the most basic storyline of Russian literary history, according to which it was only the onset of Sentimentalist and Romantic sensibilities that enabled new types of historical interpretation and writing. This reading of the ode also captures the relationship of the panegyrist and panegyric discourse to the royal subject at the challenging intersection between history and allegory: history seeks to narrate events (even if according to a constructed literary template[20]), and allegory elevates the specific and the singular to the realm of mythical archetypes. Thus, the transition in the thinking about history—first as pivot-ing around archetypes and mythical models, and then as unfolding within particularized narratives—a shift commonly dated to the beginning of the nineteenth century, can already be detected as a series of gradual and incre-mental adjustments within the Russian eighteenth-century ode itself.

MIKHAIL LOMONOSOV

Lomonosov, the Russian panegyrist of greatest rhetorical elation, whose ode-writing career commenced in the reign of Anna Ioannovna (r. 1730–1740), culminated during, and in fact became synonymous with, the rule of Eliza-beth (r. 1741–1761), and finally faded with the enthronement of Catherine II (r. 1762–1796), recast empresses as goddesses with great consistency and suc-cess. Lomonosov's allegorizing strategy relied neither upon some elaborate parallel plotting of fictional and real worlds nor upon a playful or deferential veiling of the allegorized identity. On the contrary, time and again we see his odes shrink, if not entirely eliminate, the distance between their allegories' tenor and vehicle, and insist upon the empress's and goddess's fundamental sameness. The achievement of his odes consists as much in the coherence of the eulogized identity they create as in their masterful configuration of impe-rial panegyric space.[21]

In an illustrative (though not particularly common) example of this strat-egy, Lomonosov presents Catherine's accession (1762) as divine endowment: "[The Most High gave] us a Goddess for a Tsarina" (*Boginiu nam* [*Vyshnii*]

poda[*l*] *Tsaritsei*), a phrase whose very syntax accommodates both sides of
the allegorical equation within a single poetic line.[22] Neither of the capitalized words subsumes the other; neither appears in nominative case as a subject. In this line (uncharacteristically for Lomonosov, devoid of all ornament),
each word evokes a key element in the structure of eighteenth-century Russian monarchy: sacralization (*boginia*), the people (*nam*, in this case of course
understood not as the Romantic Volk, but as the tsarina's subjects), the Godhead (the subject of the verb *podal*), and the institution of the monarchy itself
(embodied by the *tsaritsa*). While "goddess" is an epithet that denotes the
empress's—here, Catherine II's—inalienable virtues (the premise of her legitimacy and the promise of her rule), "tsarina" marks a place or institution of
earthly power which that virtue is sent to occupy. The essence is godly; the vest-
ments, royal. A similarly intentioned line, "Minerva has ascended the throne"
(*Vzoshla Minerva na prestol*), underscores the essentially epithetic quality
of Lomonosov's Olympian allegory, but redistributes the weight between the
place of power and its godly essence. Even though Minerva is this sentence's
subject, the lofty position of the human throne is what makes its predicate,
the ascent to power, possible. A goddess *rises* to the seat of earthly authority,
even though ascent is markedly a movement from the earthly to the celestial
domain. Thus, Lomonosov again accomplishes a difficult allegorical equilib-
rium between (i.e., an identity of) goddess and empress in an ode that celebrates, however anxiously, Catherine II's ascent to power.

As instances of intermittent and condensed allegory, these succinct pairings
of the divine and the human preclude the sort of divergent interpretations
or even misreadings of the empress's identity and legitimacy that a lengthier
narrative allegory might inadvertently provoke. As will become even more
apparent upon closer examination, the Lomonosovian panegyric insistently
restricts interpretation through several figurative moves: through the exaggerated (in this case, syntactic) proximity of the imperial allegory's tenor and
vehicle; through the unqualified figure of equivalence between empress and
goddess; and, more generally, through a concerted effort of semantic conden-
sation whenever the empress's person is concerned.[23]

The proximity of the Olympian to the human realms enables the synthesis
of sacralization. Unlike the Christian symbolic repertoire, the pagan pantheon
tolerated, if not espoused, the amalgam of idealization and embodiment while
legitimizing and elevating the ruler in sacral but not sacrilegious terms.[24] In
Greco-Roman mythology, Olympian life is coextensive with human life; the
godly Olympian territory is separate yet contiguous with the human lowlands.

While the powers wielded by the gods are of a higher order, the gods' social and emotional conduct resembles the human. The gods possess immortal and infinitely transformable bodies, but these transformations often proceed along an anthropomorphic course, on occasion leading mortals to mistake gods for human beings. Finally, ancient myth sees Olympus as perpetually agitated by the all-too-human troubles of parentage, family, and power. Olympian allegory thus allows the poet to present the human and the divine as extensions of each other, as tending toward each other in their resemblance. As an allegorical vehicle, Olympian imagery generates description that never departs too radically from its tenor, emerging not as a poet's accidental invention, but rather as a logical synthesis of the ruler's traits.

There is a complex interdependency between Olympian allegory and the ode's historical vision. The moment Catherine is called Minerva, her actual military and legislative undertakings grow fainter in the contrived archetypal light. Minerva indeed is an archetype for all too many women who espouse wisdom and warfare, and as such, her figure collapses all historical distinctions. The comparison of Catherine and Minerva both glorifies the empress's exceptionality and renders her fundamentally comparable to others in the past. While modern historical narration (which we owe in large part precisely to Lomonosov's era) rests on the fundamental premise that the past and present are distinct, allegory minimizes this distinction. It is a trope that discovers, simultaneously, the semblance and difference between the signifier (here goddess) and signified (the empress). This figurative understanding of the present conceives of the empress as an otherwise impossible hybrid of the unprecedented and the recurrent, as the sole object of poetic attention and as only a part of a greater historical canvas, which includes numerous other epiphanic points. As such, allegory endorses—and also invites the reader to question—the repetitiveness, cyclicality, and interchangeability of distinct historical moments.

At least rhetorically, if not always ideologically, Lomonosov emphasizes the equivalence of the present, concerned with topical issues of court politics and the perils and rewards of writing about it, with the mythical Olympian past of the timeless Golden Age. He repeatedly draws equations between the current and previous reigns, where the latter acquire mythical dimensions in the very act of comparison. The same 1762 ode on Catherine's accession recognizes the event as identical to Elizabeth's accession of 1741: "Thus had Elisabeth ascended the throne!" (*Tak shla na tron Elisavet!*).[25] The history that emerges in the ode is thus punctuated by periodic triumphs, repetitive but (from the standpoint of Classicism) never monotonous. The ode threads history—both the human with the divine and the present with the past—as a series of miraculous epiphanies: Catherine II is like Elizabeth, and both restage a scenario of divine visitation. Odic history is one of reincarnations, propelled by an allegorical imagination that envisions the particular historical moment as an instantiation or recurrence of others.

It is not by accident that my initial remarks on the construction of history in the Lomonosovian ceremonial ode emerge primarily from a close examination of accession day odes. Unlike such other odic occasions as royal lifecycle festivities or military victories, the accession celebrations offer the opportunity, rare in the odic canon, for reflecting upon historical fluctuations and regime changes, as both unique and recurring. Accession day odes account for a third of Lomonosov's ceremonial ode corpus; of these, five are dedicated to Elizabeth's enthronement, thus successively reinventing her accession's circumstances and import. The dual premise of all the poet's Elizabethan texts is that the empress both transforms and fulfills the course of earlier Russian history. Thus, the Ode of 1746 casts the advent of Elizabeth as the arrival of morning and light to a country that had been plunged in night and darkness after the deaths of Peter I and Catherine I. Celebrated for its topos of *tishina* ("quiet, peace"), the ode of 1747 praises Elizabeth for turning from military to peaceful pursuits (including the advancement of science), thereby founding a model of governance both new and, at the same time, already extant in the reign of Peter as a hopeful futurity. The Ode of 1748 introduces the metaphor of seasonal change, another topos common in odes celebrating the ruler's advent. Here Elizabeth brings about spring, a welcome renewal after the barren season of the more than decade-long "interregnum" separating her reign from Peter's. While revisiting the image of Elizabeth as a new light, the Odes of 1752 and 1761 strike a more retrospective pose, reviewing her reign as a fulfillment and even transcendence of several legacies: that of her father, Peter I, all Russian princesses, and, finally, all Russian rulers of prominence. The accession day ode can thus be read as a ritualistic genre, constantly re-experiencing novelty and promise within an already well-established regime and performed on an occasion that calls for retrospection. As such, it epitomizes the paradoxical nature of Lomonosov's historical allegorism, its two codependent animating principles: a reliance on a multitude of precedents to ground and legitimize its contemporary subject, and an emphasis on that subject's exceptional nature and status.

On a smaller scale, the archetypal allegorical vision, foregrounding as it does the figures of equivalence (Elizabeth is like others) and exceptionality (Elizabeth is unlike others), also facilitates a legitimizing narrative of the royal family's uninterrupted continuity, stitching over the many places where the eighteenth-century familial fabric wears thin. Once the contemporary moment is in this manner examined for triumphal analogs with heroic precedents rather than in juxtaposition to the immediately preceding past, it becomes possible, for example, to rewrite post-Petrine history so as to exclude Anna Ioannovna's reign (1730–40) or the easily forgotten reigns of Peter II (1727–30) and Ivan VI (1740–41). Odic celebratory history in the second half of the eighteenth century skips over Anna's decade entirely, moving with suspect poise from Catherine I (r. 1725–27) straight to Elizabeth (r. 1741–62); Anna, after all, did not belong to the family.[26] In the case of Elizabeth, Peter's daughter, the rhetoric of family resemblance to Peter's line virtually suggests itself as a basis for the language of continuity and celebration. And though in the case of Catherine II, ascertaining family resemblance to Peter I becomes problematic, the figurative structure is powerful enough to enable the panegyrist to make a convincing case for heredity.

In the 1746 accession day ode, Lomonosov proclaims Elizabeth heir to both her parents, strikingly different though they be. The daughter of Peter and Catherine is similar to her glorious mother and father, but also exceptional in combining the traits of both:

> *Таков* Екатеринин лик
> Был щедр, и кроток, и прекрасен;
> *Таков* был Петр врагам ужасен,
> Своим Отец, везде велик.[27] [Emphasis mine]

> [Just so was Catherine's [Peter's wife's] countenance, / Generous and gentle and resplendent; / Just so was Peter, a terror to his enemies, / A Father to his own, everywhere great.]

This motif of heredity as semblance reappears in the 1748 ode; only now heredity is reformulated as Elizabeth's synthesis of her parents rather than as an act of duplication ("just so . . . just so . . ."):

> Мы видим, что в тебе *единой*
> Великий Петр с Екатериной
> К блаженству нашему живет.[28] [Emphasis mine]

> [We see that in you, united [in you solely] / The great Peter and Catherine / Live for our felicity.]

As we see, the same occasion of enthronement tolerates here the discourses of both repetitiveness and uniqueness: in fact, far from being counterposed, the two reinforce each other, creating a historical narrative that satisfies dynastic history's simultaneous need for reinstatement and renovation, for being grounded in the past and for subsisting into the future. In a feat of ingenious reappropriation of the heredity scenario, Lomonosov congratulates Catherine II upon the New Year 1764, using the continuity of his own poetic career and his own unflagging loyalty to his royal addressees to smuggle Catherine II into the Russian royal family as Peter's granddaughter:

Что ныне, чтя Петрову внуку,
Пою, как пел Петрову дщерь.[29]

[That now, honoring Peter's granddaughter / I sing as I have sung of Peter's daughter.]

In addition to highlighting the stable core of both post-Petrine female rule and the poet's career, these lines weld the two together in a symbiosis that does not admit of variation or unpredictability.[30] Catherine is recast here from a foreign princess into a legitimate heiress, Peter's granddaughter. And the procedure of equating disparate moments in Russian history, which we should by now recognize as the ode's crucial pattern, is rationally justified by the putative familial resemblance between Peter's daughter and "granddaughter."

In the ceremonial ode, the substance of history—at least of post-Petrine, modern history—is always uniform, and the historical narrative is not that of progression but of repetition and synthesis, a conclusion that seems to apply to realms both political (e.g., royal dynasties) and personal (e.g., Lomonosov's presentation of his poetic career). This emphasis on the coherence of history provides the conceptual brace for the ode's otherwise atomized chronologies of the present, its disparate battles, public festivities, processions, manifestoes. Lomonosov's goddesses linger between the epithetic and the fully allegorical, adumbrating, but never permitting to develop, a parallel Olympian world—a world that could conceivably contain, exceed, or even question and trivialize those fragments of imperial realpolitik that always fill the ode's historical canvas. The figure of resemblance and, ultimately, equivalence between the heroic past and a present ever in need of articulation concentrates and controls the ode's meaning. And the figure of synthesis makes the novelty of each successive reign both less threatening and more potent.

The desire for synthesis permeates Lomonosov's odes, manifesting itself particularly in places where the empress's uniqueness is conceived in terms of cumulation and cohesion. We have already noted how Lomonosov presents Elizabeth as inheriting the legacies of both Peter I and Catherine I ("in you, *united* / The great Peter and Catherine"). Both the coherence of imperial history and the success of the monarch's sacralization depend on the establishment of the empress as a singular being. Surfacing time and again, the reiterated *edinaia* ("one" in the sense of "singular"/"only" and also "unified"/"indivisible") integrates the turbulent eighteenth-century history, the tenor and vehicle of the Olympian allegory of sacralization, as well as the queen's spiritual virtues and physical endowments (which, incidentally, never go unnoticed). The emphasis on singularity in the representation of the empress is furthermore clearly evocative of the central tenets of both monotheism and monarchy.

In the service of representing the virtues of a specifically female monarch, Lomonosov discovers a happy formula, "beauties of soul and body" (*dushi i tela krasoty*), which he applies to both Elizabeth in 1748 and Catherine in 1764.[31] Occasionally expanded to contain a more specific enumeration of virtues of the two kinds, this formula compellingly brings into view the rationale behind representing the empress through the figure of synthesis. The queen's body here is not a Hobbesian symbolic container for the political wills of her subjects: indeed, Lomonosov only invokes these subjects' wills when they come together in unanimous praise of the empress. Rather, it is an unmistakably physical woman's body whose only symbolic extension can be found in the inimitable bodies of Olympian deities. And it is not simply that the masculine attainments of the intellect are meant to compensate for feminine sensuality and superficial beauty; the queen's physical body is itself equally deserving of admiration, and the female monarch is herself a figure of synthesis, defined through a combination of traits (or through a negation of undesirable traits, as we will see in Derzhavin), and not through a forceful isolation of any single trait or cluster. Whether as an antidote to the discordant politics she engenders, or by virtue of the harmony that as a feminine presence she is supposed to establish, the queen in the Lomonosovian ode is always necessarily an integrative, rather than discriminating, unity.

In the 1748 accession day ode, just before proclaiming Elizabeth a synthesis of her parents Peter and Catherine, Lomonosov characteristically brings together all the key topoi of this type of representation—spiritual virtue and physical beauty, divine aura and royal parentage—and accomplishes the connection between the goddess-tsarina and her polis by naming her human parents as intermediaries:

Тебя, богиня, возвышают
Души и тела красоты,[32]
Что в многих разделясь блистают,
Едина все имеешь Ты.
Мы видим, что в Тебе *единой*
Великий Петр с Екатериной
К блаженству нашему живет.[33] [Emphasis mine]

[You, goddess, are exalted / By beauties of soul and body. / What in many shines
separately / You have all in yourself alone. / We see that in you, united [in you
solely] / The great Peter and Catherine / Live for our felicity.]

While the divine here remains purely epithetic—the goddess is not even
named—and the naming of Peter and Catherine signals Russia's imperial and
Elizabeth's familial lineage and legitimacy, it is the reiterated figure of unity
or synthesis that casts Elizabeth's accession and reign as a unique historical
highpoint and gives rise to the ode's distinctive elation.

Written in a period of official recognition and promise for Lomonosov, the
1748 accession day ode enjoyed tremendous success at court and even garnered
its author 2,000 rubles from the empress, a prodigious honorarium for a poet
at the time. The ode cleverly inscribed elements of topical reportage, which
atomize Lomonosov's contemporary Russian history (affairs at the Academy of
Sciences, the Library and Kunstkammer fire of 1747 and concurrent Moscow
fires, Elizabeth's plans to travel to Moscow, escalating Russo-Swedish tensions)
within the overarching theme of integration. Russia's many and various ethnic
groups, and her vast imperial territories, also converge in admiration for the
empress—the motif of congregation and consensus typical for the panegyric:

Народов Твоея державы
Различна речь, одежда, нравы,
Но всех согласна похвала.
Единым гласом все взываем [. . .][34] [Emphasis mine]

[The peoples of your land / Differ in speech, costume, and mores, / But all agree
in their praise. / In one voice do we all exclaim . . .]

Compare this construction of synthesis to a similar one that Lomonosov
resorts to in his much less successful and somewhat delayed ode celebrating Catherine II's troubled accession of June 1762. Through the figure of

equivalence, Lomonosov portrays Catherine's triumph as a resurrection or reincarnation of the previous regime, and, in a gesture of synthesis, Catherine is made to embody both human and divine characteristics, while her rule is portrayed as a synthesis of the reigns of her two female predecessors (Catherine I and Elizabeth) as well as a union of church and state ("church and palace," *tser'kov' i chertog*):

Воскресла нам Елисавета:
Ликует церьковь и чертог.
Она или Екатерина!
Она из обоих *едина*!
[. . .]
Тебя толь счастливу считаем,
Богиня, в коей признаваем
В *единой* все доброты вдруг:
Щедроты, веру, справедливость,
И с постоянством прозорливость,
И истинной Геройской дух.[35] [Emphasis mine]

[Elizabeth has been resurrected for us: / Church and palace rejoice. / She or Catherine! / Of both, She is one! (. . .) We consider you so fortunate / Goddess, in whose united person we recognize / All virtues at once: / Munificence, faith, justice, / Constancy and sagacity, / And true Heroic spirit.]

The lines "She or Catherine! / Of both, She is one!" call attention to the ode's synthesizing agenda. The choice of predecessor between Catherine I and Elizabeth is entertained for but an instant, before the first fractional "She" (Elizabeth) is displaced with the second unifying "She" (Catherine II). Standing for two different empresses, the same pronominal signifier inevitably points toward the miraculous sameness of their identities and missions, even as the stanza concludes with Catherine II's absorption of Elizabeth's legacy.

Finally, even the poet's rhetorical enthusiasm, what Nicolas Boileau might have here complimented as the *beau désordre*, that enabler of the ode's intended affective authenticity, can be seen as stemming from the poet's inability to dismantle the synthesis and focus on the empress's individual characteristics:

Когда воспеть щедроты тщимся,
Безгласны красоте чудимся.

Победыль славить мысль течет,
Как пали Готы пред Тобою?
Но больше мирною рукою
Ты целой удивила свет.[36]

[Should we endeavor to sing your bounty, / Speechless we marvel at your
beauty. / Should our thought move to glorify your victories, / How the Goths
fell before You? / But more with a peaceful hand / You have astonished the
whole world.]

At the mention of one, all of the empress's superb qualities crowd into the eulo-
gist's mind, just as the syntax of these lines becomes inextricably tangled by
their interdependencies. A bountiful reign requires that all rhetorical bounty
be assembled at once. Disordered and sudden though this assembly might
seem, it indexes not only the poet's lyrical afflatus, but more crucially, an
entire worldview putatively shared by the ode's writer and reader (one that
we will see becoming increasingly untenable in the 1800s). Inasmuch as the
ceremonial ode engages in history-telling, its account of historical time, articulated through the figures of equivalence and synthesis, presents it as a series
of triumphal peaks. Odic historical time includes only the highpoints. It portrays exceptional moments that can nevertheless be replicated and represents
at once a series of unprecedented climaxes and a uniform straight line that
resists historical ebb and flow.[37]

Two mainstays of eighteenth-century odic poetics—the figures of equivalence and synthesis, and their concomitant worldview—pull a cruel trick on
Vasilii Petrov (1736–99), Catherine's court poet and favorite ode-writer. In
December 1796, less than a month after Catherine's death, Petrov enlists
these figures in the service of bemoaning his recently deceased patroness and
celebrating her son's accession within a single generically hybrid poem—an
inventive, but failed, variation on the accession day ode, entitled "Russia's
Lament and Consolation to His Imperial Majesty Paul I, the Autocrat of all
Russia":

Услышен свыше глас:
«О Павел! облекись во праотцев порфиру
И, не косня, покрой Россию оной сиру;
Покрой, и покажи, что в сыне мать жива.
Ты счастья к ней залог, ты телу днесь глава.

Чтоб свет узрел, кто ты, во грудь твою *едину*
С великим я Петром вмещу Екатерину[. . .]³⁸ [Emphasis mine]

[A voice from on high was heard: "O Paul! Array yourself in your ancestral purple / And cover with it the orphaned Russia without delay; / Cover, and show
that the mother is alive in the son. / You are her pledge of happiness, now you
are the head to the body. / So that the world sees who you are, in your breast
alone / With the Great Peter I'll lodge Catherine . . ."]

Needless to say, Catherine's heritage was precisely what Paul was intent on
downplaying when devising precedents for his reign. It was indeed impossible
to pretend that the reign of Catherine II and its ideological reversal, the reign
of Paul I, were both equally glorious moments within a uniform flow of Russian history. A new rhetoric had to be invented on the spot, but neither Petrov
nor the ode seemed to possess the requisite adaptability. God's coupling of
Peter with Catherine ("in your breast alone / With the Great Peter I'll lodge
Catherine") appears ironic in light of Paul's rehabilitation of his father Peter
III and the ceremony of reinterment that Paul orchestrated to reunite his parents in death and restore to his father the power that Catherine had so violently captured from him in the coup of 1762. Of course, the Peter that Petrov
ritually conjoins with Catherine, betraying his waning political acumen, is
Peter the Great, whom Paul indeed enlisted as a much-vaunted model of masculine virtue, but never in association with a female autocrat, let alone with
his loathsome mother.

If Paul's reign did require any poetic regime, it was no longer the one that
legitimated and celebrated the monarch as a force of integration and reconciliation. And Catherine II, unlike Anna Ioannovna, was not an empress one
could easily overlook. Nor could the representation of monarchy after the
French Revolution make a convincing case for a historical status quo whereby each new enthronement would predictably echo previous ones, each new
reign synthesizing the triumphs of the ones before. The voices challenging
the fantasy of triumph and stability were now simply too loud to ignore, and
Lomonosov's was one celebratory vision of history that did not survive the
eighteenth century intact. But the shift in poetics not only echoed a shift in
politics, it also signaled equally momentous though gradual changes underway
within the odic procedure itself, changes that we will now trace in Gavrila
Derzhavin's creative trajectory. If the mid-century poetics of analogies and syn-
theses can be seen as characteristic of a cultural situation of intense receptivity

and reception (whether of secular, sacred, poetic, historical, or political paradigms), Derzhavin, who is less versed in and hence less dependent on Classical and European models, and has a longer native poetic tradition behind him, conceives a much more idiosyncratic panegyric project.

GAVRILA DERZHAVIN

The relationship between empress and panegyrist was negotiated particularly successfully and dynamically in the writings of Derzhavin, the poet who, for nineteenth-century critics like Belinskii, came to represent the very "spirit of the Russian eighteenth century" and who, in the view of his early and still influential scholar Iakov Grot, produced poetry that was "closely tied to external life [and] history," and thus was—and was perceived to be—both the product and the spokesman of his age.[39] The "Bard of Felitsa," as readers over the past two centuries have come to call him, Gavrila Derzhavin made his reputation with the so-called Felitsa cycle of poems. This cycle played with "continued"—even across several different texts composed over the span of almost a decade—narrative allegory, which also doubled as a direct and at least ostensibly casual dialogue with the empress, an allegory lifted out of her own writings and continued through a clever revision of the allegorical signified.[40] In these texts—"Felitsa" (1782), "Gratitude to Felitsa," ("Blagodarnost' Felitse," 1783), "Murza's Vision" ("Videnie Murzy," 1783–4, 1790), and "Felitsa's Portrait" ("Izobrazhenie Felitsy," 1789)—Derzhavin both perfects the fundamentals of Russian Classicist poetics and precipitates its disintegration.

Quite typically for Derzhavin, who was intent on fixing his poetry's meaning in extensive self-commentary, ample information on the history of the poems' creation has reached us in the poet's own words. "Felitsa," the first and best-known ode of the cycle, was written in response to Catherine II's didactic tale "Tsarevich Khlor" (1781), dedicated to her grandson, the future Alexander I. In the tale, the bright and beautiful child-prince Khlor, kidnapped by a Kirghiz khan and sent to a place tellingly called the Menagerie (Zverinets) in search of a thornless rose (a symbol of virtue), encounters several characters, some determined to help, some to hinder his quest. Felitsa, the khan's virtuous daughter, dispatches her son Reason (Rassudok) to guide Khlor away from crafty and loquacious or lethargic and pleasure-seeking noblemen, and from a mob of crude tradesmen. Only because Reason firmly insists on the straight but arduous path of virtue does Khlor ultimately triumph in his quest, which is as much about the recognition of the dangerous perversions inherent in aristocratic lifestyles as it is about the discovery of the actual rose. Though clearly a parable of the tension between autocrat and nobility, Catherine's tale draws no direct parallels between its characters and the actual figures in young Alexander's life, save for the obvious one between Khlor and Alexander himself.[41] Thus, when Derzhavin appropriates the figure of Felitsa as a rhetorical mask for Catherine, he interprets the tale somewhat liberally, but also heeds its playful parting challenge: "Here will end the fairy tale; whoever knows more [should] tell another" (*Zdes' skazka konchitsia, a kto bol'she znaet, tot druguiu skazhet*).[42]

Derzhavin's "other" tale continues the allegory of Catherine's "Prince Khlor" in more ways than one. The first stanza recapitulates and converts the parable into the odic form and idiom, refocusing the original plot on the character of Felitsa, who in the parable was a markedly unobtrusive figure for benevolent wisdom:

> Богоподобная царевна
> Киргиз-Кайсацкия орды!
> Которой мудрость несравненна
> Открыла верные следы
> Царевичу младому Хлору
> Взойти на ту высоку гору,
> Где роза без шипов растет,
> Где добродетель обитает,—
> Она мой дух и ум пленяет,
> Подай найти ее совет.[43]

[God-like princess / Of the Kirghiz-Kaisak horde! / Whose unsurpassed wisdom / Revealed the right steps / To the young prince Khlor / For ascending that high mountain / Where the thornless rose grows, / Where virtue resides,—/ She captivates my spirit and mind, / Grant me guidance to find it.]

This opening disposes of the fairy-tale fictionality of Felitsa's assistance to Khlor and of the characters in general by mentioning the original parable's masks and plot as a summary reminder of apparently well-known, real facts interposed among similarly recognizable panegyric elements: the odic stanzaic structure, the apostrophe of the sacralizing address and the requisite odic ascent to allegorical heights. Plainly reminiscent of Lomonosov's most famous lines in the opening of the 1739 Khotin ode—"A sudden rapture captivated the mind / And leads to the summit of a high mountain" (*Vostorg vnezapnyi um plenil, / Vedet na verkh gory vysokoi*)—the first stanza of "Felitsa" draws attention to the by now conventional Lomonosovian pedigree of its form, as well as to the novelty and playful inventiveness of the speaker's relationship to the empress, her collaboratively invented allegorical mask and her ethical, rather than purely mythical, clout. What follows is an extension of the schematic narrative of Catherine's parable, on the one hand, and of the conventions of the panegyric ode codified by Lomonosov, on the other. It is precisely as an extension of both that "Felitsa" tests the limits of the two allegorical forms.

The ode equates Catherine with Felitsa and hence with virtue, at the same time transposing from her original tale a mask for the poet himself: Murza, the speaker of the poem, is a more creative, outspoken, and autobiographical embodiment of the tale's marginal character, the indolent hedonist Slothful Murza (*Len'tiag-murza*), who tempts Khlor with the pleasures of food and sleep. The effect of these allegorical equations is distinct from that achieved by the figure of equivalence in Lomonosov's odes: rather than reducing the difference between the allegorical tenor and vehicle, Derzhavin's figures are clever narrative extensions that please precisely by shifting, expanding, and variously specifying the diverse identities of the referents of Catherine's original Felitsa and Murza. Thus, Felitsa grows to encompass a range of meanings (wisdom, virtue, felicity, Kirghiz princess, Russian empress, Catherine II), while Murza, originally a cardboard figure for the vices of sloth and gluttony, emerges as the semi-anonymous poet-Derzhavin (both of Asia and of Petersburg), who for all his coy self-deprecation is an appealing voice in his own right. As a result, the ode's relationship to the parable embodies the kind of enlightened cultural exchange promulgated by Catherine: the conversational ideal where courtiers follow their empress's creative lead, whether on the stage, in periodical publications, or like Derzhavin, by way of a modification in genre from the parable to the ode.[44] The ode's now "continued" allegory embodies the possibilities and limits of the faux public sphere, both encouraged and constrained by Catherine II, the exceptional but also quintessential Russian female ruler of the eighteenth century.

If "Felitsa" is rather playful in its appropriation of the tale's characters and plot, it appears far more punctilious in the way it espouses the Enlightenment values advanced by Catherine's parable. The parable concerns the rational overcoming of temptations and distractions on the road to virtue, the triumph of reason, and the value of proper guidance. In continuing and extending Catherine's allegory, Derzhavin's ode reshuffles all of these themes. Its

structuring dichotomy distinguishes the poet-Murza—who, like mankind
generally ("Thus, Felitsa, am I corrupted! / But the whole world is like me"
[*Takov, Felitsa, ia razvraten! / No na menia ves' svet pokhozh*[45]]), spends his
days in aimless indulgence—from the Empress-Felitsa, who leads a rational,
righteous, and well-ordered life. Because the odic speaker does not embody,
but only purportedly covets these virtues ("Grant me guidance"[46]), the virtues
are rendered more mobile: a matter of conscious and difficult, if not impossible, choice, manifested through consistent conduct of various specific kinds,
truly attainable only by one semi-godly being.[47] The parable's structure resembles its lesson, rigidly eschewing the digressions presented by the worlds of
its minor negative characters, and insisting on a linear path of virtue, a goal-
driven schematic narrative. By contrast, the ode's structure, while similarly
determined by the position of its speaker (now a non-rational and non-
virtuous lowly human), promotes digressions to its center. Such rational
guidance as aids Khlor's mission and emerges as the true hero of Catherine's
tale is, at least ostensibly, also what Derzhavin's ode solicits from the empress.
Far greater attention, however, is directed here at documenting or imagining
Felitsa's and Murza's contrasting daily regimens.

While dutifully disparaged, Murza's life of dissipation is consistently presented in the affirmative; Felitsa's virtuous life, by contrast, materializes out of
a recurrent negation of Murza's (e.g., "You do not play cards / As do I, from
morning to morning," *Podobno v karty ne igraesh', / Kak ia, ot utra do utra,*
etc.).[48] Even as it thus unfolds within the framework of sanctioned Enlightenment values, Derzhavin's dialogue with Catherine's text broadens its range
of vision and loosens its didactic rigor. It complicates the parable's dichotomy
of virtues and vices through an extended narrative reconstruction of the lifestyles of characters who originally merely embodied the two extremes, and
through the elaboration of their grammatical and ethical interconnectedness.
As a result, "Felitsa" establishes a dual relationship between the poet and the
queen: the hierarchical one of subject to ruler, with its Lomonosovian scenario
of ascent; and a parallel, horizontal exchange between two authors engaged
in the same creative and moralist project, a model that pretends to take at face
value Catherine's Enlightenment mission of privileging the life of the mind
and diversifying the intellectual outlets for her elite.

The range of allegorical attitudes modeled by "Felitsa" extends further, however, than this initial duality of the relationship between poet and empress.
Derzhavin hesitated in publicizing his ode because of its transparent criticism
of Catherine's courtiers, "in her taste [. . .] though with no slander, but with

plenty of mockery and teasing" (*vo vkuse eia* [. . .] *khotia bez vsiakogo zlorechiia, no s dovol'noiu izdevkoiu i shalost'iu*).[49] While the odic "I" in "Felitsa" ostensibly refers to the poet-speaker Derzhavin, it also combines the negative traits of several of Catherine's most prominent grandees: the "murzas" Prince Grigorii Potemkin, Count Aleksei Orlov, Count Petr Panin, and Prince Alexander Viazemskii. As a response to Catherine's efforts of the 1780s to curb courtier opposition and consolidate power, "Felitsa" offers a series of satirical jibes at members of her milieu who are all, strangely, hypostases of the same odic first person. The mobile character of the first person in "Felitsa" opens the ode up to narratives other than the central odic scenario of poetic transport. While the subject attempts to emulate Catherine, he mockingly yet candidly puts forward—offering "truth [. . .] with a smile" (*istinu* [. . .] *s ulybkoi*[50])—a variety of experiences that exist beyond the empress's purview, shifting the focus from the ideal to the mundane through a seemingly guileless "whereas I" (*a ia*): "Whereas I, having slept till noon, / Smoke tobacco and drink coffee" (*A ia, prospavshi do poludni, / Kuriu tabak i kofe p'iu*).[51]

"Felitsa," indeed, sustains its sizable length precisely by means of the numerous behavioral options it conjures up, and gains its momentum in several extensive lists of amusements (smoking, drinking coffee, visiting Masonic lodges, attending to fashions, playing cards, frolicking with one's spouse, etc.), associated via the repeated conjunctions "or . . . or . . ." or "now . . . now . . ." (*il'* . . . *il'* . . . and *to* . . . *to* . . .).[52] Here is an example of one famous passage, a list that ironically brackets off the domain of conventional odic praise as it satirizes Potemkin:

А я, проспавши до полудни,
Курю табак и кофе пью;
Преображая в праздник будни,
Кружу в химерах мысль мою:
То плен от Персов похищаю,
То стрелы к Туркам обращаю;
То, возмечтав, что я султан,
Вселенну устрашаю взглядом;
То вдруг, прельщаяся нарядом,
Скачу к портному по кафтан.[53]

[Whereas I, having slept till noon, / Smoke tobacco and drink coffee. / Transforming workdays into holidays, / I spin my thought in chimeras: / Now I steal

booty from Persians, / Now I point arrows at Turks; / Now, having imagined
myself a sultan, / I frighten the universe with a glance; / Now suddenly, tempted
by an outfit, / I gallop to the tailor for a caftan.]

The "I" of this excerpt is a difficult amalgam of the odic speaker and the
object of satire, a full-fledged epideictic subject: Derzhavin directing his verse
at Catherine, on the one hand, and Potemkin all of a sudden exposing the
flawed life of his imagination in a mediated first-person soliloquy, on the other.
The list of this hybrid speaker's activities combines military, political, and sartorial ambitions as figments of an idle imagination, a narrative thread nor-
mally unbefitting an ode. Meanwhile, at least the first three "or's" (*to*) here
enumerate actions that would have been quite appropriate in a conventional
ceremonial ode, but their new context signals this rhetoric's gradual corrosion:
military ambition is belittled by its very proximity to the foppish pursuit of a
new caftan, while even the little that might be praiseworthy as constructive
action becomes laughable as an idle fantasy. A similarly playful disparage-
ment of the imagination reappears in the opening section of "Murza's Vision,"
thus becoming the cycle's satirical refrain. The odic structure—both performative in its address to the empress, and formal in the poem's loyalty to the
traditional odic stanza—frames Potemkin's satirical cameo appearance. Yet, as
a narrative that points outward, away from the ode's vertical relationship to the
empress, this satirical appearance also inescapably destabilizes the odic frame.

The unstable ethical position and multiple identities of the odic speaker
highlight the individual and collective subjects' insurmountable distance from
the ruler as well as the diversity of their motivating passions and interests (cf.
the undifferentiated subjects in Lomonosov's odes, who raise univocal praise
to the empress/goddess). Even as these subjects become absorbed into an
essentially moralistic narrative, they nevertheless acquire partial autonomy in
their very status as Felitsa's foils. To a much greater degree than in Lomonosov
or in any other ode writer of the earlier generation, Derzhavin's odic output, particularly when it consciously departs from its precedents, is about
explicit and implicit narrative possibilities that exist beyond the ode's panegyric intent. This lack of deliberate concentration was noticed already by
Derzhavin's early readers. Thus, still during Derzhavin's lifetime, Aleksei Merzliakov (1778–1830), influential professor of the Moscow University and one
of the most prominent critics from Zhukovskii's generation, drew a lasting
contrast between Lomonosov's and Derzhavin's poetics: "Lomonosov is ever
the slave of his subject; Derzhavin directs it at his will. [. . .] In his style,

Lomonosov is purer, more precise, more economical and coherent. Derzhavin is more colorful, varied, and sumptuous."[54] Lomonosov, Merzliakov continues, resembles a river that never exceeds its banks; Derzhavin, by contrast, might be compared to a waterfall maneuvering among rocks. To extend Merzliakov's reading, one might say that the rhetorical agility of Derzhavin's odes translates into an imagistic sumptuousness or variety, one that exceeds (or spills over) odic boundaries.

Despite being known for his lyrical afflatus, on the one hand, and for contentiousness, on the other, Lomonosov nonetheless both theorized and practiced a rhetoric far more concentrated than Derzhavin's in its production of condensed images, its strict adherence to distinct genres and registers, and, as we have seen, its conception of new historical milestones as essentially recapitulating the past. In other words, his odic poetics curtailed such narrative and interpretive possibilities as might transcend the panegyric frame. By contrast, Derzhavin's poetics, particularly during the 1780s, tends toward a voice almost preternaturally skilled at shifting from the serious to the comical, and toward extreme experiential description that, in the ode, disperses the panegyric focus. It is perhaps for this reason that Derzhavin, obsessively aware as he was of the multi-directionality and narrative potentials of his verse, left behind voluminous exegetic commentary bordering on the reductive in its attempts to tie his poetic choices to specific occasions.[55] This commentary's most fundamental impulse is to offer a key to the poet's allegories, but, as a result, Derzhavin's entire poetic project is revealed as deeply allegorical and anxious about figuration.

The main force sustaining the Lomonosovian ode was centripetal, bringing the empress into a close alignment not only with her allegorical representations, but also with her univocal admirers, imagining her subjects crowding in at the center from the most remote corners of her empire, and compressing the space between the figural and the historical. Derzhavin's ode, by contrast, establishes the centrifugal narrative potential of various kinds of private and public experience—the possibility of living and thinking elsewhere and improvising the allegorical signified along several divergent vectors—all the while acknowledging Felitsa/Catherine as the only being who can rein in this chaos.

As in the opening of "Felitsa," which pays homage to the Lomonosovian formulas of rapture and ascent, the rhetoric of praise that ultimately emerges to contain the overflowing lists of Murza's pastimes is that of Catherine as a unifying force, granting coherence and stability to the chaotic movements of her subjects' irrational wills:

Тебе *единой* лишь пристойно,
Царевна! свет из тьмы творить;
Деля Хаос на сферы стройно,
Союзом целость их крепить;
Из разногласия *согласье*
И из страстей свирепых счастье
Ты можешь только созидать.
Так кормщик, через понт плывущий,
Ловя под парус ветр ревущий,
Умеет судном управлять.[56] [Emphasis mine]

[It befits you alone, / Princess! To create light out of darkness; / Dividing Chaos into spheres with precision, / To strengthen their whole with a unity; / From discord, accord / And from violent passions, happiness / You alone can construct. / Thus a helmsman steering through a sea, / Catching a roaring wind under his sail, / Knows how to guide his vessel.[57]]

This stanza's unity and the clarity of its panegyric intent hold together the odic structure of the poem, which otherwise threatens to become diffused in its digressions and masks. As an allegory of enlightened rule, the stanza's final image of the helmsman structurally plays the same unifying and containing role for this stanza, repeatedly rent as it is by the "discord" of "violent passions," as does the stanza itself within the greater odic space of "Felitsa," whose panegyric integrity is also repeatedly threatened by Murza's colorful and self-indulgent, though everywhere apologetic, dissent.

Always contained by this unity, narrative in "Felitsa," as we have seen, insinuates itself on a number of levels. The ode originates as a narrative extension of Catherine's parable. As a signifier, Felitsa embodies a "continued" (rather than, as in Lomonosov, "intermittent") allegory from the parable's abstract princess to the ode's Catherine. The odic speaker combines in himself several potential life narratives, and is constituted by the multiplicity of actions he enumerates and by the tension between the panegyric and the satirical voice his persona projects. The empress herself, whose allegorical representation in the pre-Derzhavinian ode depends upon the erasure of her individual features by the rhetorical figures of equivalence and synthesis, is in Derzhavin's text individuated through the elaboration of her habits and her behavior's negation of her subjects' vividly specific foibles. This individuation coexists pleasingly, albeit uneasily, with Catherine's allegorical persona. If the panegyric

force of Lomonosov's allegories resided in the almost direct, reductive correspondence of the allegorical goddess to the ideal ruler, Derzhavin's ode fills
up the empress's ideal contours with a reality that vacillates between the referential and the ideal.[58] Thus when, upon reading "Felitsa" in the Academy's
Sobesednik liubitelei rossiiskogo slova, Catherine was moved to exclaim, "[What
author] could know me so well?" (*menia tak tonko znaet*[59])—one might speculate that she was reacting not only to the referentiality of Derzhavin's language and Felitsa's close resemblance to the self-image she had cultivated for
herself, but also to Derzhavin's seamless integration of recognizable referents
into a welcome and familiar idealizing genre: the semi-realistic narrative of
the empress and her courtiers embedded in an archetypal myth of Enlightenment. She was admiring the frame as much as the mirror.

   In his attempt to resurrect Derzhavin as a meaningful figure for the development of nineteenth-century Russian literature, Vladislav Khodasevich
(1886–1939) highlights precisely the narrative potential of Derzhavin's ode,
arguing in an article dedicated to the centenary of the poet's death that "When
Derzhavin later wrote that he was the first to 'dare proclaim Felitsa's virtues
in the amusing Russian style,' he of course took pride not in discovering
Catherine's virtues, but in being the first to speak in the 'amusing Russian
style.' He understood that his ode was the first embodiment of Russian everyday life (*byt*), that it was the embryo of our novel. And perhaps had 'old man
Derzhavin' lived to see at least the first chapter of *Onegin*, he would have heard
in it echoes of his ode. The pre-Derzhavinian lyric was almost everywhere
bound by convention. Poets depicted both the external world and their own
feelings in their 'ideal,' somewhat abstracted, purified and simplified way."[60]
Polemicizing against almost a century's worth of readers who could not get
past the limitations of the "unsympathetic" odic form of Derzhavin's works,
Khodasevich somewhat anachronistically exaggerates the precedence of the
narrative or novelistic over the odic for Derzhavin. In this appraisal, Derzhavin
becomes the first in the line of writers who presage realism and the novel,
rather than the last in the line of Russian odic poets.[61]

   In his 1931 literary biography of Derzhavin, Khodasevich returns to this
idea: "One should not, however, consider 'Felitsa' a transformation of the ode.
In fact, it was not a transformation, but a demolition. Of course, the significance of 'Felitsa' in the history of Russian literature is enormous: with it (or
practically with it) originated the Russian realistic genre, and thus it even facilitated the development of the Russian novel; it did not, however, transform
the ode as such because it ceased to be an ode, so great was its break with the

odic tradition of Russian-French classicism."[62] In my view, it is precisely the
unstable conjunction of the odic and narrative, the idealizing and individualizing impulses in "Felitsa" and the text's revision of the odic parameters, that
constitute Derzhavin's momentous, though not revolutionary, achievement.[63]
Derzhavin does not break, but rather distends the odic contours, even rendering periodization and historical differentiation possible from within the genre.
Therein lies the ambiguity of Derzhavin's legacy for the nineteenth century.
On the one hand, Derzhavin does create a space for the narrative mode—
sequential plotting[64] and descriptive detail—so highly valued in the novel-
oriented 1800s. On the other, this space, at least in the Felitsa cycle, remains
within precisely that odic power structure, which would prove incompatible
with the nineteenth-century novelistic ideology and form.

While by no means constituting an early novel, "Felitsa," due to the narrative elements it introduces into the odic genre, espouses a radically different, narrative rather than odic, vision of history. At their most individuating,
Lomonosov's figures of equivalence and synthesis, which we have seen plot
the historical continuum as a series of essentially identical epiphanic moments
of ascent, accommodated only celebration of the empress's specific feats and
battles. Even those accomplishments, however, served to confirm the empress's
belonging and resemblance to the rest of the royal line originating with Peter I
(and in some texts even earlier). They validated her divine allegorical representation and configured historical time as fundamentally uniform, repetitive,
and dominated by the figure of the ruler. By contrast, Derzhavin's empress,
her allegorical trappings notwithstanding, is not to be mistaken for anyone
else. An idealized monarch appearing under a multi-layered allegorical mask,
Catherine-Felitsa nevertheless emerges largely out of an identifiable historical time and place and comprises fragments of her own strategies of self-
representation. Saturated with markers of a specific historical moment, the
Kirghiz fantasy is a mask easily seen through: the "steppes" are colonized by
clubs and Masonic lodges and traversed by English carriages; its inhabitants
read Russian *lubok* literature (*Polkan* and *Bova*) and play cards. Catherine's
ethical superiority asserts itself over the chaos of the specifically contemporary manifestations of human foibles. Thus, her reign is no longer, or at least
not only, an Olympian reincarnation, but rather a historical period marked
by lifestyles of its own.

In this regard, perhaps as radical as Khodasevich's discovery of the novelistic in the ruins of the allegedly Derzhavin-destroyed ode, but much more
accurate, is Petr Viazemskii's recovery of Derzhavin's verse for its memoiristic

historical value. In his *Notebooks* (*Zapisnye knizhki*), themselves a record of an entire era, everywhere conscious of their documentary value, Viazemskii seems to discover a precursor to his own memoiristic project in Derzhavin's verse: "His poems, exactly like Horace's, can on occasion substitute for the memoirs [*zapiski*] of his age. Nothing escaped his poetic eye."[65] Here the comparison of Derzhavin to Horace is no longer motivated by the archetypal envisioning of the worlds the two poets respond to as essentially identical (a view implied in the formula current in the Derzhavin era, and even later, of Derzhavin as the "Russian Horace"—following the "Russian Pindar," Lomonosov—even if this view no longer corresponded to the underlying historical vision of the users of such formulas). The point of the analogy is, rather, Derzhavin's Horatian appreciation for the particular, a value cultivated in nineteenth-century historicist criticism, which espouses reading poetry precisely for the unique world it registers. As a result, Derzhavin's poetry becomes for the nineteenth century, or at least for a critic of Viazemskii's sensitivity, the most brilliant eyewitness account (and perhaps the only one performed poetically) of the eighteenth.

While as an ode that pursues ethical enlightenment, "Felitsa" strives for universal and hence trans-historical meaning, the ethics it envisions, even in its most eulogistic passages, is always applied, rather than theoretical, and grounded in a specific social milieu and historical moment.[66] This insight sheds a new light on the advice that Murza solicits from Felitsa at the beginning of the poem, a request that frames the entire ode: "Grant, Felitsa, instruction / How to live sumptuously and uprightly" (*Podai, Felitsa, nastavlen'e, / Kak pyshno i pravdivo zhit'*).[67] In the course of the poem, the quest for a life that is both "sumptuous" and "upright" turns out to adumbrate the dynamic coexistence of the ode's two temporalities: though the images of luxury and daily routines are rooted in the tongue-in-cheek observation of contemporary mores, the pursuit of a non-contingent morality surpasses the contemporary. As a result, even as it distorts the parameters of odic allegory, the contemporary also comes to elucidate and amplify the archetypal, while the archetypal raises the contemporary to a greater, more lasting significance. In this sense again, Derzhavin's ode augments and extends rather than outright destroys the odic structure with its constitutive allegorical tensions.

If the Lomonosovian ode always aimed to align the reign it praised with a transcendent allegorical realm, but inevitably exaggerated the ruler's ideal and trans-historical persona, Derzhavin's "amusing style" (*zabavnyi slog*) creates the possibility of a new historical vision in the ode, one that gives equal weight to the historical and allegorical domains. "Felitsa" suspends the empress between a very specific ambit of her life among courtiers in the capital and the idealized realm she occupies as odic addressee, but one whose geographical and temporal markers lie quasi-veiled in questions easily read as not entirely rhetorical:

Где совесть с правдой обитают?
Где добродетели сияют?
У трона разве твоего!

Но где твой трон сияет в мире?
Где, ветвь небесная, цветешь?
В Багдаде—Смирне—Кашемире?
Послушай: где ты ни живешь,—
Хвалы мои тебе приметя,
Не мни, чтоб шапки иль бешметя
За них я от тебя желал.[68]

[Where do conscience and truth reside? / Where do virtues shine? / Unless it is by your throne! // But where does your throne shine in the world? / Where, heavenly branch, do you bloom? / In Baghdad? Smyrna? Or Kashmir? / Listen, wherever you live,—/ Having noted my praise, / Don't think I wished to receive / A hat or a beshmet for it.]

The empress here retains her divine allegorical status (occupying a heavenly throne, likened to a "heavenly branch") but also, having at her disposal very material, playfully Oriental gifts, participates thereby in the historically specific practice of patronage. This passage attempts to pin down the empress's whereabouts to a concrete place, but the options given for that place are themselves allegorical: not Petersburg or Moscow, but their Oriental allegorical equivalents of Baghdad, Smyrna, Kashmir. The question of Felitsa's location can ultimately be construed here as a meta-commentary, in which Derzhavin recognizes, without resolving, the tension between, and the interlayering of, the particular and the archetypal, the localizable and the transcendent within the panegyric.[69]

In the poem's closing stanza, which follows the above-quoted passage on Felitsa's uncertain geographical station, Murza's ritualistic Orientalizing self-abasement directs itself even further, at the empress's body:

Прошу великого пророка,
Да праха ног твоих коснусь,
Да слов твоих сладчайша тока
И лицезренья наслаждусь![70]

[I ask the great prophet / To let me touch the dust under your feet / To enjoy the most sweet flow of your words / And the beholding of your face.]

While the speaker edges ever closer to the empress, the figure that he approaches in his imagination continues to elude his physical and rhetorical reach. What the poet can dare wish to touch and enjoy are only the metonymic extensions of the empress's body: the dust under her feet, the flow of her words, and, most strangely, the compound noun of beholding (*litsezrenie*) that shifts the focus from the empress's face (*litso*) to the process of vision (*zrenie*) which the poet hopes to deserve. Even as it playfully reasserts the speaker's Oriental origins through ornate rhetoric (dust under the ruler's feet, her words' flow most sweet) and appeal to the prophet, this stanza is serious in both acknowledging the impossibility of the allegorized empress's embodiment and achieving it through its very reticence.

The Empress's Body

The empress's body poses a problem for both allegory and history.[71] It calls for the artist to superpose two long-standing traditions of eulogistic representation—praise for a woman with praise for a monarch—and to create a point of view and voice that can correspond to both forms of celebration. We see this duality openly acknowledged in some representations of Catherine II, both in visual and verbal media. Consider as a particularly emblematic example Vigilius Eriksen's *Portrait of Catherine II at a Mirror*. Painted shortly after Catherine's enthronement and copied and engraved repeatedly throughout her reign, this portrait gained the empress's immediate favor and was very popular precisely, I would suggest, for its recognition of her multiple roles.[72]

Despite decorations that make it impossible to mistake her for anyone other than the empress, and the viewer's concomitant placement slightly below her, the three-quarter view figure in the foreground is brought so remarkably close to the picture plane that the space that separates her from the intended observer's station point shrinks, becoming almost intimate.[73] Captured in motion as she turns to face the viewer, inadvertently revealing an almost

Vigilius Eriksen, *Portrait of Catherine II at a Mirror* (between 1762 and 1764). The Hermitage.

Vigilius Eriksen, *Portrait of Catherine II at a Mirror* (detail).

coquettish satin shoe, and holding a fan with her elegantly curved fingers, this figure is first and foremost a beautiful woman, captivating with her charm more than her authority. But arguably the real focus of the composition, one toward which the woman in the foreground points, is in fact the stately profile in the mirror, instantly recognizable as the empress because of its resemblance to the official image on medals and coins. The mirror marks the framing of a living body into its formalized representation. If the three-quarter view is essentially dynamic or unfixed, the staid likeness in the profile emphasizes the intransience of monarchal power. The mirror conceit establishes an equivalence between the two images, which is further underscored by the mirrored profile's reciprocal pointing back at its original, the only animating gesture that resists the profile's stasis. Extending the diagonal of the empress's ample and radiant skirt, the scepter—though playfully intersecting the high society lady's fan in Catherine's right hand—is the linchpin of the entire composition, hidden in plain view. While the other regalia displayed on the console table are merely reflected in the mirror, the scepter is actually extended through it, bridging what in our analysis of allegorical representation we have identified as the imperial allegory's tenor and vehicle. If we read the mirror frame as containing not just a reflected image, but a painted one—a painting within a painting—the scepter in fact seems positioned so as to pierce that other picture plane and thus highlight the contiguity of the two representations. Yet the mirror conceit also draws attention to the obvious discrepancy between the two versions of Catherine II: the human and the royal, the idealized mimesis of the full figure and the allegorical signification of the bust. This relationship between figure and ground (precisely because seeing the image in the mirror as ground would be unthinkable) is ambiguous and dynamic. Is there a hierarchy between the two images, whereby one predetermines or supersedes the other? If the balance in the composition itself emphasizes this ambiguity, the portrait's iconography is clear.[74] Both analogical and contrastive, this double vision of the empress's image is precisely what Catherine II encouraged in her subjects; the co-presence of the human and trans-human in the sovereign is, after all, the enabling premise of enlightened monarchy. We have already seen, and will now examine further, this equivocation in the texts of Derzhavin that attempt to make sense of Catherine's physical and allegorical being.

    In a manner still more complicated and self-reflexive than that of Eriksen's painting, the Derzhavinian ode grapples with the allegorical problem of translating the real into the archetypal or ideal, and the epistemological problem of knowing (and then representing) what can only be known through figuration rather than embodiment. The embodiment of virtue—e.g., Lomonosov's above-quoted envisioning of a "Goddess, in whose united person we recognize / All virtues at once" (*Boginia, v koei priznavaem / v edinoi vse dobroty vdrug*)—is a key topos of odic praise. However, the panegyrist conceives his task along essentially neo-Platonic lines, as discerning the ideal form in its contingent physical incarnation.[75] As a result, the ode moves both toward and beyond the empress's body, which is understood not primarily as an object for vision, but rather as the goal of cognition and comprehension.[76] Clothed in the ahistorical trappings of allegory, the empress's body in the ode—unlike in the fantastic and historical fiction of the 1830s, which we will examine in Part II—is exempt from temporality, whether of aging, impulse, or any other kind of narrative development. Can Derzhavin's narrativized ode, then, truly accommodate historical narrative in representing the empress? And how precisely does the Felitsa cycle envision the overlap between the empress's corporeal and ideal presence?

Generations of Derzhavin's readers have commented on the pictorial richness of his texts, identifying visualization as one of his main poetic strategies.[77] In the Felitsa cycle, however, the representation of the empress emerges both as a distinct challenge to Derzhavin's developing visual poetics and as the focal point in his particularizing and narrativizing experiment with the ode. How much of a body does Derzhavin's Catherine possess? To Lomonosov's formula "beauties of soul and body" (*dushi i tela krasoty*), Derzhavin of the Felitsa cycle adds a similar one of his own: "an angel in the flesh" (*angel vo ploti*), an allegorical vision that seemingly strays little from Lomonosov's, as it again solders the spirit and body of the odic protagonist. This spirit and body are of course already allegorized in both Lomonosov and Derzhavin by virtue of having stepped onto the public stage of history, but Derzhavin's formula emphasizes more explicitly the hierarchical distinction between the two, implied in the very process of incarnation or epiphany. Thus, one of the definitions of Catherine's geographical location in "Felitsa" sees her as an angel summoned to assume earthly power: "Where a gentle angel, a peaceful angel, / Concealed in porphyry lightness, / Has been sent down from heaven to hold a scepter!" (*Gde angel krotkii, angel mirnyi, / Sokrytyi v svetlosti porfirnoi, / S nebes nisposlan skiptr nosit'!*).[78] In "Felitsa's Portrait," Catherine-Felitsa is invoked as an "angel incarnate" (*Felitsa, angel voploshchennyi*) and in "Murza's Vision" as a "god" and "angel in the flesh" (*Moi bog, moi angel vo ploti!*).[79] There is no doubt that Derzhavin's formula places a greater emphasis on the empress's revealed angelic essence than on her physical existence (embodiment), which is of course never in question. And yet, unlike in Lomonosov, for whom the pithy formula itself is a valuable endpoint of figuration, for Derzhavin both the angelic and the fleshly components of the empress's image, both the sacralizing and the embodying stimuli behind her representation, become equally productive.

Derzhavin presses with great insistence and inventiveness for his empress to achieve embodiment, all the while questioning its possibility and upholding her as an ethereal ideal. If the pre-Derzhavinian ode attempted to mask this discrepancy between the physical (hence historical) image of the empress and her immanent ideal (and hence trans-historical) substance—a discrepancy indeed inherent in all allegory—Derzhavin displays it at the very center of his panegyrics to Catherine. His is in so many ways not a poetics of equivalence, but of difference. Thus, in "Felitsa" we see the princess exhibit a healthy physical body, walking "on foot" (*peshkom*) while her courtiers take fancy carriages, eating "the simplest food" (*pishcha samaia prostaia*) where others indulge in gastronomical excess,[80] and yet inhabiting an unreachable and unmappable realm in which she is defined not through her body, but through the negation of others' bodily habits and through the attainments of her spirit. In "Murza's Vision"—a dreamy plea for creative autonomy doubling as a heartfelt eulogy— the empress flits over precisely this divide between the sacral and the bodily. As a panegyric scenario, *videnie* ("vision" in the sense of daydream) allows the speaker to experience and communicate the empress's image as an object of both sight and cognition, the imaginative poetic senses whose inadequacy in comprehending Felitsa Derzhavin thematizes. She is seen only briefly and cannot be touched, and the speaker's soul hurries after "his" angel, predictably never catching up with her:

> Мой бог, мой ангел во плоти! . . .
> Душа моя за ней стремилась,
> Но я за ней не мог идти,
> Подобно громом оглушенный,
> Бесчувствен я, безгласен был.[81]

[My god, my angel in the flesh! . . . / My soul hastened after her, / But I could not follow her, / As if deafened by thunder, / I remained insensate and mute.]

The speaker is weighed down by his flesh (unable to walk—*ia . . . ne mog idti*) and deprived of all sentience and expression ("insensate" and "mute," *beschuvstven, bezglasen*) as a result of his fleeting encounter with the empress. His contact with her is never sustained or satisfying, and the very brevity and one-sidedness of the exchanges that his panegyric inspiration affords constitute Derzhavin's paradigmatic odic situation: while the empress admonishes the poet in his presence, he regains his voice only in evoking and invoking her in her absence. Again in "Murza's Vision": "She spoke—and a radiant cloud concealed / From my unsated eyes / Her divine features" (*Rekla—i svetlyi oblak skryl / Ot glaz moikh nenasyshchennykh / Bozhestvenny ee cherty*).[82] If Lomonosov's rapture can lift the poet to the Parnassian heights, Derzhavin's speaker, dumbstruck by a feeling whose description equivocates rather pleasingly between civic, religious, and erotic ecstasy (an equivocation fully possible only in the address to a female ruler), is tethered to the earthly domain. Meanwhile, the empress comfortably inhabits both realms. In fact, the very tenuousness of her presence, combined with the speaker's unfulfilled aspirations to capture, localize, and preserve it, comprise the organizing tension in Derzhavin's creative position as he constructs it in the Felitsa cycle. "Murza's Vision" is built upon the need to resuscitate and legitimate the panegyrist's voice, both in the wake of post-"Felitsa" criticism and, more immediately, in response to Felitsa's admonishing apparition within the text.[83] The ode progresses from the poet's muteness to his assertion of his own symbiotic relationship with the empress: "I will extol you, I will glorify you, / Through you I myself will become immortal!" (*Prevoznesu tebia, proslavliu, / Toboi bessmerten budu sam!*).[84] Thus, by the end of the poem, the anxiety over perception (both sight and cognition) that the poet endures in his encounter with the empress is drowned out in this climactic affirmation of the poet's power of speech, and a newly engaged position for the subject vis-à-vis the empress is enabled as a result.[85]

The later ode "Felitsa's Portrait" addresses the same strained relationship of perception and expression, and of visual and verbal representation, inherent in all panegyric figuration and in the very encounter between the ode's speaker and addressee. On the one hand, the ode discovers the limitations of imperial subjects' perceptual and cognitive knowledge of the empress; on the other, one of the key claims of the genre, as established by Lomonosov, is the rapturous capaciousness of poetic communication in representing her beyond her visible contour. The poem ultimately arrives at the same empowered position for the poet as that staked out in "Murza's Vision," but, unlike in that text, where the poet confronts Catherine as an apparition and is thus aware from the start that her physicality is only illusory, "Felitsa's Portrait" entertains the possibility of comprehensively rendering the empress in painting. As the poem accretes its encomiastic detail, its initial conceptualization as an ekphrasis whereby the future spectator-poet directs the commission, and the artist wields some control over the representation, becomes untenable. The text's impressive length and masterful *beau désordre* only underscore the contrast between the inclusive space of the panegyric and the limited space of the portrait, between the translocal and the local, the mind's eye and the eye.

Pursuing a portrait rather than a vision, Derzhavin now commissions none other than Raphael to capture Felitsa's image in great—though ultimately intangible, excessive, and unrepresentable—detail:

> Изобрази ее мне точно
> Осанку, возраст и черты,
> Чтоб в них я видел и заочно
> Ее и сердца красоты,
> И духа чувствы возвышенны,
> И разума ее дела;
> Фелица, ангел воплощенный,
> В твоей картине бы жила![86]

[Portray her for me with precision / Her stature, age, and features / So that in them I could see even in her absence / The beauties of her heart, / The lofty sentiments of her soul, / The deeds of her reason; / Felitsa, angel incarnate, / Would live in your painting!]

The commission resembles Lomonosov's synthesizing "beauties of soul and body," but if Lomonosov is satisfied with the abstract breadth of this formula, Derzhavin's poetic conceit hinges precisely on the difficulty, if not utter impossibility, of reconciling the many hyperbolic requirements of his commission with the limitations of the visual medium even in the hands of so brilliant a practitioner as Raphael.[87] Representing incarnation is, after all, notoriously difficult, and Raphael is chosen for the task precisely because of his achievement in "painting the inscrutable" (*nepostizhimost' napisat'*).[88] Situated as it is at the opening of the poem, this excerpt already intimates both the frustration of the speaker's demands on the painter and the related proliferation of pseudo-ekphrastic odic description which will, over the long course of the poem's fifty-eight stanzas, take the place of the painting. What precisely, "Felitsa's Portrait" appears to ask, is the mechanism by which the rendering of the empress's "stature, age, and features" can be made to elicit "the beauties of her heart, the lofty sentiments of her soul, [and] the deeds of her reason"?[89] What kind of a painterly exactitude ("precis[ion]," *tochno[st']*) can compensate for the empress's absence (her being "in absentia," "sight unseen," *zaochno*) or ineffability? What, in other words, are the status and effect of representation when presence is difficult to secure?

The ekphrasis of the projected portrait strains against, and pushes beyond, the constraining frame presupposed by pictorial representation. For example, the text incorporates a lengthy quotation of the empress's speech (thirty lines) as part of the commission, thus requiring the impossible preservation of word in image, lest imprecision result in the crime of *lèse-majesté*. The commission's recurring subjunctive ("so that . . ." *chtob* . . .)—e.g., "So that, having descended from the throne, she would bestow / A tablet of sacred commandments; / So that the universe would accept / In them the voice of god and the voice of nature" (*Chtob, sshed s prestola, podavala / Skryzhal' zapovedei sviatykh; / Chtoby vselenna prinimala / Glas bozhii, glas prirody v nikh*[90])— evokes the disparity between the future tense of the as-yet-unexecuted painting and the past tense (a grammatical requirement for the subjunctive in Russian) of performative speech accomplished by the poet in the very act of verbalizing the commission. As we learn in the final stanza, the portrait in fact materializes not on canvas, but in the poet's heart. Even the visual details that the commission includes never describe the empress mimetically, but rather press for elaborate similes whose many elements cannot plausibly coexist within the same pictorial frame, and instead showcase the poet's supple imagination:

Как утрення заря весення,
Так улыбалась бы она;
Как пальма, в рае насажденна,
Так возвышалась бы стройна.

Как пальма клонит благовонну
Вершину и лицо свое,
Так тиху, важну, благородну
Ты поступь напиши ее.[91]

[Like the spring morning's dawn, / That's how she would smile; / Like a palm-tree planted in paradise, / That's how, slender, she would rise. // Just as a palm-tree

bends its fragrant / Top and face, / That is how her quiet, dignified, and noble /
Gait should be painted by you.]

Yet another challenge to the painter is posed by Catherine's well-known claims
to both masculine and feminine virtue. Instantiated particularly memorably
by her reign's inaugural spectacle, whereat Catherine assumed power dressed
in an officer's uniform; physical and ethical cross-dressing in fact constituted
one of Catherine's most compelling legitimizing performances. But when
Derzhavin exhorts Raphael to "clothe in golden armor / And in courage [ety-
mologically, 'manhood'] her beauties" ([o]de[t]' v dospekhi, v broni zlaty / I v
muzhestvo ee krasy[92]), the request underscores the essentially allegorical enterprise of moral representation in physical form, the problem of making virtue
legible in painting, even of so highly emblematic and reading-oriented a sort
as was produced by Derzhavin's neo-Classicist contemporaries.[93]

The poem in fact poses a challenge to the coherent and readable composition cultivated by neo-Classicist painters. Visual representation is exploded
by the speaker's desire to read everything at once:

Представь в лице ее геройство,
В очах величие души;
Премилосердо, нежно свойство
И снисхожденье напиши;
Не позабудь приятность в нраве
И кроткий глас ее речей;
Во всей изобрази ты славе
Владычицу души моей.[94]

[Represent heroism in her countenance; / Spiritual greatness in her eyes; / The
tender quality of mercy / And leniency you should paint; / Do not forget the
amiability of character / And the gentle sound of her speech; / Depict in all her
glory / The mistress of my soul.]

Even as the poem discovers that a painting can hardly be pressed to incorporate and contain all of the diverse attributes of Catherine's moral being,
Derzhavin also articulates alternative, poetic structures for the absorption of
such miraculous diversity. "In" (v), for example, is the poem's most frequently
used preposition (there are eighty-two instances throughout the ode). But
rather than mark only the space of the picture, "in" delineates an affective

space of the speaker's soul, as in the formulations "she'd live in my soul" (*v dushe moei zhila*) and "I see in my heart" (*ia v serdtse zriu*). The "mistress" of his soul (*vladychits[a] dushi moei*) and the "mistress of hearts" (*vladychits[a] serdets*) is the painting's subject. The portrait that emerges in the poem is an aggregate of innumerable depictions and history paintings that can only be truly assembled by the poet's imagination: "[Paint such that] like a mother, she would save her children; / Like a tsar—for [the nation's] pride she would move her troops; / Like God—she would cast spite down to hell" (*Kak mat', svoikh spasala b chad; / Kak tsar'—na gordost' dvigla voiski; / Kak Bog—svergala zlobu v ad*).[95] All of these images point in different discursive directions, and yet are held together by the poetic structure, by the poet's soul, and by the multifaceted majesty of the empress. To match the empress's integrity (united, *edinaia*), the poet attempts to reconstitute her completely (all, *vsia*) as an affective presence in his mind.

For her subjects, the ruler represents a totality, and, as a result, the commission is bound to erode its own foundation: the desire for a particular and individuated image of the empress.[96]

Черты одной красот ей ложно
Блюдися приписать в твой век;
Представь, каков, коль только можно,
Богоподобный человек![97]

[The traits of a single woman's beauty / In your own age take care not to falsely ascribe to her; / Imagine, as far as one can, what would be like / A godlike human being!]

If painting, no matter how well-executed, might inevitably tie the empress to a certain physical contour, "a single woman's beauty," then the ode ultimately rescues her image from such definitional strictures. The painter is here caught irretrievably between the injunction to imagine (*predstav'*) and that threshold of sacralization where imagining becomes impossible (*bogopodobnyi chelovek*). The poet, on the other hand, both amply satisfies and displaces the need to visualize the empress, constructing the transcendent from the multiple versions of the particular.

Who is the real addressee of this plea for visualizing the empress? Because it is an ode, we would expect it to be the empress herself. Why then would a portrait, a genre that in aspiring to likeness would only show her what she already knows, prove a winning bid for her favor? In "Felitsa's Portrait," as in the portrait by Eriksen, the empress is called to witness not just this or that image of herself, but also the way she projects her power for her subjects and the way her power is projected back at her through representation. The portrait is here a mirror as much because of its magnifying allegorical force as because of its mimetic historical accuracy.

Every text in the Felitsa cycle stages the encounter between empress and subject and scrutinizes the procedures for its representation. In "Felitsa," this encounter stands as the negative reciprocity of the courtiers' weakness in the face of the empress's strength, taking shape in the narrative extension and diversification of the basic parable structure of Catherine's Khlor tale. In "Murza's Vision," the encounter is most direct, crystallizing as a dialogue—albeit not of equals—between empress and poet, but also as the poet's hallucinatory creation of the empress in a "vision." In "Felitsa's Portrait," this encounter is at its most mediated, a portrait that appears nowhere and everywhere, entirely a product of the poet's imaginative will, yet ultimately also one that takes possession of his entire being. All of these portraits generalize the empress's particular accomplishments, turning her figure into a mythology, the ruler into power itself. Yet they also carve out a space of engagement for her observer/poet/subject, who strangely understands himself as a contemporary of the mythical figure he himself helps to deify. If, as Louis Marin argues, the king "can be seen only to the extent that he looks at us, since one contemplates only when taken and seized in the limits of *his* scopic beam, [and] the eye is theoretical only on the condition of being seized in and by the gaze of what it sees,"[98] Derzhavin's Felitsa texts generate precisely such a theoretical vision of power and history, in which the ode's allegorical and historical capacities for conceptualizing the contemporary are brought into alignment.

In the nineteenth century (and in many cases up to the present day), the complexity of this representational structure has gone largely unappreciated. On the one hand, the ode receives condemnation as a genre of subservience[99]; on the other, critics and scholars champion the rehabilitation of both Lomonosov and Derzhavin as poets who worked toward some sense of creative independence, as in their renditions of the Horatian "Exegi Monumentum."[100] And yet, as I hope to have shown, to talk about either servility or autonomy here is to ignore the odes' symbiotic procedure in which the allegorical and the historical are not easily isolated. The reason the ode's dynamism falls into the nineteenth century's blind spot, then, could very well be the post-Classicist move toward strictly historical and narrative modes of understanding the contemporary and the past.

In the next chapter, we will see the gap between the historical and the allegorical—between Catherine's mortal (and indeed, dead) body and her transcendent spirit—become the premise of Derzhavin's commemoration of the recently deceased Catherine in her beloved habitat, Tsarskoe Selo. Everything in the estate reminds its visitor of the "spirit" of Catherine's age, but also inescapably proclaims the impending physical disintegration of her material world. Derzhavin's elegiac rhetoric in "Ruins" ("Razvaliny"), which observes and records the undoing of Tsarskoe Selo, was, as I have shown in this chapter, already prepared by the double vision of his odes. Taking account simultaneously of the abstract and the mundane, the ideal and the bodily, the ruler and the subject, this double vision transformed the Lomonosovian odic history, distending its contours and diversifying its narrative repertoire.

2

Catherine's Passing
Hybrid Genres of Commemoration

Хотя бы окружен был тмою сей кумир,
Но в нем владычицу свою познал бы мир.

—G. R. DERZHAVIN, "To the Statue of Catherine II" (1797)

THE PERSISTENCE OF PANEGYRIC DISCOURSE

Catherine II's death on November 6, 1796, and her heir Paul I's subsequent symbolic repudiation of her legacy created a peculiar crisis for panegyric discourse.[1] On the one hand, it was difficult to represent Catherine's much-celebrated thirty-four-year reign as darkness or winter, redeemed only through the light and spring of Paul's succession, a contrastive topos we have seen Lomonosov exploit in his accession day odes to Elizabeth. If anything, uncertainty regarding the direction the new rule would take could only foster anxieties over its representation. A given panegyric ode's distribution of attention and praise between the Catherinian past and Pauline future could be construed as expressing the ode writer's personal biases and thus endanger his position at court. On the other hand, Russian literary culture in the 1790s was quite distinct from that surrounding the accession of Catherine II in the 1760s or Elizabeth in the 1740s: the spread of Sentimentalist and early Romantic notions of authorial authenticity implied new restrictions on the adaptability of panegyric poets' political values, which previously wavered, depending on the genre framing them or fluctuations in court politics. If there was only one authentic position a poet could adopt, then Paul's accession required a new type of rhetorical elasticity, one allowing the panegyrist to praise both monarchs within a single text, and gloss over or rearticulate, while not entirely ignoring, Paul's antithetical relation to his mother.

Although there is little evidence to suggest that Paul was particularly receptive to, or encouraging of, poetic nuance, there is no question that he paid great attention to the symbolic representation of his power. Countess V. N. Golovina recalls, for example, that hours before Catherine's death Paul had already arranged his reception room in such a way that officials who had come to resolve the most trifling matters would casually pass his dying mother. This act of deliberate profanation by Catherine's heir virtually sanctioned a deflation of her posthumous status before the fact.[2] This episode portends the precarious position of any who would celebrate the new ruler as successor of the preceding one. The not yet dead body of the queen is left as a mere furnishing on the way to her imminent successor's office. Yet, the attraction of her legacy is also implicitly acknowledged in the very deliberateness and impropriety of this arrangement. Moreover, as her legitimate though ideologically and personally disgruntled heir, Paul appears to share Catherine's quarters; his accession is not nearly as disruptive as was Catherine's own, his legitimacy not subject (as was Catherine's) to doubt; and his strategy in fact is to emphasize "hereditary right" as guaranteeing both his own rule and the future reigns of his successors.[3] This kind of intricate figurative demotion—highlighting the endurance and continuity of the system and, at the same time, a shift in the new ruler's values away from his mother's—was to cue the court, and by extension court poets, to the representational demands of the newly-enthroned.

Paul's downgrading of Catherine's legacy was furthermore linked to his deep-seated distrust of the European, primarily French, Enlightenment she had promulgated, and hence bound up with his attempts to ward off the threat of a Russian political upheaval similar to the French Revolution or the coup that had ousted his father in 1762. While care should be taken not to overstate Paul's shift of political direction, his succession and concomitant disavowal of the Catherinian Enlightenment offer perhaps the first native signpost of the end of the eighteenth century (or at least of the Age of Enlightenment) in Russia. The Russian government—both Catherine's and Paul's—took great pains to distance the country from the single most important such signpost in Europe, the French Revolution, and it might be intriguing (precisely because not entirely accurate) to consider Paul's enthronement as the alternative Russian watershed for the end of the Enlightenment and the eighteenth century. In addition to slighting the memory of his mother by banishing her adherents and returning those she had banished to favor, or by crowning the remains of his ill-fated father, Peter III, and reinterring him side by side with Catherine, Paul almost immediately began to wage war on the upper classes' reliance on the visible trappings of French influence, associating the philosophical Enlightenment tradition, and by implication Catherine's westernizing practices, with the French Revolution and the Terror. French fashions were banned from the streets and foreign books subjected to the harsh censorship of the newly formed State Council censorship committee under Paul's personal supervision. While Catherine's policies and anti-Revolutionary discourse after 1789 had also demonstrated an increasing wariness of France and freethinking, they had neither cast doubt upon the Enlightenment project itself nor tied the pursuit of reason quite so unequivocally and indiscriminately to the violence of the French Revolution as did Pauline political culture.[4] Even toward the end of her life, while recoiling at the events in France, Catherine had spared no effort in fashioning for posterity the self-image of an empress-*philosophe*. If the French Revolution and the ensuing Terror had furnished a definitive ending for the narrative of a French eighteenth century grounded in the Enlightenment, with the accession of Paul ambivalence about the Enlightenment rose to the center of Russian official discourse. One of the challenges to the Paul-era ceremonial ode, reared as it was on a tradition of lauding the Enlightenment during the reigns of Elizabeth and especially Catherine, was accounting for the profound change in the prevailing ideological climate.

In Derzhavin's ode celebrating Paul's accession, "On the New Year 1797" ("Na Novyi 1797 god")—a balancing act fully cognizant, it would seem, of all these challenges—every allusion to reason and enlightenment is invariably coupled with an invocation of the kind-heartedness of Paul, a ruler "who is wise through the enlightenment of the mind / and in his heart is more generous and good" (*kto mudr uma po prosveshchen'iu, / a serdtsem bol'she shchedr i blag*).[5] While such formulas are not in themselves new, their seemingly obligatory coupling most likely attests to the representational requirements of the new regime, anxious about the destructive potential of reason alone. The excesses of reason are here curbed by a different kind of wisdom, arising—in a true Sentimentalist fashion to which we will return when considering Karamzin's and Ivan Dmitriev's panegyrics—from the heart. Thus, while as monarch Paul wields the requisite degree of stern authority, this fearsome quality is immediately offset by corresponding praise for his mild sensibility: "True to his duty, [he is] stern and just, / but in his soul tender and kind" (*Po dolgu strog i pravosuden, / No nezhen, milostiv dushei*).[6] And the instrument that proclaims the monarch's praise—emanating from both the poet and Paul's other subjects—is accordingly the heart itself:

Да мы под Павловым владеньем
Еще светлее процветем,

И век его бессмертным пеньем
На лирах сердца воспоем.[7]

[Let us under Paul's dominion / Prosper still more radiantly, / And in immortal
song let us sing of his age / On the lyres of the heart.]

If we read the topos of radiance/light (morning, springtime, etc.) as representing the rise of the new monarch as well as alluding to the new regime's putative
or actual adherence to the values of the Enlightenment, then for the portrayal
of Paul's accession the topos becomes a most sensitive pressure point, unavoidable yet potentially harmful. Derzhavin skillfully inserts the topos here (*svetlee*,
"more radiantly," or literally "with more light"), but suggests alternative ways
of conceptualizing the Enlightenment and the new ruler's stance toward it.
Derzhavin's "heartfelt" ode still incorporates the praise of reason, but redefines
the value hierarchy such that reason is now surpassed in importance by sentiment. In this context, the tribute to Paul's love of peace and justice grounds
these virtues in a different, late eighteenth-century version of the Enlightenment: in the refinement not primarily of the monarch's mind, but rather of his
heart. By implication, the continuity of Russian eighteenth-century history—
inasmuch as it can be characterized by the pursuit of enlightenment—is preserved intact, while Paul's reorientation of its values is also acknowledged and
valorized.

Before turning to a more polemical representation of Paul's accession in this
chapter's central Derzhavin text "Ruins" (1797), a formal hybrid which, by contrast, revalorizes Catherine's reign and Catherine's version of the Enlightenment, I would like to dwell in greater detail on "On the New Year 1797" as
well as on three other texts by late eighteenth-century poets of diverse political and literary orientations. These four texts respond to the double challenge
posed at this moment in Russian literary history to, on the one hand, the ode
writer's powers of political judgment and divination, and, on the other hand,
to his discursive flexibility, increasingly crucial in the context of the destabilized genre hierarchy and the newly valorized coherence of biographical persona with lyric subject. All the texts that precede "Ruins" in my analysis were
written in the first months after Paul's enthronement.[8] In celebrating his recent
accession, the authors—Petrov, Derzhavin, Karamzin, and Dmitriev—also
inevitably draw epochal distinctions, assessing Catherine's role and projecting
a program for Paul's future achievements, both as it is intimated in his own
manifestoes and as envisaged by his critical subjects. The hybridity of form in

the case of these texts complements the plasticity of ideological discourse, and this complementarity presents Russian literary historians with a key moment when political and formal considerations, history and literary history, align.

Russia's Lament and Consolation

For Catherine's court poet Vasilii Petrov, the empress's death was undoubtedly a major blow. Shortly afterward Petrov himself, like his patroness, suffered a stroke and upon recovery faced the urgent need to secure his status at the new court. His attempt to panegyrize Paul's accession was "Russia's Lament and Consolation to His Imperial Majesty Paul I, the Autocrat of All Russia" ("Plach i uteshenie Rossii k Ego Imperatorskomu Velichestvu Pavlu Pervomu, Samoderzhtsu Vserossiiskomu"). Composed in late November–early December 1796, Petrov's poem is an immediate and, ultimately, miscalculated response to the change of regime. The title itself suggests a poetic structure split between contrasting sentiments and genres, and a narrative of transition from sorrow to joy. At 260 lines, "Russia's Lament and Consolation," not an ode, but something closer to a pageant script, is constructed as a series of interconnecting monologues—Russia's protracted dirge upon Catherine's death; God's designation of Paul as Russia's deliverer; Paul's pledge to Russia to ensure its wellbeing—followed by brief joyful remarks from all three parties, proclaiming the prosperous future of Russia under the new monarch. While it is not uncommon for the ceremonial ode and other para-odic eighteenth-century genres to incorporate quoted speech, allotting these other voices almost three-fourths of the total lines seems indicative of a deliberate poetic strategy. In merely framing the speeches by Russia, God, and Paul, the poet's own brief impersonal interpolations—bordering on stage directions in their function—consistently attribute both sorrow and joy to entities other, and greater, than himself. As a result, the emotional charge of the text appears magnified and universal, distinguished (though not entirely detached) from the poet's personal investment in events. Petrov's hybrid text—pageant, elegy, ode—scripts this specific moment of transition by expanding its perspective to a personified odic universe that includes Russia as nation and land, the Godhead, and the ruler.[9]

Even more crucially, the poem's pageant structure allocates distinct segments of the text to the expression of bereavement, of divine promise, and of joy. Because Petrov's poem unfolds as a sequence of monologues, the first one, by Russia, occurs as if prior to God's election of Paul, at a moment when the country is cast into anguished uncertainty in the absence of a new leader.

This temporal gap between the first monologue and Paul's election is of course pure invention on the part of Petrov since there was no moment of interregnum in 1796, but it enables the representation of pure grief untainted by the symbolic requirements of the new reign or even, as it were, of any knowledge of the new reign's imminence:

Увы! (то мысль моя воображать отмещет,
Язык мой вымолвить трепещет)
Екатерины больше нет?
Екатерины нет! о горе, о беда!
Привыкшей славы к блескам,
Ко торжествам и плескам,
Сраженной тако ль быть вдруг вышла мне чреда![10]

[Alas! (My thought refuses to imagine that, / My tongue shudders to pronounce it) / Catherine is no more? / Catherine is no more! O grief, o woe! / Having become accustomed to the splendors of glory, / To festivities and ovations, / Am I fated thus suddenly to be vanquished!]

Russia's lament is situated in the interstice between the question of Catherine's passing ("Catherine is no more?") and its confirmation ("Catherine is no more!"), or between the interrogative and the emphatic intonations. It moves from a refusal to imagine (*voobrazhat'*) and articulate (*vymolvit'*) the fact and the immediate consequences of Catherine's passing to the realization of their irrevocability (the tsarina's "eternal sleep"; *besprobudnyi son*). This is in fact a progression of sentiment typical of the elegy, a performance of the work of mourning whereby the very acknowledgment and rehearsal of loss produce consolatory closure.[11] But in Petrov's text the steps toward consolation are both more explicit and externalized, undertaken not by the grieving subject (here Russia), but, as we shall see, by the intervening God. Thus we might think of Russia's lament as an elegiac fragment that, for all the intensity of the grief it expresses, is deliberately truncated through the interference of other voices and other poetic genres.

Petrov's torrent of tears reaches universal proportions precisely because there is nothing as yet in the poem to counteract Russia's grief:

На сей великий труп, на мертво божество,
Слез миро льет со мной днесь тварей естество,

Мне горы, мне леса, мне морь состонут волны,
Во бреги бьют, ревя, слезами реки полны.[12]

[Upon this exalted corpse, upon the dead deity, / Today with me [all] creatures'
nature sheds the myrrh of tears, / With me moan mountains, forests, and the
waves of seas, / And roaring, rivers pound their shores, full of tears.]

As soon as this lament concludes, however, a divine beam of light immediately
(*i v toi zhe chas*) stretches toward Saint Petersburg and, quick as lightning
(*molniebystr*), alights upon Paul.[13] The transition between Catherine and Paul
is figured as both a pause of suspense, sufficient for representing Russia's pend-
ing deliverance as an unforeseen miracle, and as a swift transformation, a
vision that ensures that there is no break in the royal lineage. If sequenc-
ing the monologues is key to justifying the prolonged expression of grief in
the poem, the immediacy of the transitions from speaker to speaker—and
here from plaint to resolution—confirms the presence of divine intercession
in Paul's empowerment. The possibility of misreading the poem's sequential-
ity as hesitation about Paul is thereby precluded. As soon as God elects Paul,
the tsar steps in as Russia's new protector: "God spoke, and Paul instantly
donned and spread / The expanse of royal purple, and covered Russia with
it" (*Bog rek, i Pavel, vmig nadev, rasprostiraet / Porfiry shirotu, Rossiu kroet
toi*[14]). While the lament hints at the prospect, if only for the brief duration of
the poem's first ninety lines, that the empire could die along with Catherine
("Oh! Breathless is she, through whom I breathed," *Akh! Bezdykhanna ta, ia
koieiu dykhala*, exclaims Russia), God's swift intervention and Paul's readiness to lead obviate this mistaken sense of doom.

As if hastening to offset the exaggerated tears that mark its beginning, the
poem somewhat imprudently moves to assert continuity between Catherine's and Paul's reigns. God promises to "lodge Catherine and Peter in [Paul's]
breast" (*vo grud' tvoiu edinu / s velikim ia Petrom vmeshchu Ekaterinu*[15]) and
instructs Paul to follow in his mother's footsteps; Russia promises to serve the
new tsar as she had the previous ones ("as I had served the Great Peter, / And
Catherine Most Wise, / Thus shall I serve Paul now"; *kak sluzhila ia Velikomu
Petru, / Premudroi kak Ekaterine, / Sluzhit' tak Pavlu budu nyne*). And Paul
himself vows to "restore what has fallen, / Correct what has not been finished,
/ Eradicate vice and malice wherever they have taken root, / And plant virtues"
(*upadshee vosstavliu, / Nedokonchannoe ispravliu, / Gde vnedrilsia porok il'
zloba,—izgoniu, / Dobroty vkoreniu*[16]), as if such maladies could somehow have

arisen in the nonexistent interval between his mother's demise and his accession. (For the poem, with its sacralization of Catherine, does not tolerate the suspicion that vice could have accompanied her reign.)

In its basic structure, the poem replicates the inaugural manifesto of Paul's reign, which combines the news of Catherine's passing and Paul's accession. But Petrov expands—in the process interpreting and misinterpreting—what in the manifesto could read as mere official formulas: "with deep regret" (*k krainemu priskorbiu*), "we call upon God Almighty" (*Boga vsemogushchego prizyvaem*), "toward the prosperity of Our loyal subjects" (*ko blagodenstviu vernopoddannykh Nashikh*).[17] It is hardly surprising that Petrov's vision of this transitional period was not congenial with the one intended by Paul's laconic manifesto or insinuated in his multiple subsequent bids to symbolically depose his deceased mother. Petrov's missteps were many, and attest to a profound assimilation of the Catherine-bound odic discourse in his verse. Despite departing quite radically in "Russia's Lament and Consolation" from the ceremonial ode's genre parameters, Petrov preserves its constitutive discursive moves: the imagery of light and darkness, which here necessitates the creation of a temporal gap between Catherine's death and Paul's enthronement; the sacralization of the empress and her unequivocal association with the fate of the empire; and most crucially, the insistence on the continuity of the dynastic line and on the new monarch's synthesizing relationship to his predecessors, which Paul in his espousal of hereditary right by no means repudiates, but, on the other hand, does not need as much as did Catherine and Elizabeth. The elegiac opening further confuses the tone of the poem. Even though the tears of the "lament" are clearly intended to render the triumph of the "consolation" all the sweeter, they also serve to distribute panegyric attention equally between Catherine and Paul. Petrov, needless to say, was associated with Catherine far too closely, and his text can be read as a response to the impasse faced by a court poet incapable of completely changing his tune, of disregarding his previous patron in favor of the new one. Petrov's solution—a hybrid text—only complicates his predicament. The allotment of separate spaces to grief and consolation results in a work that, for all its ultimate celebration of Paul, lacks certainty and strains too glaringly to transition from the utter barrenness of the Russian landscape sans Catherine to its instantaneous resurrection upon the advent of Paul.

Far less overtly experimental than Petrov's, Derzhavin's solution to the "problem of Catherine" takes advantage of the apparent limitations of the genre system, which distinguishes the ode and the elegy as domains dedicated to different affective content. If an ode like "On the New Year 1797" virtually dictates a Paul-centered narrative and as a result justifies Derzhavin's ostensible disregard for Catherine, then a different type of text, such as the elegiac "Ruins," would accommodate historical reflections focused entirely upon Catherine and comfortable with erasing Paul. The conflicting attitudes that Petrov—imprudently in his immediate circumstances, albeit compellingly for a modern literary scholar—combines in a single text, Derzhavin distributes between two different texts belonging to two different genres.

A New Year, a New Monarch

The title of Derzhavin's "On the New Year 1797" seems intended to attract attention: if the text celebrates Paul's coming to power, then its focus is strangely displaced from the monarch to the date. This ostensibly annalistic response to history, akin to a chronicler's, masks the belatedness of Derzhavin's celebration of Paul, but also enables him to omit virtually any consideration of Catherine. This titular refocusing suggests, on the one hand, that the advent of the new ruler is only incidental to the progress of chronological time and, on the other, more pertinently, that the renewals of monarchy and chronology are providentially in sync. The convenient alignment of the beginning of Paul's reign with the beginning of a new year—much more powerfully echoed some four years later in the alignment of Alexander I's accession with the beginning of a new century—allows the ode-writer to pay tribute to the novelty of Paul's reign without having to set it against the contrasting previous one. If at the end of 1796 one cannot help but be reminded, as is Petrov, of the tragedy of Catherine's passing, at the beginning of 1797 there remains nothing to detract from the poet's enthusiasm about Paul. Celebrating the new year becomes a way for the poet to dodge any extended discussion of Catherine, thereby also disposing of a key feature of the accession-day panegyric: retrospection. The scenario is simple and convincing: a new year brings with it a new monarch.

The opening stanza swiftly performs this shift of epochs by commencing just prior to the close of 1796, the last year marked by Catherine's presence:

Занес последний шаг—и, в вечность
Ступя, сокрылся прошлый Год;
Пожрала мрачна неизвестность
Его стремленье, быстрый ход.

Где ризы светлы, златозарны,
Где взоры голубых очес?
Где век Екатерины славный?
Уж нет их!—В высоте небес
Явился Новый Год нам в мире
И Павел в блещущей порфире.[18]

[Lifting its foot for the last pace—and, into eternity / Stepping, disappears the past Year; / The dark unknown has devoured / Its flow and fast movement. / Where are the radiant, golden chasubles, / Where is the gaze of the blue eyes? / Where is the glorious age of Catherine? / They are no more!—In the lofty skies / A New Year has appeared to us in peace / And Paul in the shining royal purple.]

The ingressive verb "lift" (unlike its English translation, in Russian *zanes* belongs to the ingressive Aktionsart) both literally constitutes the beginning of the poem and promises a beginning of a certain action or state; this initiation is immediately countered by the finality of the adjective "last" (*poslednii*), situating the tension between prospective and retrospective vision in the poem's very first line, but also quickly suggesting its overcoming. This tension was in fact graphically represented by a vignette of the two-faced Janus which accompanied the original edition of the poem and was reprinted with commentary in Iakov Grot's edition of Derzhavin's collected works in the 1860s. The tension persists, if only briefly, beyond these initial words in the suggestive dash that serves to transfer the passing year's last infinitesimal step into boundless eternity, an eternity already in the third line engulfing the year 1796 so utterly as to obliterate its every trace. The few feeble attempts to invoke the Catherinian past through a handful of laconic references to topoi from Derzhavin's own earlier tributes to Catherine (blue eyes, glorious reign) are definitively dismissed by the firm "they are no more!" (*uzh net ikh!*), and the glorious appearance of the new year and Paul resolve the initial tension between past and present already by the end of the first stanza.[19] If Russia's lament in Petrov was elegiacally situated in the interval between questioning and ascertaining Catherine's death, Derzhavin's ode from its very beginning brackets off both the query ("Where is the glorious age of Catherine?") and the assertion ("They are no more!") as the past rendered irrelevant by Paul's appearance. This ode, its opening suggests, will be emphatically oriented toward the present and the future.

Compare this opening of Derzhavin's "On the New Year 1797" to a very similar, identically titled short poem by his friend and frequent poetic interlocutor, Vasilii Kapnist:

Как дождевая капля в море,
Так в вечность канул прошлый год,
Умчал и радости и горе,
Но, улетев, отверстый вход
Оставил в мир им за собою.
Почто ж могучею рукою
Не затворил он тех дверей,
Чрез кои горесть к нам втекает?
Никак: он вход им заграждает,
Оставя Павла у дверей.[20]

[Like a raindrop in the sea, / So has the past year sunk into eternity, / Whirling away both joys and sorrows, / But, having flown off, it left behind / An open entrance for them to the world. / So why with its mighty hand / Did it not close those doors / Through which grief flows to us? / Not so: it bars them entrance, / Having left Paul at the doors.]

The poem—structurally an odic fragment—contemplates the danger of inheriting the misfortunes of the previous year unmitigated, the risk of leaving the implied (if unstated) sorrow of Catherine's passing without closure. This is the very same problem that is treated so expansively by Petrov. Just as in Derzhavin's opening stanza, in this text, too, Paul provides salutary resolution, blocking the precarious threshold between past and present, and reorienting the poem toward the future. By virtue of its extremely laconic form, however, Kapnist's text grants proportionally far greater space to distressed retrospection than to enthusiasm for Paul, which is quite restrained and limited to a single line where the new tsar appears, moreover, as direct object rather than subject of the sentence. It might of course be misleading to treat Kapnist's stanza as a complete poem, but even if we compare it to the first stanza of Derzhavin's ode, the subtle difference in their treatment of the transfer of power from Catherine to Paul becomes apparent. Kapnist's point seems not, as in Derzhavin, hurriedly to clear a space for the praise of Paul, but rather to suggest a way for Russian subjects, confronted by the demands of a new regime and by new possibilities of thinking about history, to put the past behind them.

Hence the emphasis placed here on the dangerous passageway into the past ("doors through which grief flows to us") that Paul is summoned to secure. Once Paul's intervention is assured, the text has run its course.

Derzhavin's ode, by contrast, only really begins at this point of Paul's arrival, using the framing image of the new year to lend renewed credibility to the poet's odic voice, which, to the ear of the new ruler, might seem compromised by his long and successful career as the "Bard of Felitsa." There is no doubt about the pragmatic intent of Derzhavin's ode; the poet penned it to regain Paul's favor after a brief falling out in the very first weeks of the tsar's reign and openly acknowledges his motives in his commentary: "Derzhavin was much distressed by his family's complaints and finally decided, without any outside assistance, to regain the Monarch's favor by resorting to his talent. He wrote an ode on his accession to the throne, which was published in the second part of his collected works under the title 'Ode on the New Year 1797' and sent to the emperor through Sergei Ivanovich Pleshcheev. It was favorably received and enjoyed success. The Emperor allowed him through his adjutant Prince Shakhovskoi to come to the palace and be introduced, and at the same time an order was issued to the chief of the cavalry guard to admit him to the cavalier hall as before."[21] The commentary retraces Derzhavin's highly mediated and ritualized process of gaining coveted admission to Paul's person. Curiously, one could say that the poem itself is also about the barriers the poet has to overcome to regain admission to ode-writing in the post-Catherinian age. Like its opening line, the poem as a whole—both in its pragmatic intent and its lyrical content—ventures that *step* that would in fact convey the poet from the 1796 of Catherine to the 1797 of Paul.

The framework of a new year's celebration enables a historical vision unencumbered by the need to reflect upon the past or honor Paul's predecessors. In fact, the text that follows the first stanza makes only minimal reference to the past, explicit only in the following brief attempt at the requisite positioning of the new ruler among the heroes of his dynasty whom, in Derzhavin's version, Paul unequivocally outshines: "Who is this, more magnanimous than Catherine, / And still more zealous than Peter?" (*Kto sei, shchedrei Ekateriny / I revnostnei eshche Petra?*). Without further explicit allusions to Catherine, Derzhavin proceeds to applaud Paul's relative political moderation, his projected peaceful policies, his mercy for Catherine's prisoners, and rejection of luxury—all, it is implied, in contrast with the practices of Catherine's reign (cf. Petrov's placement of vices in the imagined interregnum between Catherine and Paul). If Petrov can scarcely arrest the gushing stream of figurative

tears that he and the entire universe shed over Catherine's corpse, Derzhavin
finds himself able in this particular ode to withhold even the merest sigh, provided Paul's reign delivers upon its promise:

> О бывшем не вздохнем блаженстве,
> Коль будет дух наш благ полней,
> Коль предуспеем в совершенстве,
> В делах и мира и войны.[22]

[We will not sigh for the erstwhile bliss, / If our spirit will be filled with more
blessings, / If we thrive in perfection, / In the affairs of both peace and war.]

The past (*byvshee*) is overtly, though still conditionally (signaled by "if," *kol'*),
contrasted with the future (indicated by the verb form "will be," *budet*), but
only insofar as the latter will surpass its precedents in degree, not quality
of accomplishment. Because historical time here is rendered as a matter of
chronological progression, Catherine's presence, which would have been essential in a poem with a ruler-centered periodizing narrative, is here only mentioned twice in passing. By the ode's penultimate stanza, from which this
excerpt with its oblique reference to "erstwhile bliss" is taken, the memory of
the empress is all the fainter.

The annalistic order wherein one year predictably follows another with
no regard for political conflict also restores order to dynastic history, whose
fragility, in the case of Paul's accession, lay not, as in the case of his predecessor, in contested legitimacy, but in the subtler matter of a new understanding
and representation of power:

> Лети, о Новый Год! ты смело
> С сей вестью росских в слух сынов;
> Свершай предположенно дело
> Судьбами искони веков. [. . .]
> Надень на Павла багряницу [. . .]
> В залог нам века золотаго.[23]

[Fly you, o New Year! Bravely / With this tiding to the sons of Russia; / Perform
the deed predestined / By fates from the beginning of times.[. . .] / Vest Paul in
the royal purple [. . .] / As our pledge for the golden age.]

Preordained (*predpolozhenno*) by the order of things, annalistic progression renders royal succession a likewise never-ending phenomenon. Furthermore, if the new order is predetermined from time immemorial (*iskoni vekov*), the logic of the stanza makes conceivable for Russia under Paul both a return to the golden age as an archetype of imperial prosperity and an achievement of an entirely new golden age, which suggests that Catherine's reign—*pace* the odes that had glorified it—was never a golden age at all. For the ode under Paul, this is ironically a return to the archetypal image of the golden age previously deployed vis-à-vis Elizabeth's and Catherine's reigns, but rendered problematic in 1797 both because of Paul's own political flailing and because archetypal historical thinking and its repertoire of imagery are in this very period giving way to other modes of representing history.[24] In Paul's case, the new archetypal imagery comes not from the Olympian pantheon, but from Classical and Christian history: Marcus Aurelius, Titus, and the Archangel Michael.[25] In contrast to the Roman emperors to whom Paul bears a putative resemblance of character, the Archangel's link to Paul's reign is not solely analogical, but rather also calendrical, suggested by the coincidence of Archangel Michael's day on the saints' calendar with the timing of Paul's accession. Here again, the calendar as an incontrovertible structure for ordering time yields potent figurative frameworks for marking the end of Catherine's and the beginning of Paul's reign. This text's equation of a new reign with a new year thus proves exceptionally productive; above all, it results in a subtle shift in the ceremonial ode's content away from the immediate past, allowing the post-Catherinian poet to maintain a semblance of a coherent and authentic personal voice in the face of the new regime.

It is instructive to contrast Petrov's and Derzhavin's strategies for representing the fraught transition from Catherine to Paul with Karamzin's in the "Ode on the Occasion of the Oath of Moscow Citizens to His Imperial Majesty Paul, the Autocrat of All Russia" ("Oda na sluchai prisiagi moskovskikh zhitelei Ego Imperatorskomu Velichestvu Pavlu Pervomu, Samoderzhtsu Vserossiiskomu").[26] Karamzin has left many important pronouncements on Paul's reign, including, in *The Memoir on Ancient and Modern Russia* (1811), a virtual indictment of Paul as the monarch "who has made [us] hate the excesses of autocracy," similarly to the way "the terrors of the French Revolution had cured Europe of its yearnings for civil freedom and equality."[27] In this retrospective assessment, Catherine emerges, by contrast, as a wise ruler who knew how to temper despotism by legislation, and her reign as "the happiest for the

Russian citizen."[28] Immediately after Catherine's passing, however, Karamzin appears less certain and harsh; he is far from saddened by the demise of Catherine (an increasingly reactionary ruler in her final years) and somewhat enthusiastic about the accession of Paul, whose Masonic sympathies and knightly aspirations seem to presage liberalizing reforms.

Sentimental Citizenship and the Ode

Catherine's name is conspicuously absent from the ode on the Muscovites' pledge of allegiance to Paul, and the Catherinian past is invoked only as a disparaged contrasting background to Paul's promising future. Karamzin celebrates dynastic continuity on the one hand by suggesting that Paul had for a long time been ready for the Russian throne—"So Paul the First is on the throne? / The wreath of the Russian Minerva / Has long been designated for him . . ." (*Itak, na trone Pavel Pervyi? / Venets rossiiskiia Minervy / Davno naznachen byl emu . . .*)[29]—and, on the other, by echoing Paul's own manifestoes and associating him solely with Peter the Great:

Для нас течет Астреин век:
Что росс, то добрый человек.

Петр Первый был всему начало;
Но с Павлом Первым воссияло
В России счастие людей.
Вовек, вовек неразделимы,
Вовеки будут свято чтимы
Сии два имени царей![30]

[For us Astraea's age is flowing: / Every Russian is a good man. // Peter I was the beginning of all; / But with Paul I shines / People's happiness in Russia. / Forever, forever indissoluble, / Forever held sacred / Shall be these two tsars' names!]

The association of the Age of Astraea with Paul rather than Catherine frees this allegorical personage, conventionally linked to female rule in eighteenth-century Russian verse, from its gendered specificity; the same is true of the mention of Minerva in the poem's opening. If in the Catherine-era poetics "Minerva's wreath" would have appeared virtually synonymous with "Catherine's wreath," in Karamzin's usage of December 1796 the phrase acquires a double meaning. On the one hand, the suggestion is indeed that Catherine's throne could have long been occupied by Paul I, who was forty-two at the time of his accession; on the other, as a personification of justice, Minerva appears to place her wreath only upon Paul rather than his predecessor. In this latter reading, rather than giving Paul Catherine's wreath, Karamzin proclaims the long-awaited restoration of the Astraean golden age, which might or might not have characterized the previous reign. This is in fact a different kind of legitimacy than that arising from Paul's placement in the context of his immediate heredity, a rhetoric of legitimation reminiscent in its intent of the rhetoric of preordainment in Derzhavin's ode on the new year. Karamzin decouples the previously synonymous Catherine and Minerva or Catherine and Astraea, even as he recycles these canonical figures of the Russian ceremonial ode and thus presents Russian odic discourse, if not royal policy, as continuous.

If Karamzin preserves the odic form and at least some of its traditional allegorical imagery, the vision of monarchal power in "On the Oath of Moscow Citizens" is in many ways new for the Russian ode. Scholars have read this long text as outlining directions for Paul's future policies, a suggestively programmatic quality which might arguably be recognized already in some of Lomonosov's odes.[31] Rather than examining here the content of Karamzin's program (certainly a fascinating topic in its own right), I would like to focus instead on the poem's discursive framing of this program, which seems indeed to constitute the text's true innovation within the odic genre. The central project of "On the Oath of Moscow Citizens," I would suggest, lies as much in envisioning a certain kind of relationship between ruler and subjects as in hinting at more or less specific desired reforms. As an odic occasion, oath-taking is patently distinct from the monarch's accession or coronation, the latter two entailing the tsar's physical presence and focusing the odic vision solely on the tsar. Oath-taking, by contrast, occurs throughout Russia soon after the accession and involves communal honoring of the monarch *in absentia*. If we recall how intently Lomonosov's and Derzhavin's odes had focused on the empress's person, the significance of this distinction would surely become apparent. This unorthodox choice of odic occasion allows the ode-writer to zoom in closely not upon the monarch's personal heroic biography, but rather on the body politic, and narrate not the accession but rather a peculiar social contract that, far from disposing of the monarch's sacrality or granting any real rights to his subjects, legitimizes this accession in ways other than the ruling dynasty-centered heredity scenario. This is precisely the kind of welcoming of the subjects' perspective that had characterized the Enlightenment of the first decades of Catherine's reign (e.g., the famous *Nakaz*), but under Catherine it was conceived as a juridical rather than a sentimental project, originating entirely from and ultimately attesting to the empress's absolute authority.[32] In the 1790s, the codependence of ruler and subjects is certainly a more serious and difficult argument, in part because of the violent consequences of the disjuncture between the two manifested in the French Revolution, which Karamzin had so memorably described in his *Letters of a Russian Traveler*. But in large part this was also an argument that could be fully heard after Catherine's death precisely because of decades of entertaining such arguments under Catherine and ultimately failing or being blocked in their implementation. In "On the Oath of Moscow Citizens," Karamzin claims that the reciprocal relationship between monarch and subjects is already in place in Russia, thereby profoundly transforming the articulation of power and history possible in the odic genre (though not, of course, in the realm of Russian policy). I am far from suggesting here that earlier Russian odes did not invoke Russian subjects and their admiration for the monarch; suffice it to recall the imperial topos of the peoples of the Russian Empire assembling from all of its remote domains to marvel at the tsar. Karamzin, however, does not invoke the populace in order to represent the imperial expanse and variety of Russian territories, nor is this invocation merely one among several odic topoi in the text's repertoire. Rather, the poem gives equal representation to monarch and subjects, whose admiration and love are mutual; highlights the sentimental core—individuated and universalizable—of this particular social contract; and employs the reciprocity of monarch and subjects as the structuring concept for the entire text.

The emphasis on the tsar's subjects rather than on the tsar himself marks the opening lines of the poem in which the lyric I witnesses the congregation assembling to celebrate the new reign and take the oath of "love and loyalty to the tsar" (*v liubvi i vernosti tsariu*).[33] The tsar, it is in turn proclaimed, also "loves" his subjects ("loves Russians tenderly"; *liubit rossov nezhno*)[34]; his power is thus assured through the reciprocity of his and his subjects' allegiances and the rhetoric of love that binds them. The poem's lexical makeup is replete with the vocabulary of sensibility: "hearts" (*serdtsa*) are mentioned eleven times (not counting their habitual pairing with the cognate "zeal," *userdie*); "tears" (*slezy* and related forms) appear five times as do the various forms of "kindness" (*dobro*); love and friendship are each invoked six times. All these words are associated equally with the monarch and with his subjects; their sentiments are largely interdependent. "Peter was great, you are dear to the hearts" (*Petr byl velik, ty mil serdtsam*), exclaim the hearts of Russians, and in voicing their sentiments to the tsar, they make him feel the same in his own heart:

Рекут—в восторге онемеют;
Слезами речь запечатлеют;
Ты с ними прослезишься сам,
Восторгом россов восхищенный,
Блаженством подданных блаженный.
Какой пример твоим сынам!

[They speak—and grow dumb with rapture, / Impressing their speech with tears; / You yourself [Paul] will shed tears with them, / Rapt by the Russians' rapture, / Blessed by the subjects' bliss. / What an example to your sons!][35]

The sentimentalist rhetoric of the heart should come as no surprise in a poem by Karamzin. Indeed, this rhetoric spreads simply too widely in post-Revolutionary Europe to require commentary. In this period, it is enlisted in the service of often divergent agendas, as a language of authenticity and universalism, by radicals and reactionaries alike.[36] Those critics of the Enlightenment who see the reign of reason as having precipitated revolutionary terror (this is indeed a view repeatedly voiced in the Russian press of the period) moderate the rhetoric of enlightenment with that of sentiment.[37] In part, this kind of tempering of the Enlightenment is at stake in Karamzin's invocation of Paul's affective bond with his subjects. For similar reasons, we have already seen Derzhavin in "On the New Year 1797" present Paul as a ruler who, while valuing reason, "in his heart is more generous and good" (*serdtsem bol'she shchedr i blag*)[38] and "in his soul tender and kind" (*nezhen, milostiv dushei*).[39]

If, however, during Catherine's last conservative decade the language of private experience, including the sentimentalist discourse of feeling, could be understood as offering an alternative to the compromised public arena, language of power, and ceremonial lyric subjecthood,[40] Paul's incipient reign, as it is presented in Karamzin's ode, enables the poet to bring together the two discourses and imagine monarchal power as a private sentimental experience, shared by tsar and subjects. The ode constructs a world where there is no boundary between the political and the sentimental realms, and since it is conjured as characteristic specifically of Paul's new reign, this world is also new and, by implication, non-existent under Catherine. In this context, the lyric I's assertion of sincerity ("not a flatterer with a cold soul"; *ne l'stets, dushoiu khlad-nyi*[41]) references a change in regime, from that governed by material exchange between patron and favor-seeking subject to that held together through artless sentimental exchange or an idealized social contract. Even though unnamed, Catherine's reign is mired in a period that existed before "sincere" panegyric expression. Thus, in a text that is perhaps most reminiscent of Elizabeth- and Catherine-era ceremonial odes in terms of its form, topoi, and celebra-tory stance, Karamzin in fact proposes (if far from artlessly) a recuperation of these familiar odic structures and the ode's discourse of power for a new political reality imagined and celebrated as allowing this discourse to be more than merely formulaic.

Ivan Dmitriev's "Verses to His Imperial Majesty Paul I upon the Accession to the Throne of All Russias" ("Stikhi Ego Imperatorskomu Velichestvu Pavlu Pervomu pri vosshestvii na vserossiiskii prestol") also grounds Paul's legiti-macy in the tsar's command over the hearts of his subjects. But Dmitriev's approach toward the transition from Catherine to Paul is to praise Paul still more overtly for refashioning the values established and corrupted by Cather-inian Enlightenment and yet never to exclude Catherine from the new tsar's lineage. Both Karamzin and Dmitriev applaud Paul for inaugurating his reign by granting pardon to some of Catherine's political prisoners and recalling the Russian army back from the Persian border. Dmitriev's personal experi-ence in the first months after Paul's accession renders this praise both ironic and well-deserved: Dmitriev was falsely accused of participating in a plot to assassinate Paul, unexpectedly arrested, but soon released and granted many monarchal favors. Dmitriev imagines Paul's acts of beneficence as restoring harmony within the families and homes of individual Russian subjects, and, in a manner not unlike Karamzin's, sees these acts as granting a new kind of legit-imacy to the monarch whose subjects lend him their support on new, affec-tive terms, summed up in the poem's closing stanza:

О Павел! будешь чтим веками:
Ты начал властвовать сердцами,
Ты с первым шагом приобрел
На нашу верность новы правы.

[O Paul! You'll be honored for ages: / You began to rule over the hearts, / With your first step you have gained / New rights to our loyalty.][42]

In referring to the "new rights" that Paul's "beneficent soul" (*blagotvorn[aia]*
dush[a]) acquires over the souls of his subjects, Dmitriev offers a succinct
formulation of what in Karamzin's poem is dispersed throughout a much
longer text. While the sentimental contract gives structure to Karamzin's entire
ode, whose political and poetic universe is ordered by the desired reciprocity
between tsar and subjects, Dmitriev arrives at this articulation of their bond
only in his poem's final stanza, where it provides the explanatory frame within
which Paul's early policies can be brought to cohere.

Dmitriev's "Verses" do not shy away from references to Catherine and on
the surface appear rather incautiously to endorse the continuity between the
two reigns. "You took on Catherine's scepter!" (*Ty prinial skiptr Ekateriny!*[43])
reads the poem's very first line, and after some praise for the achievements
of her reign, Catherine is mentioned again, now among Paul's other dynastic
predecessors ("You are the son of the one who ruled over half the world"; *ty
syn vladevshiia polsvetom*[44]). For Dmitriev, Catherine's symbolic deposal is
not a matter of excluding her name or dramatically restructuring Paul's royal
genealogy (which is something Dmitriev certainly engages in, but only marginally), or of delimiting the events and chronology enclosed by the poem's
frame. Rather, Dmitriev brings about this deposal through a consistent association of the new regime with new values. If Catherine's rule was bellicose, Paul's
strives toward peace ("suddenly an altar to peace appeared"; *vdrug zhertven-
nik vozniknul miru*[45]); if the former was repressive, the latter is emancipatory
("His word is the voice of joy / To the persecuted, the orphaned, the widowed";
Glagol ego est' glas otrad / Gonimym, siromu, vdovitse[46]); if Catherine was sus-
ceptible to flattery and fostered favoritism, Paul favors true merit ("Talent,
merits, and accomplishments / Are his favorites and friends"; *Talant, dostoin-
stva, zaslugi / Liubimtsy sut' ego i drugi*[47]); and most crucially, if Russia under
Catherine had achieved glory, Paul bestowed happiness upon it ("And the
glorious people became a happy people"; *I slavnyi—schastliv stal narod.*[48]). All
these contrasts rest upon the sentimentalist preference for inner experience
(happiness versus glory) and the essential opposition between artifice and
authenticity. It is not by accident, then, that the poem's most intensely expressive assessment of Paul's achievement is also the lyric I's only appearance in
the poem: "O! Where am I, where? Is it not in a new world? (*O! Gde ia, gde?
/ Il' v novom mire?*),[49] exclaims the poet, thereby openly rendering the dynastic frame of the opening, Paul's hereditary right, subsidiary to the imaginative
hold of the new tsar's capacity for transfiguring Russian reality. If the poem's
opening stanza grants Paul Catherine's scepter, by the last stanza this scepter

functions as a symbol no longer of continuity, but rather of unprecedented miraculous transformations:

Вдруг скиптр его, как жезл волшебный,
Тел чад, сил рождших воскресил
И радости бальзам целебный
Во грудь отчаяния влил.

[Suddenly his scepter, like a magic wand / Revived the bodies of the children, the vigor of the parents, / And poured the healing potion of joy / Into the breast of despair.][50]

Dmitriev's text thus manages to combine the two familiar scenarios of odic legitimation of a new monarch, presenting Paul as both succeeding and improving upon the previous ruler. But by substituting heredity with novelty, Dmitriev also suggests that this latter scenario more accurately captures the spirit of Paul's accession. Just like "Minerva's wreath" in Karamzin, the Russian scepter in Dmitriev is more of a new object than an inherited one.

In dispatching his poem to Karamzin, Dmitriev must have insisted that his text not be read as an ode since Karamzin, whom we have seen comfortably author an ode to Paul, responds by dismissing what must have been Dmitriev's disclaimer: "Your poem is very good: whether an ode or not, it's all the same."[51] Dmitriev had amply advertised his critical position on the ceremonial ode in such earlier satirical texts as "A Hymn to Rapture" ("Gimn vostorgu," 1792) and "Another's Speech" ("Chuzhoi tolk," 1794), and yet how are we to understand the poet's rejection of this generic descriptor in the case of a text that evinces so many of the ode's generic properties? For after all, the "Verses" are written on the occasion of the accession, addressed to the emperor in an unequivocally celebratory tone, preserve the ode's stanzaic structure, and incorporate panegyric topoi. In fact, this rejection most likely refers not to the structural properties of the "Verses"—those internal textual innovations, of which the three poets we have considered before Dmitriev might in fact furnish more vivid examples—but rather to the contexts of writing and reception within which Dmitriev proposes to position his text. Extratextual intentions are of course notoriously difficult to deduce, but one might speculate that when the "Verses" praise Paul for dispensing favors based on true merit, it is implied that under Paul one should no longer read this text as soliciting rewards for its author by means of a rapture that is faked. Dmitriev rejects the ode as a system of author-patron relationships (which will become the sub-ject of chapter 3), rather than as poetic form. His poem's claim to innovation is substantiated not by any interior reworkings of its generic parameters, but by its placement within the putatively changed political world (Paul's new reign, presumably of meritocracy and sensibility) and a changed context of reception (based on the exchange of feeling rather than any measurable favors).

Most readings of the Russian eighteenth-century panegyric would associate the 1790s with its decline. This is indeed a period when other genres gradu-ally move upward within the hierarchy, and the genre hierarchy itself becomes unstable; when the demand for poetic sincerity is voiced more and more force-fully, and the ode is compromised because of its pragmatic orientation; when the Russian polite readership, while still negligible, truly expands beyond the court and begins to satisfy authors' need for reception and require genres other than patron-oriented verse. In considering the poems commemorating the change of regime in 1796, I have thus far tried to resist the temptation to priv-ilege the poetic forms that come to supersede the ode in this period or the early Romantic critique that it incurs. Instead of dismissing the late odic and para-odic texts as inferior to such Russian classics of the genre as Lomonosov's Khotin ode or Derzhavin's "Felitsa" (which from the aesthetic point of view, they probably are), I have proposed to scrutinize them as examples of verse that is clearly driven by pragmatic concerns in an age that gradually ceases to believe in poetic pragmatism. Paul's accession is a particularly valuable occa-sion for this inquiry since the project of legitimating and celebrating this new ruler turned out to be complicated by the need to legitimate the panegyric poet's voice and panegyric content in general. In reading these oft-neglected texts closely, we see them revisit some of the Russian ode's standard repre-sentational procedures, but utilize them for articulating historical and politi-cal arguments that the ode had not previously accommodated. These texts belie the mistaken popular perception that the ode, because of its fixed for-mal structure and non-mimetic protocols, was inflexible and static. In fact, as scholars of the eighteenth century have long known and as I have tried to show throughout this book's Part I, quite the contrary is true, and the acces-sion panegyric is a perfect case for demonstrating the genre's complex respon-siveness to multiple political and poetic pressures. At this late point in the genre's development, its decline also entails additional pressures and redou-bled discursive and formal plasticity.

Derzhavin's "Ruins," written a year after Paul's accession, offers a particu-larly compelling example of the ode's plasticity in this period. Informed by a greater critical hindsight on Paul's policies and their effacement of Catherine's legacy, the poem revisits the central odic tropes and topoi of her reign only to recast them in the past tense of elegy. This text challenges the commonplace of genre-bound criticism on the period that sees ode and elegy as strictly delineated, competing and mutually exclusive genres; instead, where historical reflection is concerned, we might detect a spectrum of poetic attitudes not only distributed across different texts, but also structuring individual texts.

RUINS OF THE ANACREONTIC ODE

The first word of Petrov's "Lament and Consolation" is "Russia" (*Rossiia*), the country imagined not as a geographical space or even a sum total of Russian subjects, but instead personified, endowed with a voice immediately superseding and displacing the voice of the poet, thereby raising the poem's central negotiation of Paul's enthronement to a supra-individual level. The first words of Derzhavin's "Ruins" are "right here" (*vot zdes'*[52]), a deictic utterance that not only emphasizes the setting of the poetic event about to take place, but also implies the presence of a speaker situated in that setting, ready to observe and guide the reader as if through an actual landscape. If Petrov's commemoration of Catherine is deliberately impersonal, Derzhavin's intent in this particular poem seems precisely the opposite. While no lyric "I" is ever made explicit (Derzhavin's lyricism in fact remains a contested subject), the entire poem is grounded in a subjectivity that attempts to recollect Catherine's world while mentally repopulating her former environment, retracing her steps, recapping her daily routine—all in the recognizable landscape of her summer estate of Tsarskoe Selo. If for Petrov Catherine's passing is an event of universal significance, Derzhavin's "Ruins" manages to cast it in a very intimate light, nevertheless still operating via allegory, the ode's essential figure of distancing.

The deictic opening "right here"—as well as the poem's no fewer than twenty-six other deictic phrases spread over the relatively short course of 117 lines—engages both speaker and reader in a familiar relationship with a landscape that in turn bears an intimate connection to the empress. The phrase following "right here" in the poem's opening line, "on the island of Cythera" (*na ostrove Kipridy*), transfers the text onto an allegorical plane ostensibly at odds with the specific reality the deictic opening has invoked. As a result, the landscape's beholder and the landscape itself become harder to localize. Indeed, nowhere in the text is Tsarskoe Selo specifically mentioned. Instead, the mythologized space of Cythera's island is populated with cupids, as if in a rococo painting; the goddess who used to own this space dispenses ambrosia, resides in Eden, listens to Parnassian muses, and watches nymphs dance and frolic. Just as it abounds in deictic markers, so too is the poem oversaturated with mythical figures. And yet it is precisely the unlikely superposition of the deictics onto a mythical locale that imparts a particular urgency to decoding the allegory. Especially for such readers as matched Derzhavin in social standing and familiarity with the court and its spaces, recognition complements fantasy in the projected response to this locale. In fact, no idyllic masquerade of "comely Nymphs" (*prekrasnykh Nimf*[53]) can conceal the unmistakable topography of Tsarskoe Selo, itself replete with mythological allusions in its grottoes, underground streams, monuments, theater, gazebo, swing, dovecote, menagerie—all graced by Venus-Catherine's benevolent attention in the course of the poem.[54] Nor could a reader accustomed to deciphering allegory (the central trope of odic poetry) fail to recognize Catherine in the trappings of a love goddess, and the coming of Paul's gloomy reign in the goddess's unsettling disappearance at the end of the poem. The combination of the particular and the allegorical that characterizes the poem from its first line onward implicates the reader not simply in the observation of the poetic landscape, but in the perilous interpretive act of transposing its idealized allegorical representation back onto the events of 1796–97. An accessible historical space and an allegorical poetic space wrapped up in one, Tsarskoe Selo is furthermore triply marked: as ideal antiquity; as Catherine's residence captured in all its tangible specificity; and as historical realm in decay and, therefore, in need of memorialization, or rather "mythologization."

Derzhavin's choice of Tsarskoe Selo for this commemoration was by no means fortuitous. Though founded during the reigns of Catherine I and Elizabeth, the estate had come to be linked first and foremost with Catherine II's reign, a period when landscape design was enlisted with especial skill as a language of monarchal power. And the particular version of this power recreated in Tsarskoe Selo was the Catherinian Enlightenment. In the lyrical assessment of the leading historian of Russian architecture Dmitrii Shvidkovskii, "The 'castles in the air' of Russian thought in the age of Enlightenment were embodied here in the constructions of architects."[55] In its very design, Tsarskoe Selo thus contained a narrative, available to visitors through an allegorical decoding at the early stages of the landscape's development and later in the more direct inscriptions introduced and popularized by Catherine II. The park was a product not only of the forward-thinking Enlightenment, but also of the nostalgia for and research into classical antiquity, which was part of a still

broader pursuit of historical knowledge and new historical forms throughout the eighteenth century. Following the excavations of Herculaneum and
Pompeii, the ruin became one such popular sculptural historical form.[56] A key
feature of the Tsarskoe Selo landscape as well as of Catherine's architectural
and sculptural taste in general, ruins, as Derzhavin's choice of title suggests,
gained an added poignancy after her passing, as now they not only nodded to
pervasive European fashion and the vague pan-European Greco-Roman past,
but also commemorated the actually-lived Russian past of Catherine's reign.
Derzhavin's ruins, which provide both the visual imagery for the poem and
the conceptual framework for his rethinking of Catherine's reign, are only
partly of Catherine's making. What the image indexes even more powerfully
than the Catherinian Enlightenment is its dissolution in the reign of Paul and
the heir's neglect of the empress's visible material and spiritual legacy: her
palaces, parks, and sculpture gardens.

Even as it stylized the past, the design of Catherine's park publicized Russia's eighteenth-century modernity and its orientation toward the West: Western fashions, history, and philosophical developments. The origin of Tsarskoe
Selo's stylized architectural and sculptural remains was embedded at once in
the contemporaneity of the eighteenth century and in a legendary antiquity.[57]
In fact, just as the ceremonial ode's obligatory recourse to archetypal precedents brought Russian monarchs into close contact and comparison with the
Classical or mythical past, so too did the experience of Tsarskoe Selo bind the
contemporary Russian moment and the ancient European past in an intricate,
mutually-elucidating correlation.[58] The "ruins" of Catherine's Tsarskoe Selo
vividly reminded their beholders of Russia's modernity and Europeanization,
which were in fact predicated upon an appropriation of Western history and,
most importantly for the political message of this particular landscape, upon
the legacy of the Roman empire.[59] The landscape of Tsarskoe Selo was designed
precisely to capture both the latest European fashion—for English gardens,
artificial ruins, and so on—and Catherine's modernizing orientation toward
the Roman imperial model with its martial conquests and juridical advancements. The English architectural style favored by Catherine II owed much to
its main practitioners' sojourns in Rome and to their fascination with Greek
and Roman antiquity.[60] For instance, the Cameron sculpture gallery, a key
component of the Tsarskoe Selo ensemble, housed some eighty statues of
ancient and modern heroes of the sword and pen, a pantheon bearing the clear
stamp of Catherine's Enlightenment ideals and proclaiming a direct genealogy from the much-revered classical world to the modern Russian empire.[61]

Paul's transfer of the royal residence away from these Enlightenment monuments suggested a corresponding disregard for the ideals they embodied,
a deflection from or a fissure in the meticulously constructed Enlightenment
pedigree.[62] The grand-scale glamour of Catherine's Tsarskoe Selo or Winter Palace in Saint Petersburg was instantly supplanted by the military order
and comparative austerity of Paul's Gatchina and Pavlovsk and the medieval
impregnability of the newly-built Michael Castle in Petersburg.[63] New royal
residences marked a new beginning, aspiring to association with Peter the
Great's fresh start in founding Saint Petersburg in 1703. (Although hardly living up to that precedent.) Like the heroes they represented, the many monuments celebrating Catherine-era military victories also suffered neglect. Most
dramatically, the Temple of Memory, a long, raised colonnade embellished
with sculptures, bas-reliefs, and medallions depicting battles of the Russo-
Turkish War (1768–74), was demolished on Paul's orders as early as 1797.[64]
The original design of the park as a site of historical commemoration, featuring artificial ruins in addition to celebratory statues, combined with Paul's
contempt for his mother's imagery of imperial power to fashion a space of
nostalgia in Tsarskoe Selo. Reports of excessive iconoclasm and destruction
of aristocratic estates in revolutionary France, moreover, furnished a salient
model for observers of Paul's less violent iconoclasm to experience it nevertheless as a sign of profound rupture, now translated from the arena of European politics to the more intimate realm of domestic imperial succession and
royal family feuds.

A generation raised on images of the resurrected Herculaneum and Pompeii, finding pleasure in decoding the remains of antiquity and elegiacally
picturing its own moment in ruins, saw Paul's predictable abandonment of
Catherine-era monuments (after all, it was quite typical for a new monarch to
leave the residence and symbolic trappings of his predecessor[65]) give rise to the
first set of native Russian ruins. In western and southern Europe, architectural and sculptural ruins pointed to the patrimony of ancient Greece and
Rome or to the stone masterpieces of the medieval period. Old Russian architects worked primarily in wood, exposing their structures to fire rather than
gradual fragmentation. The dilapidated stone structures that did survive were
paradoxically not recognized by eighteenth-century Russian observers as the
ruins of their own culture even when the European fashion for ruins came
virtually to demand that these be identified as a national locus of sentimen-
tality and historical depth. In the seeming absence of authentic ancient ruins,
the new fashion gave rise to sham ruins and compelled a search for a native

historical domain that could plausibly accommodate them. It is this context that allowed the depopulated Catherinian spaces to be conceived of as ruined.

Derzhavin, then, was the first to grasp the symbolic potential of the neglected Tsarskoe Selo and the changed status of its ruins after Catherine's passing. In "Ruins," he employs the lifeless architecture and sculpture of the forsaken park to recreate a contrasting dynamic world of incessant activity, brimming with the empress's many pursuits, both serious and diverting. In true Derzhavinian fashion, the poem is in fact overpopulated with creatures of different kinds, ranging from dogs to fish, swans, and cherubs. As a result, it is not only the landscape's presiding deity, Venus, that vanishes in the poem's coda, but also this entire world, a Catherinian "ecosystem" of sorts. As an image, the poem's titular ruins reference both the earlier moment of the estate's absolute vibrancy and its present condition of deathly incompleteness and silence, rendering both the Catherinian and the Pauline historical layers simultaneously present to the reader's mind. Similarly, the entire poem, with the exception of its closing stanza, is couched in an unfaltering past tense: "there stood a magnificent shrine" (*velikolepnyi khram stoial*), "here sonorous harps thundered, / And a choir of singers echoed them" (*tut arfy zvuchnyia gremeli / I povtorial ikh khor pevtsov*), and so on.[66] Like ruins, the past tense calls attention to the broader narrative of historical change, within which the rich descriptions of Catherine's pastimes acquire a somewhat different meaning. What is now—in the era of Paul—absent becomes present again, even if only to the mind's eye; what is forever present in the mythologized realm of Cythera's island comes to an end with the death of the historical empress. The archetypal and the topical time frames, harmonized in the typical ode, clash in the elegiac rearticulation here performed. The title and the past tense point to the poem's hybrid nature: while its celebratory descriptions and frequent recourse to allegory are essentially odic elements, the melancholy awareness of the pastness both of Catherine's reign and of that reign's ability to be uncomplicatedly represented through allegory suggests the speaker's—a former ode writer's—elegiac sensibility.

The greater part of "Ruins" is devoted to reconstructing Catherine's reign in exhaustive and striking detail, ordered by specific location in the Tsarskoe Selo park as well as temporally, from morning to night of the empress's typical day and by implication from the beginning to the end of her rule. These details refer the reader to well-established components of Catherine's own self-mythologization ("prowess and graciousness," Enlightenment and Love[67]) and to Derzhavin's mythologization of her in the Felitsa cycle, where Catherine's virtues are shown through her lifestyle. Derzhavin's nostalgic reconstruction welds together description and myth.[68] As discussed in chapter 1, the ode as a genre makes available to its readers two intersecting modes of understanding space and history: as specific events, places, factual references, and, on the other hand, as mythical loci revealed through hyperbole and allegory. Derzhavin's Tsarskoe Selo in fact only becomes legible in the manipulations—separating, superposing, and reconciling—of these two layers.

The poem proceeds through the space of Tsarskoe Selo as also, chronologically, through an array of the empress's real and putative daily activities, from dawn till dusk, reaching, in the anti-climactic end, the "night" of Paul's rule. This gradual progression of daily pastimes, which bring the empress to various locales in her vast domain, furnishes the greater part of the poem with narrative structure. It also serves to superpose the irrecoverable temporal span of Catherine's reign on the one hand onto the enduring and accessible physical space that had witnessed or commemorated many of this reign's private and public moments and, on the other, onto the progression of a single day, a mundane, accessible experience shared by the empress and her subjects, poet and reader. The progression also continually implicates the poet-observer and, by extension, the reader in the heuristic occupations of walking and beholding. Both activities in the late eighteenth century facilitated a move from inspection to introspection (articulated most evocatively by Jean-Jacques Rousseau and, later, William Wordsworth), and as a result in "Ruins" prefigure an introspective observer-reader, who would view history through a personal lens. While not in itself elegiac, this projected introspection certainly instantiates the poem's move away from the ode and toward a complex hybridity of genre.

The enlightened monarch/goddess begins her day in a contemplative solitude that, in turn, enables her to attend to the problems of peoples and governments:

Вот тут была уединенной
Поутру каждый день с зарей,
Писала, как владеть вселенной,
И как сердца пленять людей.[69]

[Here she was alone / Each morning at the break of dawn, / She wrote of how to govern the world / And how to capture human hearts.]

This is of course a reference to Catherine's *Nakaz*, the instruction to the legislative commission she had summoned in 1767, probably the single most important document of her reign. But the origin of this public document is here traced to a moment of solitary privacy in Catherine's day. The poem alludes to this landmark in Catherine's career as ruler not in order to comment on the actual legislation, but to fill with imagined activity the space traversed by the poet/reader and to access the empress's private core through its publicly available creative products. It is in these brief moments of attention to the private realm, an interest having since the Felitsa cycle apparently only heightened, that the poet leaves the arena of public history, where the acknowledgment of Paul would have been indispensable, and instead becomes absorbed in the empress's mind and in Tsarskoe Selo as that mind's projection. As a work of historical interpretation, "Ruins" embodies the meeting-point of Classicist and Romantic poetic sensibilities in its hybrid account of the historical individual seen through the overlapping paradigms of heroism and personhood.[70]

If the fullness of Catherine's schedule complements the richness and vibrancy of the landscape, the exclusive focus on her whereabouts and her thought and vision creates an elegiac affinity between the poem's retrospective observer and the observing, thoughtful empress.[71] From this point on, Derzhavin insists on carving out a space for serious pastimes in the cupid-packed paradise of Cythera's island. If in the morning of the poem, as at the dawn of her reign, Catherine II devotes her energies to legislation, military matters dominate her policy in the later period, and toward the end of her imagined promenade in Tsarskoe Selo she surveys victory monuments. The poem recalls the triumphs of Catherine's generals only in a highly mediated and (again) privatized fashion, by observing Catherine's inspection of her war monuments. This mediation is reminiscent of the perspectival arrangement in Catherine's last portrait by Vladimir Borovikovskii (1794) where a bonneted, kindly old lady Catherine (the empress's private incarnation) points behind her to the Chesme column (her public and, might we add, masculine extension), and is in turn observed with adoration by a spindly hound gazing up at her (recall all the creatures in Derzhavin's poem).

А здесь, исполнясь важна вида,

На памятник своих побед

Она смотрела: на Алкида,

Как гидру палицей он бьет;

Как прочие ея Герои,

По манию ея очес,

Vladimir Borovikovskii, *Portait of Catherine II, Empress of Russia* (1794). Russian Museum or Tretyakov Gallery.

В ужасные вступали бои
И тмы поделали чудес;
Приступом грады тверды брали,
Сжигали флоты средь морей,
Престолы, царствы покоряли
И в плен водили к ней царей.[72]

[And here, her appearance growing more serious, / Upon the monument to her victories / She gazed: upon Alcides, / Slaying the Hydra with his club; / And her other valiant Heroes, / Who, at the behest of her eyes, / Marched into fearsome battles, / And there did myriad wondrous feats: / By storm they vanquished fortresses, / Flotillas burned upon the seas, / Thrones and kingdoms they conquered, / Brought to her their captive kings.]

Catherine's reign marked the greatest expansion of Russia's territories both through military campaigns and diplomatic intrigue, here represented in a series of allegorical images that reference the Olympian scenario of power (Heracles and the Hydra), which, as Richard Wortman observes, would at the beginning of the nineteenth century give way to comparisons with real and primarily masculine historical personages.[73] Derzhavin thus reinstates the Catherinian mode of allegorical historical vision, a vision here focalized precisely through Catherine and her ability to see, beyond her monuments, the real/mythologized occasions they signify. As I have noted earlier, "Ruins" imbues with urgency the project of decoding its allegory of Cythera's island at the time of this place's silencing and destruction; this passage, where Catherine surveys her monuments but sees the heroic battles they commemorate, presents a model for this decoding, for the kind of resuscitation of the world behind the monument and ruin that the poem itself performs.

Most commemorative architecture and sculpture in Tsarskoe Selo was non-mimetic and allegorical. The park was meant in particular to valorize the victories of Catherine's Turkish campaign. In a letter of August 14/25, 1771, the empress outlines her commemorative landscaping plans to Voltaire, her favorite correspondent on matters of politics and gardening:

If this war continues, my garden at [Ts]arskoe Selo will resemble a game of skittles; for at each of our noteworthy actions, I put up some new monument there. The battle of Kagul, where seventeen thousand men fought a hundred and fifty thousand, inspired the erection of an obelisk, with an inscription stating simply

the event and the name of the general. After the naval victory at Chesme, a ros-
tral column was erected in the middle of a very large lake. The capture of the
Crimea will be immortalized by a large column; the descent in the Morea and
the capture of Sparta, by another. All these are made of the finest possible marble, which the Italians themselves admire. [. . .] Besides this, in a wood behind
my garden, I have had the idea of building a temple of memory, to be approached
through a triumphal arch. All the important events of the war will be engraved
on medallions, with simple and short inscriptions in the language of the appropriate country, giving the date and the names of the participants. I have an excellent Italian architect, who is drawing up the plans for this building, which will,
I hope, be a handsome one, in good taste and will commemorate the history of
this war.[74]

Comparable as celebratory genres, the monument and the ode were both non-
mimetic vehicles for historical memory in the eighteenth century.[75] Catherine's letter outlines a kind of allegorizing calculus that reduces historical events
with their multiple actors and contingencies to their symbolic monuments.

Noteworthy action	Monument
Battle of Kagul (17,000 Russians against 150,000 enemies)	Obelisk (inscription of event and general's name)
Naval victory at Chesme	Rostral column in the middle of a lake
Capture of Crimea	Large column
Descent in the Morea / capture of Sparta	Large column
Entire Turkish campaign	Temple of Memory Triumphal Arch Medallions with inscriptions

Even as they memorialize the Turkish campaign, these monuments also serve
to efface the destructive nature of actual combat. Only the "simple and short"
inscriptions of events, dates, and names of key protagonists distinguish the
Classical monuments, which are otherwise hard to tell apart. Ironically, even
though the park was meant to construct memory, the process of effacement
that non-mimetic monuments generate fuels this memory's ultimate destruction, particularly when the reign that valued these monuments and the achievements behind them comes to an end. From monuments that mark victories, the

landmarks of Tsarskoe Selo become ruins signifying only the passing of Catherine's glory. First to apprehend this process of vanishing, Derzhavin is also eager to reverse it. It is as if Derzhavin's Catherine rewrites her letter to Voltaire, now guiding her correspondent backward: from architecture to reminiscence, from her sculptures' "finest possible marble" to "burned flotillas," "conquered kingdoms," and "vanquished fortresses." The poem rearticulates the historical narratives that Catherine's artifacts at once silence and evoke, reviving the tenor behind the allegorical vehicle. More broadly, this is indeed one of the central moves of Derzhavin's poetry: to explore, distend, and collapse the distance between signifier and signified in non-mimetic representation—an exploration that, as he repeatedly argues in several other poems, poses a problem for the visual arts and is only truly possible in the verbal medium.[76] At the moment of allegory's demise, "Ruins" captures its death, and attempts its revivification.

Most widespread allegorical pairings saw Catherine not as playful Venus, but as Minerva, the goddess of wisdom, martial valor, and gardens.[77] Significantly, however, it is not the unapproachable Minerva, but the lighthearted Cythera (Venus) who dwells in the Tsarskoe Selo of Derzhavin's poem amid "comforts" (*negi*) and "delights" (*utekhi*).[78] As a result, access to her domain appears both realizable and desirable. I will soon return to the Anacreontic subtext of this identification of Catherine with Venus; here it is important to note that all allusions to martial achievements (Minerva's sphere of influence) are in "Ruins" tempered by virtue of their placement in the realm of the love-goddess, in an idyllic park setting, as static, controlled sculptural representations. Seamlessly alternating *dulce et utile*, the poet sees his heroine approach a military monument and display a serious countenance right after she has had her fill of amusement gazing upon children, doves, swans, and dogs (recall Borovikovskii's Catherine with a dog by her side and the Chesme column in the background). Derzhavin reasserts here the well-established elements of both Catherine's ideology and his own poetics. While the introduction of the private sphere (the Horatian odic mode performed here in an elegiac key) into the ceremonial ode (the Lomonosovian Pindaric mode) was Derzhavin's invention and trademark, the coupling of military and legislative successes had become a de rigueur component of any ode dedicated to Catherine II, both during her reign and posthumously.[79] Godlike in her omnipresence and humane in her femininity, Catherine was celebrated for being able to attend to everything, down to the seemingly insignificant. Because in "Ruins" Catherine is Venus rather than Minerva, Tsarskoe Selo and the reign it came to be associated with are established as a domain of peaceful, loving and above all feminine activity.

Crowded with souvenirs of battlefield success, the landscape of Tsarskoe Selo invited its beholder to contemplate military victories in a pastoral setting where the memory of war violence was moderated by monumental form. Thus, each word in the phrase "upon the monument to her victories she gazed" (*na pamiatnik svoikh pobed ona smotrela*) emphasizes the indirectness of the reader's access to history and the primacy of the empress: Catherine's *gaze*, *her* victories, the monuments themselves, and finally the pervasive past tense. The rhetorical and physical placement of military monuments in a landscape of tranquility, rather than on an actual field of battle or in the middle of a bustling town-square, commemorated these victories not as milestones of aggressive foreign policy, which they certainly were, but rather as steps toward peace.[80] When Paul ascends the throne, he, by contrast, animates his parks with ostentatious military parades—displays of actual force, rather than, as in Catherine's case, "good taste"—a contrast that is implicit in this particular passage from "Ruins" and only amplifies its polemical charge.[81] As he rewrites Catherine's legacy, then, Derzhavin reasserts its main mythologizing tenets (enlightenment, peace, and love) as well as his own famous tributes to her during her lifetime—a marked reinstatement in the context of the ideological reversals of 1797. The poem's formal innovation lies primarily in its elegiac framing of this reinstatement; Derzhavin's civic daring, in the poem's odic resuscitation of Catherine's habitat in 1797.

Despite Derzhavin's dutiful celebration of Paul in "On the New Year 1797" and several other texts,[82] the nostalgic tone of "Ruins" and its intentional neglect of the new monarch, save for the image of darkness that covers Cythera's island in the final stanza, made it impossible for the poem to be published in Russia. It first appeared in Saxony through the patronage of the exiled Count Aleksei Orlov (the brother of Catherine's favorite Grigorii), a man who had played a crucial—perhaps even regicidal—role in Catherine's 1762 coup, and whose subsequent victories were immortalized precisely by the triumphal Chesme column at Tsarskoe Selo. The eighty-year-old Orlov had been publicly humiliated during a funeral procession designed to "reunite" Paul's parents and restore symbolic power to Paul's deposed father. As punishment for his prominent role in Catherine's accession, Orlov was "entrusted" with the job of carrying the Great Crown intended for Peter III's catafalque while Catherine II merited only a smaller crown.[83]

Having himself experienced the fickleness of royal favor, particularly under Catherine in the early 1790s, Derzhavin was quite sensitive to the reversals of fortune that Paul dealt out to Catherine's grandees. The poet prided himself on daring to address disgraced courtiers. In the same year, 1797, he dedicated an ode to Count Valerian Zubov (brother of Catherine's last favorite Platon), whose brilliant military career under Catherine was cut short by Paul. Valerian Zubov had to abandon his promising campaign in Persia and take up residence in the provinces.[84] In "On the Return of Count Zubov from Persia" ("Na vozvrashchenie grafa Zubova iz Persii," 1797; published in 1804, most likely on the occasion of Zubov's death), Derzhavin offers a gripping treatment of the theme of the unpredictable fall from grace:[85]

Сбылось!—Игру днесь счастья люту
И как оно к тебе хребет
Свой с грозным смехом повернуло,
Ты видишь,—видишь, как мечты
Сиянье вкруг тебя заснуло,
Прошло,—остался только ты.[86]

[It has come to pass!—This day you see / Fortune's cruel game / And how with ominous laughter / It turns its back on you, / You see the dream's glow around you fade, / And pass,—and all that is left is you.]

But in "Ruins," the theme takes on the dimensions of a grand-scale fall from Paradise; far from accidental is the poem's placement in a garden.[87] Not only does the "dream's glow fade" around Zubov; after Paul's accession, the entire post-Catherinian world is plunged into dismal darkness.[88] "On the Return of Count Zubov" can be read within the didactic tradition, which captures the hero at a moment of failure or humiliation in order to criticize excessive self-esteem or endorse self-reliance in the face of calamity. Derzhavin himself professes that he wrote this poem on a bet to prove that he could eulogize whomever he pleased regardless of his hero's standing at court.[89] This assertion illuminates Derzhavin's proclaimed investment in the stability of personal values, which we can also read in the context of early Romantic practices as an insistence on the coherence of the poet's biographical persona with his voice. Historical upheavals notwithstanding, the poet—the ode-writer in fact—claims to uphold the same hero at a moment of triumph during Catherine's reign ("To the Handsome Man," "K krasavtsu," 1794, and "On the Conquest of Derbent," "Na pokorenie Derbenta," 1796) and in a crisis wrought by her successor ("On the Return of Count Zubov from Persia," 1797). With its undeniable allusions to "Felitsa," "Ruins" can also be read as a polemical echo, in a time of crisis, of the empress's less clouded previous celebrations.

In the 1808 edition of his collected works, Derzhavin placed "Ruins" in the third volume, containing his Anacreontic verse. In fact, just as the odes to courtiers were meant to exhibit some consistency of the poet's personal position, the bucolic mythologized landscape of "Ruins" and its repeated allusions to merrymaking also evoke Derzhavin's earlier Anacreontic treatment of Tsarskoe Selo in "A Promenade in Sarskoe Selo" ("Progulka v Sarskom Sele," 1791). This pastoral poem painted a virtually identical Edenic landscape, populated by birds and fish, and described with a similar overabundance of deictics. Cast as Themis, the goddess of justice, Catherine does not appear in the poem directly, but rather presides over it as the park's *genius loci*. As the poet and his Plenira (the name by which Derzhavin referred to his first wife) enjoy the park's many amusements, the text never completely loses sight of the empress who enables their bliss:

Какая пища духу!—
В восторге я сказал,—
Коль красен взор природы
И памятников вид,
Они где зрятся в воды,
И соловей сидит
Где близь и воспевает,
Зря розу иль зарю!
Он будто изъявляет
И богу и царю
Свое благодаренье.[90]

[What nourishment to the spirit!—/ said I in rapture,—/ How beautiful is nature's regard / And the sight of monuments, / Where they gaze into the waters, / And the nightingale sits / Nearby and sings, / Beholding a rose or dawn! / As if expressing / To god and tsar / Its gratitude.]

The admiration that in the ceremonial ode would have been expressed by the rapturous poet himself is uttered in the Anacreontic by a nightingale, but the playful convergence of the two voices—the poet's and the bird's—is obvious. Unlike "Ruins," where the only overtly sentient being is the elegiacally reconstructed empress, "A Promenade" depicts Catherine's residence as it is experienced by her subjects. Ironically, it is Catherine's virtual absence from the poem that bears witness to her unspoken, ubiquitous presence. For all its idealization, the pastoral landscape is nevertheless clearly identified; in fact, it is precisely in the setting of a royal residence that the poet's Anacreontic pastimes acquire meaning. In "Ruins," the Anacreontic is focalized differently, indeed, placed in tension with the poem's elegiac title and past tense: even as she is everywhere, Catherine is now in fact forever gone. By imagining the empress's omnipresence, the poet finalizes her absence.

Derzhavin's turn to the Anacreontic in the 1790s has been seen also as a turn away from the political and historical engagements of the ceremonial ode.[91] The Bard of Felitsa himself repeatedly advertised his withdrawal from the sphere of political poetry. Thus, in another text from 1797, "To the Lyre" ("K Lire"), a free adaptation of Anacreon's Ode 1/23 doubling as Derzhavin's Anacreontic manifesto, Derzhavin proclaims the odic poet's new path chosen at a time when his former heroes are dead (Rumiantsev) or in disgrace (Suvorov): "So enough of sonorous harmonies, / Let us retune our strings again: / We'll refuse to sing of heroes, / And shall start to sing of love" (*Tak ne nado zvuchnykh stroev,* / *Pereladim struny vnov': / Pet' otkazhemsia geroev, / A nachnem my pet' liubov'*).[92] Yet even as it renounces civic verse, this short Anacreontic text still incorporates its key elements: the names of heroes, grandiloquent rhetoric, etc. The farewell to the Pindaric vocation also becomes an occasion for its reinstatement, just as later in "Ruins" the farewell to Catherine occasions her revisualization. Even in Derzhavin's early Anacreontics, as yet unclouded by Catherine's passing, the political realm makes itself insistently felt. Thus, in "A Promenade in Sarskoe Selo"—his first poem written in iambic trimeter (a meter previously used by Lomonosov, Sumarokov, and Kheraskov for Anacreontic adaptations)—the understated presence of the political and historical realms is in fact the poem's enabling premise.[93] A deeper and more complex connection than typically thought may thus be drawn between the Anacreontic and eighteenth-century Russian poetry's more overtly political odic modes.[94] If so, Derzhavin's hybrid experiment in "Ruins" becomes clearer. The dependence of the pastoral on the political is polemically revealed and foregrounded in "Ruins," where the eclipse of the idealized landscape directly follows the end of the idealized reign.

For Derzhavin and other eighteenth-century Russian poets, the Anacreontic —though lighter and smoother than the Pindaric or Horatian modes—was clearly an odic subgenre. In "Ruins," which, I would argue, is a complex generic hybrid ultimately tending toward the historical elegy that would soon be elaborated by Konstantin Batiushkov and other Russian Romantics, the Anacreontic mediates between remembrance of the golden age of the Catherinian ceremonial ode and its elegiacally framed loss in an era whose dawning the poem captures and projects into a hopeless future. The poem's elegiac coda ends on the quintessentially Anacreontic word "love," here referencing simultaneously Catherine's Enlightenment rhetoric; the main Anacreontic pursuit; and the central sentiment of elegy, at present not fully articulated, but emerging:

Но здесь ее уж ныне нет,
Померк красот волшебных свет,
Все тмой покрылось, запустело;
Все в прах упало, помертвело;
От ужаса вся стынет кровь,
Лишь плачет сирая любовь.[95]

[But here she is no more, / The light of her wondrous beauties has dimmed, / And all is darkened and desolate; / All's fallen to dust and turned dead; / A horror now chills the blood, / And only orphaned love weeps.]

With astonishing promptness, a mere monosyllabic shifter, "but" (*no*), introduces the last stanza, which rhetorically transforms the *locus amoenus* ("bliss," *blazhenstvo*) into a *locus horribilis* ("horror," *uzhas*). I would portray the formative contrast of the poem created by its final stanza as the reader's sudden expulsion from a space of observation (characteristic of Derzhavin's stance generally) into a space of blindness. This is now a kind of obstructed or ruined Anacreontic, but this reversal also renders the past more visible and hence more desirable than the dark and desolate present. Such a reverse visibility is characteristic of the elegy, rather than the ode.[96] Recall that one of the key topoi of the accession day ceremonial ode is the diametrically opposite shift from the night of the previous to the rising sun of the new reign. By contrast, here the topos is elegiac; the shift from the reign of the sun-queen to the chilling bleakness of her absence recalls an established convention of elegiac poetry—namely, the capturing of loss in terms of natural phenomena, such as the arrival of winter or the more catastrophic eclipse.[97] But insofar as it constitutes so precise a reversal of standard accession rhetoric, this shift also implicitly signals a commentary on the tenability and tenuousness of odic discourse.

As Derzhavin admitted in his autobiographical writings, his proximity to the empress in the later years of her reign made him increasingly disillusioned with Felitsa, to the extent that he was no longer capable of odic writing on the same ecstatic level.[98] His proximity to the queen's real body undermined the Pindaric impulse, which was difficult for Derzhavin to sustain in any case and which, as we have seen in chapter 1, was fueled by the poet's distance from, and allegorizing distancing of, this body. In "Ruins," however, Catherine's persona is once again depicted in scintillating verse—in what we might call a retrospective Anacreontic mode: verse that remains untroubled when the often unflattering reality of the recent past is replaced with its edifying, allegorizing memory. The ostensibly undisturbed sincerity of the descriptions of Tsarskoe Selo seems to be facilitated precisely by the overarching context of loss in which they appear. The same rhetoric that can be identified with the ode, particularly with the Anacreontic subgenre, we can also now ascribe to elegiac discourse. For example, the inventory of Catherine's oft-eulogized attributes, familiar from the late eighteenth-century ode, is now recapitulated as an elegiac *blazon*, a catalogue deriving its value from these attributes' very erasure and inaccessibility. The text thus turns the Anacreontic mode from the odic to the elegiac.

Rearranging and reinhabiting the genre hierarchy so radically and self-consciously, "Ruins" becomes far more than a vindication of Catherine; rather, it is a vindication of the poet's treatment of public history as an experience that transcends any one genre, now gaining coherence within the poet's private historical reflections. The world Derzhavin attempts to recreate is significant precisely in that it is no longer accessible without imaginative reconstruction. Now more than ever before, the poet *must* occupy the empress's domain, as a Classicist allegorist, an early Romantic observer and experiencer of her landscape, and an elegist. The imagined Catherinian world, barely a year after the empress's death, already belongs to the past and can only be evaluated against realities created by the poet, both in his former celebratory verse and in his current lamentation. The same topos of playful sacralization of the monarch formerly employed in Derzhavin's odic celebrations is now placed in the service of elegiac mourning. As Peter Sacks observes in his influential reflections on the workings of elegy, elegiac figuration involves "a turning away from the actual identity of what was lost. Consolation thus depends on a trope that remains at an essential remove from what it replaces."[99] In some ways, this kind of distancing was already at work in the ode's allegorical procedure. In "Ruins," what is regained in turning away from Catherine as Derzhavin knew her, or from the rhetorical exigencies of Paul's accession, is the poet's voice, as well as faith in panegyric discourse (untenable though it may presently be) and the Catherinian myth. A few years later, at the auspicious start of Alexander I's reign, hopes for consolation and continuity would be pinned on Catherine's "angelic" grandson, who in the first years of his rule proclaimed it as a return to his grandmother's principles. If there is any consolation in the meantime, it seems to come, at least in "Ruins," from the act of remembering, from the poet's ability to reassemble the queen's symbolic body despite the violence it suffers from official discourse or the strictures genre imposes upon its representations.

That Derzhavin destabilizes the eighteenth-century genre hierarchy is by now certainly a scholarly commonplace, one for which in many ways Derzhavin himself laid the groundwork. The idea behind this chapter (and in part, chapter 1 as well) was, on the one hand, to ground his experimentation with genre in a specific historical moment that seemed to call for precisely such experimentation—the uncertain change of regime introduced by Paul and the challenge it posed to the panegyric rhetoric that had been associated with the praise of his mother—and, on the other, to capture Derzhavin at work on loosening the genre system and provide a close reading of a select few texts that are uniquely informed by this career-long experiment. Ceremonial odes continue to be written long after Derzhavin, too, is gone; but might we not bookmark the year 1797 as a symbolic endpoint for the political and literary culture of "the age of empresses" that panegyric discourse had articulated?

THE ELEGIAC CODA

In the eighteenth century, as Stephen Baehr observes, poetic treatments of Tsarskoe Selo constructed an "image of a place that is pleasant precisely because of the presence of the monarch."[100] But this is not the image that nineteenth- and twentieth-century Russian poetry inherits in obsessively revisiting Tsarskoe Selo. Very soon after Catherine's death, with the original *genius loci* gone forever, Tsarskoe Selo emerges as a space of poetry precisely because of the absence of the monarch, because now for the first time its sham ruins acquire a poignant historical reality; and a poetics of loss begins to articulate narratives of Russian history. Thus Pushkin's "Recollections in Tsarskoe Selo" ("Vospominaniia v Tsarskom Sele," 1814), which he so famously read in Derzhavin's presence at his Lycée examination, opens with a description of its nocturnal setting—the nighttime of elegiac utterance—and then revisits

Catherine's monuments in a melancholy deictic mode, everywhere discovering her absence and everywhere reminiscent of Derzhavin's "Ruins":

> Увы! промчались навсегда те времена златые,
> Когда под скипетром великия жены
> Венчалась славою счастливая Россия,
>   Цветя под кровом тишины!
> Здесь каждый шаг в душе рождает
>   Воспоминанья прежних лет;
> Воззрев вокруг себя, со вздохом росс вещает:
>   «Исчезло все, великой нет!»[101]

[Alas! Gone forever is that golden age / When under the scepter of the great woman / Happy Russia had been crowned with glory, / Flourishing under the shelter of peace! / Here every step gives rise in the soul / To memories of former days, / And looking round, the Russian announces with a sigh: / "All's vanished, the Great [Catherine] is no more!"]

The last line of this excerpt all but quotes the closing stanza of Derzhavin's "Ruins" or the "they are no more" (*uzh net ikh*) of "On the New Year 1797"—or Russia's groan of "Catherine is no more!" (*Ekateriny net!*) from Petrov's "Lament and Consolation." And yet again, as in "Ruins," it is from within the elegiac setting that the poet turns to the odic mode, here celebrating the more recent Russian victory in the Napoleonic campaign and hailing its renowned bard, Vasilii Zhukovskii. Pushkin's recollections remember many things: from Catherine's victories, commemorated by monuments themselves no longer intact, to recent victories not yet memorialized; and from the genre hierarchy of the eighteenth century to the genre ambivalence of the poems on Catherine's passing and of the incipient nineteenth century.

Soon afterward, even within Pushkin's own oeuvre, Tsarskoe Selo would cease to connote the loss of the specifically Catherinian golden age and become, instead, a place for self-reflexive remembrance, first of happier Lycée days, and then, in post-Pushkin poetry, of the golden age of Pushkin and many other Russian poets' myths of origin and nostalgia, from Zhukovskii to Annenskii and Akhmatova.[102] But it is Catherine's passing that first imbues the space with its nostalgic aura; the significance of her passing, moreover, certainly exceeds its implications for the Tsarskoe Selo "text," a poetic place formed by the clash of epochs.[103] Catherine's reign defines a certain version of the

Enlightenment and of the eighteenth century for subsequent generations, a version captured in the idealizing and mournful frame of Derzhavin's "Ruins" as the age of strong personalities and big projects, on the one hand, and of feminine playfulness and allegorical communion with antiquity, on the other. We will encounter numerous other versions of the Catherinian eighteenth century in this book, to be sure; but this one is the most lyrically and personally pitched.

3

Poetry Reads Power
Overcoming Patronage

Ужели жаждущие славы
Одни герои лишь кровавы
На лирах стоят петы быть?
Иль смертные одни венчанны
И их дары златосиянны
Жар в музах могут возбудить?

—A. Bukharskii, "Ode on my Birthday" (1792)

The Crisis of Charismatic Authority

Derzhavin's oeuvre attests both to the odic vision's continued sway in the early nineteenth century and to the loosening of odic strictures in the period encompassed by the poet's career.[1] If the ode constructed history as essentially a solar system where everything revolved, depending on the particular subgenre, around God, the monarch, or some lesser patron, the blurring of its generic contours also destabilized the fixedly hierarchical relationship between its author and addressee, in addition resulting, perhaps less directly, in the ode's rearticulation of historical process as affected by forces other than individualized figures of authority. This chapter begins by considering the chronological turn of the century as a thematic focal point for several revisions to ruler-centered historical scenarios developed in the verse of Derzhavin's lesser-known contemporaries: Nikolai L'vov (1751–1803), Petr Slovtsov (1767–1843), Semen Bobrov (1763–1810), and, the most famous of these, Alexander Radishchev (1749–1802). Never so implicated as Derzhavin's writings in a positive relationship with the empress (and in some cases, quite antagonistic to autocracy), these poets' works were not constrained by allegiances to the court and thus, at the turn of the century, reconstituted the recently expired age from its social if not philosophical margins. If Derzhavin consistently inscribes Enlightenment ideology within the reign (Catherine's) that promotes it, these odes—some polemically, some inadvertently—move away from reign-based chronologies toward alternative conceptions of periodization.

The ceremonial ode evolved in eighteenth-century Russia as a genre of complex pragmatic content: a text of imperial and individual celebration, a gesture of value within the system of patronage, and a manifesto of the fledgling Russian Enlightenment and secular literary language. Responding to the demands of a new, rapidly modernizing state, the ode was the genre most swiftly assimilated from the Classicist canon by eighteenth-century Russian poets. First to be imported and naturalized are the instruments of power. The serious tone of the ode called for the use of heightened diction and enrichment by poetic device. Especially in the pseudo-Pindaric form practiced by Mikhail Lomonosov, these odes frequently appeared incoherent in their brilliance of imagery, abrupt shifts in subject matter, apparent disorder of form within the individual sections, and emotional, exalted tone. Scholars of Pindar have identified a social function of the ode that seems to apply equally as well to eighteenth-century Russia as it did to Pindar's Greece of the fifth century B.C.: the genre's restorative effect upon the polis. It has been argued that by entering into a contract with his patron, the ode-writer committed his language and performance to reintegrating society's victor(s) into the community, thus strengthening the communal ties momentarily weakened by the patron's athletic superiority, institution-building or power-gathering.[2] In eighteenth-century Russia, fractured by the demands of modernization, repeated court coups, and other contingencies and uncertainties of nation-building, the ode bound the subjects and the patron/monarch within the same set of putative state aspirations. When the eighteenth century as a whole came under odic scrutiny at a time when the primacy of the ode and the importance of genre hierarchy began to be questioned, ode writers, as this chapter demonstrates, shifted their position in relation to their patrons and their social function within the nation.[3]

The poems I consider in the first half of this chapter reveal that transformations in the solemn ode occurred when the genre was used as a medium for historical reflection. In the continuum from the odic to the elegiac that in the previous chapter I posit as a necessary workspace of historical elegy, the ode itself proves not a stable and uniform generic pole, but rather a genre that expands to accommodate a tonal range, from conventional acclamation to outright criticism. This tonal range is of a different nature than the one tested by Derzhavin in the Felitsa cycle: here it has to do with a critical scrutiny of the Enlightenment as a period and ideology deserving of assessment more nuanced than rapturous idealization. Structurally, the ode preserves a stable repertoire whose main element is, as I will show, a glorifying list. This chapter's first half is devoted to identifying and explicating the makeup of these lists—the figures and events they posit as representative of their epoch—and teasing out the insights into the evolving conception of history intimated thereby; in the process, this discussion will also trace the diminishing role of the monarch as history-maker.

On the surface, these early texts appear united by little more than their occasion: the passing of the eighteenth century. Yet we might read them, in all the variety of names and events they list and of figurative language they muster for their subject, as illustrating in their very early stages two momentous processes that transfigure intellectual and literary history at the dawn of the nineteenth century. The first, which intellectual historian and philosopher Reinhart Koselleck connected with the advent of modernity,[4] is the transition in historical experience from "natural" time, calibrated by the lifespan of the autocrat and therefore renewable and ultimately cyclical, to progressive time, which extricates history at least somewhat from the constraints of hero worship, cyclical patterning, and predictability. In addition to changing the shape of historical thinking and impelling it toward a deeper engagement with abstract (rather than biographical) entities, this transformation also entailed the rise of new conceptions of acting in history, of citizenship and the provenance of individual intervention in political process: "The bearer of the modern philosophy of historical process was the citizen emancipated from absolutist subjection and the tutelage of the Church: the *prophète philosophe*, as he was once strikingly characterized in the eighteenth century."[5]

While certainly apt in describing the French Enlightenment, this assessment of modernity scarcely rings true for the eighteenth century or indeed for the early decades of the nineteenth century in Russia. As a case study, Russia might appear marginal to Koselleck's narrative, a recipient rather than setter of the trends he describes, hopelessly belated in responding to them and resigned to the power of the autocrat for far too long, even as late as the first half of the nineteenth century, which on Koselleck's timeline, informed as it is by the histories of French politics and German philosophy, is certainly the period of modernity's greatest vigor. Yet, as we shall witness in the peripheral texts I assemble here, ideas have a way of evolving faster than political systems. In the Russian case, it is poetry, rather than philosophy, that communicates the prophetic vision of "the emancipated subject" who confronts the expanded and henceforth unpredictable horizon of history. While commonly associated by scholars of Russian literature with Romantic poetry's cult of genius and individualism, the imperative of prophecy—particularly if we keep Koselleck's narrative of Enlightenment and modernity in mind—can be detected in multiple late Enlightenment Russian texts, which, though placing little trust in the court-centered system, are still far less confident than the future Romantics in their projection of the individual voice, and, crucially, far more interested in finding a language for what Koselleck calls "a typical eighteenth-century mixture of rational prediction and salvational expectation."[6] Perhaps, then, when seen in this context, the significance of the texts we are about to examine lies, on the one hand, in their assessment of the Russian eighteenth century from within the period itself and, on the other, in the alternative pre-history they illuminate for the particular hold the poet-prophet had on Russian letters of the 1820s–'30s.

The period's second relevant innovation affected the rapidly developing Russian literary field of the first decades of the nineteenth century. As the reading public expanded and more venues became available for writers to disseminate their work, patronage, though still a meaningful reality up until the 1830s, gradually relinquished its centrality, giving way first to writers' familiar associations, and later to the growing literary market.[7] Indeed, here we might locate the supersession of epochs, the difference in the spirits of the eighteenth and nineteenth centuries that this book attempts to frame in multiple ways and with recourse to diverse textual evidence, in the growing skepticism regarding ruler-centered historical narratives (dictated no doubt by late-Enlightenment philosophy and the Revolution, as Koselleck suggests) and, as though by a ripple effect some twenty years later, in the Romantic rejection of patronage as a social practice and as the enabling premise of Classicist lyric expression. Thus, in the second half of this chapter, I turn to consider "Derzhavin's moment," which writers of his generation symbolically bring to a close by looking for history elsewhere than at court, as it is assessed in retrospect by Pushkin in his multiple pronouncements on patronage. Just as the first half of this chapter focuses on the possible ways, available within the poetic idiom of a certain period, to think of history, so will its second half show patronage to be not merely a topic in Pushkin's journalistic polemics with his detractors, but also an abiding theme in his poetry, where it is treated with much ambivalence and is integral to Pushkin's emerging historical vision of Russian modernity.

Even when not appealing to a patron directly, poetry written under the conditions of patronage can be read as, explicitly or implicitly, a form of address that preserves, and rarely if ever questions, its trust in a poetic utterance's potential for reception. Throughout his career, Pushkin tests precisely the extent to which this trust can be maintained under the new conditions of literary production and circulation—conditions whereby, on the one hand, the axes of cultural, political, and moral authority are constantly revised and, on the other, the horizon of reception by individual readers, whether authority figures or friends, is eclipsed by the anonymous reading public. If Part I has explored "Derzhavin's moment" as one that foregrounds both the investment of eighteenth-century poets in the culture and power structures associated with royal authority and literature's eventual departure from this centralized system of value in the final decades of the century, at the end of this chapter I briefly consider other ways of demarcating this period—for instance, as Karamzin's or Radishchev's moments—which Pushkin might have entertained in gauging his own artistic path and method against the recent history of Russian literature.

The Eighteenth Century and "Deep Time"

The genre of the solemn ode is remarkable for the enormity of its spatio-temporal dimensions: it envisions vast imperial territories, extends along the vertical axis toward the heavenly realms, reconstructs distant pasts, and divines the future. In the ode, this immense panegyric repertoire is dedicated to the exaltation of the empress; it is accessible only by virtue of its connection to her image, and is thus under her command. The poems we are about to examine inherit the strategies of spatio-temporal expansion from the ceremonial ode, but dispose of its ultimate gesture of convergence, transferring the ode's focus from the ruler to the historical process itself. What we thus observe is the expansion of the very frame of history, its figuration as more than what is encompassed by human agency: as pertaining to the nation in L'vov; as intimating an elegiacally tinged, terrifying, timeless, and universal landscape in Radishchev; as intriguingly combining new geological with old religious notions of time in Slovtsov; and as amounting to a virtual cosmogony in Bobrov. All these strategies of understanding history portray it as exceeding cognizable reality and thereby imply the poet's position of knowledge and divination, but, unlike in the ceremonial ode which enables this transcendence only as a function of the monarch's aura, in these texts the poet's vision has no such political-pragmatic anchor.

N. A. L'vov's framework for Russian history is in a sense the least idiosyncratic: replicating other eighteenth-century ode writers' invocations of the golden age as the ultimate mythical horizon of hope, L'vov places his hope for a Russian golden age in the dawning nineteenth century.[8] The nineteenth century was to be a *Russian* century, implicitly perhaps in contrast to the Western eighteenth. Enthusiastically proclaiming these aspirations, L'vov concludes his "People's Exclamation on the Entrance of the New Century" ("Narodnoe voskliknovenie na vstuplenie novogo veka," 1801) by asserting divine intervention in Russian affairs and in the arrival of the new century:[9]

Бог русский и творец вселенной!
И меч и щит твой искони
Услышал глас твой вдохновенный,
Он век послал благословенный
Восстановить златые дни.[10]

[The God of Russia and creator of the universe! / [He,] your sword and shield from time immemorial, / Has heard your inspired voice, / And sent a blessed age / To restore the golden days.]

L'vov is one of the first poets to use the phrase "Russian god" (*russkii bog*), which in the texts he dedicates to the new century consistently references the providential blessedness and specifically national contours of the age now dawning.[11] We see similar pronouncements in "The New Nineteenth Century in Russia" ("Novyi XIX vek v Rossii," 1801), where the odic persona exclaims: "O chosen tribe! O brave Russian! / [. . .] Your god has raised your head over all the tribes of the universe" (*Izbranno plemia! khrabryi ross!* / [. . .] *Prevyshe vsekh plemen vselennoi* / *Tvoi bog glavu tvoiu voznes*).[12] Neither poem alludes to individual Russian leaders or monarchs or specific historical events. Both works aim instead to inscribe the commencing century in a history of Russian national character. "The People's Exclamation" develops as a dialogue between the Russian God and the Russian people: the God promises Russia prosperity, and the people, "in an infinite echo" (*v bezmernom ekhe*), respond: "The Russian God is great! great!" (*russkii bog velik! velik!*).[13] In the next line, however, an individuated authorial voice appeals to the "Creator" to establish a golden age in "*my* fatherland" (*v otechestve* moem—emphasis mine); the voice of the nation is thereby conflated with the voice of the poet. The same encomiastic devices of speaking for a collective that the ceremonial ode had used to sustain the autocratic order now bolster a burgeoning nationalist ideology. Yet if the former was embedded in the hierarchy-bound inequality of poet/collective and patron/singular, the latter effaces this element of patronage by accentuating instead the harmonious symbiosis of poet and nation.

L'vov asserts one of the key tenets of early Russian nationalism, which, to quote Hans Rogger, saw "the power of [Russia's] arms and the respect they commanded from friend and foe [as] Russia's strongest claims for recognition."[14] To L'vov, these attainments are self-evident:

Исследуй кто россиян свойство,
Труды их, игры, торжества,
Увидит всяк: везде геройство
Под русским титлом удальства.[15]

[Whoever studies the Russians' nature, / Their work and play, their festivities, / Will see: heroism everywhere / Under the Russian title of daring.]

In identifying *udal'stvo* (an etymologically Slavic term for "daring" rife with people-wide folkloric associations) as the proper Russian designation for the broader term *geroistvo* (habitually applied in ceremonial odes to individual heroes), L'vov transforms the ode's approach to history, redirecting it toward representing the nation as no longer bound to the iconography of individual charisma, state, and empire.[16] New historical agents require new vocabulary and new strategies of representation.[17] Thus Classicist allegory—the stuff of marble statues of Roman gods—gives way to infinitely dynamic human strivings, presided over by a Russian God who, unlike the image of Minerva as empress, resists embodiment and allegorization. (It may also be that by its nature, nationalist discourse militates against the odic Christian/Classical syncretism noted in chapter 1, and is more strictly "Biblical."[18]) L'vov constructs Russian character out of the epic-inspired images of *bogatyr*s battling for amorous and military rewards, abandoning hearth and home to revel in danger and glory. The vastness of the Russian territory is realized not as a function of the poet's hierarchical elevation, which had in Lomonosov's odes lifted him closer to his royal or aristocratic protagonists, but by virtue of the poet's capacity for swiftly traversing horizontal space in his imagination. The sublime is now not vertical but, as in the epic, horizontal.[19] Epic heroes issue from the feminine and infantile realm of domesticity, with its circumscribed emotional and spatial attachments, into the unbounded terrain of military exploits:

Напрасно мать, жена и дети
Терзают их слезами грудь.
Где зрят опаснее им сети,
Там к славе краткий видят путь.

[In vain do mother, wife, and children / With their tears torment the [heroes'] breast. / Where they foresee the greatest danger, / There they find the shortest path to glory.]

"The New Nineteenth Century in Russia" thus brings the folkloric motifs of the medieval and mythical world of the epic to bear on the realm of modernity, thereby asserting the relevance of the revalorized pre-Petrine Russian history and literary idiom for the new century.[20] In effect, L'vov offers an interpretation of the eighteenth century by erasing it: his epic retellings of Russian history draw a continuous line from the unspecified heroic past of the epic to the imminent future opened up by the arrival of the nineteenth century. Ultimately, however, L'vov's patriotic rhetoric of coherence and continuity, issuing from a man of broad education and unmistakable Enlightenment sympathies,[21] contains an argument not *against* the century of westernization, but rather *for* embracing new national consciousness, a move that was itself in accord with the latest European trends. While autocratic power so soon after 1789 could not appear anything but provisional, national character and the pursuit of national self-definition could indeed reinvigorate the odic discourse of power, stability, and optimism, which L'vov projects into the nineteenth century.

In its very title, Radishchev's "The Eighteenth Century" ("Os'mnadtsatoe stoletie," 1801), formally much closer to the elegy (written in elegiac distichs) than the ode, presents a perspective very different from L'vov's. Its focus is not on the future or on Russia's national history of a very long and schematically outlined durée, but rather on the content and legacy of the century just expired.[22] While professing admiration for the ruling dynasty—little else could indeed be expected from an emotionally troubled poet, traumatized by long Siberian exile, pardoned yet still fearful for his future, and only a year away from committing suicide—the poem conceives of the eighteenth century in moralizing Enlightenment terms, as marked by a relentless conflict between Reason (scientific progress) and Folly (military and political upheavals). The century is mad (*bezumno*), on the one hand, and wise (*mudro*), on the other. And this conflict, the archaic prophetic diction as well as the elegiac (rather than odic) structure in which it is rendered, combined with the poet's failure, for all his ostensible effort, to resolve it, affords Radishchev's version of the eighteenth century its particular haunting power. The poem's most frequent image is that of blood (mentioned six times in the course of a fairly short text), and if it imagines historical process as the incremental flow of water dripping from "the urn of times" (*urna vremian*) into streams and ultimately into the boundless and bottomless sea of eternity, the stream that the eighteenth century contributes is crimson.[23] This violent estuary engulfs and crushes virtue, felicity, and liberty, reminding the reader of the century's many wars and coups, which culminate in the violence of the French Revolution and Terror. The eighteenth century thus envisioned ultimately faces damnation ("you shall be eternally damned," *budesh' prokliato vo vek*).

Suddenly, as if the poet realizes the impossibility of sustaining such a grim vision, Peter and Catherine miraculously appear amid this bloody landscape as two rocks that grant direction and hope to the flow of history and enable the poet to consider the century's positive legacy of scientific and philosophical progress. The damned century is momentarily reimagined as a blessed one: "O unforgettable century! You grant to happy mortals / Truth, liberty, and light, a bright constellation forever" (*O nezabvenno stoletie! Radostnym smertnym daruesh' / Istinu, vol'nost' i svet, iasno sozvezd'e vo vek*). Its uniqueness thus presented through a series of contradictory and irreconcilable assessments, the century emerges as polarized by its creative and destructive impulses: "Kingdoms have perished by you [. . .] Kingdoms you build" (*Tsarstva pogibli toboi* [. . .] *Tsarstva ty zizhdesh'*). Enlightenment freethought, of which Radishchev just might be the most remarkable proponent, can only be countered by the assertion of God's existence; its scientific advances only recognized in both their daring and their limitations; the despair suffusing any who would behold the century's aftermath as Radishchev describes it, dispelled only through recognition of divine providence and virtue as eternal. But neither providence nor virtue is a remedy for the ills of the departed century, and the new epoch, barely begun, is already covered in blood: "The morn of the new century appeared before us still bloody" (*Utro stoletiia nova krovavo eshche nam iavilos'*). The poet desperately needs this hopeless landscape to yield hope, but that dream only becomes more elusive the more compellingly he renders his apocalyptic vision. In the last five lines, Radishchev makes a move that is unexpected, given his visionary take on history: he falls back on the tried and true odic code, abruptly ending the poem in an apotheosis of the ruling monarch and dynasty:

Мир, суд правды, истина, вольность лиются от трона,
Екатериной, Петром воздвигнут, чтоб счастлив был Росс.
Петр и ты, Екатерина! дух ваш живет еще с нами.
Зрите на новый вы век, зрите Россию свою.
Гений хранитель всегда Александр будь у нас . . .

[Peace, justice, truth, liberty flow from the throne, / Erected by Catherine and Peter for the prosperity of the Russian. / Peter and you, Catherine! Your spirit is still with us. / Look upon the new century, look upon your Russia. / Always be our guardian angel, Alexander . . .]

The values that now emanate from the throne are the very same that were crushed and then upheld by the eighteenth century.

Charged with contradictions, the poem's course replicates the course of the century, both ultimately escaping a definitive reading. Formally and thematically, the poem equivocates between elegiac grieving and odic celebration. On the one hand, Radishchev seems to suggest that the conflicts endemic to the eighteenth century are unprecedented and extreme, yet on the other, he seeks consolation in presenting history in general as rife with discord, of which the eighteenth century offers only the most glaring examples and over which reason (*premudrost'*) ultimately prevails. On the one hand, Radishchev conceives of the historical process on the grand, trans-individual scale of eternity, and on the other, he forcibly inserts Peter, Catherine, and Alexander into a narrative that otherwise hardly attempts to reconcile eternity's all-subsuming power with the purported ability of these mortals, however illustrious, to resist it. The poem's ultimately incoherent vision of recent history stems, I would argue, from Radishchev's failed attempt to integrate universal and dynastic Russian history, or reconcile the stance of the poet-prophet defying the powers that be with that of the poet-servitor repressed by the autocracy and attempting to find his way back into the good graces of the monarch's patronage. This failure is unavoidable and perhaps intentional; it rather vividly marks, moreover, the moment at the dawn of the nineteenth century when the two systems established in the eighteenth—that of enlightened intellectual liberty and the essentially feudal relationship between poet and ruler—come up against each other and against their own limitations.

When Radishchev turns to enumerate the eighteenth century's scientific advancements, he offers a rather long and involved list of its victories over nature:

Смело счастливой рукою завесу творенья возвеяв,
Скрыту природу сглядев в дальном таилище дел,
Из Океана возникли новы народы и земли,
Нощи глубокой из недр новы металлы тобой.
Ты исчисляешь светила, как пастырь играющих агнцов;
Нитью вождения вспять ты призываешь Комет;
Луч рассечен тобой света; ты новые солнца воззвало;
Новы луны изо тьмы дальной воззвало пред нас;
Ты побудило упряму природу к рожденью чад новых;
Даже летучи пары ты заключило в ярем;
Молнью небесну сманило во узы железны на землю
И на воздушных крылах смертных на небо взнесло.

[With a happy hand you have bravely lifted the veil of creation, / You have peered into hidden nature in the faraway cache of things, / From the Ocean there emerged new peoples and lands, / From the depths of the night you made appear new metals. / You tally heavenly bodies, like a pastor the frolicking lambs; / By [their] guiding thread you summon back the Comets; / You have split the ray of light; / You have called forth new suns; / Called before us new moons from the distant darkness; / You have induced nature to bear new progeny; / You have even harnessed the volatile vapors; / The heavenly lightning you have enticed down to earth into iron bondage / And on airy wings raised mortals to the sky.]

Within a poem painting history as a turbulent apocalyptic landscape beyond human control, this list, rendered in deliberately archaic diction but containing quite specific allusions to eighteenth-century events, depicts human confrontation with nature as both the century's most heroic accomplishment and a sign of its doom-fraught hubris. If the temporality of progress would have no trouble envisioning a future for this record of scientific development, Radishchev's particular combination of the ideologies of Enlightenment and millenarianism invariably checks these projections against the immutability of eternal truths.

A similar conflict underlies Petr Slovtsov's attempts to etch his eighteenth century on what he imagines as the bas-relief of antiquity (a vision no doubt inspired by the late eighteenth-century architectural imagination alluded to in the previous chapter). Despite his obscurity relative to Radishchev, Slovtsov is a Russian Enlightenment figure whose career echoes all of the drama of

Radishchev's. He spent his formative years in the Alexander Nevsky Seminary in Saint Petersburg, at that time a center of Russian freethought, where he became fascinated with Enlightenment philosophy and formed a life-long friendship with Mikhail Speransky, the future architect of Alexander I's liberal projects. Upon graduation, Slovtsov assumed a teaching post in philosophy and rhetoric at the Tobolsk Seminary and delivered sermons at the local church. He was soon denounced for seditious speech, arrested, and sent to serve penance in the Valaam Monastery. In all likelihood he composed a part or all of "Antiquity" ("Drevnost," 1793–96) in this seclusion.[24] Slovtsov was soon released and advanced to a post in the chancellery of the Petersburg governor under Paul I by another of this tsar's acts of anti-Catherinian benevolence, but in 1808, on charges of corruption that were most likely trumped-up, he was arrested again and exiled to Tobolsk, where, despite his eventual acquittal and petitions to return to the capital, he would spend all thirty-five years remaining until his death in 1843. Now mostly known for his writings on Siberian history and lore, cited on these subjects to this day, Slovtsov in his early verse, too, evinced a scientific sensibility, invoking in "Antiquity" a historical system based on recent advances in science, primarily geology, that often went against the grain of accepted religious doctrine.

If there is an enlightener type, then Slovtsov could serve as a model: a priest who does not mince words in extolling the rule of reason, championing the *philosophes*, and criticizing the autocracy. Unlike Radishchev's, Slovtsov's earlier, Catherine-era poem is the manifesto of an undoubting believer in the Enlightenment, which for him emerges as the only lasting legacy of the eighteenth century. Slovtsov polemically ousts rulers from his historical pantheon, concluding his ode not with their rushed apotheosis, but rather by asserting the triumph of Reason, perennially embattled, but always victorious:

Знай—один лишь разум просвещенный
В поздных переломится веках!
Хоть над жизнью гениев почтенных
Тучи расстилались в облаках,
Тучи, град и дождь на них лиющи,
Но по смерти их, над темной кущи,
Над которой буря пролилась,
Мирна радуга для них явилась,
Половиной в древность наклонилась,
А другой—в потомстве оперлась.

[Know: enlightened reason alone / Shall break through in later ages! / Though the life of esteemed geniuses / Has been shrouded by clouds, / Clouds that poured rain and hail upon them, / But after their death, over the dark canopy / Where the storm had passed, / A peaceful rainbow appeared for them, / Bent with one half toward antiquity / And the other resting upon posterity.]

The image of the rainbow, recalling the covenant of God and Noah, presents history as a providential pact, ensuring a continuity of values even as that of geopolitical formations or dynastic lines is revealed as inherently transient. Slovtsov censures the world of political intrigue: instead of the monarch, his interlocutor is History itself. Reinventing the Last Judgment as the judgment of history, Slovtsov still works within the odic formal and thematic framework, in which the poet is placed in a dialogic relationship to the patron, but his patron is Antiquity, which now arbitrates between the censured monarch and the visionary poet, and gives the ode and the world its coherence and meaning.[25]

Antiquity was itself a new object of poetic apostrophe. The historically abstract and menacing *eternity* of Radishchev had indiscriminately effaced the distinguishing traits of epochs and consigned the feats of heroes to oblivion. But *antiquity* preserved some registry of the most noteworthy historical events and names ("You who see into the chronicler's tablets / And there inscribe the names of the glorious!"; *Zriashchaia v skrizhali letopistsa, pishushchaia slavnykh imena*), differentiating to a greater extent than *eternity* between the momentary and the momentous. As such, "antiquity" can be seen as an intermediate stage between "eternity," the image of time dominant in the eighteenth century,[26] and "history," the center of intellectual attention in the nineteenth century. The bridge of some 150 lines between Slovtsov's solemn introductory appeal to antiquity and his concluding affirmation of Enlightenment reason constitutes one of the most idiosyncratic summations of the eighteenth century I have yet encountered.

Slovtsov holds up as the century's most timeless achievements the accomplishments of Benjamin Franklin, Abbé Raynal, and Derzhavin; the century's most ignominious moments are for him the partitions of Poland:

Древность, мавзолей свой украшая,
Лишь над нами упражняет гнев
И, осьмнадцатый век удушая,
Высечет лишь новый барельеф.
Франклин, преломивши скиптр британской,

Рейналь с хартией в руке гражданской,
Как оракул вольныя страны,
И Мурза в чалме, певец Астреи,
Под венком дубовым, в гривне с шеи
Будут у тебя иссечены.

Но кака там тень среди тумана
Стелет по карпатским остриям? [...]
Это падшей Польши тень парит.

[Antiquity, adorning its mausoleum, / Exercises its wrath only on us, / And smothering the eighteenth century, / Shall merely carve out a new bas-relief. / Franklin, who broke the British scepter in two, / Raynal with a civic charter in his hand, / As the oracle of a free nation, / And Murza in a turban, the bard of Astreia, / In an oak wreath, with a *grivna*[27] on his neck, / Shall be, [antiquity,] carved in your [bas-relief]. // But what shade amid the fog / Drifts over the Carpathian peaks? [...] / Hovering thus is the shade of fallen Poland.]

Slovtsov's chosen representatives of eighteenth-century heroism hail from three different nations and represent three different approaches to the pursuit of civil liberty and its mythologization (to which Slovtsov himself was clearly committed). Both Franklin and Raynal—the former in practice and the latter in theory, but both in nations fundamentally transfigured at the end of the century by the American and French Revolutions—reconceive political process as vesting decision-making in broader publics, rather than the tyrannizing autocratic state; both, for example, advanced subversive ideas concerning the rights of people to revolt and to give or withhold consent to taxation. Derzhavin was hardly a spokesman for dissent on the scale of Franklin or Raynal, but he could nevertheless be seen as opening up in his Felitsa cycle a comparable space for individual representation, akin to the popular representation advocated by these revolutionaries in the political arena. In short, Slovtsov's list could be read as no less than a bid for democratization *avant la lettre*. In this context, the lament for Poland in the next stanza emerges as a perfectly logical extension of the argument: the partitions of Poland wiped an entire nation from the European map and deprived it of freedom and the right to any representation, popular or otherwise. Thus for Slovtsov the partitions of Poland mark the deplorable persistence of the repressive power of the state, unguided, despite all its claims to the contrary, by enlightened reason. Like Radishchev, Slovtsov dramatizes the archetypal clash between Reason and Folly, only he locates it within the political realm itself rather than in the opposition between scientific progress and political violence.

While Slovtsov does not enumerate eighteenth-century scientific discoveries explicitly, they in fact shape the very structure of his argument and historical vision. His conception of antiquity gradually emerges out of a series of elaborately archaicized stanzas that mix the latest scientific discourse with Biblical imagery.

> Праздны черепы, сии избытки,
> Мать-земля расплавит в новы слитки;
> Внутрь ее зияли, где погряз
> Геркулан со знамям и щитами,
> Лиссабон с хоругвью и крестами,
> Плавится людей оседших связь.
>
> Мнится, что миры людей дремучи,
> Кои прилегли к земной груды,
> С спящих мышц стряхнут надгробны кучи
> И в чреду проснутся на трубы;
> Так как мир, кой оюнев днесь паки,
> Предкам зиждет по кладбищам раки,
> Может быть, из-под сырых холмов
> Воспрянул, чтоб лечь в земной утробе;
> Так не все ль мы в раздвижном сем гробе
> Переводим с древних дух веков?

[Idle skulls, these surplus things, / Mother-Earth will melt into new ingots; / Her insides gaped, where / Herculaneum sank with its banners and shields, / Lisbon with its gonfalon and crosses; / The bond of sedimented people is fused. // 'T would seem that the slumbrous human multitudes / Who have lain in the bosom of the earth, / Shall shake off their tombstone piles / And in their turn awake to the trumpet's sound; / While the world that has this day [the Biblical *dnes'*] become young again / Is erecting tombstones to its ancestors, / It has perhaps itself come up from the damp mounds / To rest in the earth's womb; / Are we not all then in this adjustable coffin / Catching our breath after ancient centuries?]

If Christian doctrine of the period reckoned the Earth to be six thousand years old, new estimates from burgeoning geological and paleontological research proposed, rather blasphemously, that the transformations evidenced by rock formations and fossils could only have occurred over vastly greater spans of time. Evidence for this discovery had been accreting over the course of the preceding century and, starting in the late 1600s, various hypotheses (e.g., plutonism, catastrophism) proposed to explicate it, still largely from within the Biblical paradigm. But the most authoritative and radical analysis was formulated in the 1780s by one of the key representatives of the Scottish Enlightenment and the father of modern geological science, James Hutton, who maintained that the Earth was millions of years old, and that its terrain was shaped not only by catastrophic events such as the Great Flood so beloved as a historical origin by Biblical exegetes, but also by the "ordinary" and slow processes of plate tectonics and the water cycle.[28] Geology emerged in the eighteenth century as an essentially historical enterprise, dealing with what Hutton called "deep time" and demonstrating that in the forms of the present one could discover the key to the past (even and particularly the most ancient) and could understand and imagine worlds that had disappeared. "An adjustable coffin," at once burying past strata and melting them into new forms, the Earth (in Hutton's geological account), or Antiquity (in Slovtsov's poetic one), by virtue of its unfathomable age, also problematized the late Enlightenment's sense of its present's lasting significance, for neither was it now to be effaced entirely (as in Radishchev's picture of eternity) nor was it to be preserved in the contours familiar to contemporaries. The persistence of the past was now understood as a much more dynamic and unpredictable metamorphic process.

While Slovtsov might not have been familiar with Hutton's recent discoveries, he most likely knew the work of his acknowledged predecessor, Peter Simon Pallas, who spent most of his scientific career in Russia, and whose research into Russia's natural history was supported and publicized by the government.[29] We might now rethink Slovtsov's image of antiquity's bas-relief as representing a natural, geologic rather than sculptural record, and the final stanza's prediction that Reason would "break through (*perelomitsia*) in later ages" as likewise an image couched in terms of early scientific notions that would eventually come to articulate what we now know as the "rock cycle." For all its certainty in the triumph of reason, Slovtsov's assessment of the eighteenth century is a project precariously positioned between, yet managing to combine quite seamlessly, two models of historical explanation: one drawing on the Biblical prophetic timeframe and preparing for the Last Judgment; the other implying (somewhat sacrilegiously) that in the great span of natural history no judgment can be last, and that history might be an eternally productive melting pot.

Slovtsov's profoundly radical ode is remarkable both for the gravity of the political argument it advances and for the integration of different modes of historical thinking it achieves. In comparison Semen Bobrov's texts on the turn of the century[30] might appear less considered and perhaps even marked by that graphomaniac turgidity so mercilessly mocked by his younger contemporaries (Batiushkov, Viazemskii, Pushkin). But although it lacks the apocalyptic solemnity of Radishchev or Slovtsov, Bobrov's sense of historical progression is not so much superficial as it is profoundly optimistic.[31] In a tone of hopefulness, his verse pursues the dual project of "rational prediction and salvational expectation" we recall from Koselleck's characterization of this period's historical thinking, a view that has been central to my readings of both Radishchev and Slovtsov (although L'vov, as I have argued, pursued a very different, nationalist, project). Keen on metaphorizing history, Bobrov avails himself of a broad repertoire of imagery, from the mechanistic ("the centuries' wheels"; *vekov kolesa*) to the mystical ("the death of the world," *smert' mira*; "the sigh of the ages," *vzdokh vremen*).[32] He paints an eclectic historical expanse, which accommodates dark nocturnal images in the manner of Edward Young,[33] somber pronouncements by an Ossianic elder,[34] "fiery oceans" and "bloody rivers" akin to those in Radishchev's apocalyptic eternity, and even a Slovtsov-like monumental edifice as an allegory of Russia's escape from oblivion. Complementing the eclecticism of his figurative repertoire is Bobrov's preternatural ability to associate seemingly incongruous events, personages, and images, rendering his picture of the eighteenth century, for example, the most populous and varied I have seen.

His four poems dedicated to the turn of the century can thus be seen as a record of the events and figures of the recent past that preoccupied a Russian intellectual of the time. Bobrov's enthusiasm for the eighteenth century's scientific innovations, for example, knows no bounds; the only check on their appeal is the cautionary tale of Newton, whose madness Bobrov ascribes in "A Hundred-Year Song" to the shocking audacity of his discoveries. (It is now believed that his madness resulted from mercury poisoning.) While the poems' scientific scope is broad and cosmopolitan, their political concerns are confined to Russia and the (predictable) celebration of its monarchs. Crucially, however, Bobrov sees the two domains—European science and Russian politics—as manifestations of the same pursuit of progress comprising a singular narrative of the century. Thus, marveling at William Herschel's 1781 discovery of Uranus, Bobrov sees Peter the Great as a similar discoverer of the "half-planet" (*poluplaneta*) Russia. Just as future generations would always acknowledge the existence of Uranus ("In the kingdom of the Sun, [Herschel] ensures / The familiarity of future ages / With Uranus, as with some new-comer"; *On v tsarstve Solntsa uchrezhdaet / Znakomstvo budushchikh vekov / S Uranom, kak s prishel'tsem nekim*), so too, even in the absence of a physical monument to Peter such as Falconet's, would Russia always stand in testament to the monarch's grandeur as both his greatest discovery and a monument of his own making:

Пусть не было б Петру ваяний,
Пусть летописи умолчат!
Пусть памятники все исчезнут!
Россия—есть его ваянье,
Есть памятник, трудов цена;
Она—его бессмертно зданье,
Полупланета есть она,
Где был он божеством ея.[35]

[And even if there were no sculptures of Peter, / And the chronicles were to fall silent! / And all the monuments disappear! / Russia is his sculpture, / His monument, the reward of his labors; / She is his immortal edifice, / She is a half-planet, / Where he was her deity.]

Similarly, in "The Prognosticating Response," monarchs and scientists appear side-by-side, as eighteenth-century figures are imagined reincarnated in the nineteenth:

Иль *Петр,* или *Екатерина,*
Другой *Невтон,* и *Локк* другой,
Или другой здесь *Ломоносов*
Торжественной стопою внидут
В врата *Кумеиных* времен.[36] [Emphasis in the original]

[*Peter,* or *Catherine,* / Or another *Newton,* / or another *Locke,* / Or here another *Lomonosov* / Will enter with triumphant step / Into the gates of Cumaean times.]

If Radishchev's stance vis-à-vis recent history is one of bafflement, and Slovtsov's one of rational discernment that endeavors to distinguish only the century's most salient characteristics, Bobrov does not exclude any event in the eighteenth century or rule out any possible outcome in the nineteenth, at least never polemically so. Thus, in extolling Peter he admits that nature might need to rest several centuries after giving birth to such a giant; but he allows for the possibility that the nineteenth century, too, would be a period of intellectual and political demiurges. While L'vov's nationalist scenario attaches no particular value to modernity, and Radishchev and Slovtsov relativize its merits in reassessing the Petrine demiurgic narrative within the grander ethical, scientific, and apocalyptic frameworks, Bobrov unequivocally enthuses over Russia's modernization as a victorious path originating with Peter and predestining the coming nineteenth century for greatness. Bobrov's eulogistic invocations of monarchs might strike us as conforming to the ruler-centered vision associated with the ceremonial ode, but the framework within which he places them is quite original, invoking them not as patrons but as milestones, listed alongside the poets that extolled them (Lomonosov) and the scientists who in profound and radical ways were responsible for destabilizing their symbolic power.

Bobrov's basic premise is that the past is set off from the future by a gate (we might recall this conceit from the verses of Derzhavin and Kapnist on Paul's accession, discussed in the previous chapter); presiding over this gate is Janus, the divine supervisor of transitional times. By the end of his long monologue in "A Hundred-Year Song," the all-knowing hoary elder of the eighteenth century is rejuvenated as a rosy youngster of the nascent nineteenth, but in shuttling back and forth between past and future, the poem implies that the older face always persists on the other side of time's doorway. This model indeed befits the political rhetoric of 1801, when Alexander openly proclaimed the return to Catherine's political course (a little less openly understood as an anti-Pauline one) as the new vision for his rule, ironically presenting this reliance on the past as a sign of progress. The eighteenth-century history that Bobrov succeeds in accessing and recording through the speech of the elder also continuously reverberates in the present: the "Janus" shape of chronology places the relevance of the Russian eighteenth century in history's capacity for reincarnation, a conceit allowing Bobrov to perceive Russian history as a continuum coherent within itself and with European history, predictably extending from Peter through Catherine to Alexander as its most recent apogee, and thence into the future.

Unreservedly celebrated by Bobrov, the eighteenth century's uniqueness—all the achievements of its rulers and scientists—in fact opens up the possibility that in the course of the nineteenth century, the eighteenth would no longer appear unique, but would rather be seen, in its true significance, as only the beginning of a new era. The predictive passage quoted above culminates in the poem's coda, where the *pointe* of the prognosis is placed precisely in the poet's inability to prophesy anything with certainty:

А может быть—переселится
Восток и *юг* чудесно в *север;*
Не отрицай сих чувств—и жди,
Как путник на брегу морском![37] [Emphasis in the original]

[And perhaps the east and south will relocate / Miraculously to the north; / Do not deny these sentiments—and wait, / Like a traveler on the seashore!]

Though perhaps less coherent or compelling than those of the other poets discussed in this section, Bobrov's vision lends itself particularly well to concluding my survey of the alternative models of historical cognition exhibited by Russian poetry at the dawn of the new nineteenth century, precisely because of the optimistic way in which his poems emblematize the multiplicity of the historical frameworks then in circulation, the predictive imperative directed at Russia's future and unconstrained by, though aware of, the politics of dynastic succession. Bobrov's is the "emancipated subject" who does not find himself in an oppositional relation with the authorities; in fact, his emancipation is that of vision rather than of political agency. These poems are not patron-bound because their imagination, enabled by the scientific, poetic, and political innovations of the eighteenth century, in a much broader sense knows no bounds.

The end of the eighteenth century was in many ways an unprecedented occasion for odic historical interpretation. Granted, there was no shortage of odes that seized upon the near-coincidence of this temporal landmark with Alexander's enthronement to celebrate the monarch rather than the expiration of an epoch.[38] But the texts we have examined in this section evince a new spirit of history-mindedness (or historical consciousness, as it comes to be known later in the nineteenth century), only tenuously connected to the topical changes of regime. In these texts, we see the poet as a figure invested in historical interpretation unconstrained by the ruler's demands; this is interpretation and prediction on a broader scale than hitherto imagined, articulable only by a subject who conceives of his voice as striving for autonomy and engaging with a public and projects greater than those of the monarch. These new, expanded historical horizons had been opened up, to be sure, by the poetics of the ceremonial ode, but they could no longer be contained therein.

The poet's predictive and prophetic capacity modeled in these texts did not yet isolate him from the polis, as indeed no such isolation was viable or necessary in the ode (recall its Pindaric restorative function). But in the decades to follow, the prophetic stance would in effect become private and insulating, as part perhaps of a more general movement toward the intimization of poetic speech and space. In these decades the odic genre would also undergo multiple revisions, gradually losing its status as the most vocal arbiter of history and the public realm, to a large extent because the prophetic voice would come to reside elsewhere, in the shorter lyric, while the historical eye, as will be examined in Part II, would come to dwell especially in prose. It is in the context of these transformations that we might ponder Pushkin's lyrical considerations of patronage (here treated primarily as the condition of odic utterance, rather than in all the specific circumstances of reception and remuneration) as he revisits this question in the late 1820s with the hindsight of these literary developments, and having himself formerly retreated into private poetic genres and made major pronouncements in the tradition of the isolated poet-prophet.

"I HAVE NOT PRAISED THE EARTHLY GODS"

Pushkin's lyric repeatedly reflects on the social, historical, and affective status of the poet's voice, assessing its reach and negotiating its addressees' varying levels of participation in meaning-making. Differently focalized at different biographical and historical junctures, the present in Pushkin's lyric is often portrayed as a time of transition between different models and institutions of literary production, reception, and consumption. These two central themes might in fact be examined as mutually illuminating. We might consider the problem of the lyric voice—posed by Pushkin throughout his career, and raised in an array of forms, from the public genres of high prophecy to the private genres of intimate address—as couched in historical questions of personal maturation, literary succession, society's development, and history's flow. The problem of the voice is in fact the problem of the world in which it is heard or muffled, and of the systems of reception this world gives rise to. Thus,

Pushkin is born into a world where poetic expression is still intended for the patron and conjures vast realms only to lay them at the feet of a single addressee; he becomes a poet in a world where that former system mixes with, but also gives way to, circumscribed and personal poetic visions aimed at audiences intimately connected with the poet—with this new understanding of lyric utterance devaluing the attainments of the previous system. In the 1820s, the possibilities of literary reception as Pushkin experiences it become both more diverse and more challenging: in the course of this decade, his voice must reach his various audiences from exile, cope with their attrition after the Decembrist Uprising, contend with increasingly strident critics, and reinvent itself in the face of the new commercial readership, anonymous and demanding. All of these changes affect the lyric voice, and also engender the historical consciousness of that voice's placedness within a specific period, of its different capacities at different moments in the poet's past. In this light, we might reevaluate Pushkin's varying treatments of patronage throughout his career as implicit opportunities for testing the reach and power of the poet's voice at particular moments of the nineteenth century. This section examines Pushkin's changing attitudes toward patronage, from his early participation in its dismantling to the late 1820s–'30s, when he reassesses it against the backdrop of his much-altered nineteenth-century world.

Let us first consider the young poet's subtle but forceful rejection of patronage in two of his early epistles. The 1818 epistle "To Zhukovskii" ("Zhukovskomu"), which was fervently admired by Viazemskii (and by Zhukovskii himself) as a manifestation of young Pushkin's preternatural poetic ability, paints Zhukovskii at a moment of poetic afflatus (an exalted soul, an impatient hand on his lyre, a magical haze, a quick chill of inspiration), only to shift abruptly to the pragmatics of this inspiration (writing for the select few, for the exacting friends of talent):

Когда, к мечтательному миру
Стремясь возвышенной душой,
Ты держишь на коленях лиру
Нетерпеливою рукой;
Когда сменяются виденья
Перед тобой в волшебной мгле,
И быстрый холод вдохновенья
Власы подъемлет на челе,—
Ты прав, творишь ты *для немногих*,

Не для завистливых судей,

Не для сбирателей убогих

Чужих суждений и вестей,

Но для друзей таланта строгих,

Священной истины друзей.

Не всякого полюбит счастье,

Не все родились для венцов.

Блажен, кто знает сладострастье

Высоких мыслей и стихов!

Кто наслаждение прекрасным

В прекрасный получил удел

И твой восторг уразумел

Восторгом пламенным и ясным!³⁹ [Emphasis in the original]

[When, to the dreamy world / Aspiring in your lofty soul, / You hold on your knees a lyre / With your impatient hand, / When visions flit / Before you in a magical haze, / And the quick chill of inspiration / Lifts the hairs on your brow,— / You are right, you create *for the few*, / Not for the envious judges, / Not for the beggarly collectors / Of others' opinions and news, / But for the exacting friends of talent, / Friends of the sacred truth. / Fortune does not love every man, / Not all are born for laurels. / Blessed is he who knows the voluptuousness / Of lofty thoughts and verses! / Who has received the enjoyment of beauty / For his beautiful lot / And comprehended your rapture / With his own, ardent and lucid!]

The poem as a whole can be read as a fellow poet's commentary on Zhukovskii's ideal audience, but it is the identity of this elite readership that emerges as a hidden stumbling block in this otherwise eulogistic epistle. The italicized phrase "for the few" (*dlia nemnogikh*) in fact comes from the title of a bilingual German-Russian collection *Für Wenige/Dlia nemnogikh* that Zhukovskii published in several installments starting in 1818 for the Grand Duchess Alexandra Fedorovna, the wife of the soon-to-be emperor Nicholas I.[40] Zhukovskii's friends were troubled by his alliance with the court, seeing in it a compromised tribute to the outmoded pseudo-sincerity of eighteenth-century patronage structures and a betrayal of the new affective fellowship of the poet and his readers.[41] In this light, the lines "Fortune does not love every man, / Not all are born for laurels" revise the initial italicized meaning of "the few" (*nemnogie*), relocating this select audience from the court space, which threatens to isolate Zhukovskii from his friends, to the intimate space opened up by the epistle's performance of dialogue between its speaker and addressee. This new space of reception can accommodate both audiences. Alexandra Fedorovna's feminine court, which has ceded its institutional authority over the poet, can now offer him appreciation commensurate with his gift: in the epistle's conclusion, the poet and his ideal readers mirror each other in their rapture. The epistle as a genre and as a speech act effects a similar mirroring of the roles of speaker and addressee: the poem is both about Zhukovskii as poet and Pushkin as his reader, and about Pushkin as poet and Zhukovskii as epistle recipient. Thus, while not entirely suspending the possibility of dialogue with the court, "To Zhukovskii" clarifies the conditions allowing this now tenuous dialogue to continue in the post-Derzhavin age, "when the union with the tsars has been dissolved."[42] More generally, the poem brings the bard and his select few listeners/readers into a relationship that grows increasingly intimate as we move from the first to the final lines, implying the Romantic ideal of impassioned interpretation as co-creation on the poem's horizon.

In another poem of the same year, "To N. Ia. Pliuskova" ("K N. Ia. Pliusko-voi"), written in response to a "challenge"[43] to compose a panegyric to Alexander I's wife Elizabeth, Pushkin similarly seeks a new mold for casting the poet's relationship to the mighty of this world, and articulates a non-courtly scenario of reception in a poem commissioned by the court:

На лире скромной, благородной
Земных богов я не хвалил
И силе в гордости свободной
Кадилом лести не кадил.
Свободу лишь учася славить,
Стихами жертвуя лишь ей,
Я не рожден царей забавить
Стыдливой музою моей.
Но, признаюсь, под Геликоном,
Где Касталийский ток шумел,
Я, вдохновенный Аполлоном,
Елисавету втайне пел.
Небесного земной свидетель,
Воспламененною душой
Я пел на троне добродетель
С ее приветною красой.

Любовь и тайная свобода
Внушали сердцу гимн простой,
И неподкупный голос мой
Был эхо русского народа.[44]

[With my modest and noble lyre / I have not praised the earthly gods / And for power, in my unbound pride, / I have not burned incense. / Learning to praise liberty alone, / Sacrificing only to her my verse, / I was not born to amuse tsars / With my bashful muse. / But, I admit, near Helicon, / Where flows the Castalian spring, / I, inspired by Apollo, / Secretly sang of Elizabeth. / An earthly witness to the heavenly, / With my soul enflamed, / I sang virtue enthroned / With its amiable beauty. / Love and hidden freedom / Suggested to the soul a simple hymn, / And my incorruptible voice was the echo of the Russian people.]

Throughout the poem, the space inhabited by the speaker is one of secrecy: his lyre is humble, his muse bashful, his song to Elizabeth furtive. In addition, this space is beyond the physical borders of the Russian state and exists only on the mythological map of inspiration, in the shadow of Mount Helicon, watered by the Castalian spring, and visited by Apollo. Before proceeding with his eulogy, the speaker has made sure to remove himself and his voice from the public sphere, where the poem's pragmatic intent might easily be misjudged. Similar manipulations shape the temporality and addressee of the poem: the panegyric takes place in the past, while the poem itself is only a narrative of the panegyric act, which in its highly mediated and framed form is directed not at Elizabeth (who remains in the third person throughout) but at some implied reader, perhaps Nadezhda Iakovlevna Pliuskova, Elizabeth's lady-in-waiting, or perhaps the people (*narod*) whom the poet's voice claims ultimately to echo.

This non-panegyric panegyric is split into two unequal parts: the first eight lines reject the panegyric stance (all the verbs are negated), while the final twelve rehabilitate it on new conditions and as a supposedly new set of poetic attitudes. The praise of Elizabeth escapes the poet as a confession ("I admit," *priznaius'*) of an ardent (*vosplamenennaia*) soul. Here again the relationship between poet and empress, compromised by its history as an institution of flattery, insincerity, and material exchange, is reinvented as one of spiritual affinity (here, of the poet's "enflamed soul" for the virtue and beauty on the throne), emanating from a voice emphatically professing its own independence. Tellingly, the language of this emancipated panegyric is very similar to that used for the rejection of the odic situation in the beginning of the poem: the poet does not "praise earthly gods" (line 2) and yet bears witness to "the heavenly on earth" (line 13). We might also recall the formula "virtue with beauty" (*dobrodetel' s krasotoi*) from Lomonosov's odes to a different Elizabeth, composed within precisely the framework of the high panegyric form and of patronage, both in a sense codified by Lomonosov. Thus, "To N. Ia. Pliuskova" amends the language of the panegyric only superficially, while instead radically reinventing the odic situation and genre.[45] The two parts of the poem, initially appearing in conflict with each other, contraposed by the conjunction "but" (*no*), are in the end meant to be superposed, with "liberty" (*svoboda*), the lyrical object of the first part, merging with Elizabeth (*Elisaveta*), the lyrical object of the second. What in Lomonosov's age would have been an ornate panegyric is now a "simple hymn," which we in fact never read, but are invited to imagine as an echo of a similarly imaginary voice of the people. In the end, "To N. Ia. Pliuskova" remains a commentary on the *challenge* of writing a panegyric in Alexander's Russia, the framing fragment of a text whose construction is both encouraged and at the same time avoided. The two poems can thus be read as early manifestoes of the new poetic possibilities available to a poet who divests himself of a hierarchical relationship to his consumers at court, and believes in the imminence of spiritual kinship and the potential for co-creativity with the reader, while also continuing to contemplate past genres and institutions of reception.

Perhaps the most momentous transformation in the tenor of Pushkin's reflections on patronage and readership appears in a series of poems written in exile, in which the figure of Ovid becomes both Pushkin's double or kindred spirit and his negatively assessed model predecessor. This scenario is further complicated by the increasing sway of Byron's competing models of displacement, itinerance and poet's relationship with reader. Pushkin finds himself in Ovid's place of exile and is keen to retrace the Ovidian scenario, but with several key modifications suggested by his critical modern perspective.[46] Knowing that Ovid appealed for mercy to the emperor Augustus (who turned a deaf ear), Pushkin repeatedly sees his path diverging from his predecessor's specifically in this respect. Echoing the finality of his rejection of patronage in "To N. Ia. Pliuskova," Pushkin restates his position in "From a Letter to Gnedich" ("Iz pis'ma k Gnedichu," 1821): "To Octavius—in blind hope / I do not sing obsequious Te Deums" (*Oktaviiu—v slepoi nadezhde—/ Molebnov lesti ne poiu*), and again in his most poignant exile poem "To Ovid" ("K Ovidiiu," 1821) elucidates the motivations and mood behind this stance.

Кто в грубой гордости прочтет без умиленья
Сии элегии, последние творенья,
Где ты свой тщетный стон потомству передал?

Суровый славянин, я слез не проливал,
Но понимаю их; изгнанник самовольный,
И светом, и собой, и жизнью недовольный,
С душой задумчивой, я ныне посетил
Страну, где грустный век ты некогда влачил.[47]

[Who in harsh pride shall read with no emotion / These elegies, the last creations, / Where you conveyed to posterity your vain moan? // A stern Slav, I did not shed tears, / But understand them; a voluntary exile, / Displeased with the world, myself, and life, / With pensive soul, I have now visited / The country where you once dragged out your sorrowful age.]

The hopelessness of a supplicatory epistle to Augustus/Alexander stems not only from the ruler's unwillingness to grant mercy, but, more crucially, from the erosion of the nineteenth-century petitioner's belief in the possibility of dialogue with power, and more broadly the possibility of dialogue between a poet and his contemporaries. This poem's governing mood is that of quiet discontent, for which there is no living interlocutor and which only finds its release in the unpeopled natural expanse. If Ovid sheds tears, Pushkin's lyric subject can understand, but finds no such outlet for himself. If the previous texts were ultimately about the untenability of the ceremonial ode in the nineteenth century, "To Ovid," taking the elegiac form, is about the silencing of the elegiac voice, the misrepresentation committed by the elegiac vision (Ovid and Pushkin see the Moldavian landscape in radically different ways), and about the futility of the elegiac utterance; the lyric thereby also calls into question those forms of poetic communication, forms privileging intimacy and sincerity, that had come to supplant the older odic modality. If the first two poems we examined showed Pushkin reformulating the poet-reader relationship in the panegyric, his exile poems attempt elegiac contact with friends, the reading public in the capitals, poetic predecessors and posterity, but inevitably discover that the conditions of physical and spiritual exile obstruct most circuits of communication—a far more troubling discovery, indeed, than that of "Augustus's" indifference.

If in the 1810s and early '20s, the Russian Romantic project entailed active disavowal of such immediately preceding poetic and social systems as Classicism, the ode, and patronage, in the late '20s–'30s these were no longer an active threat, or at least not one comparable to that posed by the literary market or the ascendancy of prose over poetry. This was a time to reconsider, or cast a mindful, history-conscious look at, the "unsympathetic" forms of the eighteenth-century past. Pushkin's stance on patronage, as evidenced by his brief but not inconsiderable pronouncements on the subject, was a key part of his reflections on the place of the eighteenth century and his own aristocratic class in a progressively more diverse nineteenth-century society and, specifically, within the increasingly commercialized literary culture of the 1830s. His attitude toward patronage fluctuates, but the cluster of themes and questions evoked by it remains constant. Thus, in a letter to Viazemskii of June 7, 1824, Pushkin declares, "[P]atronage has gone out of fashion. None of us would want *the magnanimous support of an enlightened grandee (prosveshchennogo vel'mozhi)*. This has grown old together with Lomonosov" (emphasis in the original).[48] But by the 1830s, for example in "A Journey from Moscow to Petersburg" ("Puteshestvie iz Moskvy v Peterburg," 1833–34), his critical backward retracing of Radishchev's famous journey, Pushkin defends Lomonosov from charges of captation and insincerity, claiming that addressing one's work to a sophisticated noble patron might in fact be less disreputable than currying the favor of some deceitful journalist: "Lomonosov and Crabbe deserve the respect of all honest men, despite their humble dedications, and the gentlemen NN are still contemptible, even though in their little books they preach independence and dedicate their compositions not to a kind and intelligent grandee, but to some scoundrel and fibber much like themselves."[49] This is a view much amended by several years of the so-called "literary aristocracy" debates,[50] one of the first polemics to examine the Russian literary sphere on the basis of its social composition rather than aesthetic values or national affiliations. These debates also inevitably revolve around the status of the eighteenth century, Russia's first literary modernity, when the social position of the writer differed fundamentally from that in the 1830s. Thus, in the same section of the "Journey," Pushkin declares that, in belonging to the gentry, Russian writers of his milieu cannot avail themselves of the favors of their equals, a state of affairs that "has endowed our literature with a distinct physiognomy,"[51] distinct from both Western Europe and eighteenth-century Russia. Precisely because patronage is thus seen as no longer belonging to Pushkin's present, even as it so profoundly structured the preceding, formative period, his critique reclaims it as a lens through which to assess his own time.

Primarily a social phenomenon, tethering authorship to specific hierarchies of authority and property, patronage as a subject of critique also opened up historical questions of periodization and the comparative inquiry into the "spirits" of ages, both Pushkin's age, spanning Alexander's and Nicholas's reigns, and the age of Lomonosov and Derzhavin, governed by the empresses. In a period obsessed with historical inquiry and imagination, with pondering its own novelty in comparison to the past, patronage became a marker of historical difference, a principle that had ordered the social comportment and literary sensibilities of earlier writers, readers, and benefactors, but quite rapidly lost its relevance in the new post-Napoleonic world order. Thus, the reconstruction of the eighteenth century, one of Pushkin's chief preoccupations in the 1830s, often brought him to reconsider patronage, requiring a conscious reformulation of nineteenth-century norms. Treated as a distinctly eighteenth-century practice, patronage, then, can be read as a problem as much of historiographical inquiry as of social critique.

To illustrate these two ways of approaching patronage in the 1820s–'30s, let us consider the reception history of the epistle "To the Grandee" ("K vel'mozhe," 1830), the inaugural poetic text for Pushkin's engagement with the lifestyles of the eighteenth century, or "bytopisanie," to use Vadim Vatsuro's term for this particular Pushkinian project. The main problem with the epistle, in the eyes of Pushkin's contemporaries, was that it addressed what sounded too much like unreserved praise to Prince Nikolai Borisovich Iusupov (1750–1831), a rich and famously hedonistic grandee of the Catherine era. Much in the poem, including its stylized elevated poetics, seemed to cast Pushkin in the role of a supplicant or flatterer, or at least a poet who sincerely attempted to resuscitate and inhabit one side of the patronage relationship. Satirical journalistic attacks followed immediately.[52] A particularly mean-spirited jibe from Nikolai Polevoi portrayed Pushkin as an Italian abbé eager to be treated to a weekly dinner by a rich nobleman.[53] Even Pushkin's own cohort, however, were surprised to see in his verse such an idealized portrait of Iusupov, one clearly shoehorned to fit eulogistic convention.[54] Without recapitulating the ensuing polemics, at times clever, at times hurtful, one can identify two basic assumptions governing this early reception of the text: a) that the biographical figures of Pushkin and Iusupov fully corresponded to the lyrical figures of the epistle's speaker and addressee, and b) that therefore the act of lyric communication staged the biographical subject's pragmatic relationship with the epistle's biographical addressee. According to this interpretation, the poem is about Pushkin *the man*'s navigation of social space. The debates thus ignored a paramount principle of Romantic self-fashioning; namely, the Romantic irony that would underscore the textuality and constructedness of both the poem's lyric subject (the visitor to the grandee) and its addressee.

About a decade later, however, when the poem had receded from the stage of pressing social debate,[55] Belinskii redefined its purview as pertaining more to the historical than to the social sphere: "Some loudmouthed fools, having misunderstood the poem, had the nerve to cast aspersions upon the great poet's character in their polemical escapades, seeing flattery where one should see only the highest degree of artistic insight and a depiction of an entire epoch through the figure of one of its most remarkable representatives."[56] For Belinskii, standing at an even further remove than the poem's earlier critics from the realities of patronage and the eighteenth century, and moreover writing with the hindsight of such other Pushkin works as "The Queen of Spades" and *The Captain's Daughter*, "To the Grandee" was a poetic act of historically conscious archaeology and restoration, one that comprehended "the age of Catherine" more incisively than her contemporaries ever could: "This portrait of a grandee of the old era is a marvelous restoration of a ruin into the original shape of a building" (*divnaia restavratsiia ruiny v pervobytnyi vid zdaniia*).[57] This reading of the poem magnified the distance between its first and second person, setting them upon entirely separate epochal planes, and thus depriving the poem's lyric communication, which earlier critics had deemed purely pragmatic, of its potential for reciprocity; in this view, this ostensible epistle was in reality a uni-directional inspection of eighteenth-century detritus by a man of the nineteenth. (In this book's final chapter, we will see Turgenev's narrators espouse a similar attitude toward the century preceding them.) The line of argumentation that Belinskii offers here would lead later readers of the poem to place it together with "The Queen of Spades" and Pushkin's other projects of eighteenth-century reconstruction. The social and the historical are thus the two contexts in which patronage has been seen to signify in Pushkin's work, and it is certainly instructive to observe the limitations that either approach, pursued exclusively, imposes on the poem's meaning.

Neither Pushkin's early critics nor later scholars have analyzed the poet's statements on patronage, in this epistle as well as other texts, for their possible *metapoetic* implications. After all, patronage and its distinctive dedicational forms had, besides a social function, a profound impact on the creative process of eighteenth-century poets, or at least on their representations of this process; recall, for example, Lomonosov's lyrical afflatus and expansive pane-gyric spaces, or the improvised masks of Derzhavin's Felitsa cycle, or the diversity of conceptual frameworks enabled by the departures from patron-age in the texts discussed in the previous section. In this context, interrogating patronage in the nineteenth century might have meant questioning not only eighteenth-century poets' sincerity, but also their very *modus operandi*, since patronage seemed to presuppose notions of inspiration that differed dramat-ically from the Romantic. I would argue that "To the Grandee," though never explicitly commenting on poetic craft, reinhabits forms of inspiration that had circulated in the eighteenth century, but had since lost their currency.

Before examining this 1830 epistle more closely, however, let us briefly turn to an earlier one, "To Mordvinov" ("Mordvinovu," 1826), a poem that responds to the post-Decembrist crisis of political and moral authority by revisiting the question of patronage from social, historical, and aesthetic angles. Nikolai Semenovich Mordvinov (1754–1845), Iusupov's contemporary, was strikingly unlike Iusupov both in his comportment and in the way he was perceived in Pushkin's milieu.[58] A "grandee-citizen" (*vel'mozha-grazhdanin*), as Evgenii Baratynskii called him,[59] Admiral Mordvinov was also inscribed on the ban-ner of the liberal movement by such poets as Kondratii Ryleev, Petr Pletnev, and Baratynskii himself, and this was even before Mordvinov became the only member of the Supreme Criminal Court to object to the execution of Decembrist leaders and to capital punishment in general. In an April 1824 letter to Viazemskii, Pushkin credits Mordvinov with "compris[ing] the en-tirety of the Russian opposition."[60] In other words, for poets of the Pushkin generation, Mordvinov presented a curious and inspiring combination of the Catherine-era grandee and the energetic liberal politician of the reign of Alexander I—that is, someone who could be addressed both in the Pindaric eighteenth-century mode and in a friendly, albeit formal, epistle.[61] Unlike other eulogies to Mordvinov, Pushkin's text approaches its subject indirectly. Instead of addressing Mordvinov, the lyric speaker invokes the aging Vasilii Petrov's, Mordvinov's proto-panegyrist's, enthusiasm for the young courtier in an ode of 1796. The appeal to Petrov's visionary celebration of the hero so early in his career allows the young poet, Pushkin, to highlight the constancy of Mordvi-nov's merits: "You have justified his lyre, you have never betrayed / The hopes of the prophetic poet. / How gloriously you have fulfilled his prophecy!" (*Ty liru opravdal, ty vvek ne izmenil / Nadezhdam veshchego piita. / Kak slavno ty sderzhal prorochestvo ego!*).[62] These lines also imply a continuity between Petrov's and Pushkin's texts and panegyric sentiments. This insight can help

us understand the emphasis placed upon the age difference between the old
Petrov and the young Mordvinov in the poem's opening. ("At that time"—in
the poet Petrov's last years—"you arose; your ray warmed him," *V to vremia
ty vstaval: tvoi luch ego sogrel.*) At the end of the poem, Mordvinov's own
aging, his metaphorical embodiment in a "gray cliff" (*sedoi utes*) now echoing Petrov's status as "gray eagle" (*sedoi orel*) at the beginning, makes room
for the next young man to come forward—the invisible author Pushkin, parallel to Petrov's young Mordvinov. The poem thus casts the Pindaric relationship
of poet and hero not in terms of pragmatic hierarchies, but rather in terms of
generational and cultural reciprocity and continuity, as a chain of inspiration.

Claimed as a conduit for Pushkin's panegyric energy, Petrov's ode itself was
already highly unconventional, imagining the poet-hero relationship as a creative and prophetic symbiosis and friendship, a complex (and never simply
vertical) interplay of "thou" (*ty*) and "I" (*ia*):

Не обща в море служба,
Но дар небесный, дружба,
Творит, что есть твое,
Как собственно мое.

Мое наследие—молва приятна она,
Котора о тебе, теча,
Распространяется и паче лирна звона
Пленяет сердце мне, звуча.[63]

[Not our common service at sea, / But the heavenly gift, friendship, / Makes
what is yours / Mine proper. // My legacy is this pleasant talk / Of you, that in
flowing / Spreads and, stronger than the lyre's chime, / Captures my heart with
its sounds.]

Pushkin validates his poetic praise of a grandee—by the 1820s a proposition
decidedly damaging to a poet's reputation—not simply by presenting it as a
realized prophecy of an eighteenth-century poet (by definition less problem-
atically implicated in the patronage system), but also by referencing the particular ode of that poet that in fact redefined the Pindaric pact itself, bringing
its new articulation quite close to the early Romantic affective models of the
poet-addressee dialogue and friendship, but nevertheless still preserving its
enabling frame of inequality and deference. As a result, in addition to praising

Mordvinov, Pushkin emerges as Petrov's successor and rememberer, while the poem thematizes panegyric inspiration itself and implicitly considers the possibility of accessing it in an age that has abandoned its traditional generic forms.[64]

"To the Grandee" similarly places the poet at the end of an entire line of Iusupov's interlocutors, primarily the French *philosophes*, that is, the voices of the eighteenth century. As in "To Mordvinov," "To the Grandee" makes extensive use of eighteenth-century lexical and syntactic structures, modeling both a stylistic and a physical immersion in the age of Catherine ("I am suddenly transported to the days of Catherine"; *ia vdrug perenoshus' vo dni Ekateriny*).[65] The epistle's Iusupov is a member of the European "republic of letters," equally at ease in Voltaire's study, at the court of Louis XVI, and in front of a Spanish belle's balcony à la Beaumarchais. Scholars have described Pushkin's long list of Iusupov's Enlightenment-era encounters as a "gallery of historical paintings,"[66] a single "gigantic historical painting," or a "gigantic historical panorama."[67] Some have invoked a more dynamic structure and compared it to the European Grand Tour.[68] These interpretations see "To the Grandee" as a survey of European culture and history of the eighteenth century, whose pictures come in for the treatment of Pushkin's restoration artistry, but seem to imply no particular personal investment on his part, and certainly not the desire for patronage. Little attention has been paid, however, to the relationships that Iusupov establishes with his interlocutors, relationships that prefigure and complicate the terms of Pushkin's own encounter with the prince; a closer focus on these might yield an alternative to interpreting the poem along either purely social or historiographical lines.

The first encounter mentioned is Iusupov's visit to the aging Voltaire, the sort of exchange between young and old we have already seen constitute a historical continuum in "To Mordvinov"; but Iusupov's youth is also associated with Russia's eighteenth-century status of a "young" nation craving the culture of "old" France. (Hence, too, the epistle's deliberate alexandrines.)

Явился ты в Ферней—и циник поседелый,

Умов и моды вождь проныривый и смелый,

Свое владычество на Севере любя,

Могильным голосом приветствовал тебя.

С тобой веселости он расточал избыток,

Ты лесть его вкусил, земных богов напиток.[69]

[You arrived in Ferney—and the grey-haired cynic, / The crafty and daring leader of minds and fashion, / Cherishing his rule over the North, / Greeted you with his sepulchral voice. / On you he lavished the surplus of his gaiety, / You partook of his flattery, the drink of earthly gods.]

While the address to Iusupov is cast consistently in a solemn and formal tone, the description of Voltaire borders on the satirical, potentially undermining the weightiness of his praise of Iusupov. Echoing, in the earlier "To N. Ia. Pliuskova," the young poet's misgivings about his panegyric commission, "earthly gods" (*zemnykh bogov*) recalls the sacralization of human authority in the ceremonial ode; but the praise issuing here from Voltaire also models a critical relationship to power in its vaguely oxymoronic pairing of the earthly and the divine. The reconstruction of the Voltaire-Iusupov encounter pokes gentle fun at flattery even as it signals its omnipresence in eighteenth-century cultured society. But the passage also resurrects and questions a particular brand of inspiration associated with excess (*izbytok*), inspiration that is effervescent rather than prophetic. Up until the end of the eighteenth century this kind of inspiration was feared as irrational and damaging to the social order.[70] But by the beginning of the nineteenth century, early Romantic philosophy reevaluates inspiration, which now begins to describe a very different creative state associated with poetry and prophecy.[71]

Iusupov's encounter with Diderot elicits a similar kind of enthusiasm in the *philosophe*:

За твой суровый пир
То чтитель промысла, то скептик, то безбожник,
Садился Дидерот на шаткий свой треножник,
Бросал парик, глаза в восторге закрывал
И проповедывал. И скромно ты внимал
За чашей медленной афею иль деисту,
Как любопытный скиф афинскому софисту.[72]

[To your austere feast / Now the worshiper of providence, now the skeptic, now the atheist, / Diderot would sit down on his shaky tripod, / Would throw off his wig, close his eyes in rapture, / And preach. And humbly would you listen, / Over the slow cup, to the atheist or deist, / As a curious Scythian would [listen to] an Athenian sophist.]

While the descriptors pertaining to Iusupov and his realm are "austere" and "humble" (both characteristics apparently quite far from the historical reality), Diderot is distinguished by a protean mutability of belief, by dramatic gestures and high emotion (all apparently resembling Pushkin's own comportment and matching well his documented preference for the Mozartian forms of artistic genius and inspiration).[73] There is a lurking suspicion that his and Voltaire's enthusiasms, so easily marshaled for Iusupov's pleasure, might just be a form of flattery, and of a particular eighteenth-century kind of entertainment to which intellectuals would treat their patrons. Finally, sincere or not, Diderot's enthused sermons, along with Voltaire's languidness, are framed by the ironic hindsight that perceives the French Revolution as their direct consequence and realization.[74]

Aroused only by the beauties of Seville, Iusupov is touched neither by his interlocutors' intellectual passion, nor by the political events of the turn of the century ("You alone remain the same"; *odin vse tot zhe ty*). Iusupov's equanimity, in addition to his frequently mentioned aesthetic taste and cultivation of beauty—qualities also modeling a certain level of aestheticized detachment—becomes the basis for Pushkin's epistolary encomium. It is both a feature of his Russianness ("a curious Scythian"; *liubopytnyi skif*) vis-à-vis Europe and of his aristocratic status and wealth vis-à-vis those who would regale the esteemed wayfarer with their talents. The contrast between Iusupov's composure and constancy and the world's penchant for frenetic agitation and change persists throughout the poem's 106 lines.[75] If the Derzhavinian ode, for example, returned time and again to the transience of the individual life, Pushkin's epistle seems to propose a powerful reversal of this vision: the eulogized individual (Iusupov and perhaps more generally a certain type of aristocratic eighteenth-century survivor—the Countess in "The Queen of Spades," in an openly parodic key) is imbued with constancy amid historical perturbations, unaffected by the Mozartian enthusiasms of their servitor-*philosophes*: "You, not participating in worldly unrest, / At times archly look at them through the window, / And see in everything a cyclical rotation" (*Ty, ne uchastvuia v volneniiakh mirskikh, / Poroi nasmeshlivo v okno gliadish' na nikh / I vidish' oborot vo vsem kruzoobraznyi*). Pushkin temporarily reanimates the *philosophes* with a kind of satirical nostalgia, but the satire is compromised by the speaker's own position in the poem as visitor to Iusupov's estate.

If, that is, in coming to pay his respects to Iusupov, Pushkin resembles the grandee's own former role as "curious Scythian," does the poet here not also play the part of the vaguely jester-like Voltaire and Diderot? Can his role be described solely as that of a historian on a research trip? Implicit in the poet's visit to a patron is a strained reciprocity of desires, particularly in the nineteenth century, when the terms of such an encounter (one, as Pushkin would likely remind us, of two equal members of the aristocracy) are so tenuously defined. If Pushkin the historian arrives at Iusupov's Arkhangel'skoe estate to browse in the old gentleman's library and record his stories, Pushkin the poet—at least perhaps in the eyes of the eighteenth-century grandee—is himself the day's entertainment, whose poetic enthusiasms are to be observed with a mix of indifference and indulgence. Pushkin might have had (or attempted) his own conception of the *philosophes*, his own Voltaire and Diderot. But with Iusupov's advantage of real-life eighteenth-century experience, this gentleman's *version* as it were of the *philosophes* must necessarily interfere; the poet must follow specifically *their* path (their socially unequal, quasi-entertaining and strangely foreign path) to the person of the grandee, and inhabit their relationship to him. Thus Pushkin is only a historian in part; he is also the experiencer of a different mode of inspiration. We might then amend Belinskii's interpretation of the particular archaeology performed in this epistle: here Pushkin excavates not only anecdotes and material culture, but also poetic states and attitudes toward power and creative work; he stands as a historian not of the eighteenth century as *other*, but of the eighteenth century as *self*, as offering to an intellectual a set of distinct versions of selfhood, only partially tenable under the nineteenth-century conditions.

The scholar M. A. Maksimovich, a correspondent of Pushkin's who took the poet's side in the polemic around this epistle, found the poem's Iusupov to be spiritually empty. To this apparently accurate estimation, Pushkin replied: "It's alright! He won't notice!" (*Nichego! Ne dogadaetsia!*).[76] This admission, strengthened no doubt by Pushkin's dismay at Polevoi's accusations of servility, points to the essentially reflective rather than reflexive character of Iusupov as constructed in the epistle. Iusupov's greatness stems from the epoch having imprinted its image upon him, not from acts of his own personal agency. The poem tacitly equivocates about Iusupov's prized constancy, a quality indeed praiseworthy in Mordvinov, in whom it is manifested in an unabating responsiveness to the world, but in Iusupov potentially amounting to little more than a kind of blankness or opaqueness of spirit. Pushkin's reflection on the "spirit of the age" is directed at the spirit of the individual and runs into an impasse as it discovers the reciprocal unintelligibility of the new world to the old grandee and the grandee to the nineteenth-century world.

It is in this context that we might now briefly consider the relationship of
Pushkin's epistle to Derzhavin's famous 1794 ode "A Grandee" ("Vel'mozha"),
one of the key Derzhavin texts to have articulated a civic discourse in the
Russian ode and to have empowered the poet to chastise the powers that be—
indeed, a text whose clear civic vision might very well have inspired Slovtsov's
inscription of its author into the bas-relief of antiquity. Derzhavin maintains
that the true grandness of a grandee resides not in the material trappings of
power, but in the spirit, and it is first and foremost the artist who can tell the
difference:

> Кумир, поставленный в позор,
> Несмысленную чернь прельщает;
> Но коль художников в нем взор
> Прямых красот не ощущает,—
> Се образ ложныя молвы,
> Се глыба грязи позлащенной!
> И вы, без благости душевной,
> Не все ль, вельможи, таковы?[77]

[An idol, erected as a spectacle, / Lures the senseless mob. / But if the artist's
gaze / Does not sense in him real beauties, / Then this is an image of false
renown, / And a block of gilded dirt! / And you, when lacking spiritual grace, /
Are you not all thus, grandees?]

For Pushkin, the word "grandee" (vel'mozha) is most likely a Derzhavinian
term tied to this particular critique of authority and its revision of the power
relationship between poet and patron. In Derzhavin this term casts the poet's
role as adjudicating the grandee's worth for the polis, rather than, as in the
Pindaric patronage model, reintegrating the patron into the polis. An echo of
Derzhavin's chastising voice can be heard in Alexander Herzen's later reading
of Pushkin's "marvelous epistle" (chudnoe poslanie[78]), and of Iusupov's generation (liudi XVIII veka[79]) as a whole, in My Past and Thoughts (Byloe i dumy,
1852–68). In a caustic rejoinder to Pushkin, Herzen presents Iusupov's patronage of the arts as a hedonistic cover-up for moral vacuity and profligacy:
"First and foremost in this Moscow circle was the brilliant and wealthy Russian grandee, European grand seigneur and Tatar Prince N. B. Iusupov. Next
to him there formed a whole galaxy of gray-haired ladies' men and esprits forts,
all those Masal'skiis, Santis and tutti quanti. They were all highly developed

and educated; left with nothing to do, they flung themselves into pleasures, titivated themselves, loved themselves, good-naturedly absolved themselves of all sins, raised to a Platonic passion their gastronomy and brought down to some kind of a gluttonous delicacy their love of women. An old skeptic and epicurean, Iusupov, the friend of Voltaire and Beaumarchais, Diderot and Casti [. . .] luxuriantly faded away at the age of eighty, surrounded by marble, drawn and live beauty."[80] For Herzen, Iusupov's beautiful belongings epitomize what he perceives as the main flaw in the Catherinian grandee's lifestyle and a crucial one in Catherine's version of Enlightenment generally: the pernicious substitution of action and purpose ("[some]thing to do") with superficial cultivation, acquisitiveness, and pursuit of pleasure.

Pushkin's epistle intimates no aspiration to the role of public moralist on the scale of Derzhavin or Herzen, but focuses consistently, almost in an antiquarian fashion, precisely on the material, metonymical trappings of Iusupov's greatness, ultimately leaving unanswered the question of this idol's true worth, beyond his tasteful possessions. If holding a man of the eighteenth century to a moral standard of action and agency (as Derzhavin advocates for all grandees, and Herzen performs in the case of Iusupov and his milieu) entails a universalist understanding of history and ethics, Pushkin's refocusing of attention on Iusupov's space accentuates an individual lifestyle governed by the norms of a particular epoch, and only partly accessible to a universalizing logic. And yet this refocusing, too, is not entirely a rejection of Derzhavin's position, but rather its adjustment to an emergent historicist vision, which allows for a more relativistic assessment of character and value, and to a postodic moment in Russian literary history, when the relationship of poet to power is fraught with ambivalence.[81]

Just as he reinhabits the inspirations of Voltaire and Diderot by visiting and entertaining Iusupov, might Pushkin not also be reinhabiting, both playfully and by way of critique, Derzhavin's inspirational mode, his civic consciousness and questing for heroes to eulogize, as one through which poet emancipates himself from patron—or used to do so, back when it was still possible to maintain Derzhavin's moral clarity? Pushkin's own moment has apparently outlived the odic mode of Derzhavin's, and the poem's explicit critique is directed not at the old grandee, but at the young and senseless world around him. More significantly, Pushkin's creative situation, while ostensibly leaving behind the former constraints of genre and patronage hierarchies, is not that far removed from the time of Derzhavin, when the poet's voice had also to struggle to free itself from accusations of flattery on the one hand, and the

demands of the patron on the other. After all, is not Nicholas I's commitment
to act as Pushkin's personal censor, announced very soon after his coronation
in 1826 and with the full memory of the Decembrist insubordination, only a
more ominous and heavy-handed reenactment of the patronage scenario? As
I hope to have shown, patronage was a quintessential eighteenth-century practice against which Pushkin (the nineteenth century's most creative historian
of the eighteenth) modulated his understanding and critique of a whole range
of past and present social relations, historical distinctions, and forms of creative life. The unsettling conclusion was that, for all intents and purposes, the
oppressive "union with the tsars" might in Pushkin's age, too, not have been
"dissolved" just yet.[82]

Pushkin's Eighteenth-Century Options

Pushkin's poetic strategy vis-à-vis his precursors often involves partially
inhabiting their worldview and voice, the more ironically to lay bare the experiential strain of such a displacement. The previous section explored his
temporary adoptions of the worldviews of Ovid, Petrov, the French *philosophes*,
Derzhavin, and even perhaps Iusupov himself in that nobleman's "curious
Scythian" guise. Much has been written about Pushkin's "proteanism," the ease
with which he assumes various creative stances, navigates various forms of
writing and conduct. The comparison to Proteus celebrates Pushkin's flexibility and versatility, emphasizing his oeuvre's playfulness, its stemming from a
seemingly preternatural mastery of multiple discourses and an impulse toward
their ironic overcoming. And yet Pushkin's engagement with his eighteenth-
century precursors appears only partially motivated by this dynamic of creative one-upmanship. Suffice it to recall, for instance, that in the late 1820s,
neither Petrov nor even Derzhavin preserved a relevance sufficient to jus-
tify the ironic appropriation of their rhetoric; moreover, they are invoked—
whether openly in "To Mordvinov" or implicitly in "To a Grandee"—as creators
of a powerful alternative discourse about human character and poetic judgment, a discourse that in fact still challenges newly arisen poetic stances (rather
than merely paling in comparison with them). This complex dynamic—the
activity of seriously engaging, even inhabiting the recent past, while at the
same time recognizing its inadequacies and limited relevance for the present—
lies at the core of all Pushkin's treatments of the eighteenth century, whether
in the lyric as briefly discussed here or in the prose of the 1830s, the central
subject of the chapters to follow.

Identifying this capacity of Pushkin's texts for concurrent acceptance and rejection of historical phenomena enables us to account for the inconsistencies in Pushkin's attitudes toward most eighteenth-century figures and practices, including patronage and the panegyric. Does he visit Iusupov in search of a patron, as his opponents claimed, thus hoping misguidedly to perpetuate a practice no longer acceptable to nineteenth-century literati? Or is he, as Belinskii believed, decidedly alienated from Iusupov, chronicling and judging his world from a historical remove? Might we not see this particular form of Pushkin's proteanism—his ability to be part of the world of the past, yet stand apart from it—as making a serious case for the non-linear workings of history, whereby modern man can no longer be guided (like his Classicist predecessors) by historical analogy, nor yet accept without qualification the notion of progressive change as leaving the past behind?

Renegotiated and radicalized in the Romantic period, yet ever constrained by the conservatism of sociopolitical structures, the circuits of exchange between writer and power provide Pushkin with an opportune testing case for this particular version of historicist thinking. Especially in his volatile relations with Nicholas I, Pushkin repeatedly attempts to transcend the conditions of subjection rooted in the eighteenth century, but invariably comes up against the intransigence of these conditions. If Petrov and Derzhavin embody the practice of placing literature at the service of the state or patron (however cleverly or moralistically), the French *philosophes* make use of the monarchs' (Frederick's, Catherine's) pretensions to enlightened authority, engage in flattery and witty correspondence with their patrons, all the while maintaining their independence (philosophical if not financial) and the consciousness of their French cultural hegemony. Another eighteenth-century scenario of conduct that Pushkin sporadically entertains is no doubt Radishchev's rejection of autocratic power and its attendant discriminatory relations, patronage among them. It is perhaps for this reason as well that Pushkin's most extensive reflection on patronage appears in *Journey from Moscow to Petersburg*, in which Pushkin replicates Radishchev's position of solitary traveler-thinker and his particular travelogue form, but neither Radishchev's itinerary nor his chastising voice find its nineteenth-century equivalent.

Standard literary history would more readily associate the period I call here "Derzhavin's moment," and which in some Soviet-era criticism was forcibly yoked to Radishchev and his political philosophy,[83] with Nikolai Karamzin, a seminal figure who exemplifies the turn-of-the-century fascination with sentiment and historicity, transforms Russian letters so profoundly that it is scarcely possible to classify his career as belonging to either century, and sits comfortably with multiple epochal paradigms. Karamzin's relationship to centralized power also epitomizes this transitional moment inasmuch as his monarchism presents itself as a matter of intellectual choice and finds expression in a variety of genres, including the panegyric, but culminating in *The Memoir on Ancient and Modern Russia* and especially in his magisterial work of nation-building ambition, *The History of the Russian State,* To be sure, the latter two were written on commission, but they nevertheless emanated from a historian who was emphatically autonomous.[84] Karamzin offered to Pushkin perhaps the most compelling model of an intellectual's public conduct that both originated in the eighteenth century and transcended it. Indeed, the possibility of such respectful and mutually beneficial communication with the monarch, a connection not (or at least not openly) contaminated by the inequity of patronage relations, is the abiding and mostly frustrated aspiration behind Pushkin's historical work in the 1830s. And if historical fiction ultimately extricates its author from the impasse-laden dialogue with power that both the panegyrical and the documentary historical genres constitute, it is only, as we will see in chapter 4, to implicate him in the new bondage of commercial readership.

PART II

The Fictions
of the Eighteenth Century

Вот то-то, все вы гордецы!
Спросили бы, как делали отцы?
Учились бы, на старших глядя:
Мы, например, или покойник дядя,
Максим Петрович: он не то на серебре,
На золоте едал; сто человек к услугам;
Весь в орденах; езжал-то вечно цугом;
Век при дворе, да при каком дворе!
Тогда не то, что ныне,
При государыне служил Екатерине.
А в те поры все важны! в сорок пуд . . .
Раскланяйся—тупеем не кивнут.
Вельможа в случае—тем паче,
Не как другой, и пил и ел иначе.

—A. S. Griboedov, *Woe from Wit* (1825)[1]

Тут был в душистых сединах
Старик, по-старому шутивший:
Отменно тонко и умно,
Что нынче несколько смешно.

—A. S. Pushkin, *Eugene Onegin* (chapter 8, 1829–1830)[2]

В 18-м веке резкие, угловатые характеры были гораздо обыкновеннее, чем в наше время, когда более распространенное между всеми сословиями и притом более искусственное воспитание подводит всех под один довольно общий уровень образования и на всех кладет однообразную печать сдержанности и приличия.

—IA. GROT, *The Life of Derzhavin* (1880)[3]

Prologue

As a point of entry into the second half of this book and a counterpoint to some of the more ambivalent assessments of the eighteenth century it contains, let us consider a long passage from Prince Petr Andreevich Viazemskii's *Notebooks* (*Zapisnye knizhki*, 1813–48), one of the most perceptive, idiosyncratic, and extensive documents of the nineteenth century.[4] None of the prince's contemporaries strove to grasp the essence and legacy of Russian eighteenth-century culture so tenaciously and yet in such an episodic and nimble semi-diaristic form. The reason seems to be that Viazemskii perceives this legacy as alive in the nineteenth century, and its analysis as capable of elucidating the spirit and inadequacies of his present. His earlier notebook entries are filled with observations on the differences between his own time and the Catherinian past, which Viazemskii tends to idealize. As he grows older and becomes disillusioned with his circumstances and with Russia's cultural course under Nicholas I, Viazemskii begins to connect Catherine's reign, so formative for his generation, with the first decades of the nineteenth century, which we now associate with Pushkin and which Viazemskii in fact helped shape. In coexisting within the same extensive though fragmented timeline and self-narrative, these approaches to the eighteenth century, distinct though they may be, nevertheless reveal an important point of coherence in the *Notebooks*: this is a project of self-understanding that is achieved in large part through self-historicization, where the "self" is both Viazemskii (and, by extension, any individual of similar cultural background) as a critical subject, and a communal entity that Viazemskii presents now as generational, now as pertaining to the intellectual elite as a class, now as organizing Russian society as a whole. Thus, when read in its entirety, the *Notebooks* yield a peculiar answer to this book's underlying query about the dating and interpretation of the origins of Russian modernity: Viazemskii casts the two Russian modernities—one inaugurated by the eighteenth, the other by the nineteenth century; one political, the other literary (hence also political)—as at the same time alternative scenarios of Russian civilization and contiguous periods, forming a single though disjointed narrative.

In this particular entry from November 7, 1830, Viazemskii's impressions upon reading a biography of A. I. Bibikov (an important political and military figure of Catherine II's reign) occasion a series of far-reaching reflections on the nineteenth century's departures from Russia's recent past. Viazemskii laments what he identifies as profound changes in the quality of political culture, social climate, and even physical appearance and sense of selfhood that differentiate the society of the 1820s–'30s from that of the eighteenth century:

> How our spirits have flagged since the time of Catherine, that is, since the time of Paul. Some manly life breathes in the people of Catherine's reign, how noble their interactions with the empress; it is obvious that she considered them members of the body politic. And their very being at court, their very obsequiousness had something chivalrous about it, in large part due to the tsar being a woman. Afterwards, everything acquired some servile humility. The whole difference is that the higher lackeys put on airs before the servants and oppress them, but before the master they are the same voiceless lackeys. Take, for instance, Panin and Nesselrode, this lackey dwarf—leaving aside morally, for in that sense he is not a dwarf, but some sort of excreted embryo [. . .], but physically he is a dwarf: is his relationship with the tsar the same as Panin's was with Catherine?[5] Say what you like, but Russia also needs its dignitaries to have stately physiques. Who needs these liliputians? Paul's words, this summation of despotism, sachez qu'à ma cour il n'y a de grand que celui à qui je parle et pendant que je lui parle [know that at my court one is only a grandee when I speak to him and while I speak to him], became our principal dictum. Still, under Paul, despite all the fear he inspired, some Catherinian customs remained in effect; but during the reign of Alexander, for all its mildness and many enlightened views, especially at the beginning, personhood [lichnost'] was completely effaced. The people grew smaller and lost their voice. All the remaining forces were applied toward roguery, and the power of this or that high official came to be judged by the impunity with which he abuses it. The idea that a minister might have his own opinion has vanished even from legend. There is no doubt that since the time of Peter the Great we have made great strides in education, but at the same time, how our souls have

shriveled. Peter's rule was, one might say, tyrannical in comparison to the rule of our time, but the rights to contestation and lawful resistance have dwindled to nothingness. At least in France it was Richelieu who made people kowtow and reduced their souls to tatters, but who brought about this change in us, and how? It was not the consequence of a system—and so much the worse.[6]

In this tirade, not coincidentally a response to the perusal of a biographical narrative, the pathos of epochal distinctions lies precisely in their discernibility in the evolution of individual, and hence also communal, character.[7] As posed by Viazemskii, the question of character—or *lichnost'*, a term more capacious and vague than this English equivalent, and denoting a range of concepts, from individuality and identity to personality, character, and personhood—renders physical appearance, moral conduct, and political autonomy interdependent and mutually illuminating. Individual character, both as possessed by a specific person and as more abstractly demarcating the range of behavioral possibilities available to an individual in a given period, becomes the most visible bearer of the epochal imprint.

For all its idiosyncratic idealization of the Catherine era, Viazemskii's appraisal is echoed by other, often less enthusiastic, mid-nineteenth-century commentators. As the ideological progeny of Peter the Great (conveniently, a giant both in his physical build and transformative vision), the men and women of the eighteenth century seemed somehow larger than their posterity: their prospects unobstructed by civilization precisely because of their confidence in the civilizing process; their autonomy untrammeled precisely because of their voluntary sacrifice of that autonomy to the causes espoused by their autocrats; their vices excusable precisely because not furtive and small-minded like their descendants, but rather large-scale and forthright—their "luxurious amusements, their conscientious, childish dissipation" (*roskoshnye zabavy, ikh dobrosovestnyi, rebiacheskii razvrat*), to quote Lermontov's description of his generation's forefathers in the well-known "Reflection" ("Duma," 1838).[8] Paradoxically, the nineteenth century, a time when many eighteenth-century civilizing projects finally come to fruition, is seen to betray the spirit of that originary epoch. In this excerpt, for example, it is through the propagation of hierarchical consciousness, undoubtedly a byproduct of Petrine modernization, that the individual becomes a "lackey," implicated in, and rendered subservient to, the social order, and thus stripped of his autonomy. The transition from the eighteenth to the nineteenth century is reconceived as a kind of fall from grace, a sullying of innocence by education or historical experience.

Written soon after the July Revolution in France, this entry indeed attests to Viazemskii's dispirited awareness of the gradual defeat of progressive hopes during the reigns of Paul, Alexander, and Nicholas, and in particular following the suppression of the Decembrists. It is all the more significant, then, that the excerpt's most profound realization, its real *pointe*, comes in its very last sentence, which refuses to hold the government—a "system" of suppression akin to Richelieu's in seventeenth-century France—accountable for this emasculation of nineteenth-century Russian man, but instead implicitly indicts this diminished man himself for allowing, through his complacency, the momentous transformations that separate the spirits of the two centuries. These transformations are first and foremost of the *lichnost'*, and only then of the political order.

Even as it bemoans the modern individual's loss of political autonomy, this type of argument, precisely by holding the individual responsible, reclaims that autonomy, making the individual the agent of his own fall and thereby redirecting social critique from the autocrat (a monarch-centered vision residual from the eighteenth century) to his subjects (both subjects of the government and critical subjects who think and feel, both communal and individual selves). In judging the nineteenth century, Viazemskii employs a critical approach that at least in Russia belongs mostly to the nineteenth century itself, the period in which such concepts of Enlightenment political theory as the "body politic" could finally be mapped onto Russian reality by the educated elite. Likewise, the veneration of the age of Catherine is, Viazemskii's rootedness in eighteenth-century culture notwithstanding, a specifically nineteenth-century sentiment, born of a historical consciousness that imbues periodization with explanatory power and explicates phenomena by means of their placement in history. As we shall see in the following chapters, a writer need not, like Viazemskii in this passage and elsewhere in the *Notebooks*, idealize the eighteenth century to enlist it as a polemical point of contrast with the nineteenth-century present.[9]

The eighteenth century definitively recedes into the past in the 1830s in large part because in this period Russian intellectuals debate and assimilate historicist thinking in its multiple forms, from the prophetic historicism of Romantic poetry to the fictionalized, domesticated histories of Sir Walter Scott's novels to the nationalist and progressive ideologies grounded in the historicism of German idealist philosophy, which in Russia gains traction toward the end of the decade. In obsessively considering the present as historically determined, historicist thinking (of which Viazemskii is in fact one of the earliest and most distinguished Russian practitioners) tends to discern epochal divisions and residues of the past everywhere and, most notably, in the individual. This epoch-manufacturing tendency cast historical process as movement forward and the present as a mosaic of historical layers, where representatives of different generations and objects from different periods occupy a common physical space, but belong to different temporal strata. Thus, in the 1830s, the period that incessantly thinks of itself in terms of novelty and progress, the people, lifestyles, and material effects of the preceding century appear noticeably outdated, and hence vulnerable to critique, satirical or fictional reappraisal, incomprehension and dismissal.

Time and again in the *Notebooks*, Viazemskii apprehends transformations in the lifestyles of his countrymen, perceptible though difficult to characterize, and correlates these changes with the more palpable and crucial political shifts distinguishing the age of Nicholas from the age of Catherine. Indeed, numerous tangible transformations separate the two epochs. If the Russian eighteenth century seems truly relegated to the past only in the 1830s, the Decembrist fiasco was no doubt partly responsible for the newly perceived antiquation of Russia's Enlightenment. After the disillusionment of the revolt's immediate aftermath, new forms of political process arose, and eighteenth-century political practice seemed scarcely pertinent to the new, nineteenth-century realities. If the monarchy in the 1700s was bound by its commitment to the Enlightenment project, by the mid-nineteenth century that project itself had undergone multiple amendments and been subjected to skeptical scrutiny, with the status of the monarch as arbiter of cultural policy considerably diminished. After Alexander I, Russia's last tsar with intellectual roots in the eighteenth century, the monarchy felt no longer compelled to legitimize itself via adherence to Peter and Catherine's vision. The frequent alterations of Russian social hierarchy eventually produced a world in which the new class of intelligentsia was perceptibly at odds with the government; by contrast, eighteenth-century cultural elites—not yet an intelligentsia proper—had seen themselves as the monarch's associates. The makeup of the cultural elite, moreover, also changed dramatically, becoming more diverse, if not yet democratic. Finally, the Russian literary scene in the 1830s bore little resemblance to the court-centered, genre system-bound, and poetry-oriented literary culture of the eighteenth century, or to the literature of the 1810s and even 1820s, which still in many ways contended with the "first" epoch's legacy and limitations. On the other hand, the 1830s—a decade which, to follow its greatest spokesman, Belinskii, was "critical for Russian literature"[10]—were characterized by a new preference for prose genres, particularly the novel; by the commercialization of the literary field and writers' professionalization; and by shifts in the content of literary polemics, away from concerns with the contours of the Russian literary language or Romantic literary form and toward questions of literature's social engagement and relationship to reality.

The pastness of the eighteenth century thus no longer in question, its relationship to the nineteenth becomes less topical but at the same time more problematic. Wherein lies the continuity between the two centuries? And what is the extent, the value of the inheritance bequeathed by the age of Peter and Catherine to the nineteenth century? Are there, conversely, unbreachable gaps between the old and new modernities? And if so, what are the implications of a national historical narrative whose discontinuity is only partly concealed in the celebratory rhetoric of the Petrine and Catherinian myths? In short, what does it mean for the country and its intellectuals to have *had* an eighteenth century, specifically the one Russia experienced?

Prose fiction, in addition to being the preferred literary format of the mid-1800s and therefore deserving our close attention, poses these questions with particular subtlety, for one of its most pressing concerns in the period is precisely to place the individual in a historical world, to reconcile private and public (hi)stories in an artistically compelling fashion. Culled primarily from the fiction of Alexander Pushkin and Ivan Turgenev, the material presented in Part II accesses the eighteenth century when it is no longer a lived past, but rather an increasingly tattered (though still hallowed) object of multiple re-interments. The more this past is apprehended thus—as residue, as relic—the less it is in fact apprehended, the less meaningful it becomes. Under redoubled scrutiny, the object paradoxically disappears. Thus, when my narrative in Part II moves from Pushkin to Turgenev, the opaqueness of the eighteenth century in the oeuvre of the latter will be seen as a consequence not only of the greater distance separating Turgenev from the 1700s, but also of the 1700s having been repeatedly processed through historicist discourse, becoming, by the mid-nineteenth century, otherwise inaccessible.

Because they preserve the century's legacy in marginal textual and material forms (anecdotes and reminiscences, snuffboxes and family portraits), these narratives might seem to trivialize the eighteenth century, to assume a distance from it. But precisely because of the gravity of historical questions regarding the eighteenth century's legacy—questions that, I would argue, motivate the appearance of even the most negligible caricature of a Catherinian *grande-dame*, the most cursory mention of a Catherine-era trinket—the "fictions of the eighteenth century" have to be read as advancing or, alternately, chipping away at large-scale political arguments about Russian history. On the one hand, in capitalizing on their professed fictionality, these fictions subtly challenge the present moment from its ostensible margins, casting doubt upon official narratives of national character and historical continuity, and suggesting alternative relationships to the past. Colonized by fictional and even fantastical plots and characters, the recent past emerges as a site where readerly adventure is only barely constrained by fact, but also, crucially, as a site of readerly engagement, interpretation, and dissension. On the other hand, by virtue of literature's new commitment to mimetic representation and to documentary and pseudo-documentary literary forms (such as those cited as well as performed in Viazemskii's *Notebooks*), the prose fiction of the mid-1800s exceeds its fictionality and locates history—including its readers' personal histories, which fiction renders narratable by analogy—in its serendipitously observed and preserved fragments and margins, in *lichnost'* and all its quotidian manifestations and personal effects. The eighteenth century that emerges in this second half of the book is thus nothing like the heroic and centralized one that we have examined in Part I; rather, it is reconstituted through a multitude of particularized and individualized pasts, which, like Viazemskii's *Notebooks*, ultimately render the epochal spirit a question of the individual.

4

The Verisimilar Eighteenth Century
Historical Fiction in the 1830s

Мы живем в веке историческом; потом в веке историческом
по превосходству. . . . Теперь история не в одном деле, но и в
памяти, в уме, на сердце у народов. Мы ее видим, слышим,
осязаем ежеминутно; она проницает в нас всеми чувствами.
Она толкает вас локтями на прогулке, втирается между
вами и дамой вашей в котильон. «Барин, барин!—кричит
вам гостинодворский сиделец,—купите шапку-*эриванку*».
«Не прикажете ли скроить вам сюртук по-*варшавски?*»—
спрашивает портной. Скачет лошадь—это Веллингтон.
Взглядываете на вывеску—Кутузов манит вас в гостиницу,
возбуждая вместе народную гордость и аппетит. Берете
щепотку табаку—он куплен с молотка после Карла X.
Запечатываете письмо—сургуч императора Франца.
Вонзаете вилку в сладкий пирог и—его имя Наполеон! . .
Дайте гривну, и вам покажут за гривну злосчастие
веков, Клитемнестру и Шенье, убийство Генриха IX и
Ватерлоо, Березину и Св. Елену, потоп петербургский и
землетрясение Лиссабона—и что я знаю! . . Да-с, история
теперь превращается во все, что вам угодно, хотя бы вам
было это вовсе не угодно.

—Alexander Bestuzhev-Marlinskii, review of N. A. Polevoi's
"Kliatva pri grobe Gospodnem. Russkaia byl' XV veka" (1833)

The Sight of Historical Fiction

This account by Alexander Bestuzhev-Marlinskii (1797–1837), glib and sensationalist though it might sound, identifies a cluster of epochal attributes that
can productively frame this chapter's examination of the most spectacularly

successful genre of the early nineteenth century: the historical novel.[1] As if heeding Ivan Kireevskii's appraisal of the 1820s–'30s as the decades when "defining the dominant direction of the age has become a common goal for all thinking people,"[2] Bestuzhev characterizes the spirit of his age as universally obsessed with history. If we are to read this passage as playfully gesturing toward an early definition of historical consciousness, then, for all its requisite invocations of "the memory, the mind, the hearts of peoples," it locates this consciousness primarily in the strikingly interconnected realms of sensual experience and commercial activity. For Bestuzhev history was inseparable from the new commercial modernity in which it helped to sell commodities. After all, as a best-selling author Bestuzhev both capitalized on a commercialized conception of history and helped to shape it.

As material objects, saleable commodities engage history differently than monuments designed for its commemoration. Instead of memorializing history, marketable goods deploy it to boost their own memorability and commercial appeal. If triumphal arches, such as those of Tsarskoe Selo (considered in chapter 2), loom as signifiers for History the great signified, the market economy reverses the direction of meaning-making, transforming substantive commodities into the main "good" and relegating history to the status of brand-name: biting into a napoleon is the primary experience—recognizing this label's connection to Napoleon is only secondary. In this sense, the historical imagination of the 1830s, at least as described by Bestuzhev, radically departs from the allegorical protocols of the eighteenth century. If in Classicist poetics, historical allegory was essentially a neo-Platonic procedure, explicating topical events by associating them with their more famous precedents, with eternity, antiquity, or the divine, at this late Romantic moment the focus of historical representation shifts to the idiosyncratic individual and the concrete object, whose appeal derives only partly from their historical embeddedness. Thus, when the ode as the primary genre of historical representation in the eighteenth century is replaced in the nineteenth by historical prose (in parallel to, but more successfully than, the elegy and historical drama),[3] the allegorical striving for history's totality is superseded by a metonymic procedure of meaning-making befitting the post-Napoleonic fragmentation of historical vision and experience and the commodification of culture. The precise payoff of metonymy, however, is difficult to define: what does it mean for a horse to be called a Wellington or for Kutuzov's image to advertise a hotel? Bestuzhev recognizes the arbitrariness of these signs—"history is nowadays being changed into everything you could wish for, even if you don't in the least wish it." And yet, he also implicates, in what he decries as contemporaneity's fragmented vision, his readers who populate this same contemporaneity, who are perpetually distracted by a synchronous array of tempting new commodities and confused by these goods' professed links to history. The passage, then, ultimately both raises a profound epistemological question and participates in the very cultural dynamics that render it so pressing: how is historical knowledge produced under the new conditions of consumerism?

This chapter reads the Russian historical novel of the 1830s as a site where such knowledge is both produced and questioned. Reviews of historical novels in the period center largely on their historical truthfulness and deem the greatest possible merit of such works precisely their ability to deliver knowledge of the past. Yet for all the concern with the novels' veridical value, what mattered to their readers (or at least the popular reader), I shall argue, was not so much the history they referenced, but rather the novelistic procedures that augmented the referential. The astounding popularity of these novels, these marketable aesthetic objects, owed as much to their compelling fictionality as it did to their claims to veridiction. However insistently contemporary criticism attempted to cast it as historiography's popularizing supplement, the historical novel emerged in large part as an alternative—"a literary challenge"—to historiography and its epistemological and representational frameworks.[4]

Part of this challenge no doubt came from the novel's validation of private experience as historically marked and significant. The historical novel brought the possibility of cogent narrative into a world that otherwise confronted the Russian city-dweller, for example, with elusive and incoherent traces of the past (a *Wellington* horse and a *Napoleon* pastry among them). While linking a pastry with the emperor who had mastered a continent seemed frivolous to contemporaries like Bestuzhev, the historical novel offered a more convincing connection between private, seemingly ahistorical, experience and the world of public history. If, as Boris Eikhenbaum has suggested, the 1830s were concerned primarily with comprehending "the relationship between private life ('the story of the heart') and historical life, the life of the people,"[5] the novel held up, as its organizing theme, the codependence of "the story of the heart" and history, offering a framework within which this relationship could be elaborated. In this domestication-by-novel of history, new light could be shed on obscure spaces of familial lore and the national language. But most significantly, especially in Sir Walter Scott's novels, this framework hinged upon a particular kind of protagonist—namely, the "mediocre" or "middling" hero celebrated by critics, most famously Georg Lukács, who praised this invention as "the clearest proof of Scott's exceptional and revolutionary epic gifts."[6] Insofar as such a protagonist could scarcely be said to have played a significant role in events, his involvement in history consisted largely in witnessing and observing; as a result, the Scottian historical novel engaged its protagonist in what amounted to both participation in history and a reception of history (with all its attendant blind spots and misconstruals). These two modes of engagement in turn formed the basis for readerly interest and identification in Scott's novels. Like the protagonist, the reader too lived and made decisions in a historical world whose contours became visible only in retrospect; at least provisionally, the reader could gain legitimate and desirable knowledge of this world by reading about a different everyman's historical experience.

To a much greater extent than the novel genre as a whole, the historical novel explicitly foregrounds its proximity, much vaunted in this case, to the real, whether by privileging the experience of the everyman; or through detailed ethnographical and topographical descriptions and dialect transcriptions, seemingly unmotivated by anything other than the novel's claim to represent what actually occurred; or a nuanced scholarly apparatus, complete with footnotes, references to the studies of professional historians, and accounts of the author's fieldtrips; or the Romantic mystifications of provenance (Scott's denials of his own authorship prominent among them) and the conceit of the found manuscript—attempts to pitch the entire novelistic text as a documentary artifact (such for instance is the narrative frame of Pushkin's *The Captain's Daughter*).[7] By the same token, most early discussions of the historical novel in the 1830s foregrounded questions of its accuracy, not its narrative innovations, which were in fact largely responsible for concealing the artifice sustaining it, and reinforcing such texts' claims to verisimilitude in the first place.[8]

Verisimilitude indeed emerges as an asset desirable in literature precisely in the early nineteenth century. This term only becomes widely confused with historical accuracy, it seems, around the time Scott's novels first appear; but its morphological components—truth and semblance—signal a distance from history "as it happened," a *novelistic* strategy that *creates* an illusion or "semblance of truth," rather than recreating any presumed historical reality.[9] Contemporary dictionary entries on verisimilitude (*pravdopodobie*) expose its ambiguity both in English and Russian. Examples in the *Oxford English Dictionary* reveal that up until the beginning of the eighteenth century, "verisimilitude" was used negatively, as synonymous with "dissimulation," but, starting in the late eighteenth century, it also began to denote narrative sophistication.[10]

The Dictionary of the Russian Academy (1806–22) also registers both of the word's valences. Under *pravdopodobnyi*, it lists an example that in fact distinguishes verity from verisimilitude: "A verisimilar story is not truthful" (*Pravdopodobnaia istoriia ne istinna*). Meanwhile, *pravdopodobie* is illustrated with a more affirmative example: "In epic works, verisimilitude should be preserved" (*V epicheskikh tvoreniiakh nabliudat' dolzhno pravdopodobie*), but here epic stands for an extreme of fictionality which, apparently, is best harnessed with some modicum of the real.[11] On the one hand, verisimilitude is fiction's realistic virtue or conscience; on the other, it keeps fiction fictional, a "truth" or mere *approximation* of truth, a repository of probabilities and potentialities. This semantic uncertainty foregrounds one of the key questions in the reception of the historical novel: does such a work create an imagined world, or recreate a formerly real one?

Responses to historical novels reveal the unprecedented eagerness on the part of nineteenth-century readers to mistake verisimilitude for truth, to believe in the novel's recreative power. Theorizing the significance of descriptive detail in the nineteenth-century novel, Roland Barthes has famously pinpointed a transformation in the relationship between the verisimilar (*vraisemblable*) and the real: "The whole of classical culture was for centuries nourished by the idea that there could be no contamination of the 'vraisemblable' by the real. At first because what is 'vraisemblable' is never other than the thinkable: it is entirely subject to (public) opinion. [. . .] Then because it was thought that what is 'vraisemblable' is general and not particular, as is history [. . .]. Finally because, with the 'vraisemblable', the opposite is never impossible, since description is founded on majority, but not unanimous, opinion."[12] In the nineteenth century, the new fascination with history evinced, alongside the Hegelian questing after zeitgeist noted by Kireevskii, a rival (and opposite) craving for the minutest details of past life-styles. Evidence can be gleaned not only from the extraordinary popularity of historical fiction, which zoomed in on ordinary characters of different social classes, genders, ages, and claims to notability, but also from the rising appeal of archaeology and ethnography; the redirected interest of collectors in original and ancient objects, including those of the everyday, as opposed to beautiful copies of beautiful originals; and the related growth of museum holdings in applied art. Where the past could not be recreated with desired minuteness, plausibility substituted for reality, often without disclaimers, and thereby the distinction between "verisimilitude" and "verity" imperceptibly faded. Barthes continues, "The motto implicitly prefacing all classical discourse (obeying the ancients' 'vraisemblance') is: *Esto*

(Let there be, suppose . . .). The kind of 'real', fragmented, interstitial descriptive *notation* we are dealing with here does not appeal to this implicit introduction, and it takes its place in the structural fabric with no hint of such a hypothetical qualification. Just for that reason, there is a break between the old 'vraisemblance' and modern realism; but for that reason also, a new 'vraisemblance' is born, which is precisely what is called 'realism' (taking this term to refer to any discourse which accepts statements whose only justification is their referent)."[13] Even as verisimilitude sheds its hypothetical meaning, the category of the real—decades before the capacious term "realism" was coined in France in 1856—subsumes both the mimetic and the hypothetical. The truth of history and the truth of fiction gradually coalesce.

In the historical novel, skillful narrative construction fabricates the "vraisemblable" and, conversely, verisimilitude disguises narrative artifice. Readers demanded verisimilitude, or what Barthes calls the "referential illusion,"[14] not because of its complete alignment with "fact," but because a verisimilar novel induced a thrilling sense of illusion, of mediation, of representation, at the same time concealing this excitement under the pretexts of pedagogical value and truth. Paradoxically, then, historical novels were enjoyed not for the reasons openly professed by readers—not, that is, for their accuracy—but for the multitude of ways in which they deviated, and concealed their deviations, from the established version of the past, for the machinery of verisimilitude which they constructed and upon which they relied.[15]

It is in the reception of the historical novel, for all its practitioners' sophisticated deployment of Romantic parabasis, that the distance between the supposedly uncontaminated facts of history and their verisimilar novelistic rendering is either left unacknowledged or, when its concealment appears no longer sustainable, deemed a failure on the part of the author. Dmitrii Iakubovich, one of the earliest scholars to study Scott's influence in Russia, aptly formulated the set of concerns underpinning readings of the historical novel, both by Pushkin's contemporaries and by commentators of Iakubovich's own and subsequent generations, as "questions of historical accuracy, documentation, anachronism, [period-specific] language, and integration of historical personages into fiction."[16] The impulse to deconstruct the novelist's feat of verisimilitude privileged positivist intertextual pursuits disentangling fact and fiction.[17] Thus, in an early Russian debate on historical fiction, Faddei Bulgarin, author of one of the first Russian historical novels, *Dimitrii the Pretender* (*Dimitrii Samozvanets*, 1829), defends himself from the Pushkin camp with reference to his high standard of accuracy and the epistemic limitations of the historian: "I have tried to depict all historical personages in exactly the way history represents them. My novel can be likened to a window, through which a contemporary looks at Russia and Poland of the early seventeenth century: many historical figures are seen through the window, yet they are described only inasmuch as the historian's eye could see them and inasmuch as they participated in a given event."[18] The metaphor of the window exposes the expectation of an unmediated access to history, a seeing-through. Insofar as the passage privileges a direct mimetic relationship of text to historical referent, the metaphor of the window makes the barrier between viewing subject (the reader) and object (the "epoch," historical figure, etc.) transparent. The window renders access to a past reality not some intricate matter of time travel or imaginative visualization, but an act of pure sight, unbiased, though fractional and delimited by a frame. The window-frame corresponds to narrative composition, which is, however, also described in terms of vision—"inasmuch as the historian's eye could see"—and not of artistry or manipulation. This recourse to the visual is likely not premeditated on Bulgarin's part (but rather, as will be elaborated below, epochally inevitable), but it does allow him to circumvent the vexed issue of narrative choice-making, and to reformulate his opponents' charges of inadequate understanding as the less blameworthy, as it were, physical shortcoming of limited eyesight. The conceit did not help Bulgarin: the main objection to his novel was not that it owed too little to historical reality, but rather that it owed suspiciously too much to Pushkin's unpublished *Boris Godunov*, which Bulgarin had read as a royal censor, despite his protestations to the contrary. Nevertheless, Bulgarin's defense illuminated the preferences, if not requirements, for historical fiction held by its early readers and critics: not simply verisimilitude, but window-like transparency. The text was expected to make history not merely imaginable but visible, and such expectations destined the historical novel to a rather tedious realist critique.

Where did this emphasis on vision originate? Why did verisimilitude so readily index the reader's ability to *visualize* history? Contemporaries' insistence on the connection seems to go beyond the ancient convention tying cognition to sight (inherent in such expressions as "the mind's eye," "out of sight, out of mind," "hindsight," "foresight," etc.[19]). In fact, the culture of the early nineteenth century was particularly saturated with visual representations of history. Historical painting continued to crown the academic genre hierarchy. Even more importantly, history emerged as the preferred subject for various staged representations (historical drama, tableaux vivants) and

popular technologies of visual entertainment: dioramas, panoramas, magic
lanterns, stereoscopes, and other contraptions that displayed historical events
as sequences of pictures, sometimes projected through smoky or fiery screens
(as in the eidophusikon, a moving panorama combined with dramatic light-
ing effects and music) or accompanied by "fitting" sounds or narration.[20] Theater, and especially amateur theatricals and tableaux vivants, taught the viewer
to decode historical narrative from static scenes of frozen movement. As forms
of popular entertainment, these illusionistic spectacles privileged sensational
subjects and titillated the viewers with their quasi-reality.

The most illusionistic, "unreal" representations were praised for their mimetic success. In his important work on transformations in the status and
function of the observer in the nineteenth century, Jonathan Crary ponders
the discrepancy between these phantasmal technologies and their critics'
investment in apodictic categories of evaluation: "Certain forms of visual experience usually uncritically categorized as 'realism' are in fact bound up in
non-veridical theories of vision that effectively annihilate a real world. Visual
experience in the nineteenth century, despite all the attempts to authenticate
and naturalize it, no longer has anything like the apodictic claims of the camera obscura to establish its truth."[21] Although Crary does not directly address
the use of these new technologies for channeling historical knowledge, his
insights into nineteenth-century manipulations of vision (in fact this is the
age which, he shows, gives rise to an entire industry of such manipulations)
can also shed light on nineteenth-century manipulations of history.

By its very nature, history lingers on the threshold between the verifiable and
the imagined; like no other faculty, vision matches this ambiguity because it
is called to authenticate and witness while running the ever-present risk of suc-
cumbing to deception. In Bestuzhev's list of commodities that feed on the new
vogue for history, optical entertainments are ubiquitous, cheap, and capable
of conjuring intense visions of history's most dramatic scenes: "Spend a ten-
kopeck piece and you will receive in exchange the ill-starredness of the ages—
Clytemnestra and Chenier, the assassination of Henry IV and Waterloo, the
Berezina and St. Helena, the deluge of Petersburg and the Lisbon earthquake."
If the commodities in the list are only tenuously related to history, the visual
spectacles bought for a *grivna* (10 kopecks) are more deceptive still, for they
create an illusion, which unlike a horse or pastry, corresponds to nothing
physical at all—what Ina Ferris calls, discussing precisely this kind of equivocation in historical fiction, its fabrication of "absent presence."[22] For the
viewer or reader, envisioning the past by means of illusionistic technology or

novelistic construction means the comfortable pleasure of direct contact with history without the inherent dangers. To the show's owner or the novel's author, it makes available multiple instruments of *trompe l'oeil*. It is this illusionistic underside of the historical novel's realist artifice that Bulgarin's window metaphor, and other contemporary explorations of what it means to write, read, and crave historical fiction, ultimately obscure.

The historical imagination in the age of historical novels can thus be characterized as emphasizing vision and the illusion of direct access to the past, a knowledge gained via the senses rather than through reason. In the inaugural scene of Scott's first historical novel, *Waverley* (1814), the protagonist, reading through his family's chronicles, seems to move effortlessly and without delay from word to image, from the written page to the indiscriminate visualization of everything it contains. And the length of the passage, playfully highlighted by the narrator, seems to reference such musings' potential for infinite extension and replication:

> He would exercise for hours that internal sorcery by which past or imagined events are presented in action, as it were, to the eye of the muser. Then arose in long and fair array the splendor of the bridal feast at Waverley-Castle; the tall and emaciated form of its real lord, as he stood in his pilgrim weeds, an unnoticed spectator of the festivities of his supposed heir and intended bride; the electrical shock occasioned by the discovery; the springing of the vassals to arms; the astonishment of the bridegroom; the terror and confusion of the bride; the agony with which Wilibert observed, that her heart as well as consent was in these nuptials; the air of dignity, yet of deep feeling, with which he flung down the half-drawn sword, and turned away forever from the house of his ancestors. Then would he change the scene, and fancy would at his wish represent Aunt Rachael's tragedy. He saw the Lady Waverley seated in her bower, her ear strained to every sound, her heart throbbing with double agony; now listening to the decaying echo of the hoofs of the king's horse, and when that had died away, hearing in every breeze that shook the trees of the park the noise of the remote skirmish. A distant sound is heard like the rushing of a swoln stream; it comes nearer, and Edward can plainly distinguish the galloping of horses, the cries and shouts of men, with straggling pistol-shots between, rolling forwards to the hall. The lady starts up—a terrified menial rushes in—But why pursue such a description![23]

Ancestral chronicles inspire Waverley's youthful daydreams; the historical imagination takes its first cues from household lore to produce visions that are vivid yet manifestly speculative.[24] Through the family, history is rendered more visible, but also more amenable to mythologization. From a single line of a family record rises a swarm of romanticized characters, their agonized hearts, their terror and confusion, their feasts and battles—all registered by the narrator at a breathless speed. Waverley spends his youth not learning about or analyzing the past, but imagining and visualizing it. His engagement with history is an illusionistic experience of image sequences ("Edward can plainly distinguish"), akin to those craved by the nineteenth-century public, as Crary presents it. This ironic passage is meant, quite typically for novels of this period, to distance the book the reader holds in his hands from its rivals—mere romances that target the fancy and not the reasoning mind, and give sustenance mainly to those overly preoccupied with medieval chivalry. The description breaks off in mid-sentence precisely to mark the distinction between what the narrator calls Waverley's "internal sorcery" and the minutely researched reconstruction of the past for which Scott's novel itself presumes to stand. Waverley the young mediocre hero-in-the-making is like Don Quixote, oversaturated with romance reading and romantic ideals, and it is through its irony toward this kind of protagonist that *Waverley* the novel, just like *Don Quixote* the novel, asserts itself and even perhaps similarly inaugurates its genre. Clearly, however, what is involved in this passage, besides a deliberate contrast of Scott's historical imagination with his character's, is an implicit recognition of those traits and demands of his readers that in fact underwrite the creation of this novel and eventually enable its unprecedented success. Even as it mocks reading-as-reverie, the passage in fact presents its reader with such images as induce precisely an imaginative state. On the one hand, then, this excerpt exemplifies the early novel's typical repudiation of romances; on the other, appearing at the beginning of Scott's first historical novel, it suggests the direction its potential, or perhaps even ideal, reader's mental energies and desires should take.[25]

If the historical novel thus relied on its readers to perform an almost immediate pictorialization of its text, it also transformed their vision of their own mundane surroundings, encouraging them to attend to even the most commonplace of objects as if to historical formations, and perceive in their familiar landscape its invisible temporal layers. Bestuzhev's comments cited at the beginning of this chapter pertain to Russian culture at the peak of its assimilation of these new, post-Scottian norms of historical vision; but already Scott's earliest readers recognized his works' affinity with conjury, alluding to the writer as "the Scottish Sorcerer" and "the Wizard of the North" (thus did Pushkin and Gogol dub him, albeit borrowing these appellations from reviewers of Scott's novels). In one of the earlier documentary instances of Scott's Russian reception, an 1826 diary entry by Alexander Turgenev, who in 1828 would in fact make Scott's acquaintance and convey impressions of this meeting to his friends in the Pushkin circle, we encounter a succinct formulation of Scott's transformative powers: "He who has read Scott looks at these antiquities with different eyes (*inymi glazami*)."[26] Turgenev acknowledges, though in an admittedly metaphorical usage, Scott's power over the very apparatus of vision and cognition. But perhaps the greatest tour-de-force of visualization appears in an epistle ("To Walter Scott"; "K Val'teru Skottu," 1832) by Ivan Kozlov, the "blind bard," who in his imagination transports himself to Scott's estate in Abbotsford, where he strolls alongside the novelist through a landscape he reconstructs and synthesizes from the various fictions, thus inserting the "real" writer into his no less "real" novelistic world:

Как часто я в мечтах веселых,
От мыслей мрачных и тяжелых,
В тенистый Аббодс-форд лечу,—
С тобой, мой бард, пожить хочу,
Хочу смиренно быть свидетель,
Как небо любит добродетель!
И что ж? в мечтании моем
Уж я давно в саду твоем
С тобой хожу и отдыхаю,
Твоим рассказам я внимаю,—
Со всех сторон передо мной
Места, воспетые тобой:
Вот там Мельросская обитель,
Где часто бродит по ночам
Убитый рыцарь Кольдингам;
Вот мост Боцвеля,—он хранитель
Преданий страшных; всё кругом—
И крест холма, и дуб косматый,
И пруд под башнею зубчатой—
Оживлено твоим пером.[27]

[How often I in jolly dreams, / Away from dark and heavy thoughts / Fly to shady Abbotsford,—/ With you, my bard, I want to stay, / I want to be the humble witness / Of how heaven loves virtue! / And so? In my dream / I am long since in your garden, / Strolling with you and resting, / Listening to your tales. / On all sides before me / Places that you have celebrated: / Over there is the Melrose cloister / Where by night often wanders / The slain knight Coldingham, / Here is the Both-well Bridge—the keeper / Of frightful legends. Everything around me—/ The cross on the hill, the shaggy oak, / The pond under a notched tower—/ Is enlivened by your pen.]

This hardly unconventional enumeration of places from one's favorite novels resolves in a poignant contrast with Kozlov's actual circumstances in Peters-burg: in his reverie, the poet traverses the picturesque Scottish terrain, an activ-ity from which this man paralyzed from the waist down is otherwise barred; the novelistic landscape allows his sight to escape the elegiac confines of his blindness, which has cast him into "the languor of eternal night" (*v tomlen'i vechnoi nochi*[28]). Thus, for Kozlov, picturing the historical novel amounts to a transcendent mode of contact with the outside world, or even the virtual means of overcoming his disabilities. Scott restores to him his lost vision. The historical novel's visuality thus connoted not simply the transparency implied by Bulgarin's plea, nor merely the consumption of cheap spectacles craved by Bestuzhev's gawking flaneurs, but also, perhaps even at the same time, the quintessentially Romantic transcendence-via-imagination as foregrounded by Turgenev and Kozlov, and a radical rethinking of the textual nature of the his-torical novel as, in effect, a springboard for the reader's own artistry.

In connection with the historical novel's emphasis on visuality, we should note, lastly, another of its crucial innovations: the invention of a particular temporality, the "Sixty Years Since," or as the Victorian critic Leslie Stephen described it, employing the visual sort of metaphors the historical novel seems decidedly to elicit, "the twilight of history; that period, namely, from which the broad glare of the present has departed, and which we can yet dimly observe without making use of the dark lantern of ancient historians, and accepting the guidance of Dryasdust."[29] Scott's novels thus created a sense of intimacy with history, even for those who knew nothing of Scotland or its past; in fact, this unique temporality might, along with the middling hero, account for the historical novel's truly global appeal.[30] This formula's slight temporal remove granted readers new skills of emplotment and exoticization for conceiving of their own familial history, summoning their vision not necessarily to appre-hend some alien historical past for the very first time, but rather to recognize the lifestyles of their grandfathers, ways and doings only recently and par-tially obscured. Stephen in fact proposes that Scott's "best stories might be all described as *Tales of a Grandfather*."[31] By this remark he was discounting some of the medieval romances, which had in fact been the critics' bias from Scott's initial reception. Scott's ability to historicize the mundane and the recent seems also to be the heart of Pushkin's most famous praise for the novelist. "The main charm of Walter Scott's novels," he writes in his two-paragraph sketch on Scott, "is that we are introduced to the past, not with the *enflure* [pomposity] of French tragedy,—not with the primness of the sentimental novel, not with the *dignité* of history, but rather in a contemporary domestic manner."[32]

For a writer whose sixteen historical novels published during his lifetime (two more, which he was working on shortly before his death in 1832, appeared only in 2008) came out from 1814 to 1829, the "Sixty Years Since" formula pointed directly to the eighteenth century. It was specifically in its treatment of this century that the European historical novel of the 1810s–'30s best approximated other, factually grounded, historical prose genres, such as (auto)biography, memoir, and historiographical treatise, and pinpointed the elusive bonds between fiction and history, past and present, narration and truth. One is tempted to speculate that in a market virtually inundated by historical fiction, novels of the eighteenth century occupied a somewhat distinct niche, responding to different generic expectations. In Russia, this was perhaps especially the case. Karamzin's magisterial *History of the Russian State* (published during precisely the same period as Scott's novels, 1816–29), the most influential model of imaginative history-telling in Romantic Russia, ends with the enthronement of the Romanov dynasty, leaving the eighteenth century open, or even crying out, for further exploration. Scott's Waverley novels, the most influential model of history-telling in Romantic Europe, insisted upon directing imaginative exploration toward the recent eighteenth-century past, precisely the terrain Karamzin does not cover.[33] With its turbulent political history, the eighteenth century in Russia presented ample material for thrilling novelization; yet any novelist approaching this period of Russian history would also run the risk of advancing, or on the other hand too glaringly eschewing, political judgment as he inevitably trod the fraught territory of dynastic history, dubious successions, popular unrest, and the brutal mores and sociopolitical customs in fact surviving into the nineteenth century.

In this chapter, I offer readings of two patently dissimilar Russian historical novels which use the eighteenth century as their theme and setting: Ivan Lazhechnikov's *The House of Ice* (*Ledianoi dom*, 1835) and Alexander Pushkin's *The Captain's Daughter* (*Kapitanskaia dochka*, 1836). Lazhechnikov's novel illustrates the evolution of the historical novel genre away from Walter Scott's model, which placed equal weight on edification and amusement, and toward the model, popularized by French writers of the 1820s–'30s, in which entertainment was uppermost. Pushkin's novel, by contrast, reexamines and complicates the Scottian paradigm, establishing a poetics of recognition rather than spectacular wonder, and confronts a uniquely obsolescent context of patronage turned royal censorship, far different from the kind of readership that engendered or craved the historical novel.[34]

In Scott's Footsteps

What did it mean for a Russian writer to take up historical fiction in the 1830s? On the one hand, as with any cultural import, applying foreign novelistic conventions to national material presupposed some ideological engagement with the nation's past, a questioning of this past's consonance with, or place within, greater European history, and, conversely, some wrestling with its idiosyncratic developments and the formal adjustments these might require. In this regard, it comes as no surprise that the first major Russian historical novel, Mikhail Zagoskin's *Iurii Miloslavskii, or Russians in 1612* (*Iurii Miloslavskii, ili russkie v 1612*, 1829), appeared in the wake of Karamzin's authoritative history, and headlined its search for a Russian hero in the title and its specifically national preoccupation in the subtitle. On the other hand, this first Russian historical novel appeared quite late, at a time when the educated Russian reader had already gained familiarity with many of Scott's fictions, first translated into Russian in the early 1820s but available in French translation even earlier. In fact, the French translations were one of the most successful publishing ventures of the early nineteenth century;[35] according to E. Preston Dargan, one of the first scholars to study Scott's reception in France, Scott's main translator, Auguste Defauconpret, in whose renderings Scott was received by both French and Russian Romantics, had already translated nine of Sir Walter's novels by 1820, but "shortly after the days of '1830,' the Defauconpret translations all told ran to nearly a million and a half volumes."[36] Let us recall, too, that the complete Waverley novels appeared in England in forty-eight volumes from 1829 to 1833, the last after their author's passing, certainly signaling the completion of this particular project, if not yet the genre's exhaustion. In other words, by the time such Russian writers as Zagoskin and Bulgarin in 1829, and Lazhechnikov and Pushkin several years later, published their historical novels, their books could not have been perceived as anything other than

belonging to an entire genre of similar works, one with certain familiar protocols and well-founded aspirations to commercial success.

Any narrative of Scott's reception in Russia, or anywhere else in Europe and
the Americas for that matter, has to account not so much for the popularity
of individual texts, but the historical novel's advent as a genre. Scott himself
was aware that with the publication of *Waverley* he had put in motion a kind
of a machinery of replication, or an army of imitators: "I am something like
Captain Bobadil who trained up a hundred gentlemen to fight very nearly, if
not altogether, as well as myself,"[37] he remarked in an 1826 diary entry good-
humoredly, wondering, even so, how to keep reinventing himself in the face
of such rapid appropriation of his style by others, and worrying "like a fox at
his last shifts"[38] that these imitations might indicate that the fashion was in
fact already on its way out. Indeed, even as European readers continued to wax
rhapsodic over the "sorcery" of Scott's novels, critics already in the mid-1820s
began to question the authenticity of any work that could lend itself to such
seemingly easy imitation or be so readily distilled to a template. Thus, in the
same year as Zagoskin's and Bulgarin's novels appeared in print (1829), the
Herald of Europe ran a Russian translation of the French critic Saint-Marc
Girardin's mocking recipe for historical novels (published in the French original in 1828). While first and foremost intended to ridicule Scott's imitators,
such recipes also served to undermine the "magic" of the "Scottish sorcerer"
himself—anyone, that is, could be a magician, so long as every step was followed to the letter:

> 1st. The protagonist of a historical novel must necessarily be insignificant. The
> heroine can also do without any character. 2nd. Try to endow the villains of your
> novel with some strange virtue and give the honest men some funny and most
> unusual idiosyncrasy. 3rd. You always need to present at least one public figure
> with a grand disposition. 4th. Do not forget that among the characters of your
> novels there also needs to be a fool whom you from time to time make pronounce
> mysterious phrases. 5th. Incessantly mix the comic and tragic. And since some-
> times it is very hard to entertain the reader with truly comical situations, here is a
> method that always works: give one of your characters some word or gesture and
> force him to repeat either of these every minute; for in the historical novel, cari-
> cature is the only source of the comical, of all that can entertain the reader. 6th. As
> far as the authenticity of the mores, it will suffice if you can make your readers
> believe that you are depicting the mores of this or that century by representing
> your characters with a physiognomy *not of the present century* and if they seem

alien to your reader. 7th. In your story periodically introduce phrases from ancient chronicles and occasionally color the speech of your own time with folk phrases, and mix it all together. To this end you can be guided by some of the productions of the French theater [. . .] where a mistress or a servant appears in the costume of 1828, while a lover or a servant wears the fashions of the seventeenth century; where a tail-coat, a marquise tunic, a farthingale, a galloon dress, short underwear, and pantaloons appear all together on the same stage. It is to this happy mixture that the style of the historical novel should aspire![39]

Clearly, what had originated as a rather complex genre, and had even boosted the legitimacy of prose fiction and its devices in the wake of the dissolution of classicism, or at least successfully and interestingly responded to the nineteenth century's fascination with historical knowledge, had very soon, a mere fifteen years after its invention, lent itself to utter trivialization in the eyes of elite European opinion-makers. Scott had not yet lost his appeal amid high- and middle-brow adult readers, as he would by the time, for example, Leo Tolstoy took up the writing of *War and Peace*, but there was certainly an acknowledged and widespread awareness of his limitations already in the time of Pushkin.

Since the historical novel was so implicated in the market economy, so targeted at a mass readership or at least a broader one than was typical for other relatively high-brow genres in Russia,[40] we must attend to the projected readership as it is implied in the Russian historical fiction of the 1830s, and frame the close readings of Lazhechnikov and Pushkin that follow within the contradictions of the genre's status as both magic and formulaic.[41] Thus when Lazhechnikov and Pushkin arrive on the scene with their projects of outdoing Walter Scott in the 1830s, they both do so when Scott has already lost some of his luster, when his novels are already well-established and register more as a genre—a template or recipe—than as individual texts. In the Russian context, both are also already latecomers to the genre, entering a market awash in translations of Scott, the works of his foreign imitators and successors, and those of the so-called "russkie val'ter-skottiki."[42] If Lazhechnikov, as we shall see, revises Scott's recipe by incorporating narrative strategies of his contemporaries from the French "frenetic school" (themselves influenced by Scott), Pushkin, we might say, minimizes the amount of each ingredient, producing a text that at the same time clearly harks back to Scott's novelistic procedure, synthesizes and abridges it, and ultimately advances a critique of both the historical novel and Russian eighteenth-century history.

"The Literature of Galvanism"

Set in 1739, the last year of Anna Ioannovna's reign, Ivan Lazhechnikov's 1835 novel *The House of Ice* places its reader in a world not unlike (at least stylistically) the early nineteenth-century one inhabited by Bestuzhev's flaneurs, a world that accosts one with a multitude of sensory stimuli, focalizing one site, one temporal frame after another, as the narrator excitedly hurries the reader along. The opening paragraph inaugurates this sense of overstimulation, of the past's over-aliveness:

> My God! What's all that clamor and merriment at the court of the cabinet minister and Ober-Jägermeister Volynskii? During the rule of Peter the Great, blessed be his memory, one wouldn't ask this question because no one wondered at gaiety. [. . .] But now, even though we are only in the fourth day of Christmas-tide (mind you, in the year 1739), now all Petersburg is quiet with the silence of a cell where the condemned reads even his prayers in a whisper. [. . .] Here, we have said, people are coming home from church, sorrowful, cheerless, as if from a funeral, and only in one corner of Petersburg are people amusing themselves openly and make so much noise that one's head is ready to split. The crowd wells up and overflows. There is not a costume or dialect missing! Of course all the peoples inhabiting Russia have sent hither their representatives, a pair each. [. . .] This is truly a Satan's Sabbath! You the Orthodox, walking by this devilish revelry, spit and cross yourselves! But let us, sinners that we are, enter Volynskii's court, force our way through the crowd and find out in the house itself the occasion for such a wild commingling of languages.[43]

Casting the narrator as a guide ("but let us enter") and aligning the "now" of the reader with the "now" of depicted events, the novel insists on its realism, on the reader's palpable contact with the fictive world. The use of "we" (*my*) to mark the narrator's voice stipulates the reader's complicity in viewing the events and telling the story. The style of the opening indeed resembles scripts used to attract crowds to sensationalist visual spectacles at street-fairs taking place, perhaps, even as Lazhechnikov's book was being sold. *Come on in,* hawkers would urge, *and see history unfold before your eyes!* One is reminded again of the colorful historical scenes that could be purchased for a *grivna* in Bestuzhev's history-saturated urban space; though the covenant between Lazhechnikov's reader and narrator, the agreement granting a peek under the veil surrounding Volynskii's court, is not sealed by any direct monetary exchange (presumably the book has already been paid for), the transaction is similar. At first, the reader finds himself outside the main spectacle, but, gradually becoming aware of its exceptionality—but for this oasis of "merriment," the city is enshrouded in gloom—he buys entry into the house by acknowledging his transgressive desire ("sinners that we are") to see history. This reader, furthermore, is made strikingly aware of his own somatic presence in the novel (and hence in the historical world): first, he hears and sees and is patently perturbed; later, as in a street-fair, he achieves access to the spectacular space by "forcing [his] way" through jostling onlookers. The novel thus pretends to effect, in 1835, physical contact with a crowd from 1739. For this crowd, moreover, the memory of Peter I's reign is still alive, and thus the novel's temporal reach is at the same time extended far beyond the Scottian sixty years, but also contracted through the pretense of the fictive world's presence.

Lazhechnikov was in no way inclined to draw an equivalence, even by implication, between Anna Ioannovna's brutal reign and the present of his own Nikolaevan Russia. As a result, the novel's temporal structure is further complicated through allusions to the narrator's distance from the exoticized world of the 1730s. If in the opening paragraph, the narrator's knowledge of Volynskii's household appears to be firsthand, a mere paragraph later the mores of Bironian[44] Russia are rendered through the somewhat nostalgic reminiscences of the narrator's old nanny, themselves remembered from the narrator's childhood: "Speaking of fast messengers (*skorokhody*), I cannot help recalling the words of my nanny who once upon a time, telling me of the golden olden days, expressed regret that the fashion for human runners (*beguny-liudi*) had given way to the fashion for trotters and amblers."[45] The introduction of this highly mediated piece of information creates a peculiar tension in the novel: does the narrator inhabit the world of the 1730s or the 1830s? and can he plausibly—considering the historical novel's emphasis on realism—inhabit both epochs at once?

This tension indeed persists throughout the entire novel as it saturates its world with color and detail, foregrounding alternatively this world's exoticism—and hence the reader's alienation from the eighteenth century—and its familiarity, with the reader immersed as eyewitness in the novel's historical environment. Scott's conception of historical development, for all its thinly disguised nostalgia for the culture of the Highland clans, emphasized the notion of progress, whereby the novel's past was carefully detached from the reader's present, the former portrayed as the latter's necessary but surmounted precondition. Lazhechnikov sets his novel during a reign that was, as we have seen, habitually excised from the celebratory Russian mythologies of the eighteenth century, which tended to foreground instead the rulership of Peter I, Elizabeth, or Catherine II. Because Anna Ioannovna's reign was conceived of as an exception, rather than an integral stage, in the purposeful progression of Russian imperial history, the novelist could pluck it from among time periods as one whose relation to the 1830s is unregulated by any particular mythology or conception of historical process, as a period insulated by its exoticism and comparative irrelevance, and capable of providing a curious time-traveler the thrill of total immersion precisely because of its distance from his present. On the other hand, even as the narrator's serf-nanny laments the passing of the world of fast runners—the novel is densely populated with characters seemingly thus oblivious to their own enmirement in systems of human servitude—the narrator himself comes to occupy an ironic space, from which the cruelty of exploitation and subservience under Anna Ioannovna by contrast illuminates the progressive nature of Nicholas's reign despite, or in fact simply with a blind eye turned to, the persistence of serfdom and rank hierarchies, and the recent execution of the Decembrists.

If Anna Ioannovna and her odious advisor the bloodthirsty Biron can hardly be said to offer the novel's nineteenth-century reader worthy models or predecessors, it is through the figure of Artemii Volynskii that the book contributes a hero to the Romantic national pantheon, suggesting a continuity of national spirit as an alternative or supplement to the discontinuous historical narrative of Russian political culture and social custom. Although many of Lazhechnikov's devices undoubtedly evince the legacy of Scott, the latter's main innovation (at least from Lukács's perspective)—the insertion of an invented middling protagonist into a well-researched historical world—does not find its way into *The House of Ice*. The novel's hero Artemii Petrovich Volynskii (1689–1740) was an eminent cabinet minister under Anna Ioannovna, and Biron's known adversary. The historical Volynskii, starting in the reign of Peter the Great, had been repeatedly promoted for his administrative talents and then repeatedly demoted for corruption, bribery, and physical abuse of subordinates. In an ultimate demotion in 1740, he was beheaded, after an investigation into his embezzlement of state funds and brutal beating of Vasilii Trediakovskii in Biron's antechamber also revealed Volynskii's supposedly central role in a conspiracy to seize the Russian throne after Anna Ioannovna's imminent death. His was the last sensational execution to take place under Anna Ioannovna. It would thus soon come to symbolize the terrors and incongruity of her reign, the shameful past erased by the Russian ode (as we have already seen) and so ambivalently resuscitated by Lazhechnikov.

Lazhechnikov's recovery of Anna Ioannovna's reign for the novel's setting and rehabilitation of Volynskii as hero were not without their precedents. The Decembrist poet Kondratii Ryleev dedicated two of his *Reflections* (*Dumy*, 1821–23)—titled "Volynskii" and "The Vision of Empress Anna" ("Videnie imperatritsy Anny"; in Bulgarin's manuscript fittingly dubbed "Golova Volyn-skogo" ["Volynskii's Head"][46])—to Anna Ioannovna's cabinet minister. Here Volynskii was cast in two of Romantic poetry's most beloved roles: as a con-demned man in prison and as a ghostly severed head that comes to haunt its murderer. As a historical project, *Reflections* envisions Russian history as a sequence of hero-centered elegiac national scenes, and Ryleev's Volynskii appears as a historical revenant to remind readers not to forsake their patri-otic obligations even in the face of death. In the first poem, after expounding upon the fortitude Volynskii shows on the verge of his unjust execution, Ryleev admonishes his readers to preserve Volynskii's memory:

В его очах при мысли сей
Сверкнула с гордостью отвага;
И бодро из тюрьмы своей
Шел друг общественного блага.
Притек . . . увидел палача—
И голову склонил без страха;
Сверкнуло лезвие меча—
И кровью освятилась плаха!
Сыны отечества! в слезах
Ко храму древнему Самсона!
Там за оградой, при вратах
Почиет прах врага Бирона!
Отец семейства! приведи
К могиле мученика сына:
Да закипит в его груди
Святая ревность гражданина![47]

[At this thought, his eyes / Flashed with pride and courage; / And briskly from his jail / Went the friend of public good. / He arrived and beheld the executioner / And fearlessly he bent his head. / The sword's blade flashed, / And blood sanctified the executioner's block! / Sons of the fatherland! In tears / Come to Samson's ancient temple! / There behind the fence, next to the gate / Rest the remains of Biron's enemy! / Paterfamilias! Bring / Your son to the martyr's grave! / In his breast let boil / The sacred zeal of the citizen!]

Ryleev's elevated diction effaces Volynskii's individual features, rendering him an archetypal rather than identifiable hero. The event of the execution is sketched through a series of poetic clichés: the hero's pride, courage, fearlessness; the flashing blade of the executioner's sword and blood on the block. Such a formulaic depiction suggests that in *Reflections* Ryleev aspired not to a precise representation of historical figures, but rather to prescribing a specific attitude toward them (in this case, the civic zeal to be inculcated in the hypothetical youth through Volynskii's example). It was Lazhechnikov's novel, however, with its equally distributed appeals to the imagination and morality, rather than Ryleev's one-sidedly lofty summons, that ended up impressing Volynskii's significance upon thrill-loving readers, bringing them in droves to his grave at the Sampsonievskii Monastery.[48]

In "The Vision of Empress Anna," Ryleev takes the effacement of Volynskii's historical specificity to its extreme. We recognize the identity of the apparition only through the eyes of the sentimental moribund empress to whom it appears. (This languorous queen, incidentally, is hardly the most canonical portrait of the corpulent and cruel Anna, but might illuminate Lazhechnikov's repeated close-up portrayals of her as pensive and even embarrassed.) Grief at Volynskii's absence is followed by dread at his transfigured presence, both clichés of sentimentalist and Gothic writing that reveal nothing about Volynskii himself and merely render him the hero of an easily recognizable plot. The real focus of the poem is the ghost's speech to Anna, which again hews to an interpretation corresponding not to any documented or even verisimilar historical event involving either of these figures, but only to the perspective of a Romantic poet. The complex historical Volynskii has little significance for Ryleev; what inspires him, rather, is the discovered fit between European Romantic poetics and Russian national history, as well as the possibility of enlisting disparate Russian historical figures in the Romantic revolutionary cause. The force of the revolutionary message depends not on making history "present" to the eye of the reader through detail and differentiation, but on the repeated discovery of the same heroic features persisting through the ages (recall L'vov's depiction of the heroic Russian spirit as described in the previous chapter). The poet calls, then, for continuity, for the reincarnation of absent heroes in future patriots, rather than for the "picturesque" revivification of potentially complicated historical figures from the past.

Lazhechnikov's innovation lies, by contrast, in the vivid (almost too vivid) portrayal of Volynskii: not a portrait centered upon the cliché of his execution (ironically, the best-remembered moment of his life), but rather a researched and colorfully imagined biography, in which Volynskii emerges as a hero intelligible to Romantic sensibilities, but not limited by them. We learn to recognize the hero's tall frame and magnetic gaze (his sex appeal and virility are repeatedly noted) before we discover Volynskii's name. In introducing the hero, the narrative moves slowly, seductively toward him, starting with the merry noise at his court heard by a casual passerby amid Petersburg's icy silence, then following the couples who have just arrived for a nationalities pageant on the grand staircase of his mansion, then looking around at the tiled stoves, painted ceilings and porcelain—"our contemporaries too would have found much to marvel at in the grandee's chambers!"[49]—and comparing the space created by the hall's high windows to a camera obscura (clearly Lazhechnikov is aware of the illusionistic performance he has concocted for us), then finally homing in on the hero himself, also rendered as a beautiful, opulent object of readerly vision. The sequence concludes, "In the middle of the room, in a splendid armchair, sits a stately man of attractive appearance, in a silk, light-purple caftan of French cut. This is the owner of the house, Artemii Petrovich Volynskii. He is famed at court and among the people as one of the handsomest of men."[50] Volynskii's machismo ultimately precipitates his downfall: the hot-tempered hero sacrifices his political interests to his unbridled passions, a perfect recipe for a romanticist historical novel. Matters of politics vie with matters of the heart for dominance in the plotline, but both conspire to bring the hero to his bloody demise. Volynskii falls in love with a young Moldavian princess (or as it turns out, a Gypsy) raised first in a harem and later at Anna Ioannovna's court. Forgetting his obligations to his wife and his political cause, he exposes himself to Biron's ubiquitous spies and fatally compromises his clandestine campaign against the favorite. As in Ryleev's poem, Volynskii is here clearly Biron's honorable and heroic foil and a Romantic icon of martyrdom; however, as Lazhechnikov fills this Romantic mold with details purportedly culled from historical sources, he also endows the hero with a plotline compromised by self-indulgence and licentiousness, and striving toward, though never fully achieving, the protagonist's psychologization.

For all the author's claims to accurate historical representation and research, the distance between the fiction and the documents on which it is purportedly founded should be obvious even from the few examples cited so far of Lazhechnikov's style and my incomplete exposition of the plot of *The House of Ice*. The book's rootedness in Romantic hero-worship (albeit heavily mitigated by the novelistic requirement of an individuated, at least somewhat flawed protagonist) is matched only by the hypertrophy of passion and overwrought expressivity allotted its other characters, particularly the positive heroes and female cast; its narrative excess on the level of description, which lays heavy emphasis on affecting the reader through his somatic and visual incorporation into the novelistic Petersburg space; and a cloak-and-dagger plot that pursues several interconnected conspiratorial lines, which at the point of their intersection explode in graphically violent resolutions.

All of these features—the stuff of pulp fiction for most present-day readers, but not to the same extent for Lazhechnikov's contemporaries, inexperienced in such entertainments—reveal the novel's *siuzhet* as constantly engaged in distorting whatever historical *fabula* Lazhechnikov might have gleaned from his sources. Still, the criticism that most pained the book's author (and caused him to ruminate about it for years after its publication and stunning success among readers) concerned the novel's accuracy. The remark was offered by none other than Pushkin, a younger contemporary, yet also something of a literary idol for Lazhechnikov.[51] (We can guess at Lazhechnikov's great admiration for Pushkin by looking only at the number of explicit and oblique quotations from the latter's works in the text of *The House of Ice*.) Pushkin, who was at the time rethinking his *History of the Pugachev Uprising* (1833) as a historical novel, comments in his otherwise enthusiastic response on the discrepancy between Lazhechnikov's book and its supposed documentary base, "The historical truth is not observed in [*The House of Ice*], and in time, when Volynskii's case becomes public, this will no doubt impair your creation; but poetry always remains poetry, and many pages of your novel will live so long as the Russian language itself is not forgotten. [. . .] I confess that I am prepared to argue with you about Trediakovskii. [. . .] And we could have a talk about Biron, too."[52] Like most of his contemporaries, Pushkin in his critique treats historical and stylistic precision as the novel's autonomous building blocks: even as the short-lived historical value of Lazhechnikov's fiction jeopardizes its chances at survival, his inspired writing—"poetry"—will avert the novel's extinction. It is unclear whether what is meant by "poetry" is in fact precisely the text's ability to orchestrate multiple plotlines through a system of interconnections, guesswork, gossip, disguises, and innuendos; or whether it is the plot's convergence on the image, almost overdetermined by its allegorical and symbolic potential, of the ice palace built on Anna's orders as a venue for the marriage of her court jester; or whether the novel's poetry is its pictorial vividness and over-saturation, amounting to a successful exoticization of Petersburg and its past.[53] To judge from other contemporary reviews, "poetry" is usually invoked to compliment either some vaguely sensed inventiveness and lyricism or very precisely observed stylistic details, taken out of their broader context.

The earnestness of Pushkin's critique, however, is emblematic of how historical fiction—particularly, but probably not exclusively, in Pushkin's internal genre hierarchy—was held to different standards than those applied to other kinds. Indeed, we might not recognize in this stickler for the responsible treatment of historical material the protean author whose oeuvre thematizes our epistemological limitations and presents the confrontation between subject and world as riven, or perhaps enriched, by bias and fragmentation. Pushkin's approach to the incorporation of research into fiction seems more indebted, at least in this case, to Enlightenment rationalism than to the aporetic epistemology of the German Romantics.[54] His attitude appears in fact to accommodate the fragment (of historical events, biographies, conversations) as ultimately pointing to an epochal totality which we can strive to know—and which it is in fact possible to know—through research and fiction. Moreover, for Pushkin history-writing, whether fictional or not, is a matter of rendering service, both to the public and (starting in 1831, when he steps into the role of Nicholas's historiographer) to the state. For Lazhechnikov, no such optimistic project of sticking to the facts is viable, in large part because his novel develops an intrigue of espionage and mistrust, thereby replicating in its historical setting, plot construction, and oppressive atmosphere its author's profound epistemological suspicions about the project of historiographical research. His acceptance of Pushkin's terms notwithstanding, that is, Lazhechnikov appears deeply skeptical of the integrity of the very sources Pushkin urges him to consider: "In your letter of 3 November you reproach me for not observing historical truth, and say that in time, when the Volynskii case becomes public, this will harm my *House of Ice*. The Volynskii case? . . . In the present age of skepticism and strict historical research, will this case really be received unreservedly, as a writ upon which a historian can rely simply because it happened to be in the State Archive? Reason would ask first who compiled the case. Will the accusations be believed, and the signatures of people who were mostly enemies of the condemned, and all of them minions of the favorite, people bribed with the hope of honors and other gain, by the fear of Siberia and execution, weak people full of envy and hatred? They were all advocates of a horrible power: who was the advocate taking Volynskii's side?"[55] This thoroughgoing skepticism as to the reliability of the Volynskii archive implies that non-fictional sources, too, must be read as fictions, that is, with the same apparatus of doubt used to interrogate the historical novel, and with the same sort of allowance for characterological complexity, in this case, the archive's informants' psychological and political motivations. Lazhechnikov's retort to Pushkin makes the radical move of identifying elements of narrative construction and ideological manipulation in the very documents supposedly grounding historical research and fiction. Even (and perhaps particularly) the state archives, those guardians of reliable access to history upon which Pushkin depended, though not at all exclusively, for his own historical studies of Pugachev's "case" (surely no less subject to narrative manipulation than Volynskii's) could, according to Lazhechnikov, contain untrustworthy sources. Ironically, strict research, whose value Lazhechnikov in no way disputes (having himself supplied Pushkin with important sources for his Pugachev project), does not entail the optimistic pursuit of a history (or History) knowable from surviving sources: where writing is involved, there is writerly bias. Conversely, it may be inferred, not just from Lazhechnikov's statements but from his whole novelistic endeavor, that because knowledge is necessarily fractional and distorted, historical fiction can lay claim to it, as legitimately as does historiography.

Hardly a declaration of the instability of all historical knowledge, Lazhechnikov's response does not altogether reject the tenet of accuracy. Verisimilitude is still the main objective of any historical narrative, but it is no longer predicated solely upon documentary evidence, and accuracy in fact becomes understood, at least from what we can infer from Lazhechnikov's novelistic practice, as similitude performed through some degree of poetic license, rather than scholarly exactitude, which seems to be the procedure Pushkin privileges. For Lazhechnikov, the writer's general sense of the epoch overrides the authority of individual documents. In "My Acquaintance with Pushkin" ("Znakomstvo moe s Pushkinym," 1856), a brief memoir almost entirely dedicated to what Lazhechnikov (unlike, in all probability, Pushkin) considered an important polemic over *The House of Ice*, Lazhechnikov backtracks from the more radical claims he made in his correspondence with Pushkin and recycles, instead, the time-worn vocabulary of 1830s discussions on historical fiction ("truth," "accuracy," "research," "painting," "epoch"): "In [the novel] I forcefully defended historical truth, which Pushkin disputes. For a long time before writing my novels, I studied the epoch and people of that time, especially the main historical figures I depicted. [. . .] I conscientiously researched the main characters of my *House of Ice* in historical sources and reliable traditions. [. . .] My task was to faithfully draw a picture of the epoch which I had undertaken to depict."[56] Framed as a memoir, this later vindication is markedly more conservative than the challenge to documentary authority he had thrown down in 1835; it uncritically reinstates the writer as scholar and realist painter. The release of Volynskii's case in 1858 disclosed evidence that, as Pushkin had predicted, was at variance with Lazhechnikov's romanticized "historical truth."[57] However, readers of historical novels seemed to react favorably to features other than documentary validity; *The House of Ice* went through multiple editions in both the nineteenth and twentieth centuries, eventually relocating, as most historical novels did, from the drawing-room to the nursery (to use Alexander Dolinin's apt formulation), where it remained until very recently.[58]

What precisely is it that grants Lazhechnikov's project of historical verisimilitude its poetic license? If the disagreement with Pushkin only hints at the two writers' divergent understandings of "the real," to which the historical novel should adhere, Lazhechnikov's departure from both Scott's articulation of the genre and Pushkin's implied standards of accuracy stands out memorably in the scenes of eroticism and violence in *The House of Ice*. It is in these episodes, specifically, that novelistic verisimilitude reveals itself as a matter of the immediacy of the reader's visceral and visual experience, rather than the kind of textual consonance between source and fiction we shall see Pushkin achieving in *The Captain's Daughter*. Lazhechnikov is not entirely original in emphasizing pleasure and trauma as sites of the temporary suspension of textuality, of a text's giving way to almost immediate imagery or sensation. In fact, Scott's popularity had already been partially eclipsed in the 1830s by French writers of the so-called "frenetic" school, itself significantly indebted to Scott, but taking his legacy in a direction that could hardly be seen as congenial to his project, and eventually instrumental, indeed, to the rise of such un-Scott-like literary phenomena as the Russian natural school.[59] The freneticists (Alfred de Vigny, Victor Hugo, Jules Janin, Alexandre Dumas [père], Eugène Sue) held that knowledge in the novel—particularly under the new conditions of literary consumerism, which I have sketched in this chapter's introductory remarks—derives from unexpected sources, from an incursion into and exaggeration of life's most sensational, incongruous, unattractive, or sensuous features. Enormously popular in Russia, Jules Janin in his fiction drew on his experience as a feuilletonist, in both capacities bearing vivid witness to extreme scenes from city life. Applying similar tools of intense observation to the past, Victor Hugo reinterpreted Scott's domestication of history as license for an extreme intrusion into the occluded private spaces of architecture and psychology. Having come a long way from its esteemed progenitor's innocuous narratives, then, the historical novel had become a risqué genre, always threatening to expose the reader's secret desires as well as contemporary political anxieties.

In the 1830s Russian critics hotly debated freneticism, controversial not only for its aesthetic shock-value, but also its apparent association with the July Revolution and suspected potential to incite political unrest. Apollon Grigor'ev, first to comment on Lazhechnikov's debt to these French writers (and viewing him as "richly endowed with an unconscious perceptiveness, a feminine-passionate impressionability, but utterly lacking in self-control"[60]), would look back on the cultural climate of the decade thus: "The public then had temporarily lost interest in Pushkin, read [Bestuzhev-]Marlinskii with great enthusiasm, good-naturedly took as fact all sorts of historical novels, a dozen of which appeared every month, listened in secret alarm to the tempting echoes of the young French literature in the stories by Baron Brambeus [the penname of Osip Senkovskii, 1800–58], and now and then read translations of Paul de Kock's [1793–1871] novels."[61] Perceiving freneticism's admirers as dangerous, the Russian government shut down some publications favorably disposed toward it, which surely only heightened the appeal of the texts in question.[62] If early historical novels could be perused for moral and historical edification, the new frenetic novel, suffused with all manner of agitating devices, harbored and even perhaps inculcated subversive yearnings and unwholesomeness.

Significantly, in these discussions the names of Walter Scott and the freneticists were invariably linked. Even in the *Northern Bee* (*Severnaia pchela*), the mouthpiece of Russian conservatism, the editors Faddei Bulgarin and Nikolai Grech waxed enthusiastic over the new heirs to Scott's legacy: "Look at how people with talent have taken after Walter Scott! Having thanked the Scottish novelist for the creation of the genre, they did not borrow directly from him; working on their own ground, using their own materials, and following their own taste they have raised edifices admired by an educated readership the world over. Victor Hugo, de Vigny, Janin, Balzac, Mérimée, Sue and other novelists are original writers who use the genre of Scott and Cooper, but who do not copy them."[63] Paradoxically, then, the freneticists, who reveled in the most extreme spectacle, were cast as the disciples of Walter Scott, whose main merit was believed to be the sheer credible mundanity of the historical worlds he created. This perceived connection lends support to this chapter's initial thesis: at work under the aegis of verisimilitude in the historical novel—particularly of the more popular kind practiced by Lazhechnikov—were phenomena not documentary, but in fact novelistic and imaginative. French freneticists radicalized the novelistic strategies already in place in Scott's novels; they exposed the spectacle contained in the everyday. Heightening readers' anxieties about the past, frenetic historical novels pull the rug out from under every last stronghold of security and normalcy. To be sure, this unsettling manner owed much to the Gothic novel, which routinely situated violence and illicit sexuality in the Middle Ages, but was never embarrassed by its imaginative origin; the historical novel effected a far more involved cover-up, overtly aspiring to the status of research, yet stealthily accommodating the most fanciful desires of the new reading public.

Considering its executionary fervor and penchant for ornate pageantry, it would be difficult to find an epoch in recent Russian history more amenable to this freneticist poetics of agitation than the reign of Anna. A peculiar tension arises, however, when the freneticist pursuit of "naked nature," a concept entailing an almost hyper-realist emphasis on visualization and a belief in the universality and pan-intelligibility of passion, is paired with such principles valorized by Scott and the Scottians as the privileging of historical specificity and research, or the need to keep a judicious distance from the past. Freneticism replaces the Scottian "local color" with color per se. The middling hero, an observer whose role it had been to provide an extra layer of mediation for the historical novel's reader (who is, himself, already positioned at a temporal remove from the text), is no longer needed; the freneticist historical novel foregrounds not mediation, but access, claiming via its sensual and emotive universalism to know what historical figures feel, down to their most private thoughts and desires.

Compare, for instance, the following episodes of sexual reverie from Victor Hugo's *Notre Dame de Paris* (1831)—one of the most influential historical novels of the "young French literature"—and Lazhechnikov's *House of Ice*. Here is Hugo's licentious priest Claude Frollo (not a historical figure, but very few are in the world of Hugo, whose scholarly attention is focused primarily on Paris's architectural cityscape) fantasizing about Esmeralda, the innocent, supposedly Gypsy young girl whom he obsessively pursues throughout the novel:

Each night his delirious imagination depicted la Esmeralda to him in all the attitudes which had most set fire coursing through his veins. He saw stretched out over the captain after the stabbing, her lovely bare breast covered in Phoebus' blood, at that moment of ecstasy when the archdeacon had printed on those pale lips that kiss, which the unfortunate girl, although half dead, had felt searing her. He saw her again, undressed by the brutal hands of the torturers, letting them strip and then fix in the iron-screwed boot her little foot, her slender, shapely leg, her supple, white knee. He saw once more that ivory knee, alone remaining outside Torterue's horrible apparatus. Finally he pictured to himself the girl wearing a shift, a rope round her neck, shoulders bare, feet bare, almost naked, as he had seen her on that last day. These sensual images made him clench his fists and sent a shiver down his spine.[64]

Lazhechnikov's reader, similarly, is privy to Volynskii's lustful transports regarding Marioritsa, his illicit love interest, who unwittingly distracts the cabinet minister from his anti-Bironian scheming. Unlike Frollo, Volynskii the historical personage is known to us, albeit limitedly, from archival materials, which needless to say give no mention of such fantasies: "He was plunged into thoughts only of Marioritsa. His entire soul, all of him, became warmly, moistly elemental, and in this Marioritsa bathes her charms. Like this element, he embraces her with his ardent dream, runs down in a stream along her rounded shoulders, splashes a hot foam on her swan-neck, rolls in a wave under her breast, sinking in sweet rapture; he clings to her scorching lips with a flying spray, kisses her black curls and grips them, and his whole self, drenched in her essence, fawns upon her in a subtle, fragrant vapor."[65] Such scenes focalize readerly attention by transforming history from a domain of recorded action or custom to a titillating realm the writer is free to populate with voluptuous content (modeling or echoing his reader's desires), precisely because such content lies beyond the purview of verifiable, hence constricting, records.

Both these episodes catch the protagonists at moments of the utmost frustration, when possession of the object of desire can be achieved only mentally rather than physically. However sensuous the imagery—and here, at least, Lazhechnikov certainly surpasses Hugo in suggestiveness, conjuring a masculine desire on the verge of compromising eruption as its harborer is on his way to the royal palace—it is still just imagery. Here "just" is used not in the sense that the reader is barred access to actual sensuality by the printed page, but in the thwartedness these passages emblematize: at best voyeurs, the protagonists are most often mere dreamers. Unlike contemporary romance fiction, which is happy to frame sex scenes in historical settings chosen seemingly at random, the sensual vignettes in Hugo and Lazhechnikov, as in other historical novels of the period, undertake to test the capacity of the protagonists' and readers' imaginations, hinting at a rather unsettling affinity between the erotic and the historical, between verisimilitude and demonic temptations. In the freneticist historical novel, the erotic presents a specular image of the reader's own pursuit of history—a stalking that is obsessive, constantly sublimated by the imagination, and invariably frustrated. (It is also similar to, albeit more intense than, what we will see possess Pushkin's Hermann in the next chapter.) History absorbs some of the shock of sensuality by letting it belong to what supposedly happened, as opposed to what was merely imagined by the author/narrator in a voyeuristic dream. Conversely, the extreme voyeurism involved in our reading of Frollo's and Volynskii's fantasies is only a heightened version, a disclosure of that voyeurism which propels our interest in the novels' other passages and in history generally.

While Lazhechnikov never shies from frenetic spectacle, Pushkin dismisses this French sensationalist aesthetic as "the literature of galvanism, convict prisons, punch, blood, hand-rolled cigarettes and so on" (*slovesnost' gal'vanicheskaia, katorzhnaia, punshevaia, krovavaia, tsigarochnaia i pr*).[66] In the next section, we will have occasion to contrast Pushkin's treatment of violence and mutilated bodies in *The Captain's Daughter* (for the sexual body is virtually occluded in the novel) with the scene of shocking mutilation in *The House of Ice*. In concluding this section, I will comment only on the first term in this idiosyncratic list, since the others more obviously refer to the frenetic novel's content, whereas "galvanism" might in fact convey a particular understanding of the readerly response such novels anticipate or their general narrative strategies. As an electric shock whose effect was first discovered on dead animals (Luigi Galvani published the results of his experiments in 1791), galvanism or "animal electricity"—particularly for the Romantics who were fascinated with the subject—signaled the possibility of giving life to matter both inanimate and dead, or of matter itself containing transcendent life energies.[67] But in practice, these moments of animation subsided quickly, with galvanism enabling not contact with higher powers, but a twitch. Pushkin's elliptical indictment of the frenetic project as "the literature of galvanism," then, might be interpreted as attending to the intermittence and brevity of the style's shocking effects. Reminiscent of Galvani's experiments with dead frogs, the frenetic historical novel is marked by a desire to resuscitate history through the concentrated and briefly administered shocks of eroticism, violence, and arresting imagery; but the historical novel's greater project of resuscitation—so crucial to the genre, with its insistence on accuracy and authenticity, everyday life and human character—ultimately proves abortive, even if, for short moments, we almost feel ourselves in the presence of the past.

This "galvanic" structure of Lazhechnikov's novel, its patterning in episodes calculated to shock, might help account for the peculiar uncertainty of its temporal frame, the question with which we began this section: how can the narrator plausibly inhabit both the 1730s and the 1830s? The imperative of historical accuracy casts the writer, and the narrator as the novelistic projection of his storytelling voice, in the role of researcher treating his chosen epoch with the requisite critical distance, interspersing in the text, for instance, explanations of dated customs and mentions of his sources (e.g., the narrator's nanny or Georg Wolfgang Krafft's drafts and descriptions of the ice palace). The imperative of resuscitation, a different side of the historical novel's mimetic conceit, contracts the temporal distance between reader and setting, yielding immediate, almost magical, contact with the historical world (e.g., Volynskii's erotic musings or the self-mutilation of Marioritsa's mother, which we will encounter in the next section). If in the first model, authorly/readerly engagement in history is a matter of flipping pages and taking notes, the experience of history in the second is that of the electric charge. Lazhechnikov's project is curiously pitched to combine both.

THE LITERATURE OF RECOGNITION

In *The Captain's Daughter*, Pushkin domesticates history à la Scott, placing a naïve and confused middling hero in the midst of a sweeping historical drama, resolving the plot's final conflict through the intervention of a female protagonist, portraying a central historical personage (Catherine the Great) from the perspective of a character who does not recognize her, and locating the novel's past at a sixty-year remove from the reader's present. However, in the context of the 1830s—a time when the spell Scott had cast had to some extent worn off, and when the frenetic school was introducing major revisions to the sorcerer's original formula—Pushkin's work should be read as a deliberate (post-frenetic) display of simplicity and transparency, distinct from Scott's exoticized national narrative with its Romantic ballads, folk legends, and dialectal idiosyncrasies (examples of which, however, Pushkin allows in epigraphs and integrates in other, virtually imperceptible ways).[68] As with most of his engagements with his European predecessors and peers, Pushkin proceeds by synthesis, distillation, and interpretation. Thus does he resolve the issue of the narrator's temporal location, for example, by marking the entire text as a first-person memoir, an eyewitness account of events of the early 1770s written by the aged narrator in the early 1800s and first brought to the public's attention in the 1830s, thereby activating multiple perspectives at once, connecting the two epochs through individual biography and the lore of one family, but keeping the reader's own groundedness in Nikolaevan Russia in view. Eschewing the exotic, Pushkin, as we shall see, responds to the challenge of representing interiority and violence quite differently from Scott, as well as from the freneticists, with their importunate readiness to entertain. Unlike Lazhechnikov's fidgety narrator, Petr Grinev moderates his reactions to history's most unsettling tableaux, intensifying their effect by his very reserve: violence in Pushkin is all the more shocking in that the fast pace of narrated events means that no one bothers to be shocked by it. The language of the tale is meticulously stylized to sound very familiar and in no way forestall communication between the two epochs, and yet to include usages and textual allusions specific to the eighteenth century as well as folkloric discourse, with its carefully invented or quoted adages; the result is the impression of a shared linguistic patrimony, a multi-generational linguistic community that strains to cover up the political breaches separating the two periods. Interspersed throughout the narrative and in epigraphs, references to eighteenth-century Russian authors (Trediakovskii, Sumarokov, Kniazhnin, Fonvizin, Kheraskov) further shape the novel's verbal *byt* and adumbrate a cohesive trajectory for Russian literary history. But it is significant that these allusions, too, are evenly distributed throughout the text, constituting a verbal baseline that casts the reader's exposure to the eighteenth century specifically as to the recent past of his linguistic and literary contemporaneity. Most of the novel's innovations have the effect of rendering the eighteenth-century past unspectacular, familiar yet situated at a vague, sometimes endearing remove, like lore inherited from one's grandparents.

The young Grinev, whose imagination, not unlike Waverley's, paints chivalric locales for his future military service (though it is left unclear where in his provincial education he could have learned of such vistas), is sorely disappointed with the unspectacular setting into which he is thrown at the Belogorsk fort. The hero's Bildung is conceived in part as a process of coming to terms with the vastness of Russia and the monotony of its landscape: "I looked in every direction expecting to see fearsome bastions, towers, and a rampart, but I could not see anything except a small village bounded by a palisade. [. . .] A melancholy steppe stretched out before me. On one side I could see a few huts; some chickens were roaming about the street. An old woman was standing on her porch with a trough in her hands calling her pigs, which responded with friendly grunts. This was the place where I was condemned to spend my youth!"[69] How different is this arrival onto the stage of history from the beginning of *The House of Ice*, with its florid invitation to enter Volynskii's carnivalesque court. The battles in *The Captain's Daughter*, too, are always somehow unimpressive; the reader is never allowed to forget the fortress's inadequate size, pitiable fortifications, and its defenders' agedness and insufficient training.[70] The city of Orenburg does not fare any better. The descriptions of military action are pitched so as to redirect the reader's imagination away from the warrior-trod terrain of novelistic romance and toward a milieu represented in more mundane archival materials. (Despite his own de-romanticizing stance, Scott had not entirely excised medieval bastions—but these were simply absent in Russia.) The book stands, that is, as the terse and unheroic documentary evidence of Pushkin's historiographical research—precisely the type of evidence he urged Lazhechnikov to heed more faithfully, and within which the novel is ultimately ironically situated, as yet another document, by the editorial remarks framing its end: "Petr Andreevich Grinev's manuscript was given to me by one of his grandsons, who had heard that I was engaged in a historical study of the times described by his grandfather."[71]

Grounded in several textual traditions, the protagonist himself is almost too familiar, having roots on the one hand in the Scottian middling hero and in types engendered by eighteenth-century Russian provincial life and portrayed with great caricaturistic wit by Denis Fonvizin and, on the other, in a real-life episode of the Pugachev war, with Grinev originating in events surrounding the renegade officer Mikhail Shvanvich.[72] Everything about him bespeaks the author's desire to render a legible Russian type from a particular epoch, instantly recognizable both as a familiar fictional character and a historical prototype. In a draft of his unfinished foreword, Pushkin remarks that the event at the basis of the novel was well known in the Orenburg province and that the reader would not find it difficult "to discern the thread of the real incident traced through novelistic inventions."[73] He thus identified recognition of the book's documentary basis as a possible, if not in fact the primary, reading strategy for his historical novel.

The orientation of *The Captain's Daughter* toward recognizable characters and settings seems largely responsible for its subsequent reception as a work whose foremost feature—whether one to be lauded or not depends on the commentator—is simplicity. Thus in a diary entry of October 31, 1853, Leo Tolstoy disappointedly remarks, "I have read *The Captain's Daughter*, and alas! I must confess that Pushkin's prose is now old—not the style, but the manner of exposition. Now, in the new direction, interest in details of feeling has rightly supplanted interest in events themselves. Pushkin's tales are somehow naked (*Povesti Pushkina goly kak-to*)."[74] Tolstoy assesses the novel thus at a moment

in Russian literary history when psychological portraiture has come to dominate fiction; but he does not seem to recognize that the lack of adornment
in Pushkin's writing, its "nakedness," does not in fact represent some earlier,
underdeveloped stage of Russian prose, but rather responds to and revises the
historical novel's tendency, both in its Scottian and freneticist versions, toward
hyper-ornamentation.[75]

A mere five years before this diary entry was made, Nikolai Gogol—who
unlike Tolstoy had to contend with the same state of Russian fiction that Pushkin had faced, but who as we know took a route very different from Pushkin's,
toward narrative excess—offers puzzling yet remarkably perceptive praise of
The Captain's Daughter in his treatise on the "essence of Russian poetry" (1847):

> The thought of a novel that would narrate a simple, artless tale (*bezyskustvennaia
> povest'*) of straightforward Russian life (*priamorusskaia zhizn'*) had lately preoc-
> cupied him incessantly. He gave up verse solely in order not to be distracted by
> anything on the side and to be simpler in his descriptions, and his prose itself he
> simplified to the point that his first tales were considered to be of no value. Pushkin
> was glad for this, and wrote *The Captain's Daughter*, decidedly the best Russian
> work in narrative form. Compared to *The Captain's Daughter*, all of our novels and
> tales seem a mawkish gruel. Purity and artlessness in it are taken to such a high level
> that reality itself seems artificial, a caricature by comparison. For the first time here
> stand forth truly Russian characters: the simple fortress commandant, the captain's
> wife, the first lieutenant; the fortress itself, with its single cannon, the confusion
> (*bestolkovshchina*) of the time and the simple grandeur of simple people—all of
> this is not just truth itself, but as it were better than it. That's how it should be: that
> is the calling of a poet, to take us out of ourselves and return us to ourselves in a
> purified and better form.[76]

Gogol presents Pushkin's mimesis—the preternatural correspondence of his
writing to Russian reality—as achieved not through re-presentation, but rather
through a distillation of Russian identity, "[taking] us out of ourselves and
[returning] us to ourselves in a purified and better form" (*iz nas zhe vziat'
nas i nas zhe vozvratit' nam v ochishchennom i luchshem vide*), a vertiginous
phrase that, in a manner typical of Gogol's art, metaphorically combines the
physical and the transcendent. Indeed, while Pushkin's citation of a manuscript acquired in the course of research suggests that his text could be approached with a scholarliness, a historically-minded focus on events of the
early 1770s, casting his work as precisely the sort of event-centered narrative

Tolstoy would later deem outdated, for the novel's original audiences of the 1830s–'40s, most eye-catching is its articulation of national character. This articulation is achieved through the erasure of anything typically considered novel-worthy in the mores of the novel's characters; the jocular deconstruction of all their potentially chivalric behavioral codes, such as the writing of love songs or the practice of dueling; and particularly through Grinev's language, which, as noted earlier, tends toward the folkloric. If Pushkin's is a poetics of recognition—and we have only begun to uncover the many ways in which it is—then Gogol's reading, echoed (albeit less idiosyncratically) by many around this time,[77] sees the main thrust of this poetics as directed at the national self rather than national history per se. While not psychological, this model of reading *The Captain's Daughter* emphasizes its foregrounding of characters, understood as bearers of a national character whose eighteenth-century manifestations are in no way alien from, but only clarifying to, Gogol's contemporaries' self-understanding.

How does Pushkin's poetics of recognition approach subjects the freneticists exploit for entertainment value? After all, if so far we have considered the ways this poetics shapes *The Captain's Daughter*'s distinct but overlapping readerships—cravers of historical knowledge, and of national self-knowledge—the most basic desire that, for instance, Walter Scott taps into with the publication of *Waverley* in 1814 is for history as divertissement. Let us turn, then, to the time-tested source of entertainment that is violence and the bodily harm it perpetrates.

Mutilated bodies were a privileged site of signification in the works of the freneticist school. In *The House of Ice*, a narrative not focused on warfare except of the secretive, virtually bloodless kind attending conspiracies, a middle-aged Gypsy named Mariula disfigures herself to erase all resemblance to her daughter, Volynskii's young beloved Marioritsa, whose state of being happily settled at Anna's court depends on the ruse that she comes from a princely Moldavian family. In a fit of maternal sacrifice, the Gypsy pours molten lead on her own face: "Her hand wanders . . . finally, she grabs the vial . . . the paper stopper is cast aside, and . . . my God! What has happened to her? . . . her eye is injured . . . molten lead cuts her cheek . . . her brain is pounding in her head as though her skull were being drilled . . . suns leap before the remaining eye . . . thousands of knives in her breast . . . And only a single moan, one solitary gnashing of the teeth are her tribute to all these torments; and among these torments, the faint, distant thought of Marioritsa! This thought triumphs over all!"[78] In a world teeming with spies and denunciations, even the testimony of one's face is treacherous. Lazhechnikov's characters constantly retreat into dark alcoves, hide under masks, and write anonymous letters and denunciations. Mutilation, then, represents at the same time an extreme act of rendering one's body nameless and unreadable and a radical claim to autonomy, to choosing whether to speak or not. It is also an especially important moment in *The House of Ice*, given the historical novel genre's constant quest for credible access points to history that might replace or even exceed those available to historiography proper. The mutilated body, that is, is a diachronic presence par excellence, a reminder of the time when the body was still intact, of the conditions of its disfigurement, and finally of the power of the observer to read the body's history beneath its ruins.

Lazhechnikov savors the very process of mutilation and its unsettling effect on the reader, who is shamelessly invited to observe. And yet, as Elaine Scarry has compellingly argued, "whatever pain achieves, it achieves in part through its unsharability, and it ensures this unsharability through its resistance to language."[79] It is just such ineffability that the freneticist novel proposes to overcome through excessive somaticization and visualization of its content. (In the previous section, we already saw it challenge this resistance in the domain of sexual experience.) It is precisely in the depiction of this process, in the breathless ellipses that mark the pain of Mariula's disfigurement, that novel asserts itself over document, for the progression of the Gypsy's suffering, even had she been a real historical personage (as neither she nor her daughter is), would have been inaccessible to history, which only registers the images of before and after. What is most private does not get "spun" by political chronicles; the reader is thus invited to interpret this scene as a climax of verisimilitude, of *golaia natura*, for it is in its shocking way even truer than history, albeit also one of the novel's most aestheticized episodes.

Characteristically, Pushkin foregrounds precisely pain's resistance to articulation, leaving the incursion of pain (of which there are all too many instances in this gory history) unnarrated because perhaps unnarratable, but using the mutilated body, instead, as a far more specific historical record. In *The Captain's Daughter*, the maimed subject is identified only to become once more a candidate for torture and maiming. This is the famous scene where the commandant of the Belogorsk fort interrogates his Bashkir captive:

> The Bashkir stepped across the threshold with difficulty (he was in irons) and, taking off his tall hat, remained standing by the door. I glanced at him and shuddered. I shall never forget this man. He appeared to be over seventy. His nose and ears

were missing. His head was shaved; in place of a beard he had a few gray hairs sticking out; he was small, thin and bent; but fire still sparkled in his narrow slit eyes.

"Aha!" said the commander, recognizing by the terrible marks one of the rebels punished in 1741. "So you're an old wolf who's been caught in our traps before. I can tell by your well-shorn nob, it's not the first time you've rioted."

And, just as his torture is about to commence, the narrative continues: "[T]he Bashkir gave out a moan in a weak, imploring voice and, shaking his head, opened his mouth, in which there was a truncated stump instead of a tongue."[80] Here too the mutilated body, a body that is marked, shuttles between past and present, recognizable as a sign, invariably activating the context of its mutilation, just as a branded animal, if it wanders from its herd, can always be returned to its rightful owner. The Bashkir's appearance provides the most legitimate occasion to trigger novelistic description, for not only is he foreign and therefore limited in his communication with the Russian officers, he is also physically unable to speak for himself, and his interrogators do the speaking, just as the historian or historical novelist might paraphrase his less forthcoming sources. The novel maintains our knowledge of the Bashkir at the same level as the knowledge of his observers within the novel; we do not feel his pain, as the freneticists would perhaps have us feel it, but rather interrogate him speechless as he is. In his awe, the protagonist Grinev reads the Bashkir as a historical representation, just as he reads and is puzzled by the history embodied in Pugachev's sinewy Cossack body. The body is here conceived as a symbolic document of history's pressures. The Bashkir's datable appearance is, moreover, a metric with which to mark Enlightenment's progress; the past is figured as exotic and barbaric, yet the danger of the Bashkir's being tortured again casts doubt on the distance traversed since such unreason. What happened in the savage year 1741 threatens to reoccur in the enlightened year 1774, or for that matter in the reader's contemporary moment in the 1830s, roiling with peasant unrest. The spectacle of torture, an opportunity Lazhechnikov would never have passed up, is preempted in this case by a prior mutilation; Pushkin pursues knowledge and access, rather than spectacle, but the truncated stump of the Bashkir's tongue proves to be more productive of spectacle than of knowledge. The Bashkir emerges as a historical cipher, a character whose life trajectory is easily gleaned from his appearance by the commander, narrator, and reader. Pushkin thus denies his reader a privileged, novelistic access to the past, exposing only that which can be seen through the restrictive window of history (read historiography), but this vision is directed at a particularly painful and poignant site, the tortured, tongueless, alien body of a nameless subaltern, one for whom historiography has no place.

The poetics of recognition is encoded in the Bashkir's body. Though he cannot speak, his appearance intimates the entirety of his story, verisimilar yet unmentioned in any history of the early 1740s and Elizabeth's tumultuous accession to the throne. Similarly, as Alexander Ospovat has demonstrated, clues pointing to this earlier history are interspersed throughout *The Captain's Daughter*: Grinev's father, for example, was most likely implicated in the Volynskii case.[81] Thus, the gentle reign of Catherine harbors troublesome memories of, or even resemblances to, the merciless reign of Anna, and *The Captain's Daughter* remembers *The House of Ice*. These multiple reverberations configure Russian history, and specifically the eighteenth century, in traces and echoes. Many critics have noted that Pushkin's work on the Pugachev uprising coincided with the peasant unrest of the early 1830s, and they therefore plausibly inferred that his interest in the would-be Peter III was grounded in contemporary concerns. If popular uprisings recurred in amorphous and ominous waves, Russian aristocratic dissatisfaction with the monarchy, too, had its historical cycles, its expressions similarly displeasing to officialdom and passable through the censorship only in faint traces. Thus, just as the entertaining violence of the freneticist novel exposed it to accusations of political subversion, the poetics of recognition, too, harbored dissident potential, enabling a code by which unsettling historical parallels could be drawn, and the Russian timeline imbued with a most disturbing coherence.

Other literary concerns aside, the coded historical knowledge that distinguished Pushkin's texts from those of Scott or the freneticists most obviously stemmed from the former's unique situation of working directly under the eyes of his most powerful potential reader; this singular audience himself embodied a peculiar inheritance from the eighteenth century—that of patron/censor, in this case of the supremest rank. As state historiographer, and a writer whose every work had to pass Nicholas I's personal muster, Pushkin wielded a hitherto unprecedented familiarity with documents of recent Russian history and, at the same time, only the most limited leeway to make them public.[82] His primary audience was not the new mass readership that created the demand for the historical novel and informed its specifications, but the monarch, alternatively chastising and encouraging almost according to whim; and it was no doubt to bypass this particular reader that Pushkin first published his novel anonymously. Nicholas I was, as we know, not immune to the attractions of historical fiction: he even suggested on one occasion that Pushkin rework *Boris Godunov* as a novel à la Scott. In the system of patronage, historical writing was judged by its conformity to the requirements of the patron's self-conception and, therefore, both fictional and non-fictional historical writing was scrutinized first and foremost for its informative gist, not for its "poetry." Not only does the poetics of recognition smuggle unwanted knowledge past the censor, it also thematizes the very constraints that patronage and censorship impose on representation. The maimed Bashkir speaks through his body when deprived of physical speech, and his message is not what the commandant wants to hear; in fact, it rejects the very invitation to communicate. Moreover, as a purely novelistic construct, a mutilated body is a spectacular site that the censor, just like Captain Mironov, may neglect to examine. But in Pushkin's novelistic economy, every detail is potentially eloquent. Indeed, the Bashkir is set free only to rejoin Pugachev's adherents and wreak vengeance. Like sexuality, violence provides a point of access to history. For Lazhechnikov, it is also an opportunity to gratify his spectacle-hungry reader with shocking representation. For Pushkin, by contrast, it offers a chance to probe the violated body for its ability to gesture at what is unspoken and unspeakable, to sneakily disclose fragments of unnerving but familiar history. Pushkin's history addresses not primarily the immediate impressions of the eye, as does Lazhechnikov's, but rather, *through* sight, the associative and deductive mind, encouraging it to examine the surfaces of historical representation and documentation for signs of the deeper nexi they may repress.

We could adduce numerous other features of the novel that bespeak its structural convergence around echoes and moments of recognition or distillation. The executions of Captain Mironov and Emelian Pugachev that book-end the text have been treated in scholarship as covert reminders of the Decembrist executions that inaugurated Nicholas's reign and the autocratic power structure persisting virtually unchanged, though not unchallenged, from the eighteenth to the nineteenth century.[83] The images of severed heads (Iulai's and Pugachev's) are similarly positioned, the former as a fictional harbinger of the latter, the latter as a historical reminder of the former. When we learn that Grinev attends the "execution of Pugachev, who recognized him in the crowd and acknowledged him with a nod of his head, which in another minute was displayed to the people lifeless and bloodied,"[84] this image in the course of a single sentence manages to reference both the entire story of Grinev's acquaintance with the pretender (in which his head implies the face and mind of a human being and fictional character) and the known history of Pugachev's capture and punishment (in which the head metonymizes the object of state sanction), thus binding together the novel's fictional and historical layers. The gallows is likewise an image ubiquitous in the novel: it is noticed almost in passing at various locations, sung about prophetically in a Cossack song, mentioned by Pugachev, and incessantly invoked by Grinev himself as a kind of elegiac anchor to his experience ("The gallows with its victims loomed dark and terrifying"; "I cannot describe what effect this song about the gallows, sung by people destined for the gallows, had on me"; "I left Pugachev and went out on the street. [. . .] The moon and the stars shone brightly, illuminating the square and the gallows"[85]). Repeated as a motif or a shibboleth, the gallows acquires a ritualistic dimension wherein a single word induces the frisson of the ineffable workings of history. The Scottian and freneticist novels' descriptive overabundance is here subjected to a radical abridgement, whereby images, expressed by single words, are engaged in a complex system of echoes.

Of all the ways we detect Pushkin creating what I call here a "literature of recognition," perhaps the most crucial is the novel's recognition of its own status as literature, specifically as post-Scottian historical fiction. One of the signature features of the historical novel as practiced by Scott and the regiment of writers he had "trained up" is its number of pages—about five hundred—and the narrative possibilities concomitant with this length; while such a work is not yet quite a multi-plot novel, it is certainly a novel that requires a strong, most typically third-person narrative voice to sustain the many twists and turns in its plot. In Scott's *Waverley*, for example, this voice is capacious enough to mediate ironically between the history of the 1745 Jacobite uprising and the story of the protagonist's Bildung. Countering these conventions, Pushkin offers a hundred-page first-person narrative, where every potential opportunity for a Scott-like excess of local color, or for a freneticist emotional surplus, is passed up; it is as if Waverley were left to speak on his own, without any narrator, to explain his own disoriented movement through history or register the exotic flavors and sites of the past. On the one hand, *The Captain's Daughter* is presented as Grinev's memoir and, therefore, as I have suggested earlier, points to Pushkin's historiographical project and to the pursuits of antiquarianism generally. Indeed, as Alexander Dolinin suggests, "The ideal reader Pushkin addresses in *The Captain's Daughter* needs to know his *History of the Pugachev Uprising* and juxtapose the novelistic events transpiring in the conditional time of fiction with their historical analogues and prototypes."[86] This proximity of fiction and non-fiction intimates the synecdochal relation of Grinev's tale to the collection of Pugachev-related materials Pushkin has amassed that purportedly includes it; and it raises the possibility of not reading the novel as a novel at all. On the other hand, by playing with this very frame, Pushkin also inscribes himself precisely in the tradition of Scottian fabrication. Why, then, is Pushkin's Scottian novel so much shorter than Scott's? Given my reading's insistence on the text's self-awareness, its repeated staging of moments that are recognizable rather than new, my answer should come as no surprise: *The Captain's Daughter* relates to the Waverley novels as an ironic signifier to a well-known signified. The text stages the recognition of the genre in which it proposes to participate as well as the recognition of its very participation in that genre (through the many parallels with Walter Scott's texts), but in the process Pushkin's text revises this genre's parameters and questions its purchase on Russian history. What is created through repetition and abridgment is not a shorter Scottian novel, but that novel's critique.

How far ago is "sixty years since"? How distant was the eighteenth century from the 1830s? The historical novel in the first decades of the nineteenth century enabled a long-lasting recalibration of vision, such that this question could now be answered in a variety of ways and through recourse to a range of narrative techniques of resuscitation, rapprochement, or exoticization. For Lazhechnikov, the past—however visceral the sensations, however profusely descriptive the detail through which it is accessed—remains "a foreign country" to be marveled at, its relationship to his contemporary moment everywhere elusive. For Pushkin, the ties between the Nikolaevan present and Catherine's or even Anna's past remain unbreached, sometimes in ways that make for an uncomfortable, stifling sense of déjà vu—at least in *The Captain's Daughter*, for, as we shall see in the next chapter, "The Queen of Spades" confronts its reader with other, though in no way contrary, scenarios of periodization.

5

Mimetic Temporalities
Fashion from the Eighteenth Century to Pushkin's "The Queen of Spades"

Старинная мода есть любопытный антик; переменившаяся мода страшный скелет; царствующая мода новый и свежий цветок.

—*The Herald of Europe*, "Something on Fashion" (1813)

THE SUBJECT AND TIME OF FASHION

In Russia, fashion was coerced into becoming a visible mechanism of social regulation in the eighteenth century.[1] Vestimentary decrees were among the earliest and arguably most peremptory acts of Petrine westernization. In 1701, having mandated the Hungarian caftan for his Moscow courtiers less than two years prior, Peter ordered all Muscovites and Moscow visitors, with the exception of the clergy and peasants, to switch to German attire, described in exacting detail in his decree, which instituted a system of penalties for those who continued to wear or make Russian-style clothing. This law rearranged native categories of social distinction manifested by clothing choice, abandoning ethnicity- and estate-specific Russian costume in favor of a new contrast between urban and rural populations. Modernization was cast as a city privilege (and affliction). In 1705 came Peter's most famous injunction, the one against beards, which again visibly polarized Russian society, with one class servicing the state and thus conforming to its regulations on appearance, and others—the clergy, merchantry, and peasantry—exempt from the breakneck pace of westernization.[2] Different segments of the population now lived according to ostensibly different historical timelines: the modern Western versus the archaic Russian.

Peter's legislation, strictly speaking, had little to do with fashion per se, as this concept entails some freedom of choice coexisting with conformity to dominant trends.³ But in introducing his elite to Western modes of dress, Peter also set in motion a new temporality of change this class would experience: a temporality that was externalized, wearable, foreign, unpredictable, and ultimately accelerated. Designed to secure the permanence of the new clothing style, these laws instead paved the way for constant sartorial adjustments that, appearing with increasing frequency as the eighteenth century wore on, would correspond only tangentially to broader political transformations. Rarely if ever again would a change in clothing styles in Russia amount to a virtual revolution on the scale of the Petrine transformation, an exceptional moment when a makeover in appearance aligned completely with the political one. Keeping up with Western fashion soon meant attuning oneself to a regime of changes inconsistent with any local Russian developments and only marginally related to local history. After all, fashion, operating as it does on a fundamentally smaller scale than political and cultural revolutions, creates a temporality of constant superficial modifications that nevertheless conserve and recycle the basic shapes and principles of dress. Compared to the temporalities we have encountered thus far (the revolutionary temporality of Petrine reforms or the French Revolution; the cyclical temporality of odic allegory; the progressive temporality implicit in historical fiction), fashion is far more restless, fickle, and fine-tuned. Its changes recalibrate historical time and follow their own logic or even, as its critics repeatedly complain, defy reason altogether; as a result, the history of appearances matches political history only somewhat. Fashion counters the understanding of historical time focused on political process—and thus abstracted from and overwhelming to the individual—with history rooted in the experience of the everyday and perceived as variety and flux. If history is "public time," fashion is private time on public display.⁴

By the mid-eighteenth century, even as the vast majority of the Russian population is still hardly cognizant of what it means to follow fashion (or of the fluctuations it introduces into the experience of personal and historical time), the most affluent members of the Russian elite not only adopt European fashion culture, but espouse it to excess, even by the showy standards of aristocratic Europe. The requirement to serve resulted in the transference of Russian noblemen from their country estates—where they had belonged to a system of signification foregrounding their immediate milieu, interpersonal relations, and neighborly allegiances—to a new semiotic environment emphasizing conspicuous consumption. Once in urban centers, they entered a world with different structures of belonging and social hierarchy, in many ways signaled through fashionable display. If Peter I's clothing advertised a westernization to a great extent oriented toward states with strong or at least fledgling bourgeois traditions, the disproportionately large wardrobe of his daughter Elizabeth (r. 1741–62) pointed to a different understanding of westernization, geared toward the importation of aristocratic luxury and the culture of courtly display, particularly from France. Noted scholar of Russian economic history Arcadius Kahan identifies three stages of developmental change in the eighteenth century: "from 1700 to 1725, the Petrine period, a period of rapid institutional change and economic growth; 1725–1762, a period of consolidation and continuity after the one of extreme effort; and the third period, after 1762, a period of growth and 'liberalization.'"[5] Eighteenth-century Russian fashion history follows a similar outline: first the Petrine period of vestimentary legislation, then consolidation and even excessive fashion implementation by Elizabeth in the middle of the century, and finally, under Catherine II (1762–96), a period of native development and critique culminating in outright official repudiation of luxury (specifically of its French forms) during Paul I's reign.

During the reign of Elizabeth social commentators begin to apprehend fashion—sartorial, behavioral, and linguistic—as a convenient stand-in for other, often more weighty and less officially permissible, targets of cultural malaise.[6] Under Catherine II, it emerges as one of the central topics of the still tentative public discussions, directly encouraged by Catherine's particular brand of westernization. As a polemical focal point, fashion was particularly well-suited for communicating the delicate distinction between the forceful and appearance-oriented Petrine westernization and its discourse-oriented Catherinian extension; the latter strove to alter mentalities from within, to bring transformations as profound as Peter's, but less violent and more mindful of Russian national specificity. To quote Viazemskii's clever formula, "A Russian endeavored to make Germans out of us, and a German (*nemka*) wanted to make us over into Russians."[7] Both fashion and its critique were imports from the West, but the former became associated with Petrine reforms and the latter with the Catherinian "public sphere," however limited this realm might have appeared in comparison to that of Paris and London. Western appearances originated with Peter; the apparatus for their critique evolved under Catherine.

The censure of luxury that Russia inherits from Europe together with luxury itself is, as with most such inheritances, imported very selectively and considerably adapted. In France and England, the enemies of fashion's ubiquitous glamour comment on the new superficiality, acquisitiveness, and feminization of urban culture.[8] Conservative political commentators see fashion as one of the main culprits in the erosion of social hierarchies; in this view, fashion lays disturbingly bare "the mechanisms which register social mimesis."[9] In Europe, fashion emerges as an enabler and, subsequently, one of the most visible indicators of the rise of the bourgeoisie and its encroachment upon aristocratic privilege. More generally, as a value system of sorts, fashion reveals, beneath culture's material façade—beneath transient and perishable bodies, fabrics, surfaces—its deep-seated and otherwise intangible foundations (symbols, mimesis, desire). As society's palpable metonym, fashion thus becomes eighteenth-century European social critics' pet subject. And in Russia, fashion critique is certainly as euphemistic as in the rest of Europe,[10] but inevitably anchored in different social realities and discourse. For one thing, the bourgeoisie had famously not truly arisen in Russia even by the mid-nineteenth century, let alone the eighteenth. As a result, social mimesis—fashion's basic modus operandi—is in Russia a process whereby not the bourgeoisie but the lower or more provincial strata of the gentry emulate the aristocratic elite, which in turn encourages (if guardedly) this imitation. Such trend-following thus serves primarily to bring members of the same class closer, rather than extend some shaky bridge *between* classes; it is, moreover, explicitly directed outward, to the West, rather than self-contained as in France, the arbiter of European taste. This kind of social mimesis, essentially restricted to the gentry and oriented toward Europe, was part and parcel of the cultural mimesis put into practice by Petrine westernization and profoundly internalized by the end of Catherine's reign.

Fashion's changeability and apparent randomness, together with the vice of luxury implicit in its pursuit, habitually drew fire from its detractors, both in Russia and the West. But Russian social commentators, as we have seen, had additional reasons for resisting fashion's allure. Fashion in eighteenth-century Russia meant modernization; it pointed to a specific view of Russia's place in Europe and to specific beliefs about the nation's historical course. On the one hand, fashion was indeed erratic, random, and superfluous; yet, on the other, it was excessively meaningful, almost overdetermined. The two temporalities of political and sartorial history in this case became uniquely interchangeable. Moreover, both the westernization of aristocratic appearances mandated by Peter at the start of the century and the subsequent eighteenth-century critique of fashion were premised on one basic interpretive substitution. In a period so profoundly vested in cultural self-definition, dress was seen to reflect more or less directly the political, social, and moral identities of its Russian wearers, identities that might not have otherwise met the eye, but that needed to be proclaimed.

The choice of attire thus indexed a whole array of other, arguably more meaningful, personal and communal choices. When read in this context, Paul I's authoritarian and ultimately futile attempts to reroute Russian fashion away from France, preposterous though they might have seemed, were rooted in this common conception of fashion as manifesting ideology and were perfectly understandable in the wake of the French Revolution, the political upheaval that in France itself amounted to a complete overhaul of conventions in dress.[11] In the first days of his reign, Paul I issued decrees aimed against the latest European clothing styles, which for him embodied the dangerous ideology of the French Revolution as well as the unwelcome remnants of his mother's power. Paul I objected not only or not even primarily to the *sans-culottes*—this "barbaric" style had by then in any case been relegated to the past, the first year or two immediately after the Revolution—but rather to all French fashion, endorsing, instead, the styles and luxuries of a different *ancien régime*: the heritage of Frederick the Great. The prolific Pushkin-era memoirist Filipp Vigel recalls: "Paul took up arms against round hats, tail-coats, vests, trousers, shoes and boots with tops, strictly prohibited wearing them and ordered them replaced with single-breasted caftans with a stand-up collar, three-cornered hats, camisoles, short undergarments, and Hessian boots."[12] Princess Dorothea Lieven mentions another instance of this perceived equation between certain clothing items and specific ideological positions: "Vests are outlawed. The emperor said that it was the vests that perpetrated the French Revolution (*imenno zhilety sovershili frantsuzskuiu revoliutsiiu*)."[13] Paul's astounding determination to regulate the seemingly trivial dictates of fashion evinces the great symbolic value he and his contemporaries attached to dress. Even if stand-up collars and Hessian boots made Russians look out of sync with the rest of contemporary Europe, they also advertised Russia's immunity to the "French contagion."[14] Unsurprisingly, the contagion proved uncontainable, and French fashions returned very soon after Paul's death in March 1801, asserting their independent course.

By the early nineteenth century, as fashion industries all across Europe expanded and clothing trends underwent increasingly frequent makeovers, the correspondence between individual material possessions and political positions or even selfhood became ever more tenuous. Fashions simply changed too rapidly, and the self (a concept crystallizing precisely in this period), if it were to be premised on integrity of worldview, was presumably less adaptable than ever-changing appearances. In relating news of European trends, early nineteenth-century Russian journals such as *The Herald of Europe* (*Vestnik Evropy*), which ran a column on fashion in almost every issue appearing in the 1800s–'10s, or *The Moscow Mercury* (*Moskovskii Merkurii*), whose only four installments were published in 1803 and focused exclusively on fashion, transformed fashion into a discourse only vaguely concerned with the issue of westernization. This discourse still originated in the West, specifically in Paris (most such articles were reprinted from French sources), nor could it have been otherwise, for Russia had yet to develop either a full-scale fashion and luxury industry or trend-setting and dissemination mechanisms of its own.[15] But the news items themselves, focusing as they did on the minutest and numerous modifications in trendy colors, fabrics, and styles, compelled readers to acknowledge fashion's autonomous, even distracting, claim on modern attention.

If in the eighteenth century fashion critique had in fact voiced Aesopian challenges to modernization, early nineteenth-century fashion's presence in the life of the Russian elite could no longer be wished away: it had become an integral part of this class's daily life and even reading. Now fashion critique was increasingly directed at urban life, rather than at westernization. Russia's relationship with the West, on the other hand, also had to be defined against the backdrop of a very different political reality, a reality dissociated from Petrine cultural importation by the far more pressing challenges of the French Revolution and the entire Napoleonic era. While in the early 1700s Peter combated Russia's isolation from the rest of Europe, a century later the Russian elite's awareness of and involvement in European cultural politics was all too intense, even if still mixed with an equally intense sense of belatedness. And modernity itself—in the eighteenth century so unilaterally mandated through autocratic force and implemented by policing appearances—had by the early nineteenth century graduated from policy to actuality. Thus, early nineteenth-century Russian fashions no longer point beyond themselves (at least, not as a rule) or toward the question of modernization.

The Romantic understanding of fashion, moreover, does not emphasize its ability to externalize political affiliations; rather, the Romantics use sartorial practices to exemplify the disjuncture between the self's private aspiration and public expression (with the individual understood as always compelled and constrained by the social world around him, ever oppressed by it and fighting to overcome it). Fashionable appearance, therefore, is found to be in tension with the individual's identity rather than dependably expressing his outlook.

While the emblematic figures of Russian fashion critique in the eighteenth century are the *petimetr* (petit-maître) and the *shchegol'* (fop), the Romantic age replaces them with the figure of the *dendi* (dandy).[16] Lacking in psychological depth, the eighteenth-century types epitomize the shallowness of Russian cultural mimicry, whereas the dandy, determined to avoid the blunders of excess and bad taste, embodies the post-revolutionary suppression of character in the *comme il faut*, the limits placed on the ideal of authenticity, and the resultant disarticulation of the subject. Further separating the two figures and the two epochs they embody is what the influential psychoanalytic historian of appearances J. C. Flügel has called "the Great Masculine Renunciation," an early nineteenth-century taming of male dress, which resulted in an unprecedented divide between the expressive and colorful female and the subdued, uniform-like male costume of the nineteenth century, a dichotomy nothing in the eighteenth century had anticipated.[17] At the very least, the male dress of the Romantic period problematized, rather than facilitating, the identification of private with public character, of person with dress. By contrast, the flamboyant eighteenth-century dress now seemed impracticable, a naïve product of a more optimistic age, when private and public identities had been uncomplicatedly fused. The new nineteenth-century modernity looked different from what was proclaimed in the eighteenth century: by fashion's peculiar logic, the appearances that had only recently seemed new and even radical now appeared not only insufficiently radical, but even antiquated.

Not only did nineteenth-century men in uniform and women in dishabille look distinctly unlike their eighteenth-century forebears and each other, the very range of fashion's signification appears to have expanded as well. Sir Walter Scott's novels, omnipresent and influential across a host of intellectual disciplines and behavioral practices, indirectly contributed to the historicization of fashion. In ballrooms and at masquerades, Scott's devotees donned costumes similar to those described in his novels; his use of "local color" and ekphrastic description (including dress) furthermore suggested a new understanding of fashion as conveying information about history and the epochal spirit. Thus, fashion choices now inscribed the individual in a specific historical period. On the psycho-sociological level, fashion came to articulate an entire spectrum of attitudes of the individual toward society, from acceptance to *ressentiment*. Recall, for example, Onegin and Pechorin, the Russian Romantic novel's eternally conflicted protagonists, who cultivate appearances—be they Western or Caucasian—that mask the fundamental disharmonies in their selves and render both their characters and their Russian identities increasingly inaccessible.

More important for this study is the fact that, in addition to connoting the class affiliations and aspirations fashion had long externalized in Europe[18] and the cultural mimesis it had promoted specifically in eighteenth-century Russia, particular clothing choices now signified the individual's epochal belonging and, by extension, the historicity of everyday experience. In the first quarter of the nineteenth century, if only for a brief time, the categories of identity implicit in fashionable display thus became muddled and hard to read—though not for long.

The next important shift in the history of fashion's representation and interpretation occurs toward the middle of the nineteenth century, with the ascendancy of a particular kind of novelistic narrative concerned with social and psychological observation and representation. This early realist narrative is epitomized most amply and influentially by the works of Honoré de Balzac, whose descriptive strategies in turn find great resonance, though not always acceptance, among his Russian contemporaries.[19] In the preface to *The Human Comedy*, Balzac explains his magisterial project's approach to the artifacts of material culture and private life: "I attach to common daily facts, hidden or patent to the eye, to the acts of individual lives and to their causes and principles, the importance which historians have ascribed to the events of public national life."[20] The relationship of a writer to private life is here understood as homologous to a historian's relationship to the life of the nation: this correlation is already implicit in the historical novels of Scott, who masterfully combines the two objects of novelistic inquiry.[21] Moreover, the private sphere itself is presented as a system of signs where the material world signifies the still more private domain of the individual psyche; Balzac declares as his object "men and the material expressions of their minds."[22] Fashion blurred the line between the physical and symbolic body, encouraging not just consumption, but a constant scrutiny of others' appearance as well. Dress—which Balzac's novels describe in great detail—becomes an integral (and often the most basic) step in framing the historical and social existence of Balzacian character types. In the next chapter, we will see a similar approach to characterization surfacing in the work of Ivan Turgenev, who, though hardly a Balzac enthusiast, often employs attire to refine the epochal distinctions that are his primary focus. In this chapter, I will demonstrate that Pushkin expands the range of meanings that clothing distinctions can connote in fiction, drawing on, but in some ways exceeding Balzac's achievement. To return to my general sketch of the history of fashion representation: the realist novel, and the Balzacian novel of manners in particular, ever intent on integrating description with narration, invites readings of fashion that again, as in the eighteenth century, insist on the semblance of character and appearance, only now this semblance is conceived along multiple interpretive lines. When mid-nineteenth-century novelists appropriate fashion as an instrument of their characters' social representation, novel readers are asked to associate descriptions of appearances with entire clusters of finely catalogued social, psychological, and historical identities. The same process of association is also involved in parsing the interiors these characters inhabit, as well as all their miscellaneous belongings.

In this type of novel the profusion of detail in descriptions of persons and the spaces they inhabit is justified, despite the requirements of narrative economy, by the implied equation between the individual and his or her consumption practices. Novelistic characters, understood as both individuals and types, are shown to possess objects that distinguish them from others and, through these very possessions, represent the tastes of their generation and social milieu. This practice of mutually dependent individuation and typification is amply documented in novel theory, particularly in discussions of novelistic character.[23] But it is also an important moment in fashion history, for this literary practice is especially well-adapted to representing the process of history as that of the change in appearances; after all, fashion too is premised on the coexistence of the conflicting desires for both individual distinction and social coherence. This dynamic, as cultural historian and fashion theorist Daniel Roche suggests, is characteristic above all of the nineteenth century, "a period when both anonymity and the individual were promoted, thus bringing into play two, to some extent contradictory, animating principles: the quest for a distinctive appearance and that for uniformity and conformity."[24] These two impulses in fact create the central tensions both in fashionable display and in novelistic characterization.

For the nineteenth-century novelists who enlisted realist representation to understand and order the relationship between text and world, material culture became an important site where literary mimesis could register the complex operations of social mimesis, rather than simply mirror a specific reality or signal the real as in Roland Barthes' seminal argument on the "reality effect."[25] Through its descriptive excess, the realist text captured the very desire for social mimicry and advancement particularly characteristic of Balzacian France and its narratives of upwardly mobile young men. In Russia of the 1830s and '40s, this European experiment with fashion as socio-literary form—an experiment that ostensibly seeks to dispense with formal construction in favor of mimetic mirroring—encountered additional challenges. The very character of Russian historical and social reality was as much a source of anxiety as the future of the Russian narrative, its forms, content, and ideological purpose on the eve of the Great Russian novel. The history of belatedness and imitation, counterposed in the Nikolaevan Russia of the 1830s–'40s by such redemptive nationalist agendas as Sergei Uvarov's "orthodoxy, autocracy, nationality," called for these early realist narratives to at least hint at a stance on Russia's *cultural mimetic* relationship to Europe, the Russian "text" vis-à-vis the European "world." And here eighteenth-century fashions, so clearly emerging out of a particular program of westernization and also so visibly obsolete, provide an ideal testing ground for this Russian version of the realist experiment, directing the mimetic literary lens at the nexus of social *and* cultural mimetic practices that configure post-Petrine Russian modernity.

Having sketched the major cultural shifts that transformed eighteenth-century fashions into stand-ins for the *ancien régime* and for Russian westernization, and into objects of nineteenth-century writers' observation and historical analysis, this chapter now turns to two case studies of the afterlife of eighteenth-century material culture in Russian literature of the first half of the nineteenth century. The first examines interpretations, published in early nineteenth-century Russian journals, that incriminate fashion and luxury in the wake of the French Revolution and thus signal the subsequent epoch's separation from the *ancien régime*. The second zeroes in on the trappings of the encounter between the old Countess (the age of Catherine) and Hermann (the age of Nicholas) in "The Queen of Spades" and argues that this most read of Pushkin's novellas is a text that thinks through mimesis in its various interconnected forms: cultural, social, and literary.

LUXURY AND REVOLUTION

The early nineteenth century in Russia saw a proliferation of periodicals, some short-lived, some that would shape the voices of Russian journalism for decades to come. Not surprisingly, one of the central topics addressed by the more serious of these publications was the Enlightenment and the value for Russia of Western thought and life, only recently rendered suspect by the French Revolution. Was it desirable, or indeed even possible, to discard imported cultural forms, which included products not only of Western thought, but also of the Parisian fashion industry, the latter in a sense more difficult to disown? The *Herald of Europe*, a biweekly started by Karamzin in 1802, embodied an affirmation of Russian westward-oriented Enlightenment. The

journal chronicled European events, running original Russian-language articles alongside reprinted news as well as historical and political commentary
from numerous foreign sources. It also published a regular column titled "A
Letter from Paris" ("Pis'mo iz Parizha"), which commented in minutest detail
on current affairs in the "capital of the world," and featured in almost every
issue the column "On Fashion" ("O mode"), which detailed trends in attire as
thoroughly as the journal's other coverage did political developments. Titled so
as to polemicize with Karamzin's publication, Sergei Glinka's *Russian Herald*
(*Ruskoi* [sic][26] *vestnik*, 1808–20, 1824) offered the most contentious assessments of eighteenth-century Russian history (if couched, at the same time, in
the most patriotic terms), of Russia's modernization and relationship to the
West (France in particular), advocating domestic models of education and
comportment. As part of its critique of mores, the journal also censured fashions, to which it opposed virtues more lasting and universal. Thus, in the journal's miscellany section, Glinka placed not a single mention of fashion, but
published instead news of charitable activities, particularly those undertaken
in the Russian provinces. His focus on virtue also had a historical pathos, often
referring his reader back as far as pre-Petrine times.[27] Finally, Glinka also
voiced an antipathy for novels, echoing widespread eighteenth-century criti-
cisms that again became topical (if only briefly) after the French Revolution:
novels were seen as the most insidiously fashionable, and hence virtueless,
spawn of Europe. As Glinka proclaims in his *Russian Herald*'s first issue, which
was something of a manifesto for those to follow, "We have seen what these
novels, these dreams of an inflamed and conceited imagination, have led to
(*k chemu priveli sii romany*). And so, taking note of present-day mores, education, customs, fashions, etc., we will counter them not with novelistic fictions,
but with the mores and customs of our forefathers."[28] As was typical in such
arguments, the calamity that novels, Enlightenment philosophy (referred to
throughout the journal as *lzheumstvovanie* or "false philosophizing"), fantasies, and fashionable display had "led to" was the French Revolution, which
in the early 1800s proves the most challenging stumbling block, albeit also
an interesting one, for commentators on fashion. Glinka's is a rather simple
argument, grounded in the kinds of familiar binary oppositions—Russia vs. the
West, native vs. foreign, virtue vs. vice, reality vs. fiction, the time-honored
vs. the fashionable—that Iurii Lotman and Boris Uspenskii have proposed as
characteristic of pre-nineteenth century Russian culture.[29] But his rhetoric is
remarkable for its consistency, for the wide range of phenomena to which these
binaries are applied, and for the nationalist vocabulary it devises.

Writing in the *Herald of Europe* about French society, fashion, and the Revolution, Karamzin no doubt drew upon his experiences as a youthful sentimentalist traveler through Europe of the revolutionary period, his impressions having been recorded in the famous *Letters of a Russian Traveler* (*Pis'ma russkogo puteshestvennika*, 1791), the single most cited testimony to the immediate aftermath of the Revolution by a Russian writer. In the *Letters*, Karamzin, himself a man of fashion, waxes nostalgic for the luxury he had learned to associate with France, but which he finds seemingly banished from the streets of Paris upon his arrival in 1790: "Paris today is not what it was. A threatening storm swirls above its towers and darkens the brilliance of this once sumptuous city. The golden luxury that formerly reigned over it as its favorite capital—that golden luxury, lowering a black veil over its sad face, has vanished into the air and hidden behind the clouds; one faint ray of its brilliance has remained, which barely shines on the horizon like the dying light of dusk. The horrors of the revolution have chased the richest residents from Paris . . ."[30] Karamzin might be deifying luxury here, describing its disappearance from Paris as a kind of mournful apotheosis in the style of Classicist allegories; indeed, this description seems couched in the allegorical imagination of the eighteenth century. Another, less alienated, observer, François-René de Chateaubriand, perceives not a figurative obscuring of glitter by gloom but a bewildering coexistence of clothing styles, a kind of sartorial sedimentation: "Walking beside a man in a French coat, with powdered hair, a sword at his side, a hat under his arms, pumps and silk stockings, one could see a man wearing his hair short and without powder, an English dress-coat and an American cravat."[31] This new social landscape which erases (yet also foregrounds) the distinctions that dress used to advertise and perpetuate would later be codified in revolutionary legislation: "No-one may constrain any citizen or citizenness to dress in a particular manner, on pain of being regarded as suspect and so treated, and prosecuted as a disturber of the public peace; everyone is free to wear whatever garment or whatever outfit of their sex they please."[32] Ultimately, this legislation in fact enabled a revival of fashion, only now not primarily as a mechanism of social regulation. In 1797, fashion magazines reappeared in France, and soon the capital of couture was back on its feet.

Indeed, while to Karamzin fashion appeared to register the ebb and flow of politics much faster than any other cultural institution, it was also able, he noted, to proceed along its own course, oblivious even to the most earth-shattering political transformations. Acting unperturbed, after all, was an imperative of good taste. In the same observations on Paris in 1790, Karamzin good-naturedly remarks on the easily-distracted attention of Frenchmen, their astonishing ability to go right on participating in inconsequential literary and artistic debates while utterly ignoring pivotal political events. A decade later, Karamzin reiterates this observation in the *Herald of Europe*, now applying it to fashion, and himself committing the same sin of distraction, jumbling (sometimes literally, in the "Miscellany" ["Smes'"] section) reports of Napoleon's Egyptian campaign with fashion news. In the very first issue, Karamzin publishes side-by-side a translation of a French article entitled "A History of the French Revolution, Selected from Latin Writers," and a short piece, also lifted from a French magazine, on the latest fashion for wigs, whose surge in popularity the article erroneously ascribes to the Terror (on which more below). If the former text endows the Revolution with historical depth, in the latter contemporary fashions yield a different kind of commentary. The ancients present epic parallels to revolutionary upheavals, but the trifling, stereotypically "French" fuss over surfaces and appearances mitigates the destructive thrust of revolutionary terror, in a sense explaining away purportedly world-altering events as the result of a change in hairstyles. Instead of leading to a radically new political order, or to a sweeping alteration in human behavior, the Revolution eventuates merely in *new* fashions. With the benefit of hindsight, the Revolution is reconceived as hardly more than a call for a theatrical change of costume.

Mocking the latest vogue for wigs, the article traces their popularity to the grim events of the Terror: "The Parisian origin of this fashion is well known. A lover, mother, sister, daughter, deprived by Robespierre's guillotine of their lover, son, brother, father, wanted to preserve at least some sad remnants of their beloved, and bought their hair from the executioner and adorned themselves with it. But these hapless victims are already forgotten, yet the wigs remain. [. . .] O times! O mores!"[33] As mediators between different individuals in the body social, wigs highlighted some of the anxieties connected to consumer culture. Fashion and commerce have a troublesome leveling effect on sentiment and memory. An *au courant* Frenchman wears wigs, but forgets the victims they allegedly represent. However short-lived, fashionable commodities in their circulation still paradoxically exceed the duration of human life. Furthermore, if sentiment is individuated and specific—note all the singulars in the passage: "a lover, mother, sister, daughter"—fashionable objects begin to signify only *en masse* ("wigs"). To whom does the wig really belong—its wearer, or the donor of the hair? And what happens in the interpersonal and temporal gap between the two?[34] In eighteenth-century pamphlets, wigs are repeatedly questioned as a commodity that binds two individuals unknown to one another: if a criminal's hair makes up a wig for a young innocent, does it carry with it some psychological and behavioral residue of its original owner, potentially corrupting an otherwise right-thinking and upright girl? Karamzin seems to puzzle over precisely the disappearance of the residue, the precariousness of memory as transmitted (or not) through a purchasable object. The victim is entirely obliterated, and soon enough the wig loses its commemorative function and, as a mass-produced object, denotes trend-consciousness rather than historical awareness.

The same can be said of fashion in general. A specific trend might originate in some historical event, but what memory of that event does it perpetuate? By extension, what is fashion's relationship to history? Does it not ultimately anesthetize the wounds of historical trauma? Witness, for instance, the ever ironical Filipp Vigel recalling how as a child in the 1790s he had seen a family acquaintance flaunt a particularly unusual and fashionable hairstyle, called "à la guillotine."[35] Coiffure and the threat of decapitation are vastly incongruous concerns—as suggested by the Russian saying, "When the head's off, you don't cry about the hair" (*sniavshi golovu, ne plachut po volosam*)—an irony that escapes neither Vigel nor the reader, but seems hardly to concern the trend's originator and devotees. Like the Karamzinian wigs, the hair à la guillotine bears only a faint and even jocular memory of the Terror.

Even though as a foreigner, and especially as a Russian monarchist, Karamzin remembers the revolutionary catastrophe as a warning, the French people's failure to remember their own history with solemnity also proves to him a source of amusement. In another article, the future historian of the Russian state is stunned by the Parisian city life's quick recuperation of its pre-revolutionary commercial vigor: "Paris, which had only recently been filled with so much noise, agitation, riot and all manner of terrors, is now so calm and quiet that a foreigner seeing this will find it hard to believe either his eyes or his memory. The French are truly astonishing; one year for them is like a century, so quickly do they change! Shops are open everywhere, and all of them are filled with goods. Palais Royal is resurrected in its former splendor and serves again for the daily promenades of fops and fashionable ladies."[36] Which to trust, one's eyes or one's memory, is the question that quick-paced commercial temporality poses to a historian. The issue was especially relevant in this period when exteriors and interiors, surface and depth were discovered to exist in a perpetually discomfiting, even deceptive relationship.[37] If, as we saw in chapter 2, ruined landscapes intimated the future decay of magnificent contemporary edifices, thereby opening up a space for memory in what was hitherto only perceivable by the eye, then fashion, to the contrary, invited the subject to interpret change not as painful rupture but as pleasurable variation, as a change of costume. Fashion flattened out the rough terrain of memory, assuaging its anxieties by allowing the observer to revel in the visible and to suppress the remembered. Only a foreigner like Karamzin, then, could preserve both faculties, carving out for himself a unique position as historian and critic of modernity.

Despite Karamzin's apparent amusement at the faulty memory of the French, one senses also a satisfaction with life having returned to its normal course, with the reassuring persistence of the French *esprit de nation* (the cliché of French superficiality and obsession with trends, familiar from eighteenth-century satirical accounts). The author clearly takes comfort in listing carriage and hotel rates rather than revolutionary heroes and victims. All of Karamzin's remarks carefully project a sophisticated Russian reader who would side with the author in harboring an ironic *distance* from the French, would be eager to participate in the sentimentalist classification of peoples by their "national character" and yet curious about the price of trendy commodities in the capital of European glamour. Unlike the fickle French, Karamzin's hypothetical reader would be capable of penetrating beneath glitzy surfaces to unearth forgotten history; to rephrase Karamzin, this reader would believe his memory while also indulging his eyes.

Writing only a few years later, in a period marked by early formulations of Russian national sentiment, Sergei Glinka, by contrast, refuses to excuse French fickleness, denying fashion any redeeming historical depth and tying it strictly to the social and political ills of the age. Following a critical tradition that had flourished in Europe at least since Jean-Jacques Rousseau's emphatic rejection of modern luxury (indeed, Rousseau is the only French philosopher Glinka does not reject), the *Russian Herald*'s publisher sees in fashion and luxury the cause and evidence of the Enlightenment's moral bankruptcy, only brought to the surface by the French Revolution: "Luxury had excited the passions; from the passions proceeded the revolution."[38] To Glinka, this conclusion appears indisputable, allegedly endorsed by the prophesy of none other than Peter the Great: "France, said [Peter I] with sadness, shall perish from luxury (*pogibnet ot roskoshi*)!"[39] The author elaborates a coherent system of explanation for the Revolution originating in pernicious fashion: the *philosophes*, in his view, catered to unbridled French passions for real and imagined luxuries, transporting their fancy from their fatherland to exotic locales such as the Indies and Peru and thence to imaginary ideal societies, thus depriving them of true national feeling or Christian piety. The erosion of these virtues, so masterfully performed by the cosmopolitan Voltaire, Diderot, D'Alembert, Buffon, Marmontel, and their coterie, rendered the catastrophe of the French Revolution not only possible, but inevitable. Thus does a Russian intellectual— Glinka strives to present his journalistic persona as exemplary—summon patriotic sentiment in his countrymen, familiarizing them with their national history, which they should see as rich and instructive, once the scales of French iconoclastic Enlightenment, and its undue enthusiasm for costly fads, fall from their eyes.

The return to native values thus advocated inevitably means that the narrative of the *Russian* Enlightenment, which as a patriot loyal to the dynasty Glinka cannot disavow, must be reconceived as comprising more than westernization. The journal, primarily a forum for the publisher's own thoughts, often treads on precarious ground. Thus, in his critique of Kuznetskii most, the most fashionable Moscow street, Glinka writes of the origins of fashion: "Not only was fashion unknown in Russia until the time of Peter I, in France itself it emerged only when the French strayed from the mores and moderation of their forefathers."[40] The syntax of this sentence dangerously hints at a parallel between the abandonment of ancestral values under Louis XIV and the rejection of previous Russian culture under Peter I. Glinka dispels this potential association by purposefully distinguishing between French and Russian Enlightenment. The many articles he publishes on such Russian eighteenth-century leaders as Peter I, Catherine II, G. A. Potemkin, and A. V. Suvorov invariably emphasize their valor, charity, and national feeling, rather than their roles in the modernizing project. In the pages of the *Russian Herald*, such figures signify no break from Muscovite Russia, but occupy the same space as pre-Petrine heroes (Dmitrii Donskoi or Alexander Nevskii); Russian history is thereby reconfigured as an unbroken roll of honor indicative of timeless national character, rather than a narrative divided between pre- and post-modernization. Thus, the Enlightenment for Glinka retains its two meanings: on the one hand, it connotes the philosophical culture of the West (a culture he decries); on the other, it points to the spiritual "light" of Russia, with which he strives to reacquaint his readers. To the *Herald of Europe*'s motley reports from abroad, Glinka polemically opposes news of provincial Russian charitable activities and extensive eulogistic features on Russian monarchs and generals, thereby creating an idealized image of uncontaminated Russian virtue living on in the provinces and the past, even the recent past of the (westernizing)

eighteenth century. Charity rather than profit motivates Russia's national character, and substance rather than ostentation distinguishes her cultural commodities. This authenticity must be sought in the unadulterated heartland, and
not, as Glinka echoes the milder Karamzin to express what is by then a cliché,
in the cities: "Taste and fashion from the depths of luxury enter the square.
This is how everything changes, everything disappears; yesterday something
captivated us, but today we look away from it in vexation."[41] Concerned by
the rapid expansion of commercial life in Russia (recall, for instance, that it is
precisely in this period that Nevskii Prospekt begins to serve as a fashionable
thoroughfare), Glinka conflates commerce with superficiality, unlike Karamzin
rejecting any claim on the part of fashion to facilitate alternative experiences
of memory and time.

His thesis against fashion acquires particular forcefulness when directed
at the Russian importation of foreign literature. In the same October 1809
article, "Taste and Fashion" ("Vkus i moda"), the editor examines the flourishing book trade at the Il'inka market in Moscow: "Here are some writings
by Voltaire, here is a fashionable French calendar; and two or three works by
Jean-Jacques Rousseau. His passionate and tender Julie lies next to the Russian
Milord George [a popular page-turner by Matvei Komarov]. How magnificent
is the garb of the French authors! How many illustrious coats of arms adorn
them! Cast a glance, at least for pity's sake, on the Russian volumes that min-
gle with the pompous Gallic ones only at Il'inka. How modest are their bind-
ings! None display morocco leather or gilding! They have never been on the
shelves of princes and counts . . . they stood instead in the bookcase of some
undistinguished lover of Russian letters; poverty and need brought them to
Il'inka."[42] This passage reduces French *philosophes* and by extension the entire
Enlightenment first to a few ostentatious volumes and then to the books' gar-
ish covers; substance to surface; thought to fashion. Like Parisian fops, French
books and their Russian imitations flaunt their shiny surfaces while concealing, ignoring, or forgetting their baleful content; meanwhile, modest Russian
volumes openly point to their subject matter and to the humble circumstances
of their owners. The book market, itself a foreign import, privileges the superficial trappings of French luxury, while Russian intellectual goods linger only
as objects of pity. But of course, this framing of the market ignores the fact
that even the most modest Russian books on display, and the market itself, in
reality exist as a consequence of the Petrine turn toward the West.

Karamzin and Glinka approach the same troubling phenomenon, one that
has not ceased to perturb cultural critics to this day, from standpoints different

though by no means as contradictory as their early readers might have supposed. The ethical questions they raise interrogate the very nature of historical experience. What is the relationship of consumer culture to history?[43] If
fashion is only a facet of history, how can it recover its momentum after the
Revolution so much faster than all other aspects of experience? And why does
the realization of the West's moral deficiencies, shared in the wake of the Revolution even by commentators less reactionary than Glinka, prove so difficult
to translate into practice by discarding foreign attire, let alone the accelerated
temporality of fashion in which Glinka's contemporaries find themselves so
pleasantly enmeshed? As a historical phenomenon, fashion appears infinitely
changeable *qua* quotidian practice and equally as unshakable *qua* mentality
and temporality. Consequently, even at its most volatile, fashion also conveys
information about the past, recognizable and material though not at all defined
as to its meaning and potential for narrativization. This is the paradox that
Karamzin implicitly acknowledges and Glinka all but ignores. This is also the
paradox that, along with the critical assessments of fashion of the sort discussed in this section, forms an important backdrop for Pushkin's "The Queen
of Spades," not only, as I will demonstrate, for its descriptions of the old Countess's clothing and knickknacks, but also for its entire narrative structure and
historical argument.

"The Loathsome Mysteries of her Dress"

By the 1830s, commentary on fashion is largely subsumed by commentary
on urban life, which in turn is mined by writers of fiction and nonfiction alike
for material for both novelistic content and historicist thinking.[44] Consider
the following two passages, written only five years apart. In the first, the critic
Mikhail Pogodin contests what he presents as a widely held notion that Russia
is somehow lacking in material for native historical novels à la Walter Scott,
proposing, among other suggestions, that prospective authors look upon fashions viewable in city streets, and the people who display them, as examples of
cultural diversity and historical interest: "What variety of ranks we have! Each
has its own language, its spirit, its dress, even its gait, its handwriting. [. . .]
How easy it is in the street to pick out by his gait a shopkeeper, dressed as a
German, but with his hands [as if still] measuring ribbon; or a philosopher-
seminarian in an uncut long-skirted frock coat, braid tucked into a neckerchief,
walking with his studently pace and singing solemn cantatas in a whisper!;
or a young court clerk, his service cap aslant, cane in hand, and eyes full of

daring!"[45] This call for a Walter Scott to paint Russian streets would be answered later and in a very different, whimsical form by Nikolai Gogol, who in the opening to "Nevskii Prospekt" (written between 1831 and 1834, and published in 1835) would portray the daily rituals of a Russian city as determined by rank and wealth, and the resulting anonymity and repression of the individual. And yet it is not by accident that Pogodin's contemporary sketch is intended specifically for historical fiction. For one thing, Pogodin's portraits are imbued with both personal and national history inasmuch as they point to lifestyles that took shape at different historical moments. Scott, moreover, gives Pogodin's readers precisely the apparatus for imagining their own world as historical and on the verge of becoming a past.

If Pogodin captures the social cross-section of a Russian urban street that is only implicitly historical, Ivan Kireevskii offers a similar slice, though far less colorful and more explicitly focused on history. It is intended not for fictionalization, but rather for more serious philosophical contemplation: "Next to a man of the *old times*, you will find one who was shaped in the spirit of the *French Revolution*; further a man who was brought up by the circumstances and opinions that *followed directly after the French Revolution*, next to him a man affected by that order of things which arose on the solid ground of Europe after the fall of Napoleon; finally, among all of these, you will encounter a man of the latest age. And every one of them will have his own physiognomy, each will differ from the others in all the possible circumstances of life—in short, each will appear before you bearing the imprint of a distinct age."[46] [emphases in the original] Recall Chateaubriand's similar description of the jumbled temporality of fashion on Parisian streets after the French Revolution. This passage, Kireevskii's feuilleton-like introduction to his controversial article "The Nineteenth Century" (1832), offers no polemical revelations, but rather a common ground with the reader who might have contemplated similar layerings in his own daily life, "now that defining the dominant direction of the age has become a common goal for all thinking people."[47] Kireevskii's account voices two historicist premises: the Hegelian notion that each person can be understood as a product of a specific Zeitgeist, and the idea that a conglomeration of historical planes constitutes the novelty of nineteenth-century experience, of its own Zeitgeist. The critic calibrates recent decades into distinct epochs, notably all belonging to a French timeline: the *ancien régime*, the French Revolution, Terror and Napoleon, the post-Napoleonic decade, and the late 1820s–early 1830s, the time of Kireevskii's observations. In keeping with the notions of recent history common at the time, this classification suggests Russia's close ties to France and its political currents, in a sense unabated since the eighteenth century, as well as an unbridgeable gap between the 1780s and 1830s: too much can change from year to year, let alone between two revolutions set off by four decades. This gap will become one of the structuring points in "The Queen of Spades." The passage, however, also betrays a fascination with the confluence of epochs, exposing at once an investment in epochal categories and these categories' inherent ambiguity.

While the meaning of this palimpsest or mosaic remains ambiguous, its constituent planes are forcibly defined: Kireevskii's account makes the body wear an indelible imprint of the "spirit of th[at] age" which had most affected the person. Kireevskii has no trouble erasing the boundary between the observable individual body and the elusive epochal spirit as he detects the "spirit of the French Revolution" or the post-Napoleonic "order of things" stamped on the physiognomy of a passerby. Both Pogodin and Kireevskii adopt a rather distant stance on modern man and street life, observing from the perspective of implicitly minimal access to their characters' personal stories. These descriptions point to what in later Russian fiction would emerge as the issue of the "type." In the meantime, the two essayists' main interest lies in capturing the social totality in all its segmentation, rather than the individual as he enters that totality.

We might read Pushkin's "The Queen of Spades" (1833), patently lacking though it is in these kinds of urban sketches, as set in the psychological reality of an urban space similarly segmented by distinctions of class (the aristocratic Countess vs. her presumably impoverished-gentry ward Liza vs. Hermann, an officer in the Engineers' Corps, who at least as a literary type is constructed as a bourgeois) and non-synchronous in the historical allegiances of its members (the Countess as a Catherinian grande dame vs. Hermann, a man of the 1830s). The novella recreates this space not from a distance, but through a much closer engagement with its protagonist's internal world and vision, which focalizes both the recent eighteenth-century past and nineteenth-century contemporaneity.

Hermann approaches the Countess by passing (or, rather, trespassing) through a series of concentric circles: first, by hearing her story, then by surveying her house from the street, then by entering her room and mentally registering her many seemingly trivial belongings, then by momentarily viewing her naked body, then by conversing with her, and finally by crossing together with her, whether in dream or reality, into the supernatural world where he learns her secret. Page by page, the novella relinquishes the society tale and its urban space for the supernatural tale and its mental space. To be found somewhere in the middle, facilitating this transfer, are the closely observed elements of the Countess's dress and house décor, which on this side of the divide between reality and fantasy function as material incarnations of her alleged card secret. The objects also characterize the Countess as entrenched in the eighteenth century and serve to both trivialize and mystify this era in the novella.

When Hermann inspects the Countess's bedroom—the site of his imminent transgression—he distinguishes an array of seemingly random objects:

A gold sanctuary lamp burned in front of an icon-case filled with ancient icons. Armchairs with faded damask upholstery and down-cushioned sofas, their gilt coating worn, stood in melancholy symmetry along the walls, which were covered with Chinese silk. Two portraits, painted in Paris by Mme Lebrun, hung on the wall. One of them showed a man about forty years old, red-faced and portly, wearing a light-green coat with a star; the other a beautiful young woman with an aquiline nose, with her hair combed back of her temples, and with a rose in her powdered locks. Every nook and corner was crowded with china shepherdesses, table clocks made by the famous Leroy, little boxes, bandalores, fans, and diverse other ladies' toys invented at the end of the last century, along with Montgolfier's balloon and Mesmer's magnetism.[48]

Dismissed by Mikhail Gershenzon as Pushkin's misguided tribute to novelistic description, which here captures reality photographically instead of illuminating Hermann's psychological state,[49] the details of the Countess's living space nevertheless unveil a reality of history, if not of psychology. Along with the Countess's dress and behavior, they provide the only material point of entry into her antiquated world, its imagined mysteries, glamorous fortunes, and sexual freedoms, while also designating it specifically as a preserve of the eighteenth century—a point of entry that is on the plot level so crucial for Hermann and, if one reads the novella as a historicist text, for the reader as well.[50] The boudoir's description sheds light on the incongruous featuresof the Russian eighteenth century and its fate in the memory of Pushkin's contemporaries.

Pushkin renders every object as a period piece. All the furnishings of the Countess's world—armchairs and sofas, Chinese wallpaper and formal portraits, shepherdesses and bandalores—reference the culture of Catherinian aristocracy. Moreover, they adorn a space that itself was invented in the eighteenth century: the boudoir, a semi-private interior "linked to intimacy and [feminine] caprice" and designed to isolate the hostess and her special visitor from the cares of the outside world.[51] Crucially, when this insulated space of coy sociability and privacy is trespassed by the modern hero Hermann, its titillating intimacy proves fatal to both parties. Mirrors, wallpaper, portraits, armchairs arranged "in melancholy symmetry along the walls" were all intended to wall off feminine interiority from unwanted masculine intrusion; or, seen from a different perspective, to shield the stable interior from the mobile exterior, or the superannuated world of the eighteenth century from the dynamic nineteenth.[52] But when Hermann enters the boudoir, these would-be protective ornaments reveal their faded gilding and desuetude, casting doubt upon the possibility of arresting time. The very porousness of the Countess's walls, pierced by Hermann's inquisitive gaze and even more crucially by the story-teller, evinces the voyeuristic practices of early realism, perfected by such writers of urban tales as Balzac and Eugène Sue, but also highlights their limitations.[53] Sue seeks the "mysteries of Paris" in the gruesome underbelly of its society; Pushkin, only a few years earlier, locates the mysteries of Saint Petersburg in a less shocking, but more historically opaque urban space: the high-society boudoir strewn with objects that are striking in their dullness. It is precisely this kind of space that, in the words of Francesco Orlando, takes on the function of "an affective reliquary of defunctionalized things" for such mid-nineteenth-century writers as Charles Baudelaire and Gustave Flaubert, and, we might add, Pushkin and Turgenev.[54] Ultimately, Hermann's intrusion is parallel to, if not symbolic of, the intrusion and revisions cast by nineteenth-century modernity on the Catherinian *ancien régime*, and by nineteenth-century male writers on the occluded narrative spaces of eighteenth-century feminine interiority.[55]

But what and how does the Countess still signify in this modern world? In her private rooms, a Russian *barynia*'s religiosity coexists with an imported penchant for the occult (Saint Germain, Mesmer, three cards) and the Gothic (ghosts, haunted palaces, and haunting pasts). The Countess's bedroom teems with bric-a-brac fashionable under Catherine, ranging from porcelain figurines to original works by Elizabeth Vigée-Lebrun and Charles LeRoy, which immediately cede their claims to originality once the narrator's detached voice identifies them as familiar items from eighteenth-century aristocratic interiors. Particularly the Vigée-Lebrun portraits, omnipresent in European salons and barely distinguishable one from another, serve to display the Countess as an unoriginal product of her age, both in her consumption of art and through her representation in art.[56] Hermann's gaze glides over the idealized features of the red-faced man and beak-nosed woman, incapable of discerning the identity of the sitters, not only because Hermann is rooted in a milieu of German industry insensitive to Russian aristocratic genealogy,[57] but also because by the time he enters the boudoir the tie between these portraits' subjects—their "aura" and "authenticity," in Walter Benjamin's terms—and their pictorial surface has ostensibly been severed. In the few decades elapsed since the commission of these portraits, their status has changed radically, from objects that represent to objects that decorate. In his faith in the Countess's secret, Hermann makes an ineffectual move to recover the devotional, representational core of these ornaments—talismanic appurtenances, as it were, of the ancient magic he craves—with the Countess the most important ornament of them all.

Embedded in her typical eighteenth-century décor, the Countess becomes a decoration. Her ornamental datedness is noted with almost sinister precision in the way she exercises control over the rituals of nineteenth-century social life: "She participated in all the trivial events of high society life, dragging herself to balls, where she would sit in a corner, all painted up and dressed according to an ancient fashion, like a misshapen, but obligatory ornament of the ballroom; the guests, as they arrived, would go up to her bowing low, as if performing an established rite, but afterwards would pay no attention to her."[58] The Countess demands respect by her very presence, and her tenacious insistence on the perfunctory public ritual—as well as her ostensible command over Hermann's fortune and tyranny over her impressionable ward Liza—calls to mind other aging aristocratic ladies and the archetype of them all, Catherine the Great, the Russian empress who lived the longest of all the Romanovs.[59]

The acknowledged prototype of Pushkin's Countess, Princess Natal'ia Petrovna Golitsyna (1741–1837), served as a lady-in-waiting during five reigns, of which the longest and certainly most significant was Catherine II's.[60] While conferring honor on its bearer, the status of the lady-in-waiting also bound up her identity with that of the empress in a way that limited the lady's autonomy of signification, if not of action. Thus, Golitsyna's (and Pushkin's Countess's) long and eventful life could be perceived as an echo of Catherine's own. And Golitsyna, though a remarkable figure in her own right, could come to be inextricably associated by her younger contemporaries with Catherine II, by no means as her exact or even diminished replica, but rather as bearing within and all around her the spirit of Catherine's court, and in that sense appearing as a copy of a no-longer-accessible original.[61] That link was rendered visible and reinforced by the aging lady's adherence to the fashions of her sovereign's court.

We find a curious illustration of the conflation of empress and her female courtiers in a case of mistaken identity recorded by Vigel at the beginning of his memoirs.[62] Vigel recalls how as a child in the 1790s he encountered Countess A. V. Branitskaia (1754–1838),[63] Catherine's lady-in-waiting and a niece of Grigorii Potemkin, Catherine's most famous grandee and favorite. What Vigel the memoirist leaves unsaid and Vigel the child could not possibly have known was that Branitskaia had also been her uncle's lover. This revelation potentially complicates our reading of the passage, particularly if we consider a less probable, uncorroborated eighteenth-century rumor that she may even have been the offspring of Catherine herself. Suspecting nothing of this tacit common knowledge (precisely the sort that to Pushkin's generation would become precious as gossip of a bygone age), the child Vigel sees only the grandeur that renders Branitskaia visually interchangeable with the empress:

> Her favorite outfit was to copy the empress's costume: a long undergarment with long and narrow sleeves, which [garment] covered her bosom almost entirely; it was girded by a narrow, almost unnoticeable belt with one huge, wide and long buckle; and on top of it was worn another dress, short, sleeveless and completely open in the front, which was called a "Greek" [grechanka]. All of this was reminiscent of the East and the novelistic-state designs [romanichesko-gosudarstvennye vidy] that Catherine II had upon it.
>
> The portrait of that miracle-working tsaritsa, copied by the skillful hand of De Meys from the original portrait of the famous Lampi, was hanging in the guestroom of the house the state had provided for us. When someone happened to look at it, he would all but cross himself; I myself positively considered it an icon. Suddenly it came to life before me: in the middle of the room I saw a woman who to me seemed just as majestic, wearing the same dress, the same ribbon across her shoulder, people standing obsequiously around her. Is it any wonder that in the mind of a five- or six-year-old boy the concepts of majesty became mixed up, and he mistook the subject for the sovereign?[64]

Soon after this episode Vigel recalls developing a particular fondness for the Countess, his childish affection for her now having little to do with her cultivated resemblance to the empress. But the resemblance proves so resilient as to obliterate any traces of this former affection when Vigel meets her again in the 1820s and again cannot see past her Catherine-era image: "About fifteen years ago I saw her for the last time and now no longer looked at her with the same eyes. She is no rose, but lived next to one, and the imprint of Catherine's

majesty shone in her for a long time still. She is still alive, but in her extreme
old age she remains as [Catherine's] half-ruined memorial."[65] As Catherine's
aged replica, Branitskaia, like the Countess in "The Queen of Spades," can no
longer conceal the creases on the living image of Catherine she purports to
embody faithfully. As in chapter 1, here too the body becomes that difficult
meeting point where the imaginations of allegory (body as incarnation) and
realism (body as matter) clash.[66] The aging body may be clothed according to
the spirit of the empress's era, but it still betrays the passage of time and signals that the old Zeitgeist is unsustainable.

Pushkin's Countess is simultaneously an object that represents the Age of
Catherine; an object that decorates nineteenth-century salons; and a unique
subject who might be assumed to think, speak, act, and even possess a secret.
She is at the same time a ghostly automaton and a flesh-and-blood human
being—a copy of Catherine and her age but also an original. Her compound
status generates the central tension and mystery of "The Queen of Spades."[67]
Along with Hermann, and even the more knowledgeable and serene narrator,
we possess only limited, fragmented insight into all three of the Countess's
dimensions. How exactly does the Countess reference the 1770s as the peak
of her own erotic appeal and Catherine's reign? Where, if at all, does she cease
being a mere decaying replica of that more glorious world and assert her relevance for the 1830s? These are questions we might rethink as reflections
upon the relationship between the two epochs in general.

The novella never catches the Countess thinking; in fact, it insists on her
visible lack of interiority: "Her dim eyes were completely empty of thought."[68]
To a much greater degree than all other characters, she is described through
the detail of her dress and daily ritual, and at the same time left psychologi-
cally opaque. What the Countess says throughout the novella is also remarkable not for its originality, but for the gruff familiarity with which she verbally
controls her world, evident especially in her consistent use of the informal *ty*
and unrefined terms of endearment, such as *moi milyi, batiushka, mat' moia,*
matushka, all echoes of eighteenth-century forthrightness and the patchy
civilizing process.[69] The Countess is behind the times: she does not realize
that Russian novels exist—recall the situation at the Il'inka market lamented
by Glinka—and disparages the beauties of the 1830s; she is entirely im-
pervious to new stimuli and insensitive to the distress she causes Lizaveta
Ivanovna with her caprices. In fact, she bears a striking resemblance to the
old ladies of Catherine II's 1770s comedies: those Khanzhakhinas, Vestnikovas,
and Chudikhinas who insist on spinning, like the three fates, the destinies

Richard Brompton, *Portrait of Alexandra Branicka with a Bust of Catherine II* (1781). The Tropinin Museum, Moscow.

Giovanni Battista Lampi the Elder, *Portrait of Catherine II* (1793). The State Hermitage Museum, St. Petersburg.

of the young.[70] Yet, unlike the naïve, garrulous characters of a comedy of manners—ultimately cardboard cutouts—the Countess reveals very little of herself. She is stereotyped both as a copy of Catherine II and as one of those ignorant and hypocritical old ladies Catherine II, in her role as enlightened monarch and playwright, had ridiculed. The Countess is grounded in a past which the novella codes as undiscerning and senseless, but at the same time tantalizing and radically open to signification. Glimpsed only briefly amid the furnishings of her house, and portrayed for the reader via her caricatured old-fashioned speech, her empty eyes and emotional numbness, the Countess stands apart from her younger contemporaries most demonstrably, and most complicatedly, in the deliberate renderings and juxtaposition of her dress and body.[71]

From the beginning, the reader is asked to pay unceasing attention to the Countess's outdated fashions and the gradual removal of these coverings, the denuding of an illegible withered body. The fashions are meant to reference the Countess's high-spirited 1770s youth, but they only underscore the passing of time, the relentless decay of the body under the dress. First, in her 1770s Paris boudoir, the young Countess—la Vénus Moscovite as the Parisian elite then called her—removes her beauty spots and hooped petticoat as she confronts her docile husband with the news of her loss at cards (willful eighteenth-century women, Catherine II chief among them, having become a cliché in the nineteenth century). A symmetrical scene sixty years later transfers us to the Petersburg house of the 87-year-old Countess—by now a princesse moustache[72]—where in the morning she still habitually titivates herself in the same 1770s style. A third parallel occurs as Hermann observes the Countess's maids undressing her after a ball.

Repeated with slight but significant variations, these scenes furnish the structural carcass for the novella's temporal organization. The present-day couchée ritual in the Petersburg mansion echoes that of the past in Paris, tracing the historical trajectory of the Countess's life. More generally, the scene also alludes to those proverbial rituals of semi-private levée and couchée first instituted by Louis XIV, but since extinct—or driven to extinction, violently, along with the old regime itself. In the Petersburg boudoir, time proceeds uninterrupted, blissfully unaware of historical upheavals, suggesting an "alternate history," a timeline essentially Russian and aristocratic precisely in its reverence for the French ancien régime. The ritual is also one of many that had been repeated twice a day at the Countess's rising and retiring for the past sixty years, thus establishing a cyclical temporal structure both for her own days

and, by extension, for history. As we shall see, the novella presents two competing versions of historical time: one linear/progressive/modern (populated
by originals and mocking old fashions) and another repetitive/cyclical/ritu-
alistic (populated by copies and preserving old fashions). The former allows
the young men of the 1830s a comfortable detachment from the past, while
the latter keeps them ever on a short leash; the past grips the present in its
controlling "dead hand," and only through excessive interpretation can it be
exorcised and buried.

In its seemingly detached treatment of surfaces, but fascination with them
all the same, the narrative emphasizes the ritualistic recurrence of the novella's
rhythms. Let us consider the first instance of the Countess's described levée:
"The old Countess N. sat in front of the mirror in her boudoir. Three cham-
bermaids surrounded her. One was holding a jar of rouge, the second one
a box of pins, and the third one a tall bonnet with flame-coloured ribbons.
The Countess did not have the slightest pretensions to beauty, which had long
since faded from her face, but she adhered to all the habits of her youth,
strictly following the fashions of the 1770s, spending just as much time on,
and paying just as much attention to her toilette as she had sixty years before."[73]
This scene contains several of the novella's recurrent motifs: the Countess's
unyielding power over every other character (in this case her maids); the separation between, if not incommensurability of, the old body and its adornments (rouge, pins, bonnet, ribbons); and finally, the persistence of habit in the
face of historical change. These motifs, furthermore, rehearse certain clichés
of the time of Catherine.

The attention devoted to the unsuitability of such lavish costume to the
Countess's advanced age had a parallel in the satirical representations of Catherine II at the end of her reign. The empress's final liaison, with her 22-year-
old favorite Platon Zubov, provoked criticism even among her close associates.
Catherine was depicted as a grotesque libertine not only in foreign pamphlets,
but also, if less directly, in late-eighteenth-century Russian satire. Witness, for
instance, the famous fable-writer Ivan Krylov's satire "on persons," which masquerades as satire "on vice," in his early novella "Nights" ("Nochi," 1792): "She
is sleeping, and all her charms are laid out on her dressing table: her magnificent teeth are arranged near the mirror; her head is as clean as a turnip,
and the hair, which caused astonishment, now is carefully draped over the
mirror; her tender blush and captivating pallor are standing in their jars prepared for the morning. [. . .] Don't assume, dear reader, that this lady lacks
presence of mind. If someone were to steal her charms, she would still have

one more left [. . .]: eloquence is her strongest weapon [. . .]. Her letters to her lovers are very persuasive despite all adhering to the same pattern, beginning as follows: 'The Government Loan Bank hereby promises to pay to the bearer etc.'"[74] Pushkin was undoubtedly acquainted with this tradition of portraying Catherine II. Krylov's narrator, like Hermann, observes the empress unawares, at a moment when her body is at its most static, vulnerable, and exposed. In tongue-in-cheek manner ("Don't assume, dear reader"), he manipulates our perception of the interplay between body and fashion. By day, one might marvel at the old lady's hair and skin, but at night they are revealed as artificial coverings; the satirist's task is to unmask his subject. Transferred to Pushkin's novella, these disparate views, diurnal and nocturnal, yield alternative records of history, public and private—a distinction increasingly significant as demand explodes in this period for biographical and memoiristic writing.

All the "charms" that Krylov scatters around his "sleeping beauty" are material objects "in their jars" rather than her own inalienable attributes. Likewise, the multiple scenes of the Countess's dressing and undressing in her boudoir callously detach the costume from the self. Catherine's and the Countess's inadvertent exposure in the bedroom point to the indecorous sexuality that came to be associated with the libertinage of the Catherine era.[75] While power has no age constraints and is often consolidated at a more advanced stage of life, convention has it that sexuality is constrained by age and physical vigor. Krylov criticizes Catherine II for flaunting a complementarity of old age, power, and sexuality, which "decency" should presumably keep separate. Just as Catherine's erotic appeal is vouchsafed by her ability to grant wealth and power (in Krylov's satire, the genre of her eloquence is that of promissory notes), the Countess regains her appeal for a young man of the nineteenth century because of the power she wields over his fortunes. Andrew Wachtel convincingly proposes to explain Hermann's attraction to the Countess by emphasizing their competing models of wealth. "The accidental nature of fortunes," so generously granted by Catherine to her favorites, is superseded in the nineteenth century by the middle-class values of labor and frugality espoused by Hermann at the beginning of the novella, but subsequently lost in his enthrallment to the secret of the cards. "Everything in his nature and his background, from his engineering profession to his German blood, and including his desire to grow his already large capital by 'calculation, moderation, and industry,' are strikes against him in a world that still lives and dies by *ancien regime* codes relating to money."[76] All the objects Hermann espies in the Countess's boudoir belong to that *ancien régime* world, which alone is capable of satisfying the suppressed fantasies of the man of a commercial age. In beholding the commodities of the world he so passionately desired, Hermann was approaching his goal: the Countess herself, the most desirable commodity of that world, an emblem of bygone and present power, wealth, and erotic autonomy.

There is something improper in reviving the age of Catherine in the age of Nicholas—the age of female power, flamboyant dress, and libertinage in the age of male control, uniforms, and regulation.[77] This embarrassment is nowhere more intense than when the reader is asked to observe "the loathsome mysteries of [the Countess's] dress" and imagine her as a sexual object, sustained beneath and with the help of all her adornments. Hermann is oblivious to the Countess's detachment from his nineteenth-century world and does not shrink from any fantasies or ploys, even the wildest and most unsavory: "The anecdote about the three cards fired his imagination [. . .]. 'What if [. . .] the old Countess revealed her secret to me? [. . .] I could be introduced to her, get into her good graces, become her lover if need be, but all this requires time, and she is eighty-seven: she may die in a week—in a couple of days!'"[78] Throughout the story, the Countess is presented as a sexual object. A former "Muscovite Venus," she had denied her husband the pleasures of her bed when the latter refused to pay her gambling debt (financial and carnal desires being, as always, inextricably paired). She dresses and undresses incessantly. Her aged sexualized body is akin to that of Catherine herself as exposed in scabrous histories. But when the story threatens to hand the young Hermann over to her moribund embrace, the erotic charge of the encounter between modernity and 60-year-old "antiquity" can no longer be ignored.

Having sufficiently studied the boudoir's interior, and anxious for a successful conclusion to his adventure (his criminal time-travel), Hermann finally beholds the Countess's most candid undressing: "Hermann watched through a crack in the door. [. . .] The Countess began to undress in front of the mirror. The maids unpinned her bonnet bedecked with roses and removed the powdered wig from her closely cropped grey head. Pins came showering off her. Her yellow dress, embroidered with silver, fell to her swollen feet; Hermann became privy to the loathsome mysteries [*tainstva*] of her dress. At last she put on her bed jacket and nightcap: in these clothes, more appropriate for her age, she seemed less frightening and hideous."[79] In undressing, the Countess changes from a Catherinian lady-in-waiting in her ceremonial yellow dress and powdered wig to an ordinary old woman, in the unassuming clothes that "befit" her years and free her from allegiance to a specific historical period and cultural milieu. If the Countess's outdated fashions mark her as an object representing the Age of Catherine, the body beneath the clothes displays the most gripping diachronic record, connecting the seemingly severed realities of the eighteenth and nineteenth centuries and registering temporal—and indeed historical—change, from the "little feet" (*nozhki*) famously serenaded in *Eugene Onegin* to "the swollen feet" of "The Queen of Spades." Clothing strives desperately to arrest time in the repetitive rituals of dressing and undressing, but the body succumbs to time's inexorable flow: both are thus exploited as sources of historical evidence, but the temporalities they exemplify configure historical time differently.

Though presumably vouchsafed to Hermann, the view of the Countess's body is for the reader obscured; the passage closely follows only what the maids strip away (bonnet, wig, pins, yellow dress) and not what remains beneath: "mysteries" (*tainstva*) can be read here not only as the most private process of preparing for bed, but also as euphemistic for the very body, in all its functions, that the novella hints at so repeatedly and never bares completely. Pushkin rewrites the scenario of voyeuristic seduction as that of voyeuristic disgust, but the disgust is markedly focalized by Hermann, just as it is he, too, who briefly imagines the full scenario of the Countess's seduction, if only as velleity, rather than full-fledged desire.[80]

In this connection, we might reconsider the novella's indebtedness to one of the key textual sources for its allusions to eighteenth-century libertinage and dress rituals, *The Memoirs of Jacques Casanova de Seingalt*, which Pushkin mentions explicitly in characterizing Saint Germain, the original supplier of the Countess's card secret.[81] Both dress, in all its minutely perceived detail as worn by others or chosen and worn by oneself, *and* undressing, in all the variety of its attendant circumstances, are recurrent elements of Casanova's self-narrative and many erotic conquests. Moreover, Casanova was a parvenu, a man made essentially by his ability to engage in conspicuously aristocratic consumption. As suggested by Roche, who has classified all the mentions of attire in Casanova's memoirs, for this vaunted adventurer clothes "express the power of social propriety, a respect for fashion—expression of adherence to court society, the ultimate model—and the dream of never-ending seduction, in which elegance and finery were already desire."[82] Casanova's attention to fashion, otherwise remarkably steadfast, wanes only late in life, for he "feared and detested old age, which he saw as the final cessation of the power of the appearances and fashions necessary to his pleasure."[83] Finally, the *Memoirs* also abound in situations where old women are observed, with no small measure of distaste, usually in contexts where they accompany young women of interest to Casanova, and hinder or facilitate his advances—replaying an archetypal triangle that is curiously reshuffled in "The Queen of Spades," where the young maiden helps the amorous parvenu in his quest for the old woman's favors.[84] With his plagiarized letters to Lizaveta, his unloaded pistol aimed at the Countess, and time working against his vague plans to seduce her, Hermann is a character denied access: he is not only shut out of the eighteenth-century system of wealth (as suggested by Wachtel), but also—born too late—deprived of that century's discourse and culture of seduction, much of which is encapsulated in the objects—snuffboxes and bandalores—that he secretly observes by way of foreplay in his (frustrated) bid for the Countess.

Hermann's insistence on eroticizing the Countess also highlights the inherent limitations of nostalgic vision, or of any voracious desire for history, so ubiquitous in the 1830s. In its discomfiting proximity, the sight of the Countess's nakedness, so callously alluded to by Pushkin—"swollen," "loathsome," "frightening and hideous"—is as if intended to thwart nostalgia in the reader. But not in Hermann. When he descends the secret staircase, after the Countess finally gives up the ghost, Hermann succumbs to another erotic reverie, now seductive as much for its historical inaccessibility as for its belatedness after the Countess's death: "'Perhaps,' he thought, 'up this very staircase, about sixty years ago, into this same bedroom, at this same hour, dressed in an embroidered coat, with his hair combed *à l'oiseau royal*, pressing his three-cornered hat to his heart, there stole a lucky young man, now long since turned to dust in his grave; and the heart of his aged mistress has stopped beating today. . . .'"[85] Hermann is keen on retracing, or imagining that he retraces, the steps of his more fortunate predecessor, a path in fact repeatedly and successfully trod by Casanova in the period of the Countess's youth, precisely "about sixty years ago." Hermann's role is confusing. He hesitates too much between observing and participating: does he really picture another or himself as the Countess's lover? Might, after all, his body, gaining its social identity from the Engineers' Corps uniform it bears, be interchangeable beneath these trappings with the long-dead lover's, masked under an embroidered coat and the hairstyle *à l'oiseau royal*? Do epochal distinctions, advertised by fashion, disappear beneath the surface? Or are modern bodies, too, somehow changed, emasculated? Is historical time, then, linear, marching confidently forward, or precarious and cyclical, entailing regression as much as progress?

All characters in "The Queen of Spades" have parallels in the past: the Countess in Catherine II, who codified the fashions and rituals she so persistently maintains; Hermann in the Countess's imagined lover (perhaps Saint Germain himself: the French original behind Hermann's German translation); and Lizaveta, who after the Countess's death marries into a fortune and takes a ward of her own, in the Countess.[86] This vertiginous conglomeration of historical planes, reminiscent of Kireevskii's mosaic, characterizes the novella's narrative time: "The past, the events of sixty years before, appear both as something that has passed and as a foundation of the present."[87]

The intimacy of both a lover and a murderer is similar to that which a modern reader strives to achieve in relation to history. The 1830s—"Sixty Years Since," as Sir Walter Scott's subtitle-recipe for a historical novel prescribes—would dismiss the Countess along with her world, but the woman and her milieu nevertheless captivate Hermann. The nineteenth-century discovery of "the spirit of the age," the idea that each epoch possesses a unique, fleeting, and inimitable character, ultimately exaggerates the gap and miscommunication between the Age of Catherine and the Age of Nicholas, and thus breeds Hermann's fascination with the past and his fateful inner conflict. Having undeniably absorbed the Hoffmanesque tradition of the fantastic tale, "The Queen of Spades" also experiments with the Balzacian cataloguing of contemporaneity and the multiple forms of historical fiction originating with Scott. Ultimately diagnosing the pathology of the man of the 1830s, who has been taken hostage by the historicist imagination, "The Queen of Spades" tests the capacity of a variety of modes (Hoffmann's, Scott's, Balzac's) for representing the material culture through which this generation attempts to reconstruct—or in Hermann's case, appropriate—the past. For the purposes of this book, it is also noteworthy that the story takes up the eighteenth century just as it is on the verge of passing away together with its last survivors, recovering, through mimesis and fantasy, its seemingly inconsequential human and material fragments. As we move into the next chapter, several decades further into the nineteenth century, we will find that in tale after tale, Turgenev deems precisely such fragments irrecoverable.

6

The Margins of History
Ivan Turgenev's Eighteenth-Century Characters

Ко льву приходит старость:
Лишился силы он, его простыла ярость,
Зверей терзать уж перестал,
Не страшен стал.
Никто его не трусит;
Он боле не укусит.
В конуру лев засел
И никуда из оной не выходит.
Осел
К нему приходит;
Но не почтение льву тамо отдает,
А льва копытом бьет,
За прежние его тиранства отомщая.
Лев,
Душою поболев,
Бесчестие себе такое ощущая,
Сказал, стеня:
«Осел меня
Толкать уж смеет;
Какую участь лев имеет!»
—F. P. KLIUCHAREV, "An Elderly Lion" (1795)

THE UNCLES OF RUSSIAN MODERNITY

Waverley, or 'Tis Sixty Years Since (1814), a model novel for Sir Walter Scott's own numerous subsequent fictions, for the historical novels of his many followers, and for theorists of historical fiction and the novel-as-genre, anchors its protagonist's fateful ideological indecisiveness in fractious family history.[1] While young Edward Waverley's uncle, Sir Everard, upholds the family's Tory

traditions and raises his nephew on the family estate in the south of England
in an atmosphere of underhand Jacobite sympathizing, the hero's careerist
father, Richard Waverley, settles in London, supports the Whigs, and works
for the Hanoverian government. The father rules over Edward's fate from a distance but with the heavy-handedness of a state official, even as the young man's
uncle shapes his imagination and sentiments through intimate daily immersion in the Waverley family lore and way of life. And though ultimately the
novel manages to suppress its formative conflict, putting to rest the chivalric
Scottish past it had so colorfully resuscitated and returning its English hero
to the fold of domestic Englishness, Scott also leaves his readers with the realization of history's potential to polarize the most intimate spheres, to impel
individuals otherwise linked by common blood or past in opposing biographical and ideological directions, and to subdue these conflicts only hap-
hazardly, through no clear or shared moral logic. If Scott succeeds (to echo
Pushkin's praise) in representing the past "in a domestic manner,"[2] it is not
only because history in his novels is, as it were, domesticated, experienced
from the perspective of an ordinary man trying to carve an ordinary life-path,
but also because it is precisely the domestic and personal spheres' vulnerabil-
ity to the onslaught of history that gives his novels their momentum. And if
this, too, is part of Scott's recipe, it is a recipe for difference, instability, and
singularity; after all, "every unhappy family is unhappy in its own way."

Toward the middle of the nineteenth century, generational belonging becomes one of the most evocative markers of periodization, increasingly defined
via commonality of historical experience and worldview; at this point, the
novel—thriving as it does on individuation even, and perhaps especially, as
practiced by such ambitious social commentators as Balzac or Turgenev—is
called upon to develop new modes of characterization, conceiving of heroes
both as types representing a certain socio-historical milieu, and as individuals at odds with their generation's other members.[3] Thus, in Turgenev's most
influential novel, *Fathers and Children* (*Ottsy i deti*, 1862), a self-fashioned history of the recent pre-emancipation past, the fathers' generation is represented,
as in *Waverley*, by two brothers: Nikolai and Pavel Kirsanov. Both exhibit the
flawed sensibilities of the "men of the 1840s": an inability to act, sentimental-
ity, attachment to old-fashioned liberal values and Western fashions, adherence
to older hierarchical social structures. Yet the two embody their generation
strikingly differently. While the protagonist[4] Arkadii's uncle Pavel is essentially
a dead branch of the Kirsanov tree, too rigid in his espousal of the values
the novel calls into question, his father, Nikolai, given to poetic reverie and

anxious to forge a bond with his son, is defined by the melancholy naïveté of his internal conflict. Both belong squarely to their generation, but, to put it quite simply, one has a child (even two) and thus preserves a concern for, and a relevance to, the present, while the other represents an ideological and genealogical dead end. Unlike the figures of father and uncle in *Waverley*, who represent a far starker opposition, Nikolai and Pavel are on friendly, even affectionate terms with each other; they are aging members of the same generation and, as it eventually transpires, in love with the same woman. But by the end of the novel they are made to stand for two divergent scenarios of historical succession: Nikolai persists through his sons and estate, while Pavel brings his side of the Kirsanov gentry line to a full stop and abandons his native land.

Taking place mostly on the Kirsanov estate, the drama of the fathers, though not directly linked to a specific historical event such as *Waverley*'s Jacobite Uprising of 1745, showcases the relentlessness of the historical dialectic when the final reconciliation of opposites in the figure of young Arkadii Kirsanov comes at the price of not only the rebel-protagonist Bazarov's untimely death but also his opponent Pavel Kirsanov's timely banishment to Dresden—a fate that, as the novel has no qualms in telling us, is akin to burial.[5] The drama of the fathers is just as suggestive of history's pressures as the central father-son conflict, in whose margins it leaves its melancholy trace. And the uncle's residue, especially, grows faint, representing a road not taken, a cluster of foreclosed potentialities. Typically seen as constructed around a series of binary oppositions (suggested already in the novel's title), the character system in *Fathers and Children* in fact appears to work by triangulation: modifying the novel's central conflict over Russia's *future* are characters who have been or are about to be left behind in its past.[6]

Fathers and Children famously replicates its titular opposition within all three of its households: at the Kirsanov estate, in the Bazarov cottage, and even in Odintsova's manor. Along the same lines, we can detect the triangulated character system beyond the Kirsanov estate. Pavel the uncle is not the only sterile and superannuated figure in the novel. His unlikely double in the Odintsova household is the old Princess, Anna and Katya's aunt, who has passed seemingly unnoticed in the critical literature, and perhaps for good reason. She is a caricaturistic copy of Pushkin's Countess in "The Queen of Spades," similarly dressed in yellow, disengaged from the youthful world around her, demanding and self-absorbed: "Anna Sergeevna's auntie, the Princess Kh., a short, slender woman with a face pinched like a fist and nasty, steady eyes under a gray wig, came in. Scarcely greeting the guests, she lowered herself into a large velvet-covered armchair, in which no one else had any right to sit. Katya placed a little bench under her feet; the old woman didn't thank her and didn't even glance up; she merely placed her hands underneath the yellow shawl covering almost her entire feeble body. The princess loved the color yellow: she was also wearing a cap with bright yellow ribbons."[7] Bazarov thinks of her with his typical gruffness—"It's all *for the sake of appearance* they keep her, because she comes from a princely line" (*Dlia radi vazhnosti derzhat, potomu chto kniazheskoe otrod'e* [or because she is a "princely spawn"])—thus discerning in the aunt an old-fashioned marker of aristocratic prestige, a continuity of pedigree dubious (or at best irrelevant) to the *raznochinets* worldview, but presumably much vaunted by the Odintsova household.[8] Yet, by the near-symmetrical logic of *Fathers and Children*, the old Princess is a version, albeit an odd one, of Pavel Kirsanov: silenced, unloved, physically frail, historically passé, and literarily predetermined. The difference is that the description of Pavel, with its excessive attention to dress and mannerisms, only *begins* to reduce him to a historical type, hinting at, without consigning him to, the more extreme caricaturistic marginality embodied in the cameo appearance of the Princess, a character borrowed explicitly from another classic. If in Pushkin, however, the Countess's obsolescence is still a discovery to be made by Hermann and the reader, in Turgenev it is already a foregone conclusion. It is now the uncle, a man of the 1840s, who is captured in the process of forfeiting a continuous dynamic relationship with the present, even as the aunt, a woman of the Catherine era, has already completed this process and is defined above all by the barrier between her own "flatness" and the other characters' "roundness" or dynamism.[9] As an author with a particular predilection for portraiture,[10] Turgenev is acutely sensitive to the processes by which the passing of time gradually erodes the neutrality of speech and thought styles, appearances and mores, rendering them more and more historically specific and hence open to parody or, at least, to such descriptive shorthand as sums up (and dismisses) Odintsova's aunt.

   This observation is especially true of Turgenev's eighteenth-century characters, the least analyzed but in fact most populous historical layer of Turgenev's gentry milieus, and one in which the kind of character I am broadly defining as the "uncle" is particularly well represented.[11] Turgenev's works are chock full of uncles and aunts seemingly bereft of offspring, or whose children have become estranged and remain outside the narrative frame. These characters embody specific historical layers, most often the eighteenth century, in an oeuvre that is not openly or primarily concerned with capturing the past, but that rather observes the subtle ways in which history is woven into the present's texture.[12] Turgenev's descriptions of eighteenth-century characters ostensibly follow the exact same outline as his other character portraits: the narrators pause their stories to interject deliberate and unhurried expositions of the characters' social and familial backgrounds (often reaching several generations or even several centuries into the past), the layouts of their houses and the rosters of their extensive households, their clothing preferences and daily routines, their gestural and linguistic eccentricities. Less typical of Turgenev's overall technique is that these eighteenth-century portraits do not evince development through action or reflection; neither do they represent specific socio-historical types, as for example in *La Comédie Humaine*. Instead they are saddled, as it were, with the task of standing for an entire historical epoch. Deprived of even the least nuanced psychological agency, eighteenth-century characters comprise exclusively *historical* identities.

In text after text, Turgenev sketches his eighteenth-century types, but their connections to his contemporaries are repeatedly shown as tenuous, their power to resurrect the eighteenth century for nineteenth-century Russians deeply problematic. The narrators, always nineteenth-century men through and through, view these "ruins"[13] with curiosity, but ultimately also with detachment and incomprehension; even in cases when they show some desire to connect with the past, the narrators maintain their standpoint as observers. Assembled as a corpus in this final chapter of my study, these partial, often grotesque, simulacra of the Russian eighteenth century encapsulate Russia's problematic civilizing history and the detachment from this first scenario of Enlightenment that Russian intellectuals profess in the second half of the nineteenth century.[14] And yet these same simulacra persist as potential answers, by now entirely illegible, to the abiding question of the origin and nature of Russian modernity; their very presence puts the nineteenth century's belief in progress to the test. Turgenev's oeuvre, though constructing the eighteenth century as ubiquitous in the figures of far-flung relatives and distant neighbors, displaces the period of post-Petrine modernization, typically considered seminal for the Russian Empire, to the margins of Russia's history and nineteenth-century social space; but at the same time Turgenev's works insistently revisit this era.

The following table collects all of Turgenev's characterological excurses into the eighteenth century, documenting the degrees of his eighteenth-century characters' separation from their nineteenth-century observers.

Title, year	Identity of 18th-century character
"Three Portraits" ("Tri portreta"), 1846	Great uncle of the narrator's neighbor
"The Peasant Proprietor Ovsiannikov" ("Odnodvorets Ovsiannikov"), from *A Sportsman's Sketches*, 1847	The sportsman narrator's distant neighbor
"Raspberry Spring" ("Malinovaia voda"), from *A Sportsman's Sketches*, 1847	A former butler of a deceased count whose ruined manor can be found in the sportsman narrator's neighborhood
"The Quiet Spot" ("Zatish'e"), 1854	The narrator's aging neighbor's mother
A Nest of the Gentry (*Dvorianskoe gnezdo*), 1859	Lavretskii's (the protagonist's) great aunt, who raised his father, but has no children of her own
Fathers and Children (*Ottsy i deti*), 1862	Odintsova's aunt; no known children of her own
"Phantoms" ("Prizraki"), 1864	Phantoms, part of a fleeting vision
"The Brigadier" ("Brigadir"), 1866	The narrator's university friend's senile and childless neighbor
Smoke (*Dym*), 1867	A ridiculous and ignored member of émigré circles
"An Unfortunate Girl" ("Neschastnaia"), 1868	The aristocratic father of the heroine, his illegitimate daughter from a Jewish mother
Virgin Soil (*Nov'*), 1876	Fimushka and Fomushka – the childless distant relatives of Paklin's (a second-tier character's) mother
"Old Portaits" ("Starye portrety"), 1881	The narrator's mother's great uncle and aunt, who have two daughters, but are not in contact with them

We see Turgenev's interest in the eighteenth century span the entirety of his creative career and manifest itself in an array of works, including four of his six novels and eight stories and novellas. All these characters bear only a lateral, metonymic relation to those who possess narrative interest or narrative voice. They are dredged up by chance and easily forgotten. As Turgenev writes of his detour into the eighteenth century in *Virgin Soil*, "Fomushka and Fimushka [the novel's eighteenth-century characters] are an insertion which can be extracted without any damage to the whole . . . This alone condemns them irrevocably."[15] Quintessential "uncles," these characters both belong to and are easily excised from the immediate family. They embody a specific historical layer whose relationship to the present is troubling or tenuous at best.

Some of these characters are striking in the repetitiveness of their descriptions. Thus, Odintsova's aunt resembles a character from the earlier *A Nest of the Gentry* (1859), where the thematic elements of Pushkin's novella—erotic, sartorial, financial—are fitted into a mere paragraph, one among many that provide background information on the novel's protagonist, Lavretsky:

> Ivan [. . .] lived with a rich old maiden aunt, the Princess Kubensky; she had fixed on him for her heir [. . .]. She dressed him up like a doll, engaged all kinds of teachers for him, and put him in the charge of a tutor, a Frenchman, who had been an abbé, a pupil of Jean-Jacques Rousseau, a certain M. Courtin de Vaucelles, a subtle and wily intriguer—the very, as she expressed it, *fine fleur* of emigration—and finished at almost seventy years old by marrying this *"fine fleur,"* and making over all her property to him. Soon afterwards, covered with rouge, and redolent of perfume *à la Richelieu*, surrounded by negro boys, delicate-shaped greyhounds and shrieking parrots, she died on a crooked silken divan of the time of Louis XV, with an enameled snuff-box of Petitot's workmanship in her hand; the insinuating M. Courtin had preferred to remove to Paris with her money.[16]

As another echo of Pushkin's Countess, now a veritable character type, Lavretsky's great-aunt seems to make her episodic appearance only in order to imply an archetypal gentry pedigree for the novel's protagonist. If Princess Kubensky belongs to a type but nevertheless still possesses a story of her own, in his much later novel *Smoke* (1867) Turgenev sketches an outright caricature of the Countess, an "old ruin"[17] living out her days in Baden-Baden: "It seemed every instant as though she would fall to pieces: she shrugged her bare, gruesome, dingy gray shoulders, and, covering her mouth with her fan, leered languishingly with her absolutely death-like eyes upon Ratmirov; he paid her much attention; she was held in great honor in the highest society, as the last of the Maids of Honor of the Empress Catherine."[18] By the late 1860s, Pushkin's representation of the aged Catherinian beauty has assumed the form of a laughable automaton, a figure no longer of the Gothic, but of a slapstick imagination. Courted in jest by the odiously conservative general Ratmirov, the "ruin" epitomizes the moral bankruptcy of post-Reform Russian conservatism, itself a thing of the past.[19] Turgenev's caricatures comically contrast with his ever-hesitant and hazy modern protagonists; in effect "quoted" from Pushkin, they acknowledge the living presence of that great predecessor as the ultimate intertext, but do not impute any relevance to Catherine's senescent retinue. The motley émigré crowd in *Smoke* unavoidably includes a copy of Catherine. In Turgenev's novels, émigré society embalms outdated forms of Russian life, particularly forms of aristocratic pretense and superfluity. But it also allows the novelist to bring into close proximity characters who would not inhabit the same social space in Russia: thus, in Baden-Baden the novel's non-hero Litvinov is forced to observe a Catherinian relic.[20] The palimpsest of epochs and cultures, which in the 1830s seemed so exhilarating to the likes of Kireevskii and Bestuzhev-Marlinskii, in *Smoke* is recognized with aversion and melancholy. And by now the epochal palimpsest itself seems a hardened "type" of historicist description.

Turgenev's oeuvre is marked by a repetitiveness of a sort not found in the works of the other major Russian novelists of the nineteenth century, and it is certainly tempting to dismiss this feature of his corpus as a mere defect, unworthy of further comment. But what indeed is the point of minor characters who not only resemble one another, but also seem lifted from another author's work? If this is a typological description, does one instance not already stand for the entire type? Yet Turgenev's oeuvre, in covering the same characterological terrain over and over, seems also to point to some urgency of his project, as if capturing the passing Russian past, and doing it just right, might also illuminate something essential in Russia's present, from which Turgenev, too—in a way not vastly unlike his minor characters—was detached by years of voluntary exile abroad. In the introduction to his collected novels, Turgenev famously declared: "I have sought, with as much effort and ability as I could muster, conscientiously and impartially to depict and incarnate in appropriate types what Shakespeare called 'the body and pressure of time,' and that swiftly changing physiognomy of Russians of the cultured stratum, which has comprised the main object of my observations."[21] Where in the unchanging representations of eighteenth-century human relics do we locate this intended dynamism? I believe the answer lies precisely in this statement of Turgenev's purpose, for it is against the ossified backdrop of eighteenth-century modernity, a crucible of reform now forever cooled, that the rapid advancements of the nineteenth century stand out. And the more "swiftly" the "physiognomy of Russians of the cultured stratum" changes, the more ludicrously its forebears cling to their existence. (Indeed, as the latest of the three novels cited, *Smoke* offers the most grotesque portrait of the past.)

On the one hand, then, the distance Turgenev's generation has put between itself and the past distinguishes his early portraits of the eighteenth century from the later ones. But the signified itself also changes, despite all the stability of its signifiers. If in the 1840s–'50s, the men and women of the eighteenth century are still a living reality, in the 1860s–'80s the descriptions begin to lose their referential substance, intertextually replicating each other and their models. Turgenev's historicist and realist projects, the frameworks which I will revisit throughout this chapter, thus part ways. Moreover, the reception of the eighteenth century also undergoes a change in the late 1800s. Turgenev's earlier texts are written in a period when Russian readers actively disavow eighteenth-century literature and culture as anything worthwhile; this is when, for example, Derzhavin's famous biographer and commentator Iakov Grot, as noted in chapter 1, sensed the reading public's skepticism as to the value of publishing Derzhavin's collected works and admitted that the spirit of the ode was "unsympathetic" to contemporary sensibilities. The consolidation of the Slavophile position on Russia's unique course of development further challenged the "westernizing" achievements of the Petrine and post-Petrine enlightenment. This rejection of the eighteenth century persists roughly into the mid-1860s, when we detect increased interest in this period and in historical antiquarianism generally, as evinced in such periodicals as *The Russian Archive* (*Russkii arkhiv*, 1863–1917) and *Russian Antiquity* (*Russkaia starina*, 1870–1918). Turgenev's texts can be read as at the same time disowning the eighteenth century *and*, not unlike his antiquarian peers, examining its remnants with much care and attention. The eighteenth-century history his narratives simultaneously recover and marginalize is furthermore inextricably bound up with the single most important event, for liberals like Turgenev, of the nineteenth century: the Emancipation of the serfs in 1861. Many of the post-Reform sketches in particular consider the nature of eighteenth-century landowner authority—the arbitrariness, crudity, and violence of this class. It is as if the eighteenth century, now reconceived as the age par excellence of Russia's protracted feudalism, only ends in the 1860s.

Finally, the representation of minor characters takes different shapes depending on the size and ambition of the work in which they are embedded. In novels, for Turgenev a genre fundamentally focused on the present, eighteenth-century characters are marginalized far more definitively than in the shorter fiction, where the author seems to find himself at greater liberty to examine precisely the non-synchronous margins of his contemporary moment, often in fact constituting this contemporary moment through its margins. The novels, as it were, put eighteenth-century characters in their "proper" place, depicting their mindsets as outdated, abbreviating and fragmenting their life stories, segregating their habitats. Serving in many ways as workbooks for the novels, Turgenev's sketches and novellas fill out the character contours the novels leave unfinished: the shorter texts advance a very different understanding of character, a conception that, once extracted from the involved character systems that both novels and society inevitably impose upon it, emerges as all-important and deserving of close examination. Thus, Turgenev's short fictions promote eighteenth-century characters to central roles in which they—and their marginality—can be scrutinized. Eager to capture the present and follow the protagonist's story, the novels caricature minor characters; but in the accretion of characterological detail afforded by short fiction, a wistful lyricism materializes and rescues the individual from his effacement by typification. In the following sections, I examine fiction that avails itself of both representational modes and originates in pre- and post-Reform periods alike.

THE LITTLE PEOPLE

A striking device for rendering both the marginalization of eighteenth-century characters and the narrators' incomprehension in dealing with them is Turgenev's use of diminutives in his descriptions, where these terms abound to the point of tastelessness. Even the more interesting eighteenth-century characters, those likely to engage the reader, have *gubki, glazki, golosok, volosiki, melkii smekh* (little lips, little eyes, little voice, little locks of hair, little laugh), are *malen'kie, puzaten'kie, starichki, starushki v koliasochkakh* (small, possessed of tiny little paunches, little old men and women in little wheelchairs), and so on. The diminutives render these figures both touching and ridiculous, but more than anything, they highlight the perspective of the external observer uttering them, who, even in attempting conversation with these characters, remains undoubtedly removed from them, passing historical judgment, bracketing off this particular province of the past as no more than a curiosity, yet feeling inexplicably drawn to it. The diminutives essentially describe the men and women of the eighteenth century as objects, albeit art objects in the genre of miniature portraiture, which at least in Russia had its heyday precisely in the eighteenth century and, to Turgenev's contemporaries, signaled the era of Catherine the Great.

Among the textual genres that correspond to the miniature, anecdotes repeatedly supply the small conversational form so characteristic of these portrayals while also conveying the fragmentariness of our access to the eighteenth century. These are stories that eighteenth-century characters are implored to tell and that others tell about them; eighteenth-century life, it seems, cannot be reconstructed through narrative genres that might extend beyond the brackets of a briefly recollected situation or a remembered *bon mot*. Like the miniature figural representation in the plastic and pictorial arts that motivates Turgenev's diminutives, anecdotal narratives were cultivated in the eighteenth century as one of the western modes of Enlightenment sociability adopted by the Russian elite. But more significantly, the anecdote was the genre through which nineteenth-century writers and memoirists (most famously Pushkin in his *Table-Talk*) received and memorialized the eighteenth century, and Turgenev's use of the anecdote relies upon his readers' recognition of it as an eighteenth-century form as much as it does upon their interest in its content. Anecdotes are fragments of greater narratives they only vaguely adumbrate, and at the same time they constitute a complete and self-sufficient form. Like Turgenev's eighteenth-century characters themselves, anecdotes are poignant, curious, disposable, and, strangely, both autonomous from and dependent upon the greater historical narrative they are supposed to encapsulate. But anecdotes, again exactly like the characters, are also literary constructs—infinitely recyclable borrowings from another's story. Soliciting and listening to eighteenth-century anecdotes enables Turgenev's narrators to dismiss the eighteenth century while also pondering what lies behind its few preserved fragments—in other words, to privilege the anecdotal means to equivocate between satirical and allegorical readings of the eighteenth century, both a search for its meaning and its deflation.

The precise definition that miniatures and anecdotes impart to Turgenev's eighteenth-century subjects contrasts sharply with the blurred psychological profiles of his modern protagonists. And, as a result, despite the caricaturistic effect, there persists some uncertainty as to the relative merits of the pithily focalized past and the washed-out, indeterminate present. We might, foregrounding this uncertainty or "hesitation" (to use Irving Howe's apt description of Turgenev's poetics[22]), perhaps glimpse a solution to the age-old debate about the success or failure of the seemingly incongruous eighteenth-century vignette in Turgenev's last novel, *Virgin Soil* (1876). The insular world of Fomushka and Fimushka Subochev presents an antithesis to the revolutionary aspirations and indiscriminate actions of the novel's protagonists, the young radicals of the 1870s.[23] Half parody, half idyll, this scene has been appraised by critics as, alternately, the pinnacle of Turgenev's art and an embarrassing failure.[24] In

the letter to K. D. Kavelin (December 29, 1876) cited earlier, Turgenev himself attributes his foray into the eighteenth century to temptation: "I simply
could not resist the desire to paint an old Russian picture as a 'repoussoir' or
oasis if you will." In this vignette, the novel's most importunate and unpleasant
character, Paklin, conducts the accidentally assembled members of his revolutionary circle into his relatives' household, which in the 1870s still lives by
eighteenth-century codes. This is the world of Gogol's "Old-World Landowners" ("Starosvetskie pomeshchiki," 1833–34).[25]

> Imagine, it's an oasis! Neither politics, literature, nor anything modern ever pen-
> etrates there. [...] [T]he very smell [...] is antique; the people antique, the
> air antique ... whatever you touch is antique, Catherine II: powder, crinolines,
> 18th century! And the host and hostess ... imagine a husband and wife both
> very old, of the same age, without a wrinkle, chubby, round, neat little people,
> just like two poll-parrots. [...] They both dress alike, in a sort of loose striped
> gown [...]. They are exactly like one another, except that one wears a mob-cap,
> the other a skull-cap, which is trimmed with the same kind of frill, only without
> ribbons. If it were not for these ribbons, you would not know one from the other,
> as the husband is clean-shaven. One is called Fomushka, the other Fimushka.
> I tell you one ought to pay to go and look at them![26]

In this chapter, where, as Howe puts it, "the very words seem to shrink into
miniatures,"[27] the miraculously preserved eighteenth-century couple appears
as a diversion for the contemporary viewer/reader, as curiosities fit only for
Paklin's imagined menagerie of the past.

Like the dwarf they keep in the house (another now-perverse marker of
eighteenth-century social custom), Fimushka and Fomushka are freakish in
their obliviousness to historical change and their uncanny, almost androg-
ynous parroting of one another. In their idyllic symbiosis, the husband and
wife, like twin parrots, differ only by a letter in their names (presented to us,
unsurprisingly, in the informal diminutive) and a ribbon on their caps. Their
striking resemblance parodies the colorful fashions of the previous century,
which allowed male and female costume the same flamboyance and reveled
in cross-dressing and *subtle* gender difference. The couple inhabits the period
before the Napoleonic era, when, as we saw in the previous chapter, male attire
assumed its modern uniform-like shape in "the Great Masculine Renunciation." While Turgenev thus dates the pair with great precision, their fairy-tale
charm and the mixture of nostalgia and satire in their portrayal belong less to

history than to Gogol's mythologizing tradition. Fimushka and Fomushka are "old-world landowners," wonderfully autonomous and detached, as creatures of myth, from either contemporaneity or any datable past.

What kind of a contrast ("repoussoir") does Turgenev achieve in having his modern radical youths examine the travestied eighteenth century against the backdrop of their own world? Turgenev's contrasts—generational and otherwise—are notoriously unstable, favoring no one side exclusively. The visit to Fimushka and Fomushka infuses the novel with a historical expanse wherein characters are placed not only generations, but centuries apart. Even as Paklin and his friends trivialize and condemn the "antique" existence of Turgenev's "old-world landowners," the old couple's self-sufficient paradise frames and trivializes the misguided revolutionary restlessness of the young. It hardly seems an accident that Turgenev uses the painterly term "repoussoir" to characterize his device. As in a painting, where an object placed prominently in the foreground creates an illusion of depth that draws the viewer into the composition, the visit to Fimushka and Fomushka—Turgenev's comical repoussoir—brackets the world of the 1870s and thereby questions it. Through the travesty of equality and primitive undifferentiation, Turgenev links the century of women-rulers (*vek imperatrits*) with the time of the "woman question," and is skeptical about both.

Turgenev's radicals find it hard to follow their nihilistic negation of the existing world-order with constructive action. While the protagonist of *Virgin Soil*, Nezhdanov, imprudently seeks answers to his malaise in "going to the people," another world, that of Fimushka and Fomushka, is depicted— admittedly with minimal sympathy—as on the verge of slipping away. Paklin again offers unexpected insight: "[W]ould you like to know how people lived a century, a century and a half ago, make haste then and follow me. Or soon a day and hour will come—it's bound to be the same hour for both— and my poll-parrots will be knocked off their perches, and all that's antique will end with them [. . .]. [T]he very street will cease to be, and men will come and go and never see anything like this again in all the ages!"[28] In playing up the attraction of the Subochev "oasis" as something potentially vanishing overnight, to be overgrown by weeds, Paklin in his enthusiasm inadvertently conjures a dystopian future devoid of history. Ironically, this desolate world occupies the same space as the bright future envisioned by the Nezhdanovs of the novel. While the "new man," espouser of humanity as *tabula rasa*, is about to put behind him the Romantic historicist notions of the present as everywhere saturated by traces of the past, *nov'*, or virgin soil, which he will then supposedly cultivate for the first time, conceals other, equally fruit-less, historical layers.

One of the attractions to which Paklin treats his companions is Fomushka's attachment to his old snuffbox, the proverbial object that not only furnished the central prop for eighteenth-century social theater, but also became in the 1830s a metonym for the masculinities flaunted and ridiculed by Gogol: "Fomushka brought out and showed the visitors his favorite carved wood snuff-box, on which it had once been possible to distinguish thirty-six figures in various atti-tudes; they had long ago been effaced, but Fomushka saw them, saw them still, and could distinguish them and point them out. 'See,' he said, 'there's one look-ing out of a window; do you see, he's put his head out . . . ' and the spot to which he pointed [. . .] was just as smooth as all the rest of the snuff-box lid."[29] This is perhaps the most touching illusionistic trick enabled by Turgenev's repous-soir. Fomushka invites the reader to imagine what time seems to have erased. The snuffbox—a supremely ironic container, a keepsake of the eighteenth cen-tury but also its reliquary—wavers between the functions of a repoussoir and a trompe-l'oeil, revealing the past's depth and staying power, yet also undermin-ing its claims to plenitude and signification. The effaced figures on Fomushka's snuffbox embody the disembodiment, the kind of emptying out that histori-cal flow effects upon character, the gradual erasure of dynamic personhood that we have seen performed upon Pavel Petrovich Kirsanov earlier in this chapter. This process of erasure hangs a pessimistic question mark over the pursuits of Turgenev's progress-loving contemporary heroes. Why can they not see the figures, and will they not also be erased?

THE EIGHTEENTH CENTURY'S ILLEGITIMATE CHILDREN

The familial genealogical line—the very line whose generative if not ideologi-cal directness is so privileged in the Scottian historical novel or in Leo Tolstoy's fiction—in Turgenev's oeuvre follows a tortuous path; despite the obvious fact of human continuity, the main characters' roots can seemingly never be traced *directly* to the eighteenth century. Eighteenth-century non-progenitors in-sist on existing into the nineteenth; but whatever meaning they might yield becomes even murkier within the progress-oriented and ideologically agitated world of Turgenev's younger protagonists. Rather than moving in a linear fash-ion, Russian history here progresses through a series of "knight's moves," to invoke Viktor Shklovsky's metaphor for modern literary innovation.[30] One of the dominant strategies by which Turgenev relegates eighteenth-century characters to the fringes of Russian social space is their displacement to the periphery of *family* history.

Turgenev places the impossibility of a successful affective relationship with eighteenth-century characters at the center of several of his shorter works. His only eighteenth-century father-figure (not an uncle, but almost) appears in the 1868 novella "An Unfortunate Girl," where the heroine's illegitimacy casts a tragic shadow over her relationship with her aristocratic father and Jewish mother, and over her entire subsequent fate as well.[31] Similar to their grotesquely sexual female counterparts, eighteenth-century aristocratic men are often portrayed as having multiple children out of wedlock, both as a function of actual eighteenth-century mores (recall, for instance, Ivan Alekseevich Iakovlev, Alexander Herzen's much-resented natural father) and of bastardy's rich narrative potential in fiction (consider the important plot function of Pierre Bezukhov's contested legitimacy in *War and Peace*: settlement of his status launches the hero into adulthood). It is tempting to suggest as well that illegitimacy serves in these narratives to emblematize the nineteenth-century intellectuals' repudiation of the mortmain of flawed eighteenth-century modernity in their own differently modern times.

In her first-person account of her childhood, the heroine of "An Unfortunate Girl" remembers her father as incapable of affection and limited to a series of habitual gestures. He knows her to be his daughter, but never officially or even privately acknowledges her as such, and invites her instead to read to him daily from his favorite eighteenth-century *philosophes*. At first the heroine does not know Koltovsky's true role in her life and describes him in the detached manner typical of Turgenev's eighteenth-century character sketches in general: "Mr. Koltovsky was a tall, handsome old man with a stately manner; he always smelt of *ambre*. I stood in mortal terror of him, though he called me Suzon and gave me his dry, sinewy hand to kiss under its lace-ruffles. With my mother he was elaborately courteous, but he talked little even with her. He would say two or three affable words, to which she promptly made a hurried answer; and he would be silent and sit looking about him with dignity, and slowly picking up a pinch of Spanish snuff from his round, golden snuff-box with the arms of the Empress Catherine on it."[32] As the girl understands more of her position in her father's household (of which she remains a disenfranchised member, living in an out-of-the-way separate structure rather than in the manor), her attempts to challenge the hierarchical status quo and the silence governing their relationship run up, as does the changed tenor of her descriptions, against old Koltovsky's studied aloofness:

"Mr. Koltovsky continued to interest himself in my education, and even by degrees put me on a more intimate footing. He did not talk to me . . . but morning and evening, after flicking the snuff from his jabot with two fingers, he would with the same two fingers—always icy cold—pat me on the cheek and give me some sort of dark-colored sweetmeats, also smelling of *ambre*, which I never ate."[33] The ritualistic unfolding of the father-daughter encounter comes to a halt when the daughter observes the unfeeling coldness of Koltovsky's fingers (extended not to bless her, but to pat her cheek) and secretly refuses to partake in the faux-communion ("some sort of dark-colored sweetmeats") offered her by her Voltairian father.

In this story, contact with a man of the eighteenth century, even a father, emerges as an experiential impossibility. The girl is led even to question the original emotional and physical contact between her parents that had resulted in her conception in the first place: "'And she loved him! Loved that old man!' was my thought. 'How could it be! Love him!'" The logic of this question, though prepared by all the heroine's experiences, is obviously and fundamentally flawed, most importantly because it does not conceive of Koltovsky's age as a process, as *aging*, but rather as his inalienable attribute. The man of the eighteenth century is always just that, enclosed in his historical identity, beyond which the modern protagonist finds it impossible to inquire, both because of her own prejudices and because of the father's disinterestedness in the rapprochement with his daughter. Just as the old aristocrat declines to acknowledge his daughter even on his deathbed, so the girl, too, ultimately proves incapable of acknowledging her father as anything more than an eighteenth-century type. In effect, she replicates the difficulty all of Turgenev's narratives seem to discover in portraying eighteenth-century characters, the kind of narratorial blindness within the all-seeing realist narrative that, I would argue, these characters are meant to bring into focus. How can a homodiegetic realist narrator, having imposed upon himself the constraints of empiricist observation, lay claim to interiorities and sensibilities formed by values and circumstances entirely beyond his reach? And conversely, if these interiorities are inscrutable, what is at stake in continually remarking upon their existence?[34]

As an alternative approach to this quandary, we might consider how Tolstoy, indeed famed for his narratorial omniscience, constructs historical continuity within his novels' gentry family lines. Tolstoy's protagonists are direct descendants of eighteenth-century men and women, engaged in complex and dynamic relationships with them: his eighteenth-century characters are parents and grandparents. In *War and Peace*, the old Nikolai Bolkonsky, Prince

Andrei's father, bequeaths to his son along with his estate his hot temper and intense, irritable intellectualism, a line of resemblance that runs down to his grandson Nikolai, whom we leave on the threshold of his first rite of passage, presumably in the Decembrist Uprising. Pierre Bezukhov, the illegitimate son of major Catherine-era grandee Kirill Vladimirovich Bezukhov, inherits from his father his massive physique, libido, and fortune. This latter relationship, occupying relatively little space within the novel and ostensibly even more distant than the father-daughter connection of "An Unfortunate Girl"—for instance, we never see Pierre engage in an actual conversation with the old Count—ultimately evinces a certain dynamism when Pierre is declared the legitimate and only Bezukhov heir. Robust and prolific (as is much in Tolstoy), these figures leave their unmistakable imprint on their sons, persisting into the new age through their gestures and sentiments as much as their socio-economic status, both aspects of self-fashioning much amended in the nineteenth century, but always comfortably bearing the traces of the past.

Like the genealogical line, Tolstoy's eighteenth-century characters' involvement with younger counterparts is direct and uncomplicated; epochal shifts exist, indeed quite palpably, but they do not paralyze intergenerational connections.[35] These are above all *personal* relationships, introduced as studies first in individual psychology, and only then in historical typology. In *Childhood* (*Detstvo*, 1852), the protagonist, Nikolen'ka Irten'ev, is fascinated with his grandmother and deeply affected, and to some extent traumatized, by his father. Unequivocally associated with the eighteenth century, the father in *Childhood* resembles some of Turgenev's characters in his problematic relationship with the present but is never portrayed completely as an outsider or a flat character simply by virtue of his eighteenth-century origins: "He was a man of the last century and possessed that indefinable chivalry of character and spirit of enterprise, the self-confidence, amiability and sensuality which were common to the youth of that period. He regarded the young people of our day with a contempt arising partly from an innate pride and partly from a secret feeling of vexation that he could not in our time enjoy either the influence or the success he had had in his own."[36] In its epoch-awareness, this portrayal recalls Turgenev; but here the obsolescence noted is something the character consciously experiences rather than what is observed about him from the outside. The passage exemplifies the complex work of double narration in *Childhood*.[37] The mature Irten'ev rationalizes his childhood confusion about his father: the young boy understood nothing about his father's frequent absences and his mother's dejection, but the adult narrator ascribes what he now knows to have been his father's adulterous promiscuity to the mores of his eighteenth-century aristocratic milieu ("amiability and sensuality"). The father is presented as youthful, but youthful in the style of the previous century, a sharp contrast with old Koltovsky, who appears *ontologically* old. The adult narrator understands the father's secret vexation as occasioned by the supersession of epochs, and the character's psychological life becomes illuminated through the epochal understanding of historical time.

For Turgenev, this type of psychological illumination of eighteenth-century characters appears next to impossible. His 1866 novella "The Brigadier" grapples precisely with the impossibility of laying hold of the past. Its young narrator spends considerable time and effort trying to get a former brigadier of the Catherinian army to open up to him. In this context, a brigadier is a particularly evocative entity: established under Peter I in 1698, this fairly high officer rank, placing its holder between colonel and major-general, was abolished in 1800 by Paul I as part of his campaign against the old Catherinian guard. The brigadier is, in other words, the only truly eighteenth-century military rank in Russian history. Thus, when placed in the work's title, it binds the protagonist to a very specific historical period. Turgenev's "Brigadier" is also a deliberate reference to Fonvizin's comedy of the same name.[38] Composed in 1766, exactly a hundred years before Turgenev's story, the play mocked Russians' uncritical aping of Western behavior and lampooned the notion that rank at the Russian court corresponded to merit. As if to commemorate the centennial of Fonvizin's masterpiece, Turgenev's "Brigadier" takes this comical non-alignment of epaulets and importance to its extreme.[39] The rank memorializes the character's eighteenth-century achievements, but the character himself has since grown feeble and senile, and his observer is left to wonder at the lack of correspondence between his title and his mind and body, between the glorious signifier and the frail signified of the eighteenth century in the nineteenth.

It is not as though the narrator enters this encounter with any sort of dismissiveness regarding the past; indeed, he is keen to hear the old man tell of heroic feats under the leadership of the great Alexander Suvorov. But the brigadier—the would-be protagonist of a novella titled after this rank (although he is clearly no longer up to the role)—only nibbles on carrots or stares into a pond, his fishing rod drooping feebly along with his entire figure: "I could not conceive how this forlorn old man could once have been an officer, could have maintained discipline, have given his commands—and that, too, in the stern days of Catherine! I watched him: now and then he puffed out his cheeks and uttered a feeble whistle, like a child; sometimes he screwed up his eyes painfully, with effort, as all decrepit people will. Once he opened his eyes wide and lifted them . . . They stared at me from out of the depths of the water—and strangely touching and even full of meaning their dejected glance seemed to me."[40] The encounter between the brigadier and the narrator, or between the two centuries, is permeated with melancholy and mystery; it is a space where Turgenev can model a particular kind of narratorial gaze, characterized by hesitant incomprehension.[41] The story is left hollow at its very center. But it is out of this emptiness and dejection (*unynie*) that the narrator finally manages to extract meaning—a meaning, however, having little to do with his initial generals-and-battles project of historicist reconstruction.

Let us again pause here at a parallel yet divergent passage from Tolstoy in order to contrast more precisely the sources from which historical meaning is derived in the two writers' character portraits. In this passage, the old Prince Bolkonsky suppresses the news of the Russian army's retreat he has just received in a letter from his son by conjuring memories of his own time in the Catherinian military when still a dashing general in his prime: "He put the letter under the candlestick and closed his eyes. And there rose before him the Danube at bright noonday: reeds, the Russian camp, and himself a young general without a wrinkle on his ruddy face, vigorous and alert, entering Potemkin's gaily colored tent, and a burning sense of jealousy of 'the favorite' agitated him now as strongly as it had done then. He recalled all the words spoken at that first meeting with Potemkin. And he saw before him a plump, rather sallow-faced, short, stout woman, the Empress Mother, with her smile and her words at her first gracious reception of him, and then that same face on the catafalque, and the encounter he had with Zubov over her coffin about his right to kiss her hand."[42] The comparison with Turgenev's brigadier is perhaps unfair, for this passage in *War and Peace* is preceded by many others that have fleshed out the old Prince's character and prepared us to read his reminiscences as a fragment of deep psychological description, whereas the narrator of "The Brigadier" passes only an afternoon in his subject's company, even if later returning to discuss him in other contexts. More crucially, if Tolstoy is famously comfortable with entering his characters' minds, slipping in unnoticeably, Turgenev is not, and the passageways into character consciousness remain marked, at times awkwardly so, even in his late novels. Yet for all their incommensurability, both examples pose the question of how to reconcile the images of young and old man as the same person, or in narrative terms, how to grant a secondary character a long life story without disrupting narrative economy, or digressing too far from the character contour as drawn in the present of his old age. As we have seen, Turgenev's answer is not only to acknowledge the challenge, but also, crucially, to suspend the narrative in places where a connection between youth and old age, the eighteenth and nineteenth centuries, must be articulated.[43]

Tolstoy links Bolkonsky's past to his present forcefully yet sparingly. On the one hand, the passage showcases the novel's overarching faith in the continuity of Russian history, in particular one conceived as the history of Russian nobility and their service as the site of historical action. On the other, the passage's affective content—the same emotion, "a burning sense of jealousy," "agitat[ing] him now as strongly as it had done then"—instantiates Tolstoy's overall tendency to emphasize character integrity and attach certain gestures, passions, and behaviors to specific characters and character families throughout their novelistic trajectories. Bolkonsky's jealousy of his son's active place in the military transports him to a time during the Russo-Turkish War of 1787–92 when his own position was similar to or even more enviable than his son's, yet the feeling of jealousy was already there, only directed elsewhere, at the "favorite" Potemkin; the same emotional conduit conveys him to the next situation where his proximity to power was eclipsed by someone still more fortunate, this time another favorite of the empress, Platon Zubov. We recognize the old Prince in all three situations, which are, moreover, narrated in a peculiar style whereby certain features of his speech and thinking ("the Empress Mother"; *matushka-imperatritsa*) crop up amid the narrator's summary retelling ("He recalled all the words"; *I on vspominaet vse te slova*). Ambition and competitiveness are some of the qualities that stitch together the old Prince's life-narrative and make it legible; they also connect father and son through family resemblance, even as these reminiscences take the Prince away from his son's letter and the present moment. We could in fact just as easily imagine Andrei by Potemkin's side, or arguing with Zubov over the right to kiss the dead empress. Ultimately, memory does not convey the elder Bolkonsky to any fundamentally different world; it merely extends the novel's historical timeline further into the past. In Turgenev's world, modern man is insistently curious about the past precisely because he cannot imagine living in it, because he perceives identity as molded by the times, indeed stiflingly affixed to individuals by the epoch that first formed them; but it is also for this reason that these identities remain impenetrable to men of a different generation.

The moment when the Prince closes his eyes marks his descent into self-isolation, the only space where his authority and identity can still be asserted.

No one encourages him to reminisce or awaits the content of his recollections. In fact, no one observes the old Prince at all save for the omniscient narrator, whom some readers of Tolstoy describe as godlike; and this is how—that is, with an almost divine effortlessness and imperceptibility—the past is exposed. In Turgenev's novellas, by contrast, the narrator is always an embodied and enquiring presence and all sources of knowledge are marked as belonging to a perspective that is represented in the narrative. And yet this embodied narrator also conspicuously lacks an identity or story of his own and repeatedly looks to others to supply his narratives' content. Many Turgenev stories (most notably those comprising *A Sportsman's Sketches*) develop precisely from the narrator's encounters with various potential storytellers who all invariably oblige their guest with stories; gradually, the narrator's character and world-view begin to emerge as he responds to others. "The Brigadier" ultimately follows the same scenario. The encounter with the brigadier himself does little to fill the vacuum of the narrator's identity, leaving a void not only where the story seeks to find the eighteenth century, but also at the site from which observation, and by extension reading itself, takes place. Eventually, however, the narrator's friend arrives and dutifully recounts the brigadier's love story, accompanying it with a letter written by the brigadier himself when he was still young and articulate. But the appeal of the brigadier's mystery, I would argue, rests not in this love story, which is passionate yet not unusual, but rather in the impossibility of discerning even a trace of the story in his illegible, senile figure.[44] Tolstoy's narrative is ultimately optimistic about knowledge, whether historical or interpersonal, and about identity; Turgenev's, investing so much into the potential of observation to provide insight, comes up against the limitations of the mimetic approach. The experiment of observation is staged over and over again, but the results are meager, particularly when it comes to historical illumination.

In rejecting the notion that Turgenev's texts are losing their appeal to our own contemporary sensibilities because they are tethered more forcibly than Tolstoy's or Dostoevsky's to the topical realities of his day, Jane Costlow compellingly maintains that Turgenev's works have a "capacity to communicate beyond their moment and context of utterance [and] manifest a principle of rejuvenation and contemporaneity that defines them as literary."[45] It is in this context that she proposes that we recover the sense of "Turgenev's modification of the social novel by his own poetic vision and meditative concerns."[46] Here it is important to note that these works' lyricism in fact arises precisely from

their historicism, or rather from their conveyance of the inherent limited-
ness of historicism's explanatory frameworks, which attempt to fit typological
and epochal explanations to the human condition, with limited success.[47] The
failed conversation with the brigadier emblematically represents many others
in which the opaque and superficial rendering of eighteenth-century characters foregrounds the challenge they pose to realist description and historicist
interpretation. The floor gives way, and they fall right out of the very historicist narrative of progress and linearity that enables Turgenev and his contemporaries to see them as epochally defined and superannuated in the first place.
These characters become the blind spots of realist fiction, which so wholeheartedly embraces historicist modes of parsing the world. And that blindness
is nowhere more apparent than in Turgenev, but also nowhere more a problem
to be acknowledged and tackled.

Illuminating a different type of social margin, Eve Sedgwick writes about the
figure of the uncle as making legible the possibilities of alterity, for her primarily the alterity of gender relations, within the family: "If having grandparents
means perceiving your parents as somebody's children, then having aunts and
uncles, even the most conventional of aunts and uncles, means perceiving your
parents as somebody's sibs—not, that is, as alternately abject and omnipotent
links in a chain of compulsion and replication that leads inevitably to *you*; but
rather as elements in a varied, contingent, recalcitrant but re-forming seriality,
as people who demonstrably could have turned out very differently—indeed
as people who, in the differing, refractive relations among their own generation, can be seen already to have done so."[48] Could the nineteenth century have
turned out very differently? And are Turgenev's eighteenth-century characters
reminders of those alternatives? Sedgwick's seems a much more optimistic
project of reclaiming what she calls the *avunculate* as a space for imagining
genealogy as constituted through choice and difference. For Turgenev in fact,
the "uncles" seem to represent a similar space of otherness, but the projects
of its reclamation are always frustrated. This otherness is indeed closer to
abjection—Turgenev's contemporaneity "condemns [eighteenth-century char-
acters] irrevocably"—and leaves only a faint trace on the present, adumbrating a road explicitly not taken, a cluster of foreclosed historical potentialities,
and an earlier modernity that has been displaced from discourse. Eighteenth-
century characters remind us not of alternative historical paths, but of the
melancholy and restricted vision that realism and historicism bring with
them. In that sense, their particular brand of alterity, perhaps, is that which
resists inclusion in the realist-historicist family.

THE ABANDONED ESTATE

If Balzac's types are products of a characteristically nineteenth-century urban vision which excels at capturing the multiple entanglements of ages, genders, and social classes, of cultural backgrounds and financial and erotic aspirations, the majority of Turgenev's types have roots in the culture of the Russian country estate: in order to encounter them, one often really needs to be a country traveler, to move from manor to manor and village to village, as is done most notably by the narrator of *A Sportsman's Sketches*. Turgenev's Russian space accommodates enclaves of subcultures, replicating, though with diminished glee, the premise of travel that had shaped Gogol's *Dead Souls* and underlain the satirical-cum-lyrical sense of Russia's vastness bequeathed thereby to later writers, Turgenev certainly among them. This is the kind of enclave or "oasis" where, as we have seen, Paklin in *Virgin Soil* bids his friends witness the survival of eighteenth-century lifestyles in the form of Fimushka and Fomushka's cottage. While Balzac's space is everywhere richly—indeed overwhelmingly— productive of narrative, Turgenev's, as we have already seen in the case of "The Brigadier," requires an inquisitive observer to wrest stories from its pedestrian, unexpressive circumstances.

If one were to deduce a chronotope from this and similar Turgenevan stories where the narrator arrives in some godforsaken locale to become only briefly interested in another way of life, one could say that in these narratives historical layers are arranged not in a palimpsest or mosaic (the two structures of crowding I have alluded to in the previous chapter in discussing the urban space of fashion and "The Queen of Spades"), but rather in a space that is discontinuous.[49] The temporality of the present's engagement with the past is likewise episodic. Fimushka and Fomushka are, as we recall, but an insert. And even in the short fiction where narrative interest lies precisely in such episodes of close engagement with the "oasis's" inhabitants, there persists a sense of the imminent ending to the time of visitation: the hosts get tired (as does the brigadier) or the guest needs to move on (the imperative that enables the transitions between stories in *A Sportsman's Sketches*). On the one hand, this chronotope of intermittence results in a kind of trivialization of the realms thus visited so briefly: these visits will likely make no lasting impact on the visitor. But on the other hand, this chronotope also places the premium of readerly attention not on what is seen, but on how it is experienced; on a lyricism that so often, in fact, emerges from scenes verging on the satirical; or on a critique that, while in most cases remaining unarticulated, is nevertheless often implicit in the very acts of seeing, story-telling, and, for the putatively engagé reader of Turgenev's generation, reading itself.

Brought into the story by the itinerant narrator, the world beyond the enclaves serves as the historicizing and ironic gloss on each encountered idyll, ultimately undermining its reality, for, in order to be seen, the idyllic space must be focalized by someone who does not belong to or even believe in it. In "Raspberry Spring," one of the stories in A *Sportsman's Sketches*, the narrator finds himself overlooking a deceased grandee's once prosperous estate, since turned to ruins; his interlocutor, old Tuman, a liberated serf and former butler at the mansion, reminisces about his *barin's* grand eighteenth-century ways. No word in the exchange is significant, or even interesting, except inasmuch as the lifestyle it describes is implicitly evaluated and questioned from the standpoint of mid-nineteenth-century contemporaneity. Conversely, the narrator's own present becomes legible in the pauses punctuating Tuman's speech and in the tentative, questioning gestures that mark what remains unsaid between the two speakers:

> "Ah, well, those were good times [*vremechko*], though!" added the old man with a deep sigh. His head drooped forward and he was silent.
>
> "Your master, I see, was severe, then?" I began after a brief silence.
>
> "That was the fashion [*vo vkuse*] then, your honour," he replied, shaking his head.
>
> "That sort of thing is not done now?" I observed, not taking my eyes off him.
>
> He gave me a look askance.
>
> "Now, surely it's better," he muttered, and let out his line further.[50]

Just as with the snuffbox whose faded figures are ever present only to Fimushka's eye, the plenitude of the grandee's world is here visible only to his old servant, the sole surviving witness to eighteenth-century splendor. His younger interlocutor, while inexplicably drawn to Tuman's nostalgic tales, invariably counters them with moral judgment against serfdom—an indictment that ironically is presented as marked both by a greater and by a lesser vision. Tuman and the narrator temporarily find themselves in the same locale, but their separate worldviews set them apart. As in any pastoral, utopia, or dystopia, the boundary between the space the narrator enters and observes and the space he leaves behind is wrought with tension: to what extent is the liberal judgment imposed on the eighteenth century by the progressive nineteenth-century intellectual farsighted or even justified? The interaction between oasis and surrounding world creates a space (here specifically historicist) where physical markers are nearly all erased, but historical and ethical ones dominate.

This dynamic acquires added historical poignancy in the wake of the Emancipation, which abolishes the very conditions that made the pastoral possible in the first place. The Great Reform was enacted in 1861, exactly a century after Peter III had liberated the Russian nobility from obligatory state service and thus allowed, for many nobles, that settled life on their estates whose indistinct echoes Turgenev's narrators seek to attend. The liberation of the serfs also eliminated some of the rights granted the gentry by Catherine II in her 1785 Charter to the Nobility, a document that strengthened local governance and local noble privilege.[51] In Turgenev's later works, the Emancipation comes to function as a watershed separating out the times of reading, narration, observation, and lived eighteenth-century experience.

Consider the final entry in this corpus, the semi-autobiographical "Old Portraits" (1880–81), in which the narrator visits his uncle, a lifelong fervent admirer of Catherine II, and aunt, whose entire identity hinges on a moment in her youth when her beauty was noted by Count Orlov.[52] (Similarly to Pushkin's Countess, she had been known as *la Vénus de Moscou*.) The novella is split into two sections: the first assembles anecdotal conversations with the old relatives, descriptions of their dress, lifestyle, and eventual deaths, idyllically occurring a month apart; the second punctures this essentially static idyll with a discordant event that illustrates how historical reality can make an incursion into any world purportedly exempt from it: "And so I can see my old friends as though they were alive and before my eyes, and pleasant is the memory I preserve of them. And yet on my very last visit to them (I was a student by then) an incident occurred which jarred upon the impression of patriarchal harmony always produced in me by the Telegin household."[53] A serf acquired by the Telegins from their neighbor through an undocumented exchange (in the good-natured way, it is suggested, business had been done in the eighteenth century) is now demanded back by the neighbor's notoriously cruel descendant; after some negotiation, the Telegins are forced to comply, and the formerly mild-spirited serf eventually murders his new master. Even though the Telegins are hardly responsible for the crime, their very conformity with the illegitimate world order implicates them irreparably.[54] The temporality of the tale complexly corresponds to the equivocations in its ethical reading. The landowners exist almost entirely in their nostalgic reminiscences of Catherine's times; Telegin, moreover, remarks with a mix of bafflement and pride that his mother was born under Peter the Great; and yet, at the time when the narrator meets them, they already inhabit the nineteenth-century world, one where serfdom is, to be sure, not yet abolished, but already interrogated as the "serf question." The narrator's position is similarly divided between several temporal points, most crucially between the time of his encounters with the Telegins in the 1830s–'40s (not insignificantly, Telegin dies in the revolutionary year—revolutionary, that is, elsewhere—of 1848) and the time of narration (1880), when the "serf question" itself has been permanently resolved.

If Turgenev's characters, particularly his representatives of the eighteenth century, are encased in shells of historicist typology, hence often bearing only a singular identity, country estates emerge as multivalent sites where layers of historical narrative can be both unearthed and buried, sites that can signify different epochs, and recall or suppress different ethical values within the same narrative or within the same fragmented conversation. Turgenev's provincial landscapes are thus often imbued with historical meaning, not only because the essentially historical consciousness of Turgenev's narrators and characters brings them into focus, but because they serve as living spaces for many generations of such characters. (Here it is particularly significant that the social classes Turgenev most frequently represents—the gentry and peasantry—are tied to the land.) While each successive generation seeks to clear out this space, to create its own "virgin soil," the estate landscape—often precisely in the traces of its refurbishment or abandonment—tells a continuous story of use.

For a final illustration, let us return to *Fathers and Children*, Turgenev's novel most openly engaged with the issues of intergenerational continuity and rupture. At the very opening of the novel, as he rides home side by side with his sentimental father and worries about the impression his household might make upon his model-nihilist friend Bazarov, the young Arkadii suddenly experiences a pang of unexplained emotion occasioned by the unremarkable landscape of his father's estate, which he observes as they pass through it:

> The area in which they were traveling couldn't be described as picturesque. Field after field stretched as far as the horizon, first gently ascending, then descending, here and there were little woodlands and winding ravines covered in sparse low-lying shrubs that called to mind their characteristic representation on ancient maps in the time of Catherine the Great. They came upon little streams with cleared banks, tiny ponds with fragile dams, little villages with low peasant huts under dark roofs often missing half their thatch, small crooked threshing

barns with walls of woven brushwood and gaping doorways beside abandoned threshing floors, and churches, some made of brick with the plaster falling off, others of wood with slanted crosses and overgrown cemeteries. Arkady's heart gradually sank.[55]

Arkadii's pang of emotion is first and foremost meant to foreshadow his uneasy path alongside Bazarov, ultimately as a kind of fellow-traveler (*poputchik*) rather than true believer. Within its immediate context, the passage also marks the time elapsed between Arkadii's boyhood, when he presumably last saw the estate and lacked the critical distance to notice its details, and his present state of eager maturation, which equips him with a powerful defamiliarizing lens. What makes his surroundings seem strange and disturbing to him now is not their newness, but rather their triviality. Everything about his family land is small, rundown, and monotonous—nothing is picturesque. Both the landscape and Arkadii's sentiments might in fact remind us of Grinev's lackluster arrival at the Belogorskaia Fortress in *The Captain's Daughter*. Like Grinev, Arkadii is eager for historic action, yet finds himself in a space that seems to exclude the possibility of feeling or making history. On a very basic level, the landscape alerts Arkadii to the poor state of his father's affairs (next he sees "peasants in tatters"), but it also delivers a more profound challenge to his new system of beliefs, a challenge he might not yet fully appreciate.

The estate bears the marks of its age. While in following Bazarov, Arkadii aspires to a new world where nothing is inherited or predetermined, he returns to the estate that he will eventually succeed to (more a burden than an inheritance), an estate everywhere encumbered with dilapidated and abandoned structures. This is precisely the scenario of an ambivalent inheriting and forgetting of the past that will resurface again in *Virgin Soil*, when Paklin imagines weeds growing over and eventually obliterating the culture of Fimushka and Fomushka, but, ironically, even this inconsequential sediment leaves this soil no longer virgin. In *Fathers and Children*, what will soon become sediment is the gentry way of life and the culture of the estate. The Emancipation undeniably changes Russia's socio-political landscape; in this sense, ages would seem to separate the year 1859, in which *Fathers and Children* is set (and when we see Arkadii on his ride home), and 1862, when the novel is published. This three-year lapse in fact creates a space of historical irony for Turgenev's reader to occupy: any remark or observation made in the novel has to be evaluated from two temporal standpoints, before and after the Emancipation. Thus, in

1859, Nikolai Kirsanov's land appears not so much marked as a relic from the feudal past as simply inhabited, and the origins of life here—or at least the first documentary record—can be traced back to the Catherine era, to the "ancient maps" of the period that first noted this land's topography. Arkadii observes the gradual disintegration of a culture that in the age of Catherine was in its prime, but by the 1860s has been drained of its former life (these are no Gogolian old-world landowners). The estate culture still orders the existence of many Russians, from the gentry down to the peasantry, and provides the structure that renders life on the nineteenth-century estate continuous with life on the eighteenth-century one. Time might pass, but the place and the system of socio-economic relations that governs it remain the same. The Reforms do away with that continuity. And Turgenev is certainly one to welcome them wholeheartedly. But he also seems aware that with the dissolution of master-slave bonds in the Emancipation, the very premise of estate culture, its hierarchical structures of interdependence and subjugation, are also eliminated. And the decay that before the Emancipation, from Arkadii's perspective, could be ascribed precisely to the abuses of serfdom (in this novel, neglect and mismanagement; in other Turgenev stories, cruelty and violence), would after the Reforms in fact ensue as the Emancipation's consequence.[56]

Our narrative has come full circle, then, to the scene described in this book's introduction: the trip to the deserted country estates that Diaghilev and Dobuzhinskii make in search of eighteenth- and early nineteenth-century portraits and furniture for their 1905 exhibit. By then, these objects and the way of life of which they used to be part are already museum pieces. Yet another element of the eighteenth century, probably the last of its subtle symbolic legacies to survive (with the exception of the overpowering and enduring Petrine myth), was gone. As early as 1797 Derzhavin had lamented Catherine's world as an era in ruins; a century later, it finally and truly was, though as we will see in this book's conclusion, the epoch's legacy persisted into the twentieth century in multiple symbolic permutations.

In the meantime, for all the perversities and foibles touched upon in this chapter, it is hard to resist closing on a Turgenevan note, lyrical and melancholy on the one hand, and future-oriented and playful on the other. Consider two Silver Age poems: the first, a nostalgic description of a ruined estate in Andrei Bely's "Abandoned House" ("Zabroshennyi dom," 1903); the second, Vladislav Khodasevich's "Prim ladies of bygone years . . ." ("Zhemannitsy bylykh godov . . . ," 1912), which gently revises Bely's nostalgic vision and questions the grounds for the estate culture's retrospective idealization:

Заброшенный дом

Заброшенный дом.
Кустарник колючий, но редкий.
Грущу о былом:
"Ах, где вы—любезные предки?"

Из каменных трещин торчат
проросшие мхи, как полипы.
Дуплистые липы
над домом шумят.

И лист за листом,
тоскуя о неге вчерашней,
кружится под тусклым окном
разрушенной башни.

Как стерся изогнутый серп
средь нежно белеющих лилий—
облупленный герб
дворянских фамилий.

Былое, как дым?
И жалко.
Охрипшая галка
глумится над горем моим.

Посмотришь в окно—
часы из фарфора с китайцем.
В углу полотно
с углем нарисованным зайцем.

Старинная мебель в пыли,
да люстры в чехлах, да гардины.
И вдаль отойдешь . . . А вдали—
Равнины, равнины.

Среди многоверстных равнин
скирды золотистого хлеба.

И небо . . .
Один.

Внимаешь с тоской,
обвеянный жизнию давней,
как шепчется ветер с листвой,
как хлопает сорванной ставней.[57]

[An abandoned house. / Shrubs, thorny but sparse. / I lament the past: / "Oh, where are you, kindly ancestors?" // From the stony cracks protrudes / The sprouting moss, like polyps. / Hollow lindens / Rustle above the house. // And leaf after leaf, / Yearning for yesterday's languor, / Whirls by the dim window / Of the ruined tower. // How faded is the curved sickle / Amid the tenderly white lilies—/ The chipped coat of arms / Of gentry families. // The past, like smoke? / And it's a pity. / A hoarse jackdaw / Scoffs at my sorrow. // One look in the window—/ A porcelain clock with a Chinese figure. / In the corner a canvas / With a hare drawn in charcoal. // Antique furniture covered in dust, / Chandeliers in their covers, and curtains. / And you step farther away . . . And farther away—/ It's plains and plains . . . // Amid those many-versted plains / Ricks of golden wheat. / And the sky . . . / Alone. // Sadly you listen, / Breathing a bygone life, / To the wind whispering with the leaves, / To the banging of a broken shutter.]

Жеманницы былых годов,
Читательницы Ричардсона!
Я посетил ваш ветхий кров,
Взглянув с высокого балкона

На дальние луга, на лес,
И сладко было мне сознанье,
Что мир ваш навсегда исчез
И с ним его очарованье.

Что больше нет в саду цветов,
В гостиной—нот на клавесине,
И вечных вздохов стариков
О матушке-Екатерине.

Рукой не прикоснулся я
К томам библиотеки пыльной,

Но радостен был для меня
Их запах, затхлый и могильный.

Я думал: в грустном сем краю
Уже полвека всё пустует.
О, пусть отныне жизнь мою
Одно грядущее волнует!

Блажен, кто средь разбитых урн,
На невозделанной куртине,
Прославит твой полет, Сатурн,
Сквозь многозвездные пустыни![58]

[Prim ladies of bygone years, / Readers of Richardson! / I visited your dilapidated abode, / Looking from a high balcony // Upon the distant meadows, the
forest, / And sweet was my realization / That your world was forever gone / And
with it its charm. // There are no more flowers in the garden, / In the parlor, no
more music on the harpsichord, / No more the old folks' endless pining / For
little mother (*matushka*) Catherine. // My hand did not touch / The tomes of
the dusty library, / But I took joy in / Their musty, graveyard smell. // And I
thought: in this melancholy realm / All is empty for half a century already. / Oh,
let my life from now on / Be concerned only with things to come! // Blessed is
he who amid the broken urns, / In a grove untilled, / Shall glorify thy flight, Sat-
urn, / Through the many-starred wastes!]

Bely's and Khodasevich's sentiments here echo almost exactly the conclusion
to Turgenev's "Old Portraits," a narrative whose very title alerts its reader to
the pleasures and difficulties of historical distance. Remembering his relatives
the Telegins and their ill-fated serf, the narrator sighs, "Yes, one can but repeat,
in another sense, Alexey Sergeitch's words: 'They were good old times . . . but
enough of them!'"[59]

AFTER PUSHKIN

What Turgenev ultimately bids farewell to, as his narrators repeatedly call upon
the enclaves of eighteenth-century life preserved in the provincial backwaters
of mid-nineteenth-century Russia is the sense of the eighteenth century as a
lived experience: someone else's, to be sure, and only laterally connected with

the present, but nevertheless still within reach. Turgenev inherits from Pushkin and his generation both this sense of the proximate eighteenth century and the imperative of taking leave from it: recall how many of Turgenev's character studies examined in this chapter were intertextually linked to Pushkin's. To a considerable extent, then, even as they chronicle Russian history's discontinuity and the modern Russian's estrangement from the originary epoch of his country's modernity, Turgenev's excursions into the pre-Pushkin past seem meant to signal a kind of literary inheritance, a stability of intellectual attitudes, if not literary techniques, within the Pushkin-generated nineteenth-century prose tradition. If going back to the eighteenth century leads Turgenev to the discovery of Russian imperial history's brokenness, going back to Pushkin allows him to assert a continuity of modern literary sensibilities and historical experience.

In this book, I have tried to suggest a correlation between these two readings of Russian cultural history and two quests for origin: invoking Pushkin as the origin, as "our everything," also inevitably and repeatedly relegates the eighteenth century to a kind of phantasmal, collective "nothing."[60] As a result, in addition to the split between pre-modern and modern Russia performed by Peter I in the early 1700s, another symbolic, and more tenuous, fault line marks the end of the eighteenth century. This split originates in part in the new mentalities that arise throughout Europe precisely at this point as a consequence of the crisis of both monarchical power and Enlightenment ideology in the wake of the French Revolution; in part, it also bears witness to the post-Pushkin period's increasing investment in periodization and epochal categories, whereby new values become retrospectively assigned to various moments in Russian cultural history, ultimately privileging a Romantic origin that is much more recent and accessible, both linguistically and ideologically. Thus, it stands to reason that if Pushkin the Proteus finds the adoption of eighteenth-century personae or masks not only possible, but intellectually compelling, no such disguise is justifiable in Turgenev's world, whether on ethical or aesthetic grounds. The aesthetic mimicry that does hold a special allure for post-Romanticism entails a partial, and patently critical, return to the types and strategies of historical explanation developed by the Romantics: to Turgenev's minor characters are affixed the hardened masks of those from Pushkin's and Gogol's fictions; character is stuffed into the mold of historical type, and so loses its legibility.

In the arc of my study, Pushkin's heir Turgenev embodies the predicament of a generation caught in a historicist double bind: as historically conscious subjects, the men of the 1840s are drawn to study and even cherish the past; as progressive intellectuals, they seek to leave it behind. This internal conflict may be said to characterize the position of late Romantic intellectuals generally, but it acquires particular poignancy in Russia where, in the 1840s, with the crystallization of the Slavophile-Westernizer debate, the eighteenth century's westward-oriented course and its legacy render any engagement with the recent past richly divisive. The Reform era of the 1860s, the next crucial watershed signaling the ascendancy of progressivist thinking, further relegates the ethos of the earlier, Petrine, reforms to the past. It is, moreover, in this period that "historical consciousness"—a concept and sensibility some of whose early manifestations in the late eighteenth and early nineteenth centuries this book has sought to describe—comes not only to preoccupy Russian intellectuals (indeed the material I draw on in chapter 4 shows that this had already been the case in the 1830s), but, more importantly, to form their outlook from the very start, to serve as its foundation, perceived as a given rather than a novelty. The 1860s also mark the first decade when the Scottian sixty years—a time lapse that preserves the delicate balance of intimacy and imagination in one's relationship with the past—are no longer sufficient to reach back into the eighteenth century, which as a result is now gradually left beyond the bounds of the intimate span of familial history. As Bely's and Khodasevich's poems attest mere decades later, for the fin-de-siècle the eighteenth century is no longer family, but a space of only vaguely desired ancestral bonds and intuited alterity.

Epilogue

"Did the eighteenth century ever end in Russia?"—a colleague playfully retorted after I had suggested, also only half-seriously, that we consider the 1917 Revolution as one of its endpoints. In some ways of course it never did or, rather, as I hope to have shown throughout this book, the Russian eighteenth century came to connote certain resilient modes of governance and culture-shaping energies as well as particular poetics and notions of authorship and authority, even as its ambivalent and often disparaging reception by later generations (starting with Pushkin's) turned it into a handy source of analogies for whatever contemporary phenomenon one might wish to critique, whether serfdom in the nineteenth century or Vladimir Putin's vexed 2012 "succession" to a third term as president. The suggestion that the eighteenth century resurfaces time and again ultimately acknowledges our continued investment in historical analogy and archetypal thinking (which we have seen shape the historical imagination of ode-writers in the eighteenth century) even after notions of progressive change had seemingly superseded these earlier models for understanding historical development. The repeated symbolic endings of the eighteenth century paradoxically convey the sense of its non-ending, its residual, shadowy persistence on the level of Russian culture's deep structure.

Consider, for example, the key moments when elements of Soviet culture have been said to replicate supposedly analogous aspects of the Russian eighteenth century. According to the familiar claim first advanced by Iurii Tynianov, Vladimir Maiakovskii's poetics returns us to Derzhavin's moment because the revolutionary era resembles the "geological shifts" of the eighteenth century more than the "evolutionary" development of the nineteenth.[1] Though formed by a very different political climate than Tynianov, Andrei

Siniavskii (Abram Tertz) replicates Tynianov's rhetoric almost verbatim, but applies it to the aesthetic of socialist realism, suggesting that "in its content and spirit, as in its central figure, socialist realism is much closer to the eighteenth century than to the nineteenth. Without realizing it, we jump over the heads of our fathers and revive the tradition of our grandfathers."[2] If for Tynianov, the comparison draws on the eighteenth century's spirit of experimentation and grand scale, Siniavskii focuses on the two epochs' totalizing (and in the latter case, totalitarian and teleological) optimism. But what does it mean for our understanding of the Soviet period to compare it to the eighteenth century? Do we learn anything new about the futurist experiment or the socialist realist celebration of ideology? Such comparisons seem most of all to advance a narrative—and one tinged with no small irony—of Russian history's coherence, a sense that some of this history's unsettling turns have been fatefully prefigured by the first epoch of its modernity, and that the novelty of its revolutions might be mitigated by their connections to that most momentous cultural revolution of all—the demiurgic Petrine project.

What, then, is the eighteenth century for the Russian cultural imagination? In this book's introduction, I suggested that we read it as Russian culture's vanishing point, like the imaginary core, that is, that structures a perspective-governed canvas, allowing the eye, or mind in the case of our historical metaphor, to orient itself and be drawn into the image. This metaphor foregrounds the centrality of vision to our historical imagination (a pairing explored in connection with the historical novel in chapter 4). More crucially, this interpretation of the eighteenth century gives this book its structure, grounding its often expansive and digressive readings in a consistent concern with the self-understanding and legacy of the "first epoch."

Another option for conceiving of modern Russian culture's multiple invocations and forgettings of this period would be to take up the notion of the eighteenth century as a "text," akin to the "Petersburg text" as conceptualized by Vladimir Toporov; indeed, it would be, if hardly easy, not altogether impossible to assemble a lineage of texts that all reference the eighteenth century as a "synthetic übertext with which are connected higher meanings and goals"[3]—this book offers a step in this direction. But for all its appeal, this metaphor is limited, attending as it does solely to the literary manifestations of this higher, symbolic "text"; it lends itself best to philological analysis, only marginally addressing issues of cultural formation, the canon, ideology, and politics.

The metaphor I would propose in concluding this study, now that we have examined the eighteenth century's multiple traces and uses, is that of the eighteenth century as *critique*. In fact, Russian intellectuals—with the possible exception of scholars who research the eighteenth century—have turned to this period primarily as the origin of, or a point of comparison and contrast with, their own contemporary phenomena. Since the age of Pushkin, the eighteenth century has been treated as a foil to the present. Emerging as something of an ideological stumbling block first for the Romantics, then for the Slavophiles, and later for any number of cultural commentators of diverse ideological persuasions, the eighteenth century as history and myth calls for reflexive, and often polemical, evaluation of the here-and-now, of a present always and inescapably straining against the past, and against the national culture's most vital mythologies. Describing the period's lasting imprint in these relational terms, as indexing an imperative of doubt, brings into relief the paradoxically interconnected legacies of the eighteenth century's particular brand of modernity. The autocratic experiment of this epoch, that is, bequeathed to Russia's political culture certain rigid forms of behavioral process, forms whose intransigence in turn compels the emancipated modern subject's critical resistance; but this is the selfsame epoch when critical discourse itself first emerges in Russia, thereby marking modern Russian literature and cultural commentary, however much its individual practitioners might strive to dissociate themselves from this birthright, as a profoundly historical formation rooted, specifically, in the eighteenth century.

Notes

1. Quoted in Viazemskii, *Fon-Vizin*, 95. "One can say, my dear sir, that the history of our century will be interesting to posterity. How many great changes! How many strange adventures!"

2. Griboedov, *Gore ot uma*, 34. "To compare and to consider / The present age and the past age . . ."

3. Dostoevskii, *Polnoe sobraniie sochinenii v tridtsati tomakh*, 21:42. "What good is Voltaire these days? Now [we need] a cudgel, not Voltaire!"

4. Khodasevich, *Sobranie sochinenii v 8 tomakh*, 1:63. "And the dead ancestors will not grasp / Their descendants' vain speech."

5. Irina Reyfman has explored the role of what she calls the "mythogenic spirit" of the eighteenth century in Russian literary historiography that sees the period as launching a "new" literature (*Vasilii Trediakovsky: The Fool of the "New" Russian Literature*, 13). As I shall argue, this powerful myth of origin is countered by a later one reserving innovation as the province of Pushkin, and casting the eighteenth century as an epoch to be overcome.

6. For a recent collection that theorizes precisely the meaning the eighteenth century holds for postmodernism, see Clingham, *Questioning History: The Postmodern Turn to the Eighteenth Century.*

7. Lopukhin, *Zapiski nekotorykh obstoiatel'stv zhizni i sluzhby deistvitel'nogo tainogo sovetnika, senatora I. V. Lopukhina, sochinennyia im samim*, 169.

8. These were no doubt pan-European developments. Harold Mah aptly formulates the alternative and multiple temporalities available to European intellectuals before and after the French Revolution: "The Revolution did not introduce new notions of temporality, but it did unsettle them, intensifying, separating, and reifying each against the other. To many Europeans, the Revolution signaled a quickening of historical change, conveying a sense that historical events had suddenly

accelerated, so that Europe now seemed in the throes of a breakthrough into an entirely new stage of history." Mah, *Enlightenment Phantasies: Cultural Identity in France and Germany, 1750–1914*, 159. Reinhart Koselleck argues that modernity in general is characterized by an acceleration of historical time, a process originating in the gradual "temporalization" of experience underway in Europe in the long period between roughly 1500 and 1800. Koselleck, *Futures Past: On the Semantics of Historical Time*, 5.

9. There exist several influential accounts of this development broadly conceived. In the scholarship on Russia, the greatest attention has been paid to the rise specifically of the intelligentsia. Marc Raeff locates the widespread emergence of this class (defined largely through its dissenting attitudes) in the first quarter of the nineteenth century, while tracing its origins to a still earlier period, emphasizing in particular Peter III's 1762 manifesto exempting the Russian nobility from obligatory state service. Raeff, *Origins of the Russian Intelligentsia: Eighteenth-Century Nobility*. Nicholas Riasanovsky offers an alternative account, which dates Russian educated society's divergence from the government to the reign of Nicholas I (1825–55), in contrast with the strengthening ties between these entities Riasanovsky describes in the early years of Alexander I's rule (1801–25). Riasanovsky, *A Parting of Ways: Government and the Educated Public in Russia, 1801–1855*. It has been pointed out by Riasanovsky's reviewers (e.g., Richard Wortman) that the state-society trajectory he draws from full allegiance to complete break may be too stark. While I find both Raeff's and Riasanovsky's accounts illuminating (as much for the alternative arrangements of Russian intellectual history they offer as for the testimony their divergence provides to the inconclusiveness of periodizing intellectual history), here I am primarily interested not in the emergence of an opposition to the state, but in the very possibility of locating and thinking history elsewhere, outside the government or its centralized structures—a mentality in and of itself not connected with dissent. What is important for me is the decenteredness, rather than oppositionality, of Russian intellectual life at the beginning of the nineteenth century.

10. Needless to say, care should be taken not to overstate this expansion, particularly if considered retrospectively rather than from within the period itself. The demographic that was not only literate, but also interested in relatively highbrow magazines such as *The Herald of Europe* (*Vestnik Evropy*), was limited, though still sizable compared to the eighteenth century. The circulation of *The Herald of Europe* in the years 1802–30 ranged from 580 to 1200 copies.

11. Among several historians who address the broadening of the experiential range available to historical thinking in this period, Mark Phillips contextualizes a panoply of new and revised historiographical and parahistoriographical genres emerging in turn-of-the-century Britain from 1780–1820, with this period's "enlargement of the boundaries of the historical" rendering it "increasingly hard to think of history as exclusively concerned with the narrative of political action." Phillips, *Society and Sentiment: Genres of Historical Writing in Britain, 1740–1820*, 17. In Phillips's

Britain, this enlargement takes place throughout the second half of the eighteenth century, but in Russia it is internalized only with a delay of several decades, in many ways as a received notion rather than a homegrown intellectual development.

12. In this case, it is in fact difficult (and unnecessary) to maintain the precedence of the experiential over the philosophical or vice versa. Interestingly, much of what one reads in the journals and memoirs of the time, though ostensibly not informed by historicism as a philosophical development, attests to this paradigm's penetration into the popular discourse.

13. The thinkers who emphasize this shift and are generally most relevant for this book's construction of what could be thought of as "symbolic" history are undoubtedly Reinhart Koselleck and Michel Foucault, but the work of several scholars engaged with more specific circumstances of the rise of historicism in Europe has also shaped my understanding of the context of this project. James Chandler's by-now classic source on Romantic literary historicism, *England in 1819: The Politics of Literary Culture and the Case of Romantic Historicism*, has proven most illuminating and useful for my purposes. For a theoretical reading of the early nineteenth-century "desire for history" and the visual discourses it engendered (another interest that will inform much of my analysis), see Bann, *Romanticism and the Rise of History*. This introductory discussion has also drawn from Theodore Ziolkowski's intellectual history of the academic disciplines (*Clio the Romantic Muse: Historicizing the Faculties in Germany*), which demonstrates the pervasive reorganization of academic knowledge along these new historical lines. The most thoughtful account of historicism in Russia is offered by Edward Thaden (*The Rise of Historicism in Russia*), although for my purposes his study is too limited by its exclusive focus on Russian historiography and on the work of specific eighteenth- and nineteenth-century historians. There is of course no dearth of sources, particularly from the Soviet period, that interpret various literary texts through the lens of Hegelian historicism and the ascendancy of realism; see for example Makogonenko, *Problemy istorizma v russkoi literature, konets XVIII–nachalo XIX v.* While I have found many such works' specific findings valuable, their theoretical premises are too tendentious to be of use. To the best of my knowledge, there is no single source on Russian historicism that is both up-to-date in its theoretical interpretation and ambitious enough to account for the multifarious materials that manifest a consciousness of history; i.e., not only historiography or the work of specific writers, but also large-scale and varied literary and historical phenomena. Part of the reason for this lacuna is, no doubt, the speed with which this field in the West has grown and revised itself in recent decades; in part, too, the problem lies in the common perception of the Russian intellectual climate of the early nineteenth century as largely secondary to, and derivative of, that of Europe, and therefore, at least in matters of historicism, in no need of a thorough, independent theoretical consideration. While my study does not, strictly speaking, offer such a theorization, it is certainly a call for one, and hopefully a step in this direction. I have aimed to combine awareness of Russia's

indebtedness to European developments with a more attentive and wide-ranging consideration of what these developments specifically meant in Russia.

14. For the most influential account of this transition in Europe, see Koselleck, *Futures Past: On the Semantics of Historical Time*. In considering the case of early modern Russia, Viktor Zhivov (*Ocherki istoricheskoi semantiki russkogo iazyka rannego novogo vremeni*, 5–31) proposes several important revisions to Koselleck's account. I have also found relevant Mircea Eliade's account (*The Myth of the Eternal Return*) of the shift from archaic to modern temporalities, which he identifies with the abandonment of the archetypal understanding of phenomena. In a study of narrower focus, A. V. Mikhailov arrives at similar conclusions, dubbing the early nineteenth-century departure from paradigmatic forms a "categorial rift" (*kategorial'nyi slom*). "Sud'ba klassicheskogo naslediia na rubezhe XVIII–XIX vekov," in Mikhailov, *Obratnyi perevod*, 20.

15. Kireevskii, *Kritika i estetika*, 80.

16. I use this term to avoid confusion with *historians* proper who, I should emphasize, are not the main protagonists of this project. Rather, my book focuses primarily on the Russian belles-lettres and their imaginative appropriations of the eighteenth century, which arise out of the newly discovered and widely embraced sense of history.

17. In Russian Romantic historicism, the Novgorodian episode—particularly its *veche*-centered freedom and its status as a European Hanseatic city—most fruitfully represented the Middle Ages and performed the dual function of "self" and "other." On the appropriation of Novgorod as a central historical narrative from the late eighteenth century through Romanticism, see Wachtel, "A Historical Character in Search of a Genre: Vadim of Novgorod and the Prehistory of Intergeneric Dialogue in Russia"; and Hixon, "The Fall of Novgorod in Karamzin's Fiction and History."

18. This fortunate coinage belongs to James Chandler, who devotes a separate section of his book to the exploration of this formula. *England in 1819: The Politics of Literary Culture and the Case of Romantic Historicism*, 105–14. For Chandler, the problem brought to the fore by the phrase "the spirit of the age" is primarily that of contemporaneity. My book proposes to show how the pursuit of contemporaneity and its definitions was everywhere implicated in the equally urgent consideration of the past and its legacies, and vice versa.

19. Hannah Arendt sees the post-revolutionary European cultural climate as permeated with the "pathos of novelty." Arendt, *On Revolution*, 34.

20. Chandler reflects (*England in 1819*, xv) on the "new sense of period—involved with what one might call 'comparative contemporaneities,'" manifested in what in the British context he identifies as "the rash of literary invention on the theme of the 'spirit of the age.'" In his account of "comparative contemporaneities," Chandler captures what would become a longstanding issue in philosophy of history—the Marxian "uneven development" or Ernst Bloch's "non-simultaneity" (*Ungleichzeitigkeit*)— at the earliest stages of its formulation. In this sense, Chandler's firm grounding of his analysis in a specific place and period does not preclude its application to

other contexts. My treatment of the transformative pathos of both the eighteenth and nineteenth centuries in Russia is indebted to his discussion of the stakes of periodization in Romantic England as well as of the categories of our own contemporary historicist analysis.

21. Because Russian modernity is habitually characterized as belated, this term might go against received notions of Russian history; by "precocious," I mean the very early recognition, implicit in Peter's reforms, of the flexibility of historical narrative and chronology, a quality fully embraced elsewhere in Europe only at the end of the eighteenth century.

22. Marcus Levitt has recently renewed scholarly interest in what he calls, following Georges Florovsky, "a discontinuous model of Russian culture." Levitt, *The Visual Dominant*, 16.

23. In a different context, Harold Mah has identified the tendency of most influential accounts of the European Enlightenment to emphasize only a single feature or a very narrow set of its features, rather than attend to the multiplicity, instability, and uncertainty of its constituents. Mah, *Enlightenment Phantasies: Cultural Identity in France and Germany, 1750–1914*, 11–12.

24. Such recent scholarship includes: Stennik, *Pushkin i russkaia literatura XVIII veka*; and Kahn, *Pushkin's Lyric Intelligence*, which demonstrates Pushkin's intellectual grounding in the philosophical tradition of the eighteenth-century.

25. Periodization, transformed into an interpretive practice largely by Romantic historicism, has been the subject of scholarly scrutiny and critique for at least the past few decades. It is one of the key issues in Chandler's *England in 1819*. See also the essays on Romanticism in Besserman, *The Challenge of Periodization: Old Paradigms and New Perspectives*; and Fradenburg, "Group Time: Catastrophe, Survival, Periodicity." For a more general discussion of the problem for historiography, see Kelley, "Ideas of Periodization in the West." Koselleck explores the challenges of periodization in arguing that the concept of modernity (*Neuzeit*) as consciously experienced and theorized truly arises in the eighteenth century. Koselleck, "The Eighteenth Century as the Beginning of Modernity."

26. Examining this period in England, J. C. D. Clark, who initially coined the term "the long eighteenth century" in a revisionist move against the dominance of the "short" French century, sets its dates as 1688–1832 in the first edition (1985) of his seminal book and 1660–1832 in the second. In this chronology, the eighteenth century ends with the Great Reform Act of 1832, which is credited with reinforcing the emergent modern democracy in Britain. Clark, *English Society, 1660–1832: Religion, Ideology and Politics during the Ancien Régime*.

27. Dating the beginnings of the German eighteenth century to Thomasius is owed to Werner Schneiders's history of the German *Aufklärung*, "Aufklärungsphilosophien"; see also Schneiders, *Lexikon der Aufklärung. Deutschland und Europa*, 12–22.

28. Reill and Wilson's *The Encyclopedia of the Enlightenment*, for example, covers a chronology from Nicolas de Malebranche's *De la recherche de la vérité* (1674–78)

and Benedict de Spinoza's *Ethics* (published posthumously in 1677) to Goethe's *Faust* (1808–32), Lamarck's *Philosophie zoologique* (1809), and Francisco Goya's *Los desastres de la guerra* (1810–14). For a recent and already influential effort in periodizing the French Enlightenment, see Edelstein, *The Enlightenment: A Genealogy*.

29. Meinecke, *Historism: The Rise of a New Historical Outlook*, lv.

30. A recent collection of articles challenges the Enlightenment/Romanticism divide, focusing precisely on their congruence in the ample material furnished by the British novel in this period. Wallace, *Enlightening Romanticism, Romancing the Enlightenment: British Novels from 1750 to 1832*.

31. Raeff, "Seventeenth-century Europe in Eighteenth-century Russia? (Pour prendre congé du dix-huitième siècle russe)."

32. On Diaghilev's interest in the eighteenth century, also manifested in many ventures after the 1905 exhibit, see Smoliarova, *Parizh 1928: Oda vozvrashchaetsia v teatr*.

33. Ever since the death of Catherine's favorite G. A. Potemkin, who was its first resident, the Tauride Palace had been one of the Russian royal residences (with the exception only of Paul I's reign). Soon after the exhibit, the palace would house the Russian State Duma (1906–10) and then, after the February Revolution, serve as headquarters for the Provisional Government (until July 1917).

34. Zil'bershtein and Samkov, *Sergei Diagilev i russkoe iskusstvo: stat'i, otkrytye pis'ma, interv'iu. Perepiska. Sovremenniki o Diagileve*, 1:193–94.

35. Ibid., 193.

36. Chekhov, *Sochineniia v 18 tomakh*, 13:254. Mstislav Dobuzhinskii aptly describes the historical setting for the exhibit, drawing the connection with *The Cherry Orchard*: "The time was most suitable for uncovering these hidden treasures, for collecting and displaying them, since with all the various changes in socioeconomic life [*byt*], particularly gentry life, when the 'cherry orchards' came to be cut down, there set in a complete indifference toward one's surroundings, and 'the cult of ancestors' was fizzling out. As it turned out, this had to be done also because of the approach of the first revolution, which very few at the time foresaw, but Diaghilev, I am convinced, did have a presentiment and was therefore in a hurry." Dobuzhinskii, *Vospominaniia*, 223.

37. Here is one of the most memorable vignettes from Dobuzhinskii's scouting trip: "In the wooden palace of Ekateringof, we found incredibly opulent furniture from the time of Elizabeth, ebony with gold trim, painted in the Chinese style, which was in an extremely lamentable condition: the palace roof had leaked, and water was dripping in particular onto a remarkable table, and it seems it was only at this point that the steward noticed." Ibid., 225.

38. Ibid., 224.

39. In light of what has already been said above regarding the particularization of history in the late eighteenth–early nineteenth centuries, it would not appear accidental that this duality in portraiture's signification and an emphasis on "likeness"

would also date precisely to this period; see Tscherny, "Likeness in Early Romantic Portraiture."

40. Zil'bershtein and Samkov, *Sergei Diagilev i russkoe iskusstvo: stat'i, otkrytye pis'ma, interv'iu. Perepiska. Sovremenniki o Diagileve*, 193.

41. "O mode," *Vestnik Evropy* 60, no. 23 (December 15, 1811), 219–20.

42. This famous term was introduced by Roland Barthes in an influential argument for reading such detail not as mimetic, but rather as referencing the "real" generally. Barthes uses Flaubert as his example; for Pushkin, of course, Balzac's early novels provide the most meaningful context. Barthes, "The Reality Effect."

43. Pushkin, *Complete Prose Fiction*, 222–23.

44. Ibid., 223.

45. Turgenev, *The Jew and Other Stories*, 257–58.

46. Ibid., 258.

47. Here and in the title of this introduction's opening section I am recycling the structuring terms of Nikolai Karamzin's influential *Memoir on Ancient and Modern Russia* (*Zapiska o drevnei i novoi Rossii*).

48. The pictorial metaphor reflects an important preoccupation of this study: the Romantics' reliance on vision as the primary sense for the physical and figurative experience of the past.

Part I Prologue

1. Kheraskov, *Izbrannye proizvedeniia*, 88. "The curtain of time has parted! / I come to greet future days: / Russia is illumined with radiance / And the lights of joy are visible there; / Bliss, happiness, knowledge, / Extending hands to one another, / Proffer laurel wreaths; / The source of general peace, / The great Catherine / Is praised by Parnassian dwellers."

2. Baratynskii, *Stikhotvoreniia*, 124. "There is no phenomenon without a creative source, / This blessed age was the age of Catherine."

3. Pushkin, *Polnoe sobranie sochinenii v shestnadtsati tomakh*, 13:179. "Along with Derzhavin fell silent the voice of flattery—and how did he flatter?"

4. Belinskii, *Polnoe sobranie sochinenii*, 6:611. "Derzhavin's poems [. . .] were an unsightly pupa from which a luxuriously beautiful butterfly was to flutter forth to charm the eye and move the heart."

5. Quoted in Zorin, Zubkov, and Nemzer, *Svoi podvig svershiv*, 99. "In Derzhavin there is his whole age, with gold, and tinsel, and worse."

6. Eikhenbaum, *Skvoz' literaturu: Sbornik statei*, 36. "In his poetics, the 'icy' eighteenth century took on the form of a lily-white dream and established the power of light and love over the darkness of death and the chill of reason."

7. Belinskii's move is clearly rooted in the Romantic practice of self-dissociation from rhetoric, which the Romantics conceive as a pre-historicist (and pre-nineteenth century) poetic strategy, unduly preoccupied with the technical and instrumental

aspects of language. See Wellbery, "The Transformation of Rhetoric." Ultimately, Belinskii proposes the historicist framework for reading Derzhavin as the only one capable of enabling modern readers to overlook the poet's lapses in aesthetic judgment (his penchant for rhetorical inflation being the one most insistently decried by the critic), thereby also relegating eighteenth-century poetry to a subject for purely historical analysis to be approached at the requisite scholarly distance. Thus, Belinskii's bid for recuperating Russia's literary past as meaningful for the dialectical understanding of the present—a largely Hegelian proposition—also amounts to a virtual negation of the eighteenth century's power to index anything other than the historical dialectic.

8. Here Belinskii polemicizes with, for instance, the Romantic critic Nikolai Polevoi, who advocated the publication of Derzhavin's complete works in the hope that a comprehensive chronological arrangement might yield the story of Derzhavin's "inner life" (*letopis' vnutrennei zhizni ego*). Polevoi, "Sochineniia Derzhavina," 178. Pushkin appraises Derzhavin along similar lines when he describes Derzhavin's monument (*kumir*) as "¼ gold, ¾ lead." Pushkin, *Polnoe sobranie sochinenii v shestnadtsati tomakh*, 13:178.

9. Belinskii, *Polnoe sobranie sochinenii*, 6:620. It is precisely in the early 1840s that Belinskii formulates his historicist approach to aesthetic phenomena. In this sense, the articles on Derzhavin are only instantiations of the general principle the critic elucidates in his article "Russian Literature in 1841" ("Russkaia literatura v 1841 godu"): "Poetry is always true to history, because history is the soil of poetry." Ibid., 5:533. Also see Mashinskii, "Na pozitsiiakh istorizma." Andrei Zorin calls Derzhavin "the first victim of his [Belinskii's] growing historicism." Zorin et al., *Svoi podvig svershiv*, 33.

10. Belinskii, *Polnoe sobranie sochinenii*, 6:582.

11. Ibid., 602.

12. Ibid., 622.

13. As characterized in Petr Viazemskii's obituary "O Derzhavine," 20.

14. Pushkin, *Eugene Onegin*, 195. In his last years, Derzhavin was in fact preoccupied with a search for literary heirs; see Fraiman, "Derzhavin i Zhukovskii: K voprosu o tvorcheskom nasledovanii." Fraiman cites Derzhavin's fragment: "To you, Zhukovskii, I bequeath / My decrepit lyre. / Over the slippery abyss of the grave / Lowering my brow, I already stand." (*Tebe v nasledie, Zhukovskii, / Ia vetkhu liru otdaiu. / A ia nad bezdnoi groba skol'zkoi / Uzh, preklonia chelo, stoiu.*) Quoted ibid., 11. Also see Grot, *Zhizn' Derzhavina*, 619.

15. Indeed, aligning Derzhavin with one or more literary periods—from the Baroque through Classicism and Romanticism to realism—is both a point of debate and a commonplace in his scholarly reception. For an early overview of scholarly positions on this issue, see Serman, "Literaturnaia pozitsiia Derzhavina."

16. Derzhavin, *Sochineniia Derzhavina s ob"iasnitel'nymi primechaniiami Ia. Grota*, 6:443. The "different path" is a topos that goes back to Callimachus. More

pertinent in Derzhavin's case is Horace's recognition of his inability to imitate Pindar completely. Horace, *The Complete Odes and Satires*, 155.

17. The possibility of gleaning the poet's individuality, of reconstructing an inner self of a poet who belonged to a century with very weak conceptions of selfhood, is in fact what attracted numerous Romantic interpreters to Derzhavin; see Safiullin, "Derzhavin v otsenke romantikov."

18. I am influenced in this line of thinking by Mircea Eliade's powerful analysis of this archetypal-to-concrete shift (and lamenting of it as a sort of ideological Fall) in *The Myth of the Eternal Return*. Belinskii calls "naked rhetoric" what, following Eliade, we can call Derzhavin's "archetypal poetics." In essence Belinskii wants to strip Derzhavin's poetry of its analogical thinking and seeks instead the specificity and singularity of lyrical emotion discovered by the Romantics only later. Lev Pumpianskii suggests that Belinskii's inability to appreciate the eighteenth-century ode stemmed from his hostility to everything linked to the Russian state, rather than a more general philosophical prejudice against allegorical figuration. As will become apparent in chapter 1, the two explanations can in fact be seen as connected. Pumpianskii, *Klassicheskaia traditsiia*, 74.

19. In a slightly later period, Vasilii Zhukovskii could be considered a similarly comprehensive and transitional figure, whose influential poetics also eventually lose their appeal for his younger contemporaries. By contrast, Nikolai Karamzin is probably the most successful at bridging the two centuries: he seems to march in step with his time, his changing literary practice responding as if organically to the demands of the present at any given moment.

20. In chapter 1, we will see Vladislav Khodasevich inscribe Derzhavin into the history of the Russian novel as a precursor to Pushkin's *Eugene Onegin*. Most recently, an attempt to emphasize Derzhavin's early nineteenth-century work has been undertaken in Smoliarova, *Zrimaia lirika. Derzhavin*.

21. Most literary histories and graduate syllabi would consign Derzhavin to the eighteenth century. And yet, the farther removed we stand from the eighteenth century, the more frequently does Derzhavin appear as the only aesthetically salvageable poet of the 1700s, and is therefore appended to the early nineteenth century together with Nikolai Karamzin, whose membership among nineteenth-century Russian writers is more readily accepted. Still, the inclusion of Karamzin also poses far-reaching questions regarding the periodization of Sentimentalism as a literary movement and a sensibility.

22. Pumpianskii, *Klassicheskaia traditsiia: Sobranie trudov po istorii russkoi literatury*, 60.

CHAPTER 1. THE EMPRESSES' HISTORIES

1. Richard Wortman advances this persuasive argument throughout his chapters on the eighteenth century; see *Scenarios of Power: Myth and Ceremony in Russian*

Monarchy, 1:81–165. A notable exception to this claim is Anna Ioannovna. While I am suggesting here that the placement of women in the position of rule was already an instantiation of the eighteenth century's reforming ethos, the policies of female rulers were not always notably committed to the Enlightenment project. See Anisimov, *Rossiia v seredine XVIII veka: bor'ba za nasledie Petra*.

2. No. 3893, *Polnoe sobranie zakonov Rossiiskoi imperii s 1649 goda, Sobranie pervoe*, 6:496–97. For an illuminating study of royal women's real and symbolic authority in pre-Petrine Russia, see Thyret, *Between God and Tsar: Religious Symbolism and the Royal Women of Muscovite Russia*. In terms of royal lineages, it is significant to see Catherine the Great trace hers not only to the eighteenth-century female monarchs Catherine I and Elizabeth, but also to Princess Olga (r. 945–60). On the ambit of women's power in the domestic and legal spheres beyond the court, see Marrese, *A Woman's Kingdom: Noblewomen and the Control of Property in Russia, 1700–1861*.

3. It is hardly necessary to dwell upon distinctions between actuality and representational fictions in the context of this discussion, which is so deeply concerned with representation and reception. This study is thus comfortable in accepting Louis Marin's semiotic assertion (in *Portrait of the King*) of the shared nature of power and representation.

4. Brenda Meehan-Waters persuasively demonstrates ("Catherine the Great and the Problem of Female Rule") that during Catherine II's reign her femininity was a subject of discussion only among her foreign critics. Such discussion in Russia occurred only posthumously and on a very small scale. Even in the absence of open discussion, I would suggest, female rule was something that was noticed as a distinct form and associated with the eighteenth century by the subsequent generations. Also see Dixon, "The Posthumous Reputation of Catherine II."

5. No. 17.910, *Polnoe sobranie zakonov Rossiiskoi imperii s 1649 goda, Sobranie pervoe*, 24:587–89. For a cogent discussion of this law's rhetoric and implications, see Wortman, *Scenarios of Power: Myth and Ceremony in Russian Monarchy*, 1:177–78. The same *ukaz* included a section on the rights and responsibilities of an empress should she find herself occupying the throne alone. On the whole, this regulation underscored the close bond between the Church and the ruler, who is proclaimed its head, and reemphasized the crucial role of divine providence and legally-ensured continuity, rather than individual human achievement, in imperial succession.

6. An especially insightful and original response to the eighteenth century as defined by this particular convergence can be found in Prince Petr Viazemskii's *Fon-Vizin* (1830, pub. 1848).

7. Grot, "Kharakteristika Derzhavina kak poeta," 451.

8. Marcus Levitt also emphasizes the ode's historical function and points to its origin in late Renaissance literary theory (*The Visual Dominant in Eighteenth-Century Russia*, 81–82). In this chapter I trace the incremental change in the odic

conception of its historical message, from a more general one centered on glory and archetypal vision to a more concrete one focused on its present as on a specific historical moment.

9. In part, this is the rhetoric that Vissarion Belinskii so peremptorily dismisses (see the Prologue) in removing the dated rhetorical husk from what he perceives as the kernels of Derzhavin's poetic genius.

10. Here I am focusing specifically on odic allegorizing discourse, which enveils the very historical events it purports to represent. Other recent studies of the eighteenth-century ode proceed by decoding, rather than foregrounding, this rhetorical masquerade. See, for example, Zorin, *Kormia dvuglavogo orla*.

11. For a fine theoretical discussion of the distinction between intermittent and sustained allegory, see the section "The Resources of 'Continued' Allegory" in Treip, *Allegorical Poetics and the Epic: The Renaissance Tradition to* Paradise Lost, 62–65. Treip emphasizes the interpretive value of this distinction, particularly for such narrative poetic genres as the epic (131–32). As will become apparent throughout "Derzhavin's Moment," I treat the ode as a genre that consistently reaches out from the lyrical to the narrative form, particularly in its interpretation of history. Interesting in this context are the vestiges of odic discourse that one detects in the long narrative poem (*poema*) of the 1820s, most notably in the final section of Pushkin's *Kavkazskii plennik* (1820–21, pub. 1822).

12. There exists an extensive literature on allegory. For a classic study that provides some widely accepted definitions, see Fletcher, *Allegory: The Theory of A Symbolic Mode*. Most illuminating for the purposes of my study of the reception of the eighteenth century in the nineteenth is Paul de Man's seminal essay "The Rhetoric of Temporality," in which he considers the implications of the shift in the Romantic period away from allegory as a rational mode of the Enlightenment to the "supremacy of the symbol, conceived as an expression of unity between the representative and the semantic function of language" (189). De Man argues that at the heart of allegory we find an abstracting procedure and a recognition of the disjuncture between reality and representation (192) and that, significantly for my argument, "time is [allegory's] originary constitutive category" (207). Russian eighteenth-century poets' understanding of allegory is best summed up in Derzhavin's "A Treatise on Lyric Poetry, or The Ode" ("Rassuzhdenie o liricheskoi poezii, ili ob ode," 1811–15), where he lists allegory among other figurative ornaments of the lyric, explaining its purpose—quite symptomatically, as we shall see—as the subtle pragmatic elevation or demotion (in the case of satire) of the lyric addressee's status. Derzhavin, *Sochinenia Derzhavina s ob"iasnitel'nymi primechaniiami Ia. Grota*, 7:562–63.

13. Joachim Klein remarks on this expansiveness of Lomonosov's "panegyric universe" (*panegiricheskii universum*), a "fictive space [that] encompasses Russia and the world, the past and the future, the heavens and the earth, the natural and the supernatural." Klein, *Russkaia literatura v XVIII veke*, 117.

14. While this section of my study focuses on the allegorical procedure in the mid- to late eighteenth-century ode, similar rhetorical phenomena exist in the earlier genres of writing about power in Russia. Iurii Kagarlitskii, for instance, writes about the "figures of rapprochement" and the "rhetoric of likening" in the panegyric sermons of the early eighteenth century. See Kagarlitskii, "Ritorika upodobleniia i ritorika sorevnovaniia."

15. Pumpianskii, *Klassicheskaia traditsiia: Sobranie trudov po istorii russkoi literatury*, 59. In this section, Pumpianskii is concerned primarily with the evolution of Russian poetry's engagement with nature, which for the eighteenth-century ode, he argues, is scripted by the representational demands of the female ruler. My concern here is the evolution of the ode's uses of allegorical figuration, which, I suggest, is in large part motivated by female rule as well.

16. Pumpianskii distinguishes between the verse of "rapture" (*vostorg*) of the eighteenth century and the verse of "inspiration" (*vdokhnovenie*) of the nineteenth. Pumpianskii, *Klassicheskaia traditsiia*, 61. On lyrical afflatus in Lomonosov's poetry, see Gukovskii, "Russkaia poeziia XVIII veka," 47–48; Alekseeva, *Russkaia oda: razvitie odicheskoi formy v XVII–XVIII vekakh*, 189–92; Pogosian, *Vostorg russkoi ody i reshenie temy poeta v russkom panegirike 1730–1762 gg.*; Ram, *The Imperial Sublime: A Russian Poetics of Empire*, 63–120. Ram's study focuses more on the ode's conception of imperial geography and the nature and representation of the ode-writer's inspiration, whereas my concern is the emergent "portrait of the queen" and the ode's conception of historical time. For another instance of the empress's and the poet's mutual ascent, see the closing of Derzhavin's "Videnie Murzy," discussed at the end of this chapter: "I will extol you, I will glorify you. / Through you I myself will become immortal." (*Prevoznesu tebia, proslavliu; / Toboi bessmerten budu sam.*)

17. In chapter 3 of this book, we will see Pushkin as a writer of the Romantic generation assess the value of inspiration framed by patronage from the vantage point of a literary and political culture that no longer believed in the possibility of inspiration thus derived. Broadly conceived, this is of course the Romantic shift from culture to nature (external occasion) as a source of poetic inspiration (internal vision).

18. Pumpianskii, *Klassicheskaia traditsiia: Sobranie trudov po istorii russkoi literatury*, 56. Pumpianskii discusses the "objectification of the sign" in Derzhavin's ode in connection with the poet's engagement with nature, arguing that Derzhavin moves away from the poetics of "pure rapture" (the Lomonosovian paradigm) to an "inspired contemplation of nature" (56).

19. The influential, but much-contested argument for the eighteenth-century ode's orientation toward oral performance has been advanced by Tynianov, "Oda kak oratorskii zhanr."

20. The most influential argument for the figurative structures or literary modalities underlying historical narration has been offered by Hayden White in his seminal

study of nineteenth-century historical writing, *Metahistory: The Historical Imagination in Nineteenth-Century Europe.*

21. The panegyric space of the Lomonosovian ode is theorized most extensively by Harsha Ram, who argues that "[m]apping is [. . .] the most frequent outcome of allegorical personification in Lomonosov" (*The Imperial Sublime*, 76). For a more systematic catalogue of panegyric language, themes, motifs and images, particularly as they pertain to the "paradise myth" in European utopian imagination, see Baehr, *The Paradise Myth in Eighteenth-Century Russia*, 1–13.

22. "Solemn Ode to Her Imperial Majesty [. . .] the Sovereign Empress Ekaterina Alekseevna [. . .] on [. . .] Her Accession to [. . .] the Throne, 28 June 1762" ("Oda torzhestvennaia Ee Imperatorskomu Velichestvu [. . .] Gosudaryne Imperatritse Ekaterine Alekseevne [. . .] na [. . .] vosshestvie na [. . .] prestol iiunia 28 dnia 1762 goda"). Lomonosov, *Polnoe sobranie sochinenii*, 8:778. This ode arrived as Lomonosov's delayed response to the accession and did not meet with Catherine's approval. Scholars have linked her lukewarm response to the ode's supposedly subversive stance, its alleged daring to imply instructions regarding the policies Catherine should adopt. S. N. Chernov ("M. V. Lomonosov v odakh 1762 g.") meticulously traces the specific connections between Lomonosov's ode and Catherine II's accession manifestoes and draws attention to the poet's potentially subversive interpretations of these texts. My analysis eschews the arguable issue of Lomonosov's subversiveness, focusing instead on his ode's rhetorical figures.

23. In a somewhat different context, Pumpianskii defines the central mechanism of signification in Lomonosov as the "approach to the object via an already-existing word" (*otnoshenie k predmetu cherez uzhe sushchestvuiushchee slovo*). Pumpianskii, *Klassicheskaia traditsiia: Sobranie trudov po istorii russkoi literatury*, 57.

24. Many scholars have remarked upon the curious coexistence of the Christian God and pagan deities in the Russian odes of the eighteenth century. (The line just quoted above, for instance—"[The Most High gave] us a Goddess for a Tsarina"— evinces a very peculiar sort of monotheism.) For Lomonosov, as B. A. Uspenskii and V. M. Zhivov have demonstrated, pagan gods provided a legitimate and distinctive conceptual vocabulary for sacralizing the monarch without dishonoring the Church; later poets jumbled this delicate hierarchy of the incomparable, native, and singular Christian God hovering above the fragmented, foreign, and ornamental Olympus. Uspenskii and Zhivov, "Tsar' i Bog," 174–92. Stephen Baehr analyzes the transfer of images and symbols from the sacred to the secular domains that takes place in this period. Baehr, *The Paradise Myth in Eighteenth-Century Russia*, 22–34.

25. "Solemn Ode to Her Imperial Majesty [. . .] the Sovereign Empress Ekaterina Alekseevna [. . .] on [. . .] Her Accession to [. . .] the Throne, 28 June 1762." Lomonosov, *Polnoe sobranie sochinenii*, 8:776.

26. Many of these texts actually accord Anna space in Russian history, but disparage this reign to the extent of turning it into a kind of negative historical

space, mentioned only to underscore the greatness of Elizabeth or Catherine. On the representation of Anna in the 1746 ode, see Klein, *Russkaia literatura v XVIII veke*, 120. See, for instance, the allusions to Anna's despotism in Derzhavin's "Felitsa."

27. "Ode on the Day of Her Sovereign Majesty Elisaveta Petrovna's Accession to [. . .] the Throne [. . .] 1746" ("Oda na den' vosshestviia na [. . .] prestol Ee Velichestva Gosudaryni Imperatritsy Elisavety Petrovny [. . .] 1746 goda"). Ibid., 143.

28. "Ode on the Day of Her Sovereign Majesty Empress Elisaveta Petrovna's Accession to the Throne, 1748" ("Oda na den' vosshestviia na prestol Ee Velichestva Gosudaryni Imperatritsy Elisavety Petrovny 1748 goda"). Ibid., 221.

29. "Ode [. . .] to the Sovereign Empress Ekaterina Alekseevna [. . .] on the New Year 1764" ("Oda [. . .] Gosudaryne Imperatritse Ekaterine Alekseevne [. . .] v novyi 1764 god"). Ibid., 789.

30. Pumpianskii remarks upon Lomonosov's tendency to repeat the metric and semantic discoveries of his earlier odes in his post-1747 poetic output. (Pumpianskii, *Klassicheskaia traditsiia: Sobranie trudov po istorii russkoi literatury*, 76.) This, and the formulas I identify subsequently in this study, can be considered instances of such mechanization. One thing is clear: in order to mechanize these coinages, Lomonosov must have found them successful and appropriate.

31. A more obscure version of this formula appears even earlier, in Trediakovskii's verse to Anna Ioannovna: "Of a glorious body an even more glorious mind!" (*Tela slavna ume preslavnyi!*). "Verses in Praise of [. . .] the Sovereign Empress Anna Ioannovna" ("Stikhi [. . .] Gosudaryne Imperatritse [. . .] Anne Ioannovne po Slove Pokhval'nom"). Trediakovskii, *Izbrannye proizvedeniia*, 126.

32. See also "dushi i tela krasotoiu" in Stanza 6 of the 1764 ode to Catherine.

33. "Ode on the Day of Her Sovereign Majesty Empress Elisaveta Petrovna's Accession to the Throne, 1748." Lomonosov, *Polnoe sobranie sochinenii*, 8:221.

34. Ibid., 220.

35. "Solemn Ode to Her Imperial Majesty [. . .] the Sovereign Empress Ekaterina Alekseevna [. . .] on [. . .] Her Accession to [. . .] the Throne, 28 June 1762." Ibid., 772, 780.

36. "Ode on the Day of Her Sovereign Majesty Empress Elisaveta Petrovna's Accession to the Throne, 1748." Ibid., 220.

37. This is in some ways an unabashedly structuralist reading that is, however, still aware of the multiple sacrifices it makes (a disregard for the individual poems' shades of tone and intensity, or for specific agendas and histories of reception) in focusing primarily on the Lomonosovian odes' shared rhetorical structure and its implications.

38. "Plach i uteshenie Rossii k Ego Imperatorskomu Velichestvu Pavlu Pervomu, Samoderzhtsu Vserossiiskomu." Makogonenko and Serman, *Poety XVIII veka*, 1:422. In chapter 2 I will return to this idiosyncratic text and to the poetry devoted to Catherine's death and Paul's accession.

39. As cited in Zorin, Zubkov, and Nemzer, *Svoi podvig svershiv*, 79. Many of this chapter's brief references to Derzhavin's reputation in the nineteenth century are indebted to Zorin's erudite study "'Glagol vremen': Izdaniia G. R. Derzhavina i russkie chitateli" in this collection.

40. I use the term "cycle" loosely here to denote the commonality of characters and themes rather than any formal generic unity.

41. The tale is roughly based on the parable of two roads first formulated by Prodicus of Ceos in the 5th century BC.

42. Ekaterina II, *Sochinenia Imperatritsy Ekateriny II: proizvedeniia literaturnyia*, 373.

43. Derzhavin, *Sochineniia Derzhavina s ob"iasnitel'nymi primechaniiami Ia. Grota*, 1:129.

44. The ceremonial ode indeed was one genre inappropriate for the monarch to adopt, though Catherine II did engage in other genres: comedies, operas, didactic tales, and enlightened exchanges in moral weeklies, for example. "Felitsa" praises Catherine for not writing poetry—"You do not saddle up the steed of Parnassus" (*Konia parnasska ne sedlaesh'*)—leaving her exercises in other literary genres virtually without comment. *Sochineniia Derzhavina s ob"iasnitel'nymi primechaniiami Ia. Grota*, 1:134. Derzhavin's form of pseudo-dialogue with the empress ultimately proved much more congenial with her version of enlightened exchange than Denis Fonvizin's famous attempt at genuine dialogue on the pages of *The Interlocutor of the Lovers of the Russian Word* (*Sobesednik liubitelei rossiiskogo slova*) only a year after "Felitsa."

45. Ibid., 139.

46. *Sochineniia Derzhavina s ob"iasnitel'nymi primechaniiami Ia. Grota*, 1:132.

47. Harsha Ram persuasively identifies the nature of the ethical entanglement between Felitsa and her Murza: "Derzhavin introjects the state's authority, internalizing the sovereign as an ego-ideal that penetrates even the private sphere of domestic life. The enlightened despot, omnipotent but consciously self-limiting, is projected beyond the sphere of governance, to become an ethical ideal for the everyday life of the gentry." Ram, *The Imperial Sublime: A Russian Poetics of Empire*, 110.

48. Ibid., 133. Several scholars have remarked upon negation as one of the central rhetorical strategies of "Felitsa." For the most recent, see Shcheglov, "Iz illiustratsii poeticheskoi izobretatel'nosti Derzhavina."

49. Derzhavin, *Ob"iasneniia na sochineniia Derzhavina: im samim diktovannyia rodnoi ego plemiannitse, Elisavete Nikolaevne L'vovoi, v 1809 godu*, II:6.

50. "Monument" ("Pamiatnik"). *Sochineniia Derzhavina s ob"iasnitel'nymi primechaniiami Ia. Grota*, 1:788.

51. Ibid., 135. Numerous readers of "Felitsa" have emphasized precisely this discovery of the mundane, which for some amounts to a significant transformation of the ode, or even marks the ode's outright destruction as a public and state-centered genre.

52. Most recently, Iurii Shcheglov has provided a nearly exhaustive catalogue of Derzhavin's rhetorical strategies in "Felitsa." Shcheglov, "Iz illiustratsii poeticheskoi izobretatel'nosti Derzhavina." I would suggest that all of these strategies contribute to the ode's polyvalence.

53. *Sochineniia Derzhavina s ob"iasnitel'nymi primechaniiami Ia. Grota*, 1:135.

54. Merzliakov, "Rassuzhdenie o rossiiskoi slovesnosti v nyneshnem ee sostoianii," 92. On the responses to Derzhavin's comparison with Lomonosov offered by Merzliakov, see Zorin, "'Glagol vremen': Izdaniia G. R. Derzhavina i russkie chitateli," in Zorin, Zubkov, and Nemzer, *Svoi podvig svershiv*, 15.

55. This tendency to explicate the allegorical in Derzhavin's self-commentary could be redescribed in Donald Loewen's terms, as Derzhavin's prose persona's tendency to let "his identity as statesman" obscure "his identity as a poet." Loewen, "Questioning a Poet's Explanations," 383.

56. *Sochineniia Derzhavina s ob"iasnitel'nymi primechaniiami Ia. Grota*, 1:140–41.

57. Incidentally, the formula of representing the ruler as a helmsman, traceable to the "ship of state" ode of Horace, and before this, to Solon, survives in the Russian panegyric well into the nineteenth century. For a fascinating exploration of this formula in Zhukovskii, see Vinitskii, *Dom tolkovatelia: Poeticheskaia semantika i istoricheskoe voobrazhenie V. A. Zhukovskogo*, 186–200.

58. "Derzhavin's brilliance," Harsha Ram suggests in his reading of "Felitsa," "consisted of recognizing Felitsa as the empress's own self-projection, and of magnifying and then turning back on Catherine the mirror she had crafted for herself." Ram, *The Imperial Sublime: A Russian Poetics of Empire*, 108. The mirror, of course, was not merely referential, but distortive and idealizing, and we will return to the figurative potential of the mirror in the next section in discussing Vigilius Eriksen's *Portrait of Catherine II at a Mirror*.

59. Grot, *Zhizn' Derzhavina*, 199.

60. Khodasevich, "Gavrila Derzhavin: K stoletiiu so dnia smerti," 248. For a stimulating discussion of the Modernist Derzhavin revival, see Zorin, "Molodoi Derzhavin," in Zorin, Zubkov, and Nemzer, *Svoi podvig svershiv*, 144–54. Drawing connections between Derzhavin's verse and *Eugene Onegin* has become something of a commonplace in Russian scholarship focused upon literary history or historical poetics. Although his main reference point is "The Bronze Horseman," Pumpianskii, too, repeatedly draws the trajectory from the eighteenth-century ode to the novel-in-verse. Pumpianskii, *Klassicheskaia traditsiia: Sobranie trudov po istorii russkoi literatury*, 75.

61. Khodasevich's generation of Russian literary scholars repeatedly interrogated the end of the ode and the legacy of its final practitioners, much as they did the origins of the novel. Thus, for example, Iurii Tynianov contends in "Vopros o Tiutcheve" that Tiutchev follows in Derzhavin's odic footsteps, taking apart the monumental odic form in his fragments. Tynianov, "Vopros o Tiutcheve."

62. Khodasevich, *Derzhavin*, 130. In this second take on the subject, Khodasevich might also be polemicizing against Iurii Tynianov's emphasis on the ode's oratorical orientation. Tynianov, "Oda kak oratorskii zhanr." I am thankful to Boris Maslov for this suggestion.

63. Implicit in Khodasevich's reading is what we might call a revolutionary myth, a belief that the Romantics reject and destroy previous forms, most notably genre and ritualized interactions between poetic speaker and addressee. The novel in this account becomes the genre to subsume and defy all genres, an amorphous and tonally flexible hybrid. It is important to underscore, however, the anachronism in reading Derzhavin, or even the Romantics for that matter, as transcending genre strictures. For a recent study that cogently demonstrates how deeply ingrained genre thinking was in Romantic aesthetic theory, see Duff, *Romanticism and the Uses of Genre*.

64. On the absence of linear plot in the Lomonosovian ceremonial ode, see Alekseeva, *Russkaia oda: razvitie odicheskoi formy v XVII–XVIII vekakh*, 200.

65. Viazemskii, *Zapisnye knizhki, 1813–1848*, 35.

66. An even more basic point about the evolving content of late eighteenth-century Russian poetry might be worth making here: ethical and didactic commentary came increasingly to characterize Catherinian Enlightenment.

67. *Sochineniia Derzhavina s ob"iasnitel'nymi primechaniiami Ia. Grota*, 1:132.

68. Ibid., 148.

69. In a section tellingly titled "The Body Everywhere" (*Le corps partout*), René Demoris identifies as the "obsession" of classical discourse about the monarch "never to utter the place where the king is not." Demoris, "Le corps royal et l'imaginaire au XVIIe siècle," 17.

70. *Sochineniia Derzhavina s ob"iasnitel'nymi primechaniiami Ia. Grota*, 1:148.

71. In developing this brief case study, I discovered many affinities with Louis Marin's masterful analysis of power and representation in French Classicism in his *Portrait of the King*. The case of eighteenth-century Russia is further complicated by the usual disclaimers about its post-Petrine westernization: a) the forms of representation that Marin theorizes arrived in Russia as a piecemeal and nearly simultaneous import from several European courts (France, Prussia, Sweden, small German principalities, etc.) and were superposed on other, native forms of celebrating the tsar; b) particularly important for our case is the problem of female rule, which, as I have suggested throughout this chapter, requires further adjustments both from the represented and the representer of power (in this regard, Elizabeth I of England is a particularly interesting, though not an immediately relevant precedent for the challenges discovered in Russia in the "age of empresses").

72. One might be reminded here of the famous "Las Meninas" section, opening Michel Foucault's *The Order of Things*, but the resonance only underscores the differences between the two paintings: Velázquez's, orchestrating a multi-figure, multi-directional representation of power and art; Eriksen's, playing with the singularity

and multiplicity of the monarch's roles in a much more tightly composed image. Michel Foucault, *The Order of Things*, 3–16.

73. It goes without saying that the space of the observer or artist is emphatically not included in the painting itself, underscoring the empress's singularity. The ornate frame of the mirror, for example, breaks off just at the place where the viewer's space would begin. Yet, inasmuch as the entire composition poses the problem of appreciating and comprehending the empress's image, the disembodied viewer-admirer becomes its assumed, if unrepresented, part.

74. Eriksen's other famous painting is Catherine's equestrian portrait of 1762 (also in the Hermitage), another three-quarter view of the empress, now attired in the uniform of the officers of the Preobrazhenskii regiment. This portrait commemorates her seizure of power and again envisions her in two roles at once, as woman and man.

75. Alekseeva (*Russkaia oda: razvitie odicheskoi formy v XVII–XVIII vekakh*, 188–89) discusses neo-Platonic idealism in connection with *furor poeticus* in the Lomonosovian ode. For a history of early neo-Platonic interpretations of allegory, see Struck, "Allegory and Ascent in Neo-Platonism."

76. This is the principle behind odic materiality in general, as Alekseeva has compellingly demonstrated: "The panegyric ode depicts objects, as does any panegyric, not as they are seen by the flawed eye, but rather guided by a higher knowledge of them." Alekseeva, *Russkaia oda: razvitie odicheskoi formy v XVII–XVIII vekakh*, 189.

77. On visuality in Derzhavin's poetics, see the classic article Dan'ko, "Izobrazitel'noe iskusstvo v poezii Derzhavina"; see also Kölle, *Farbe, Licht und Klang in der malenden Poesie Derzhavins*; and Smoliarova, *Zrimaia lirika. Derzhavin*. In theorizing allegory, Gay Clifford establishes the visual as "[o]ne of the most important means by which interpretation is assisted and directed in allegory." (Clifford, *The Transformations of Allegory*, 71.) Indeed, visualization might offer the most compelling realistic frame in a figurative procedure that is emphatically anti-mimetic. Marcus Levitt has recently argued for the centrality of the visual to the ideological display and self-understanding of eighteenth-century Russian culture generally. See Levitt, *The Visual Dominant in Eighteenth-Century Russia*.

78. *Sochineniia Derzhavina s ob"iasnitel'nymi primechaniiami Ia. Grota*, 1:143.

79. Ibid., 272, 166. Contrast Derzhavin's adherence here to the topoi of odic sacralization with the late eighteenth-century ode's counter move, grounded in the Enlightenment philosophy of government, of praising the ruler on the merits of his/her humanness. See, for example, Derzhavin's famous line "Be a human being on the throne!" (*Bud' na trone chelovek!*) in his "On the Birth in the North of the Porphyry-Born Child" ("Na rozhdenie v severe porfirorodnogo otroka," 1779). In this text, the valorization of the human in the future ruler Alexander coexists with the by now familiar Lomonosovian scenario of the royal-sacral genealogy/succession and its figure of equivalence:

Возрастай, дитя прекрасно!
Возрастай, наш полубог!
Возрастай, уподобляясь
Ты родителям во всем;
С их ты матерью равняясь,
Соравняйся с божеством. (Ibid., 84, 86)

[Grow, o beautiful child! / Grow, our demi-god! / Grow, becoming like / Your parents in everything; / And in becoming equal to their mother [Catherine II], / Become equal to divinity.]

The appeal to the ruler's humanity is discussed as a distinctive topos of the Catherine-era ode, which constitutes a departure from the Lomonosovian paradigm, in Greshishcheva, "Khvalebnaia oda v russkoi literature XVIII v.," 143.

80. *Sochineniia Derzhavina s ob"iasnitel'nymi primechaniiami Ia. Grota*, 1:133.

81. Ibid., 166.

82. Ibid., 165–66.

83. On Derzhavin's difficult guesswork about Catherine's real opinion of "Felitsa" as giving rise to the stylized confrontation between Felitsa and the poet in "Murza's Vision," see Pogosian, "Uroki imperatritsy: Ekaterina II i Derzhavin v 1783 godu," 246–49.

84. *Sochineniia Derzhavina s ob"iasnitel'nymi primechaniiami Ia. Grota*, 1:168.

85. Maureen Quilligan has argued (*The Language of Allegory: Defining the Genre*, 15) that allegory in general, more than other literary modes, foregrounds "self-reflexivity with language." Struck locates the beginnings of this fairly commonplace "allegorical habit of claiming that allegorical literary constructions render the transcendent in the concrete, and use language to express what is beyond language," in Plotinus. Struck, "Allegory and Ascent in Neo-Platonism," 59.

86. *Sochineniia Derzhavina s ob"iasnitel'nymi primechaniiami Ia. Grota*, 1:272.

87. Elena Pogosian discusses Derzhavin's self-identification as Felitsa-Catherine's Raphael after the empress's apparent approval of the ode "Felitsa." Pogosian, "Uroki imperatritsy: Ekaterina II i Derzhavin v 1783 godu," 245–46.

88. *Sochineniia Derzhavina s ob"iasnitel'nymi primechaniiami Ia. Grota*, 1:272.

89. Eriksen's portrait moves precisely in this direction, from the empress's physical to her symbolic body, but because of the medium's limitations, the painting falls short of fully capturing transcendence.

90. *Sochineniia Derzhavina s ob"iasnitel'nymi primechaniiami Ia. Grota*, 1:275.

91. Ibid., 273.

92. Ibid.

93. Here again Eriksen would begin to approach the problem in his 1762 equestrian portrait of Catherine II.

94. *Sochineniia Derzhavina s ob"iasnitel'nymi primechaniiami Ia. Grota*, 1:273.

95. Ibid., 291.

96. Words that include *vse* ("all") abound in the poem. There are thirty instances, including, in addition to *vse* and its declensions, *vselenna* ("universe"), *vsevlastno* ("all-powerfully"), *vsederzhitel'* ("the Almighty"), *vsemogushchii* ("omnipotent," "Almighty"), *(po)vsiudu* ("everywhere"), *vsegda* ("always"), *vsiakii* ("any").

97. *Sochineniia Derzhavina s ob"iasnitel'nymi primechaniiami Ia. Grota*, 1:295.

98. Marin, *Portrait of the King*, 72.

99. Zapadov describes the charge of odic servility, which he argues does not ultimately apply to Derzhavin; see Zapadov, "Problema literaturnogo servilizma i diletantizma i poeticheskaia pozitsiia G. R. Derzhavina."

100. A recent entry in this category that, in my view, swings the revisionist pendulum too far toward an insistence on Derzhavin's civic and poetic autonomy is Anna Lisa Crone's *The Daring of Derzhavin: The Moral and Aesthetic Independence of the Poet in Russia*. A much more complicated account of the notion of poetic independence in eighteenth-century Russia is given in Klein, "Poet-samokhval: 'Pamiatnik' Derzhavina i status poeta v Rossii XVIII veka."

CHAPTER 2. CATHERINE'S PASSING

1. The epigraph that opens this chapter is from Derzhavin, *Sochineniia Derzhavina s ob"iasnitel'nymi primechaniiami Ia. Grota*, 3:370. "And even if this statue were encircled by darkness, / The world would still recognize its mistress in it."

2. Golovina, *Memuary*, 140–41.

3. See Paul's accession manifesto in *Polnoe sobranie zakonov* 24, No. 17,530 (6 November 1796). Richard Wortman discusses Paul's insistence on "hereditary right" in *Scenarios of Power*, 1:172. Cynthia Whittaker considers the hopes placed upon Paul's accession by Russian writers precisely in connection with his emphasis on the legality of his accession (*Russian Monarchy: Eighteenth-Century Rulers and Writers in Political Dialogue*, 181–83).

4. For instance, in Derzhavin's "On the Perfidy of the French Revolt and in Honor of Prince Pozharskii" ("Na kovarstvo frantsuzskogo vozmushcheniia i v chest' kniazia Pozharskogo," 1789–90), a good early example of the kind of doubly-pitched poetic text I will consider in this chapter, neither reason nor the pursuit of truth is ever held responsible for the Revolution, and the main tenets of Catherine's Enlightenment—truth and justice—in fact remain intact and reaffirmed:

Прямое духа превосходство—
Лишь к истине любовь одна;
О ней лишь может быть рачитель,
О благе общем попечитель,
Отцом отечества монарх;
(Derzhavin, *Sochineniia Derzhavina s ob"iasnitel'nymi primechaniiami Ia. Grota*, 1:324–25)

[The spirit's direct superiority / Is solely the love of truth; / For this alone can a monarch be zealous, / Of the common good alone can he be guardian, / and father of the fatherland;]

It is important to note, however, that the poem, initially censuring court intrigue, was motivated by Derzhavin's personal discontent; some of its lessons for a righteous monarch might thus stem from that original impulse, rather than some desire to juxtapose reason and enlightenment with the perversion of these ideals in the French Revolution.

5. Derzhavin, *Sochineniia Derzhavina s ob"iasnitel'nymi primechaniiami Ia. Grota*, 2:23.

6. Ibid.

7. Ibid., 25.

8. For a more comprehensive overview of panegyrics written in Paul's praise at the time of his enthronement, see Jekutsch, "Das Lob Pauls I."

9. We might compare this structure to that of Vasilii Trediakovskii's "Elegy on the Death of Peter the Great" ("Elegiia o smerti Petra Velikogo," 1725), for example. Trediakovskii, too, incorporates the quoted speech of several personified entities, including Glory, Mars, and even the Universe; but all his speakers, including the poet who mediates among them, appear in unison, and the poem itself is consistently elegiac, never attempting to celebrate the new monarch after Peter's death.

10. Makogonenko, *Poety XVIII veka*, 1:420.

11. On this structure, see the classic account of the elegy as a genre in Sacks, *The English Elegy*.

12. Ibid., 421. This passage is also interesting to consider in the context of the generic hybridity of Petrov's text, for it brings to mind liturgical topoi as well as the psalmic style codified by Lomonosov for the solemn ode.

13. Here God addresses Paul, promising to inspire him with the spirit of Catherine and Peter. I have quoted this passage in chapter 1 as an example of the "synthesis" convention in the eighteenth-century ceremonial ode, which proves untenable in the representation of Paul's accession.

14. Makogonenko, *Poety XVIII veka*, 1:422.

15. Ibid.

16. Ibid., 419–25.

17. See No. 17.530, "Manifest o konchine Gosudaryni Imperatritsy Ekateriny II, i o vstuplenii na Prestol Gosudaria Imperatora Pavla I" in *Polnoe sobranie zakonov*, 24:1.

18. Ibid., 16–18.

19. This cursory treatment of the preceding reign is in line with the practice of emphasizing the accession of the new ruler over the funeral of the deceased one, a convention observed in Russia, as Richard Wortman suggests, until the

enthronement of Nicholas I in 1825 and his elaborate funeral ceremonies for his brother Alexander I. Wortman, *Scenarios of Power*, 1:271–72.

20. Kapnist, *Sochineniia Kapnista*, 521.

21. Derzhavin, *Sochineniia Derzhavina s ob"iasnitel'nymi primechaniiami Ia. Grota*, 2:707.

22. Ibid., 26.

23. Ibid., 24.

24. In his brief discussion of this poem, Wortman focuses on its innovations in celebrating the monarch and claims that "there is no golden age imagery, no message of deliverance" (*Scenarios of Power*, 1:184). As we have seen, this is not entirely the case. In fact, the ode's achievement lies in the complex overlay of old and new modes of representation and in the successful reclaiming of old odic strategies, including the invocation of the golden age, for post-Catherinian civic verse.

25. On the importance of Archangel Michael to Paul's self-representation, see Wortman, *Scenarios of Power*, 1:179.

26. Iurii Lotman discusses this ode in the context of Karamzin's political views in "Cherty real'noi politiki," 123–30.

27. Karamzin, *Zapiska o drevnei i novoi Rossii*, 44. See also Karamzin's "Historical Panegyric to Catherine II" ("Istoricheskoe pokhval'noe slovo Ekaterine II," 1801) for an example of unequivocal praise for Catherine (whom Karamzin repeatedly calls immortal) that does not make any mention of Paul I, referring instead to Catherine's "sons," her subjects, and providing political instruction for her grandson Alexander, who had just assumed the throne.

28. Ibid.

29. Karamzin, *Polnoe sobranie stikhotvorenii*, 185. Contrast the content of this rhetorical question and its matter-of-fact resolution (after all, there is nothing surprising about Paul's assumption of power) with the question of Catherine's passing, resolved with such effort by Petrov and Derzhavin. Karamzin simply leaves the question of continuity between Catherine and Paul outside the purview of his ode, long and capacious though this text may be.

30. Ibid., 189.

31. Lotman draws the connection between Karamzin and Lomonosov in this context ("Cherty real'noi politiki," 123). S. N. Chernov reads Lomonosov's panegyric production of 1762, odes directed first to Peter III and then to Catherine II, as polyvalent texts that reconfigure the narratives of the past, interpret the future course intimated by the monarch, and possibly also offer their own program. Chernov, "M. V. Lomonosov v odakh 1762 g."

32. Viktor Zhivov ("Gosudarstvennyi mif v epokhu prosveshcheniia") locates a profound transformation in the Russian intellectuals' conception of the state precisely in the 1780s and 1790s, when the project of Russian Enlightenment ceases to be so inextricably tied to the project of Russian autocracy.

33. Karamzin, *Polnoe sobranie stikhotvorenii*, 185.

34. Ibid.

35. Ibid., 188.

36. On sentimentalism's articulation of political positions in the context of the French Revolution, see Denby, *Sentimental Narrative and the Social Order*, 139–65.

37. On Russian sentimentalism's multi-layered relationship to the Enlightenment's pursuit of reason, see Kochetkova, *Literatura russkogo sentimentalizma*, 24–74. The view I invoke here, which sees sentiment as moderating reason, certainly does not exhaust the variety of attitudes toward sentimentalism entertained by Karamzin's contemporaries or by scholars of sentimentalism. Another approach would see them as complementary or Enlightenment rationalism as actually enabling the discourse on passion and feeling.

38. Derzhavin, *Sochineniia Derzhavina s ob"iasnitel'nymi primechaniiami Ia. Grota*, 2:23.

39. Ibid.

40. See, for example, Karamzin's "Epistle to Dmitriev" ("Poslanie k Dmitrievu," 1794), where the lyric I seeks refuge from his disillusionment with public service in love, friendship, and the countryside.

41. Karamzin, *Polnoe sobranie stikhotvorenii*, 190.

42. Dmitriev, *Polnoe sobranie stikhotvorenii*, 325.

43. Ibid., 322.

44. Ibid., 323. In this section, Dmitriev also makes a rather unorthodox mention of Paul's descent from Ioann Alekseevich (Peter I's brother who had only nominally ruled Russia, all the while following his sister's line) and Ioann VI Antonovich (the tsar deposed and imprisoned by Elizabeth)—two Russian monarchs whose power had been usurped. Dmitriev thereby suggests, as did Karamzin, that the throne had been withheld from Paul. But this passing allusion, as I will soon demonstrate, is far from Dmitriev's most depreciatory treatment of Catherine in the poem.

45. Ibid., 325.

46. Ibid., 324.

47. Ibid.

48. Ibid. 325.

49. Ibid., 324.

50. Ibid., 325.

51. Karamzin, *Pis'ma k I. I. Dmitrievu*, 73. Unfortunately, not a single letter of Dmitriev's to Karamzin has been preserved: we are left to reconstruct their content from Karamzin's responses. On the makeup of the extant Dmitriev correspondence, see Vatsuro, "I. I. Dmitriev: Kommentarii," 438.

52. Derzhavin, *Sochineniia Derzhavina s ob"iasnitel'nymi primechaniiami Ia. Grota*, 2:59.

53. Ibid., 60.

54. In his meticulous commentary, Ia. K. Grot demonstrates how precisely Derzhavin's poetic images match the architectural structures on the actual estate. Ibid., 63–67.

55. Shvidkovskii, *The Empress & the Architect: British Architecture and Gardens at the Court of Catherine the Great*, 41.

56. Andreas Schönle's work on ruins has been instrumental in introducing them into the critical discussion of Russian cultural history. See Schönle, *Architecture of Oblivion: Ruins and Historical Consciousness in Modern Russia*; Schönle and Hell, *Ruins of Modernity*; Schönle, *The Ruler in the Garden: Politics and Landscape Design in Imperial Russia*; and his introduction, "Ruins and History: Observations on Russian Approaches to Destruction and Decay," to an article cluster on ruins published in *Slavic Review*. Lev Loseff identifies the "motif of ruins" in Tsarskoe Selo poetry and links it to the park's artificial ruins and "aesthetics of desolation" ("The Toy Town Ruined," 34). In an expanded earlier version of my analysis of Derzhavin's "Ruins," I have explored late eighteenth-century ruin culture and the pictorial representations associated with it in greater detail; see Golburt, "Derzhavin's Ruins and the Birth of Historical Elegy."

57. Russian antiquity at this point was also a matter of much discussion and yearning on the part of Russian Sentimentalists and amateur historians. Here might be cited, for instance, the multiple interpretations of the Novgorod story by such authors as Kniazhnin, Karamzin, and Catherine II herself (Sumarokov was the first to broach the subject in *Sinav i Truvor*). The fascination with national history also manifested itself in the appearance of amateur historical circles, e.g., that of A. I. Musin-Pushkin, whose work resulted in, if one is to follow the commonly accepted scenario, the discovery of *The Lay of Igor's Campaign* and other texts of a lesser renown. For more on this circle, see Kozlov and Buganov, *Kruzhok A. I. Musina-Pushkina i "Slovo o Polku Igoreve": novye stranitsy istorii drevnerusskoi poemy v XVIII v.*

58. Monika Greenleaf articulates the complexity of this experience along both historical and geographical axes: "While fragments of classical architecture or statuary interpolated into a northern setting cast an aura of unreality on contemporaneity, introducing the possibility of evanescence into the lived moment, living people interpolated into the classical stage set of Tsarskoe Selo began to conceive of themselves in its terms. [. . .] This ubiquitous modeling system bore a strong connection with Russian imperial iconography and ambitions." Greenleaf, *Pushkin and Romantic Fashion: Fragment, Elegy, Orient, Irony*, 59.

59. Schönle theorizes the link between "ruins" and "modernity" in the context of a different historical project; see "Mezhdu 'drevnei' i 'novoi' Rossiei: ruiny u rannego Karamzina kak mesto *modernity*."

60. For a comprehensive and illuminating study of the English influences on Russian architecture and landscape design, consult Shvidkovskii, *The Empress & the Architect*.

61. In chapter 3, we will see the pantheon as one of this period's prominent images for picturing an epoch's character and historical contribution. In his earlier poem "My Effigy" ("Moi istukan," 1794), Derzhavin imagines the placement of his own sculptural portrait among those in the Cameron Gallery.

62. Indeed, Paul and his mother harked to quite different Enlightenments; the son had a penchant for the occult and Masonic practices, exaggerated worship of Frederick the Great, and frequent sentimental outpourings.

63. The opposition between Grand Duke Paul's lesser court, with its center in Gatchina, and the empress's main court, centered in the capital and in Tsarskoe Selo during the summer, had been in place ever since Paul's first marriage in 1773. After his long-desired accession to the throne, Paul's residences, formerly associated with political marginalization, conspicuously advertised his new independence as emperor.

64. Peter Hayden, the historian of imperial gardens, mentions this episode in his overview of the landscaping history of Tsarskoe Selo in Loseff and Scherr, *A Sense of Place: Tsarskoe Selo and its Poets*, 28. Shvidkovskii notes Paul's dismissal of Catherine's foremost architect, Charles Cameron: "Paul's coronation meant a change of personnel surrounding the monarch, including the court architects. Several days after Catherine's death, Cameron was dismissed." Shvidkovskii, *The Empress & the Architect*, 33.

65. Cf. Catherine's own distaste for her predecessor's architectural preferences. Vera Proskurina remarks upon the correlation between Catherine's architectural and political programs; as soon as Catherine comes to power, "Elizabeth's architectural 'splendor' is also transferred to the semantic field of 'before': Catherine remodels and transforms the palaces of her precursor. Elizabeth's baroque tastes provoke an open aversion: Catherine does not conceal her dissatisfaction with Rastrelli, who symbolized the style of the previous reign. The aesthetic shift from Rastrelli to Falconet and Quarenghi reflected not only the stylistic turn from the baroque to classicism, but also a political strategy directed at excluding Elizabeth's reign from participation in the Petersburg myth." Proskurina, "Peterburgskii mif i politika monumentov: Petr Pervyi Ekaterine Vtoroi," 110.

66. Derzhavin, *Sochineniia Derzhavina s ob"iasnitel'nymi primechaniiami Ia. Grota*, 2:59.

67. Wortman, *Scenarios of Power*, 111.

68. A distinctive feature throughout Derzhavin's oeuvre, such an amalgamation was at this later stage of his career consumed with particular eagerness by readers and landscape viewers of the "Age of Sensibility." As John Dixon Hunt observes, "The landscape painter in the eighteenth century was torn between topography and fantasy, between his instinct for recording actual views and visions of idealized scenery." (Hunt, *The Figure in the Landscape: Poetry, Painting, and Gardening During the Eighteenth Century*, 200.) What a painter might have experienced as a conflict between the actual and the ideal in fact formed the core of an ode-writer's aesthetic and, particularly in Derzhavin's hands, became the subject of much self-reflexive play.

69. Derzhavin, *Sochineniia Derzhavina s ob"iasnitel'nymi primechaniiami Ia. Grota*, 2:60.

70. Julie Buckler proposes that the Tsarskoe Selo "text" habitually took one of three poetic forms: "official paean, private elegy, or museum catalogue—depending on the cultural moment of the palace in question" (Buckler, *Mapping St. Petersburg*, 163). I would argue that in "Ruins," these three genres (or rather, their equivalents within the eighteenth-century genre system), rather than constituting distinct options, are complexly and consciously interwoven, in part precisely in response to "the cultural moment" of Paul's succession.

71. Contrast Derzhavin's reconstruction of Catherine's day with Petrov's far less specific yet pathos-filled predictions about Paul's daily routine, which are voiced as a promise in Paul's vow to God and Russia:

Я раннюю зарю
Для пользы твоея восстаньем предварю,
Я в полдень для тебя на подвиг обрекуся,
Я в вечер о тебе, болея, попекуся.
При солнце, при свече
Тобой займусь, и труд мой будет не вотще.
И даже как на одр возлягу,
Потщуся твоему споспешен быти благу.
Не вдруг очам
Дреманье дам;
И дремля о тебе мечтати живо стану,
С тобой засну, с тобой восстану.

[The morning dawn I / Shall anticipate for your benefit with my own waking, / At midday I shall gird myself for feats for you, / At evening time I shall keenly care for you. / In daylight and by candlelight / I shall tend to you, and my labors will not be in vain. / And even when I lie upon my bed, / I'll endeavor to hasten your well-being. / I won't immediately to my eyes / Grant repose; / And slumbering will vividly dream of you, / With you I'll fall asleep, with you I'll rise.]

Here again we observe Petrov's tendency toward abstraction. Paul's day is filled not with specific activities, but with a single-minded, unspecified concern for Russia that leaves no space for the involvement—affective or otherwise—of his subjects.

72. Derzhavin, *Sochineniia Derzhavina s ob"iasnitel'nymi primechaniiami Ia. Grota*, 2:61.

73. Wortman, *Scenarios of Power*, 211.

74. Quoted from Voltaire and Catherine, *Voltaire and Catherine the Great; Selected Correspondence*, 117.

75. Vera Proskurina explicates the symbolic work that all triumphal arches perform: "To pass through a triumphal arch, decorated by all the significant emblems and inscriptions of the epoch, meant a recoding of the real space into a mytho-historical space. The state thus accrued additional symbolic capital." Proskurina,

Mify imperii: Literatura i vlast' v epokhu Ekateriny II, 168. On the odic discourse of war, see Proskurina's chapter "So shchitom Pallady: diskurs voiny" in *Mify imperii*, 147–94.

76. I have discussed Derzhavin's negotiations between verbal and visual media in Golburt, "Derzhavin's Monuments: Sculpture, Poetry, and the Materiality of History."

77. Andreas Schönle explores the connection of the Minerva image to Catherine's gardening strategies in Tsarskoe Selo. "Catherine had finally solidified this connection when in 1789 she had placed in a Tsarskoe Selo grotto a statue of herself as a colossal Minerva." Schönle, "Prostranstvennaia poetika Tsarskogo Sela v ekaterininskoi prezentatsii imperii," 63. Baehr's remark that "under Catherine II, Russia was often referred to as Minerva's garden" (*The Paradise Myth*, 82) lends support to Schönle's analysis. Given this context, Derzhavin's choice of a different goddess is all the more revealing.

78. Toward the end of Catherine's reign, associations with Venus were increasingly interpreted as subversive, alluding as they do to Catherine's sexual rapacity, seen as unsuitable for her age and detrimental to the success of her government. Her last favorite, Platon Zubov, was perceived as particularly dull and unfit for the prominent positions his proximity to the aging empress earned him. In his allegory, Derzhavin redeems the Venus image from such negative associations, which were played up by some of his literary rivals, for example, I. A. Krylov. See Proskurina, *Creating the Empress: Politics and Poetry in the Age of Catherine II*, 256–85. In chapter 5, I will return to this less than flattering image of Catherine in considering it as a model for the Countess in Pushkin's "Queen of Spades."

79. Julie Buckler sums up Charles Masson's critique of Tsarskoe Selo as that of an "already incoherent 'text,'" one indiscriminately memorializing Catherine's dogs, heroes, and lovers, and already during Paul's reign exhibiting signs of desolation. Buckler, *Mapping St. Petersburg: Imperial Text and Cityshape*, 162–63.

80. Basing his claims on the analysis of multiple contemporary sources, Baehr confirms these observations: "In the eighteenth century, when Russia was frequently at war, the image of a quiet garden [. . .] celebrated peace. [. . .] As in many other works using the garden image, there is perfect unity here between man and nature; the garden is an emblem for man's 'natural' condition of peace—a condition that had flourished along with nature in Eden." Baehr, *The Paradise Myth*, 67.

81. After his enthronement, Paul lived in Tsarskoe Selo for a total of two weeks in 1800, three years after the composition of "Ruins"; thus in 1797, when Derzhavin writes the poem, Tsarskoe Selo is in no way associated with Paul's military displays and can be contrastingly represented as a peaceful realm.

82. These include "To the Muse" ("K Muze," 1797), which allegorizes Paul's coronation as the arrival of spring; "On the Order of Malta" ("Na Mal'tiiskii Orden," 1798); and Derzhavin's translation of an ode presented by the Jewish community of Shklov, "On the Passing of Empress Catherine II and the Accession of Emperor Paul I" ("Na konchinu Imperatritsy Ekateriny II, i na vosshestvie na prestol Imperatora Pavla I," 1799).

83. Wortman, *Scenarios of Power*, 173.

84. A similar fate befell, among others, Princess E. R. Dashkova, who provides a famous account of her house arrest in Dashkova, *Mon histoire: Mémoires d'une femme de lettres russe à l'époque des lumières*. The flux of court favor, particularly during the reign of Catherine and with the accession of Paul, is indeed a recurrent topic in aristocratic memoirs of the period.

85. For a discussion of this poem in light of Derzhavin's treatment of civil service, Catherinian grandees, fate, and the sublime, see Ram, *The Imperial Sublime: A Russian Poetics of Empire*, 96–97.

86. Derzhavin, *Sochineniia Derzhavina s ob"iasnitel'nymi primechaniiami Ia. Grota*, 2:22.

87. D. S. Likhachev calls the Garden of Eden "the most important semantic prototype of all European gardens" (Likhachev, *Poeziia sadov: k semantike sadovo-parkovykh stilei: sad kak tekst*, 38). Derzhavin's evocation of Tsarskoe Selo certainly plays on this association. Stephen Baehr observes that garden imagery, especially common in ceremonial odes, became a prominent metaphor of the flourishing Russian state. He devotes the chapter "The Happy Garden State" (*The Paradise Myth*, 65–89) to exploring this metaphor.

88. Anna Lisa Crone also connects these two poems (Crone, *The Daring of Derzhavin*, 175–76), in my view overstating, however, the case for Derzhavin's political "independence" and subversive "daring." Partly following Derzhavin's own self-serving autobiographical statements, Crone considers the odes Derzhavin addressed throughout the 1790s to out-of-favor grandees (Grigorii Potemkin, Petr Rumiantsev, and Grigorii Orlov in Catherine's time; and Platon Zubov and Matvei Platov during the reign of Paul I) as signs of the poet's sovereignty. "Ruins," dedicated in 1797 to the past glory of Catherine the Great, can also be seen in this context. While Derzhavin was clearly intent on forging the poetic and civic persona of an autonomous seeker of truth, I would emphasize that such a stance was at the same time a constructed and in many ways culturally encouraged one, and that, furthermore, the Derzhavin corpus is hardly lacking in works that celebrate precisely those *in* power, including, as we have seen, odes that pay tribute to Paul I.

89. See Grot's commentary in Derzhavin, *Sochineniia Derzhavina s ob"iasnitel'nymi primechaniiami Ia. Grota*, 2:24.

90. Ibid., 1:302.

91. Serman, "Derzhavin v novom veke," 56. Leslie O'Bell convincingly argues against the excision of the political domain from our readings of the Russian Anacreontic ode, on the one hand because eighteenth-century Russian poetry was shaped first and foremost by these concerns and, on the other, because "certain of the [Greek original] Anacreontic poems are topical and need commentary as much as the ode." O'Bell, "The Spirit of Derzhavin's Anacreontic Verse," 71.

92. Derzhavin, *Sochineniia Derzhavina s ob"iasnitel'nymi primechaniiami Ia. Grota*, 2:85.

93. Pumpianskii (*Klassicheskaia traditsiia*, 111) emphasizes Derzhavin's inno-
vative adaptation of this Russian Anacreontic meter to what he describes as the content of anthological rather than strictly Anacreontic verse. Here I have chosen to
adopt a fairly broad conception of the Anacreontic, corresponding to the capaciousness of this mode in Derzhavin's third, collected volume.

94. Despite incorrectly identifying Derzhavin as a Romantic poet, Marshall
Brown makes a generally convincing case for the reassessment of the Anacreontic as constituted by its understated tensions and engagements with other genres,
and as having important ramifications for the later Romantic lyric. Brown, "Passion
and Love: Anacreontic Song and the Roots of Romantic Lyric," 388. Leslie O'Bell
maintains, on the contrary, that Derzhavin's Anacreontics cannot yield an early
Romantic lyric subject, but should rather be placed squarely within the eighteenth-
century tradition of non-introspective poetic personhood. O'Bell, "The Spirit of
Derzhavin's Anacreontic Verse." Here I have tried to find the middle ground between
these two positions, which I believe Derzhavin as a transitional figure occupies.

95. Derzhavin, *Sochineniia Derzhavina s ob"iasnitel'nymi primechaniiami Ia.
Grota*, 2:62.

96. Harsha Ram (*The Imperial Sublime*, 178) distinguishes the ode's and elegy's
historical vision in the ode's "incremental vision of history linking past and present,"
as opposed to "elegiac time [which] unfolds as an empty present that must be continually filled with the memory of a former plenitude or the anticipation of imminent death." Derzhavin's final stanza performs an abrupt shift precisely from "an
incremental vision of history" to "an empty present." In his chapter on the "elegiac
sublime," Ram examines the intricate relationship between the ode and the elegy,
but connects this phenomenon with the historical elegies of Batiushkov. I have tried
to demonstrate in this chapter that we can trace this transition to an even earlier
moment.

97. Another generic prism that might inform a reading of Derzhavin's poem is
furnished by *oraisons funèbres*, a sermon-like genre popular in the seventeenth and
early eighteenth centuries. In this genre, the mourner publicly inventories the idyllic virtues of the deceased, in the end arriving at an overwhelming loss that is shared
by the entire audience. Famous practitioners of the genre included Jacques Bossuet,
Louis Bourdaloue, and Jules Mascaron. Printed versions circulated widely during
the eighteenth century. I am thankful to the late V. M. Zhivov for alerting me to this
textual tradition.

98. Derzhavin, *Zapiski Gavriila Romanovicha Derzhavina, 1743–1812, s literaturnymi i istoricheskimi primechaniiami P. I. Barteneva*, 379. In a perfect biographical reformulation of the challenge of allegory, Derzhavin describes his writer's
block as the inability to maintain "his former high ideal when next to himself he
saw the human original with its great weaknesses."

99. Sacks, *The English Elegy*, 6.

100. Baehr, *The Paradise Myth*, 87.

101. Pushkin, *Polnoe sobranie sochinenii v shestnadtsati tomakh*, 1:79. On the complex relationship of Pushkin's text with Derzhavin's poetics, see for example Bethea, *Realizing Metaphors*, 154–72; and Crone, "What Derzhavin Heard When Pushkin Read 'Vospominaniia v Tsarskom Sele' in 1815."

102. Though focused primarily on Akhmatova, the Loseff and Scherr collection *A Sense of Place* traces some of these motifs throughout the works of many Tsarskoe Selo poets.

103. I borrow this concept from Vladimir Toporov's seminal *Peterburgskii tekst russkoi literatury*.

Chapter 3. Poetry Reads Power

1. The epigraph that opens this chapter is quoted in Gukovskii, "Vokrug Radishcheva," 230. "Can it be that only glory-hungering, / Bloodied heroes / Deserve to be sung on lyres? / Or that only crowned mortals / And their gold-glittering gifts / Can excite ardor in the muses?"

2. See Crotty, *Song and Action: The Victory Odes of Pindar*; and Kurke, *The Traffic in Praise: Pindar and the Poetics of Social Economy*.

3. This is in no way meant to suggest that all, or even most, odes of the period underwent this shift. In fact, the majority remained ruler-centered and celebrated the arrival of the new century only insofar as it was also marked by the arrival of a new ruler, Alexander I. As we will see, however, a number of poets were drawn, at this crucial juncture, to alternative readings of history.

4. Understanding modernity and conceptualizing the transformations in historical thinking occasioned by the Enlightenment and the French Revolution form a major thread in all of Koselleck's writings. For the present analysis, I found most illuminating Koselleck, "Modernity and the Planes of Historicity."

5. Ibid., 17.

6. Ibid.

7. This is the narrative developed by William Mills Todd III in *Fiction and Society in the Age of Pushkin: Ideology, Institutions, and Narrative*. On the ambit of patronage as a literary institution in the first decades of the nineteenth century, see in particular Todd's sections on patronage (51–55) and on the debate over "literary aristocracy" (83–93). To compare this evolving situation to the history of the book market in the eighteenth century, consult Marker, *Publishing, Printing, and the Origins of Intellectual Life in Russia, 1700–1800*.

8. The two poems cited here, "The New Nineteenth Century in Russia" and "The People's Exclamation on the Entrance of the New Century" appear in Makogonenko and Serman, *Poety XVIII veka*, 2:253–56.

9. Irina Reyfman comments on the "nascent nationalistic sensibilities" of L'vov's 1801 odes "The New Nineteenth Century in Russia" and "The People's Exclamation on the Entrance of the New Century." Reyfman, "Imagery of Time and Eternity in Eighteenth-Century Russian Poetry: Mikhail Murav'ev and Semen Bobrov," 104.

10. Makogonenko and Serman, *Poety XVIII veka*, 2:256.

11. The "Russian God" that in L'vov comes to bless the new century evolved, as shown by Reiser and later by Uspenskii, into a trope of nationalist discourse in the early nineteenth century, and especially in 1812 literature, where it was used to portray the Russian nation as a chosen people. The period's most famous instance of this image occurs in Zhukovskii's "Bard in the Camp of Russian Warriors" ("Pevets vo stane russkikh voinov"), a key text for Russian national ideology of the early 1800s. In his brief but comprehensive history of this term (Reiser, "Russkii bog"), tracing it from its rise with the pre-Romantics through its (partial) discreditation in the official discourse of the late nineteenth century, Reiser does not mention L'vov, who seems to be one of the first to introduce it into Russian poetry. Boris Uspenkii extends the history of the term back to the Russian middle ages and the cult of Mikola/Nikolai, suggesting that the idiom "Russian god" referred to the Russian national saint and protector Saint Nicholas. Uspenskii, "'Russkii bog': k istorii frazeologizma."

12. Makogonenko and Serman, *Poety XVIII veka*, 2:254.

13. Ibid., 255.

14. Rogger, *National Consciousness in Eighteenth-Century Russia*, 258.

15. Makogonenko and Serman, *Poety XVIII veka*, 2:255.

16. Rogger remarks that "until folklorists and writers, historians and artists could discover or create objects of national reverence, the monarch was made to serve as the symbol of national strength and greatness" (*National Consciousness in Eighteenth-Century Russia*, 255).

17. The eighteenth century witnessed a proliferation of Russian terms derived from "hero" (*geroi* or *iroi*), used to connote the half-mortal, half-divine protagonists of ancient legend and the Classical age associated with them (the "geroicheskii vek," reinaugurated on Earth, it was often suggested, by Peter the Great), as well as the less historically specific qualities of prowess and valor. L'vov's recognition of heroism under a different, Russian word—"udal'stvo," which could boast a much longer history of circulation in the Russian language—establishes an uncertain hierarchy between the two terms, the former revealed as the transcendent, pan-European essence of the nationally-specific latter term, which at the same time is recognized as newly relevant.

18. In *The Meaning of History*, Berdiaev asserts that Christianity is possessed of an "exclusive historicity and dynamism" that "differs sharply from the mindset (*sklad sozertsaniia*) of [Classical] antiquity, which was static"; he ties this dynamism to the "historical drama" (*istoricheskii dramatizm*) of the messianic idea adopted from Judaism. (Berdiaev, *Smysl istorii*, 85, 84, 70.) Drawing on this, we might note that nineteenth-century nationalism, which in effect is the apotheosis of the people and its redemption, is informed by a similarly millenarian historicity; no wonder, then, that nationalist discourse should turn from allegedly "static" Classical gods to Biblical modes of divinity befitting such a chiliastic conception of time.

19. On the ode's vertical sublime, see Ram, *The Imperial Sublime*.

20. This ubiquitous Russian heroism and L'vov's specific manner of its description are reminiscent of the then recently discovered *Lay of Igor's Campaign*, of which L'vov was a great enthusiast and interpreter. Responding to the 1790s debates on the value of the Russian epic and the European-wide Ossianist revival of epic heroism generally, L'vov composed the epic poem *Dobrynia* (1796, unfinished), where he endorsed the traditional Russian world-order and demonstrated the merits of the *bylina* (the Russian epic).

21. On L'vov's intellectual position, see Lappo-Danilevskii, "Literaturnoe nasledie N. A. L'vova."

22. Radishchev, *Polnoe sobranie sochinenii*, 1:127–29.

23. Puzzling over the synchronous increase in enlightenment and bloodshed in the eighteenth century becomes somewhat of a commonplace in the wake of the French Revolution and Terror. See, for example, Melodor's lament in Karamzin's "Melodor to Filalet" ("Melodor k Filaletu," 1795): "The Age of Enlightenment! I do not recognize you—in blood and flames I do not recognize you—amid murder and destruction I do not recognize you!" Karamzin, *Izbrannye sochineniia v dvukh tomakh*, 2:247.

24. Al'tshuller and Lotman, *Poety 1790–1810-kh godov*, 214–19. The similarity of the ideological position espoused in "Drevnost'" to Radishchev's led some scholars to speculate that Radishchev had in fact authored it. See Gukovskii, "Vokrug Radishcheva," 216–17.

25. The poem's trochaic pentameter might indicate its indebtedness to the German tradition of philosophical lyric, particularly that of Schiller.

26. For example, one of the most gripping images of human mortality and the eternity that effaces all human achievements appears in Derzhavin's famous, generically hybrid poem "On the Death of Prince Meshcherskii" ("Na smert' kniazia Meshcherskogo," 1779):

Зияет время славу стерть:
Как в море льются быстры воды,
Так в вечность льются дни и годы;
Глотает царства алчна Смерть.

[Time gapes to erase glory: / Just as quick currents flow into the sea, / So too do days and years flow into eternity; / Greedy death devours kingdoms.]

Derzhavin, *Sochineniia Derzhavina s ob"iasnitel'nymi primechaniiami Grota*, 1:90.

27. The *grivna* was a metal decoration, similar to a medal, that served as a token of distinction.

28. See, for example, Repcheck, *The Man who Found Time: James Hutton and the Discovery of the Earth's Antiquity*. I am thankful to Paul Belasky for providing much-needed guidance in the history of geology and paleontology, much of the fruit of it excised from the final version of this book, but all of it gratefully acknowledged.

29. For an account of Pallas's activities in Russia, see Marakuev, *Petr Simon Pallas, ego zhizn', uchenye trudy i puteshestviia.*

30. Bobrov composed several poems on this occasion: "To the New Nineteenth Century" ("K Novostoletiiu XIX," 1800); "A Hundred-Year Song, or the Triumph of the Eighteenth Century" ("Stoletniaia pesn', ili Torzhestvo os'mogonadesiat' veka," 1801); "A Query to the New Century" ("Zapros novomu veku," 1802 or 1803); and "The Prognosticating Response of the Century" ("Predchuvstvennyi otzyv veka," 1802 or 1803).

31. On Bobrov's optimism, see Reyfman, "Imagery of Time and Eternity in Eighteenth-Century Russian Poetry: Mikhail Murav'ev and Semen Bobrov."

32. Al'tshuller and Lotman, *Poety 1790–1810-kh godov,* 92.

33. Bobrov's Youngian imagery is explored in Al'tshuller, "Semen Bobrov and Edward Young."

34. On the Russian reception of Ossian, see Levin, *Ossian v russkoi literature: konets XVIII–pervaia tret' XIX veka.*

35. Al'tshuller and Lotman, *Poety 1790–1810-kh godov,* 95.

36. Ibid., 107.

37. Ibid.

38. Nikolai Karamzin's odes on Alexander's accession are prominent in this category.

39. Pushkin, *Polnoe sobranie sochinenii v shestnadtsati tomakh,* 2/1:59.

40. On the poetics of Zhukovskii's infatuation with Alexandra's court, see Vinitskii, *Dom tolkovatelia,* 141–62.

41. These warnings come up repeatedly in the correspondence of Zhukovskii's friends. Thus, Viazemskii admonishes in 1821: "I fear that you have the dreaminess of a courtier (*tsaredvorskaia mechtatel'nost'*). In our days the union with the tsars has been dissolved: they themselves have trampled upon it. [. . .] I am pained to see your imagination infected by court romanticism. [. . .] [I]n the atmosphere that surrounds you, you cannot see clearly, and many sentiments are dormant within you." (Viazemskii, *Ostaf'evskii arkhiv kniazei Viazemskikh,* 1:254, 260.) Pushkin complains in 1823 of Zhukovskii's epistolary negligence: "About Zhukovskii, it is a shame; how am I worse than Princess Charlotte, that he hasn't written a line to me in three years?" Pushkin, *Polnoe sobranie sochinenii v shestnadtsati tomakh,* 13:80. On Zhukovskii's problematic identity as a court poet, including its discussions in the correspondence of his friends and contemporaries, see Veselovskii, *V. A. Zhukovskii: Poeziia chuvstva i "serdechnogo voobrazheniia,"* 240–57.

42. See the previous note.

43. Pushkin, *Polnoe sobranie sochinenii v shestnadtsati tomakh,* 2/1:547.

44. Ibid., 65.

45. It is important to note that Elizaveta Alekseevna as a panegyric addressee was certainly no Elizaveta Petrovna. Alexander's wife became something of a cult figure for the Decembrists, and her goodwill and philanthropy were even imagined,

for example by Fedor Glinka and his Union for Welfare (*Soiuz blagodenstviia*), as an alternative to her husband's increasingly restrictive authority. Here we might also be reminded of Dmitriev's strategy in praising Paul I (discussed in chapter 2) where the sentimental discourse insists on the different conditions of reception and a different genre label for a text that at least ostensibly does not revolutionize the language of the ode.

46. On the Ovidian motif in Pushkin's exile poetry, see Sandler, *Distant Pleasures: Alexander Pushkin and the Writing of Exile*, 39–56. Igor Nemirovskii explicates Pushkin's recourse to two alternative life scenarios and poetic personas—Ovid's and Byron's—for presenting his sojourn in the South to the public in *Tvorchestvo Pushkina i problema publichnogo povedeniia poeta*, 19–44.

47. Pushkin, *Polnoe sobranie sochinenii v shestnadtsati tomakh*, 2/1:219.

48. Ibid., 13:96.

49. Ibid., 11:255.

50. On patronage in the context of the aristocracy debates, see Todd, *Fiction and Society in the Age of Pushkin*, 83–93; and Vatsuro, "Pushkin i problemy bytopisaniia v nachale 1830kh godov."

51. Pushkin, *Polnoe sobranie sochinenii v shestnadtsati tomakh*, 11:255.

52. On the pragmatic intent and reception of the epistle, see Vatsuro's exhaustive treatment ("K vel'mozhe"); Modzalevskii, "Poslanie k vel'mozhe A. S. Pushkina"; and most recently, Bolenko, "Poslanie A. S. Pushkina 'K vel'mozhe' kak instrument i ob"ekt polemiki: neskol'ko utochnenii." Bolenko connects the poem to "Recollections in Tsarskoe Selo," but argues that Iusupov does not emerge in the epistle as a mere copy of Catherine; rather, Pushkin transfers here a certain lyrical attitude from the earlier text.

53. Polevoi, "Utro v kabinete znatnogo barina."

54. The most famous upshot of these debates was Pushkin's polemical poem "My Pedigree" ("Moia rodoslovnaia," 1830), in which the poet defended his class and vocational independence. The entire polemic is recorded in Vatsuro, "K vel'mozhe."

55. On the quick forgetting of the poem's immediate context, see Bolenko, "Poslanie A. S. Pushkina 'K vel'mozhe' kak instrument i ob"ekt polemiki."

56. Belinskii, *Polnoe sobranie sochinenii*, 7:354.

57. Ibid., 6:622.

58. On the status of Mordvinov in Pushkin's milieu, see Stennik, "Stikhotvorenie A. S. Pushkina 'Mordvinovu' (k istorii sozdaniia)."

59. See Baratynskii's "Gnedichu, kotoryi sovetoval sochiniteliu pisat' satiry" (1823).

60. Cited in Tomashevskii, *Pushkin*, 1:132.

61. This is precisely the generic combination that Stennik discerns in the poem ("Stikhotvorenie A. S. Pushkina 'Mordvinovu,'" 174).

62. Pushkin, *Polnoe sobranie sochinenii v shestnadtsati tomakh*, 3/1:64.

63. Makogonenko and Serman, *Poety XVIII veka*, 1:417.

64. One should not overemphasize this particular line of succession as preserving significance in Pushkin's oeuvre beyond "To Mordvinov," for Petrov as Catherine's court poet was far too implicated in a system little valuing the poet's autonomy to be appreciated by the Pushkin generation.

65. Pushkin, *Polnoe sobranie sochinenii v shestnadtsati tomakh*, 3/1:219.

66. Tomashevskii, *Pushkin*, 2:391.

67. Blagoi, *Tvorcheskii put' Pushkina (1826–1830)*, 428.

68. Kelly, "Pushkin's Vicarious Grand Tour: A Neo-Sociological Interpretation of 'K vel'mozhe' (1830)."

69. Pushkin, *Polnoe sobranie sochinenii v shestnadtsati tomakh*, 3/1:217.

70. See on this Clark, "Enthusiasm and Enlightenment."

71. While becoming dominant in the Romantic period, this understanding of inspiration was in fact developed already by Shaftesbury and was certainly familiar to the Enlightenment, but only as one creative mode of the several possible. See Mee, *Romanticism, Enthusiasm and Regulation*, 23–81.

72. Pushkin, *Polnoe sobranie sochinenii v shestnadtsati tomakh*, 3/1:218.

73. On the poem's evocation of the Mozartian mode of inspiration in connection specifically to its references to Beaumarchais, see Vol'pert, *Pushkin v roli Pushkina*, 166–89.

74. Boris Tomashevskii (*Pushkin*, 2:391) connects the epistle directly with Pushkin's meditations on the French Revolution. Grigorii Gukovskii offers a similar assessment: "The poem 'To the Grandee' speaks comprehensively of the culture of the eighteenth century, its downfall in the revolution, and the birth, from the depths thereof, of a new culture." (Gukovskii, *Pushkin i problemy realisticheskogo stilia*, 287.) Gukovskii also detects in the poem thematic and stylistic signs of the supersession of epochs from Voltaire to Byron (289).

75. Dmitrii Blagoi argues that the entire poem is constructed around such contrastive structures. Blagoi, *Tvorcheskii put' Pushkina (1826–1830)*, 426.

76. Quoted in ibid., 429.

77. Derzhavin, *Sochineniia Derzhavina s ob"iasnitel'nymi primechaniiami Grota*, 1:624–25.

78. Herzen, *My Past and Thoughts*, 1:87.

79. Herzen is both one of the most vocal critics of the eighteenth century and the most influential publicist of such crucial eighteenth-century documents as Radishchev's *Journey from Petersburg to Moscow*, Shcherbatov's *On the Corruption of Russian Mores* (both published in London in 1858), and Catherine's *Memoirs* (pub. 1859). A more nuanced analysis of his position and contributions regrettably remains beyond the scope of my study. I am grateful to Ingrid Kleespies for first drawing my attention to Herzen's "men of the eighteenth century" in her unpublished paper "Dispossessed by History: '18th-Century People' in Herzen's *Byloe i dumy*," delivered at AAASS 2004 in Boston.

80. Herzen, *My Past and Thoughts*, 1:87. Catriona Kelly demonstrates that in working on his multiple drafts of "K vel'mozhe," Pushkin increasingly deemphasized sensual luxuries, which Herzen foregrounds here, in favor of the intellectual pleasures. Kelly, "Pushkin's Vicarious Grand Tour," 9–10.

81. The 1820s–'30s form a distinct, transitional and ambivalent, epoch in the history of Russian literature's relationship to political and social authority. Soon afterwards, social engagement will emerge as literature's imperative, and writers of Herzen's generation, though profoundly invested in historicist thinking, will tend to resist historical relativism and define their positions far less ambiguously.

82. Patronage and censorship (in their eighteenth- and nineteenth-century incarnations) should indeed frame all our interpretations of Pushkin's pronouncements on the eighteenth century, such as the ones offered on *The Captain's Daughter* and "The Queen of Spades" in the next two chapters.

83. One of the most extensive attempts to organize the intellectual history of this period around Radishchev is Grigorii Gukovskii's "Vokrug Radishcheva."

84. Pushkin's relationship to Radishchev and Karamzin is discussed most extensively in Pugachev, *Pushkin, Radishchev i Karamzin*. Nemirovskii has advanced the convincing claim that Pushkin gravitated toward Radishchev and Karamzin at different points in his career, as alternative models, with the former gaining relevance alongside Pushkin's disillusionment with the promise of the tsar's patronage. Nemirovskii, *Tvorchestvo Pushkina i problema publichnogo povedeniia poeta*, 304–18.

Part II Prologue

1. Griboedov, *Gore ot uma*, 33–34. "You're arrogant, the lot of you! / You ask your fathers what they used to do. / As models for you, they'd be splendid. / There's me, for instance, or the late lamented / Maxim Petrovich: Silver plates? My uncle bought / A pure gold service. Had a hundred men to serve him. / Fine horses, orders— worked hard to deserve 'em. / He spent an age at court. And what a court! / It's all so different nowadays. / It was at Catherine's court that he and I spent our days. / There used to be such big men! Twenty stone . . . / You'd bow, they wouldn't nod. They stood alone, / Another breed. While those in favour, / Their meat and drink acquired a special savour." Hobson, *Aleksandr Griboedov's* Woe from Wit, 36–37.

2. Pushkin, *Polnoe sobranie sochinenii v shestnadtsati tomakh*, 6:176. "A grey-beard too . . . with scented hair, / Who joked both cleverly and wryly / In quite a keen, old-fashioned way, / Which seems a touch absurd today!" Transl. Falen in Pushkin, *Eugene Onegin*, 196.

3. Grot, *Zhizn' Derzhavina*, 14. "In the eighteenth century, rough, angular characters were much more common than in our time, when instruction that is far more widespread among all social classes and also far more artificial has brought everyone to one rather common educational level and imprints on everyone a uniform stamp of restraint and decorum."

4. Lidiia Ginzburg's introduction to the 1929 edition of the *Notebooks* (Ginzburg, "Viazemskii i ego 'Zapisnaia knizhka'") remains the most comprehensive treatment of this text.

5. Karl Vasil'evich Nessel'rode (1780–1862), indeed quite diminutive in stature, was Russia's minister of foreign affairs from 1822 to 1856 and a key conservative statesman of the Holy Alliance. Nikita Ivanovich Panin (1718–83), one of Catherine's most important political advisors and tutor to Grand Duke Paul, headed Russian foreign policy in the first half of Catherine's reign and authored the first constitutional project in Russia.

6. Viazemskii, *Zapisnye knizhki*, 202–3.

7. Throughout his correspondence, which he consistently records in the *Notebooks*, Viazemskii urges his acquaintances to write their own memoiristic accounts, predicting that they, too, will soon furnish material for historians of the current epoch.

8. Lermontov, *Polnoe sobranie stikhotvorenii v 2kh tomakh*, 2:30.

9. Indeed, not even Viazemskii himself consistently maintains this level of nostalgia for the age of Catherine. Andrew Kahn traces the frustration of Viazemskii's attempt to locate the ideal eighteenth-century subject living in the ideal enlightened age in the person of Denis Fonvizin. Kahn, "Life-Writing in the 1830s: Viazemskii's *Fon-Vizin* and Pushkin's 'Table Talk.'" Both Viazemskii's *Fon-Vizin* and Pushkin's *Table-Talk* are essential for understanding the multiple facets of nineteenth-century Russian intellectuals' engagement with the previous epoch. Both have remained beyond the scope of this study in large part because I have found Kahn's treatment compelling as well as consistent with my book's overarching narrative.

10. Belinskii, *Polnoe sobranie sochinenii*, 6:448.

Chapter 4. The Verisimilar Eighteenth Century

1. The epigraph that opens this chapter is from Bestuzhev-Marlinskii, *Sochineniia v dvukh tomakh*, 2:415–16. English translation in Leighton, *Russian Romantic Criticism: An Anthology*, 137–38: "We live [. . .] in an age of history, moreover in an age of history par excellence. [. . .] Now history is not simply in fact, but in the memory, the mind, the hearts of men [peoples]. We see it, feel it, hear it constantly [. . .]. It jostles us with its elbows on the promenade, worms its way between you and your lady at the cotillion. "Barin! Barin!" the street vendor shouts, "buy an *Erivanka* hat." "Would you care to order a frock coat cut *Warsaw-style*?" asks the tailor. A horse comes a-prancing—it's a *Wellington*. Glance at a signboard—Kutuzov beckons you into an inn arousing both native pride and appetite at once. Take a pinch of snuff—the box is engraved with a likeness of Charles X. Stamp a letter—the seal is the Emperor Franz Joseph. Plunge your fork into a sweet pastry and—its name is Napoleon! Spend a ten-kopeck piece and you will receive in exchange the ill-starredness of the ages—Clytemnestra and Chenier, the assassination of Henry

IV and Waterloo, the Berezina and St. Helena, the deluge of Petersburg and the Lisbon earthquake, and . . . I know not what all! [. . .] Yes sir, history is nowadays being changed into everything you could wish for, even if you don't in the least wish it."

2. Kireevskii, *Kritika i estetika*, 80. I discuss Kireevskii's suggestion in the introduction.

3. This schematic account of the transition is not intended to downplay the significance of eighteenth-century novels for the development of the genre in Russia, though these hardly ever concerned themselves with historical representation; nor do I suggest that poetry entirely abandons historical subjects in this period.

4. I borrow this phrase from Mark Phillips ("Macaulay, Scott, and the Literary Challenge to Historiography"), who argues that in the early nineteenth century, literature came to destabilize the historiographic procedure, perhaps even more than did new ideas in philosophy, political theory, and science. This is in fact a familiar claim among recent commentators on Sir Walter Scott, but an interpretation that has received insufficient attention in Russian scholarship, which has until very recently tended to hew to the same fact/fiction dichotomy regnant in criticism of the 1830s.

5. Quoted in Petrunina, *Proza Pushkina*, 264.

6. Lukács, *The Historical Novel*, 33.

7. For a recent discussion of the nexus of issues surrounding history, fiction, and realism in historical fiction, see Hamnett, *The Historical Novel in Nineteenth-Century Europe*, 17–49.

8. My argument here is in line with the recent scholarship on Scott, which emphasizes precisely the novelistic conventions his work establishes for the production of accuracy. Thus, Ian Duncan has made a forceful argument for reading plot as one such convention: "Even as the novel began to totalize its mimetic range it reasserted fiction, and not mimesis, as its critical principle, in an elaborate commitment to plot. Fiction in these novels is the effect above all of plot, conspicuous as a grammar of formal conventions, that is, a shared cultural order distinct from material and historical contingency. To read a plot—to take part in its work of recognition—is to imagine a transformation of life and its conditions, and not their mere reproduction." Duncan, *Modern Romance and Transformations of the Novel*, 2.

9. In his definitive consideration of the genre, Harry E. Shaw calls attention to this feature: "Historical novels [. . .] are works in which historical probability reaches a certain level of structural prominence." Characters, events, settings in the historical novel are probable, *similar* to what could have happened. Shaw, *The Forms of Historical Fiction: Sir Walter Scott and His Successors*, 22.

10. The *OED* cites R. Flecknoe as having written in 1654: "Truth has no greater Enemy than verisimilitude and likelihood." In 1850, the English essayist Leigh Hunt writes in his autobiography, "I felt . . . that there was more truth in the verisimilitude of fiction than in the assumptions of history." In the interval between the first

and second example, verisimilitude has not only lost its immorality, it has gained narrative value.

11. *Slovar' Akademii Rossiiskoi* (St. Petersburg: Pri Imperatorskoi Akademii Nauk), 5:123.

12. Barthes, "The Reality Effect," 15–16.

13. Ibid., 16.

14. Ibid.

15. The orientations toward entertainment and mimesis might initially appear to be in conflict with each other. Characterizing the contemporaneous artistic output of Stendhal, Ann Jefferson presents the 1820s–'30s as a period of transition from what she describes as "the reader-oriented pragmatics of the eighteenth century to the mimetic preoccupation of the nineteenth." Jefferson, *Reading Realism in Stendhal*, xiii. In some ways, then, the inconsistencies in the historical novel's pragmatic orientation and reception can be ascribed to its rise in the period of a paradigmatic shift in fiction-writing that sets the two centuries apart; conversely, if one follows such critics as Lukács, it was precisely the historical novel genre that was responsible for this shift in the first place.

16. Iakubovich, "'Kapitanskaia dochka' i romany Val'ter Skotta," 168.

17. On this line of the historical novel reception, see Ungurianu, *Plotting History*, 40–54.

18. Quoted in Al'tshuller, "Pushkin, Bulgarin, Nikolai I i Ser Val'ter Skott," 288.

19. These terms are of course reflexes of a more profound conceptual linkage between knowledge and sight, as evidenced, for example, in the term *theoria* (theory), whose original Greek meaning had to do with "looking at, beholding, contemplating." For a theoretical reading of this connection's significance for Western philosophy, see Jonas's classic essay "The Nobility of Sight." Also see Jay, *Downcast Eyes: The Denigration of Vision in Twentieth-Century French Thought*. As I hope to demonstrate, the emphasis on sight in the reception of the historical novel harks only in part to this conceptual connection; vision in this case also references a kind of "scopic desire," a seeing as possessing, symptomatic of the rise of consumerism in the early nineteenth century.

20. On what she calls "the optics of history" in the late eighteenth century, see Smoliarova, *Zrimaia lirika: Derzhavin*; on the eidophusikon see McCalman, "Magic, Spectacle, and the Art of de Loutherbourg's Eidophusikon"; on these and other developments in spectacular visual culture in the heyday of the historical novel, and for a fine reading of the Scottian novel in this context, see Samuels, *The Spectacular Past: Popular History and the Novel in Nineteenth-Century France*; more broadly, on the place of visuality in the period's historical writing, see Bann, *Romanticism and the Rise of History*. Synthesizing much of the voluminous scholarship on visuality and historical fiction, Ina Ferris has recently argued that "the narrative pragmatics of Scott's historical fiction [. . .] can be best understood in terms of [. . .] an 'apparitional poetics,' a harnessing of the strange yet mundane power of

mind brought into focus by experiences like spectral illusion." Ferris, "'Before Our Eyes': Romantic Historical Fiction and the Apparitions of Reading," 64.

21. Crary, *Techniques of the Observer: On Vision and Modernity in the Nineteenth Century*, 14.

22. Ferris, "'Before Our Eyes': Romantic Historical Fiction and the Apparitions of Reading," 70.

23. Scott, *Waverley, or, 'Tis Sixty Years Since*, 17.

24. For Scott's readers in the early 1800s, the young Waverley himself, his dreams and adventures in the 1740s, in turn bear resemblance to their own household lore, and the protagonist's act of imagining the past becomes easily transposed onto the reader's imagining of the proximate eighteenth century.

25. Duncan asserts the codependence of these two tendencies of repudiating romance and grounding the novel's protagonist in romance-appropriate reading strategies: "Scott's novel undertakes a complex dialectical reversal of the project of anti-romance it began by rehearsing. Thematically, historical experience banishes romance illusion; but this progression is articulated by a labyrinthine formal logic of romance which secures for Waverley the tragic-comic destiny of a private life beyond historical process." (Duncan, *Modern Romance and Transformations of the Novel*, 13.) Paul Hamilton, on the other hand, proposes that Scott redeems romance and its interpretive procedures on new terms and in a new historical context: "While critical of Edward Waverley's romantic, jejune notions, Scott's narrative transforms them into a mature recognition that romance can best express the historical distance of a heritage or cultural ideal still esteemed valuable and potentially regulative." Hamilton, *Metaromanticism*, 116.

26. Turgenev, *Khronika russkogo*, 403. For a comprehensive account of Turgenev's acquaintance with Scott, as well as Scott's other Russian connections, see Alekseev, "Val'ter Skott i ego russkie znakomstva."

27. Kozlov, *Sobranie stikhotvorenii*, 122–23.

28. Ibid., 125.

29. Stephen, *Hours in a Library*, 219.

30. The scholarly literature on Scott's reception is extensive. For essays treating the reception of Scott specifically in Europe, including Russia, see Pittock, *The Reception of Sir Walter Scott in Europe*; and Hamnett, *The Historical Novel in Nineteenth-Century Europe*. The two classic critical accounts of Scott's influence are: Maigron, *Le roman historique à l'époque romantique: essai sur l'influence de Walter Scott*; and Lukács, *The Historical Novel*. For comprehensive studies of the reception of Scott's work in Russia, see Al'tshuller, *Epokha Val'tera Skotta v Rossii: istoricheskii roman 1830-kh godov*; and Schamschula, *Der russische historische Roman vom Klassizismus bis zur Romantik*. A less systematic but extremely insightful account is Dolinin, *Istoriia, odetaia v roman*; see also Levin, "Prizhiznennaia slava V. Skotta v Rossii." For an excellent survey of the development of the Russian historical novel, including a useful bibliography and classification of the historical novels published in the

imperial period, see Ungurianu, *Plotting History: The Russian Historical Novel in the Imperial Age*.

31. Ibid.

32. Pushkin, *Polnoe sobranie sochinenii*, 7:535.

33. The comparison between Scott and Karamzin appears to have been particularly meaningful to Russian readers of the 1830s, for whom this pair provided the two most influential models not only for reading history, but also for advancing moral judgment (the works of both touching indeed on ethical concerns in a broadly sentimentalist manner) and for defending conservative political ideology. Kozlov's epistle devotes an entire section to this comparison, basing it on the two writers' similarly profound effect on the historical imagination and similarly upright pursuit of virtue.

34. Alexander Dolinin has offered a compelling analysis of Pushkin's profound ideological departures from the Scottian understanding of historical process ("Val'ter-skottovskii istorizm v 'Kapitanskoi dochke'").

35. On Romantic readerships for the Walter Scott novel, see Lyons, "The Audience for Romanticism: Walter Scott in France, 1815–1851."

36. Dargan, "Scott and the French Romantics," 603. On Defauconpret's translations in Russia, see Davis, "From Scotland to Russia via France."

37. Hayden, *Walter Scott: The Critical Heritage*, 300. In connection with our discussion of sight in the previous section, it seems noteworthy that Ann Rigney ascribes the remarkable replicability of Scott's novels to their emphasis on the visual, Scott's "procreativity" to the "remediation" of narrative in his novels. Rigney, *The Afterlives of Walter Scott: Memory on the Move*, 55.

38. Hayden, *Walter Scott: The Critical Heritage*, 300.

39. Quoted in Dolinin, *Istoriia, odetaia v roman*, 221 (emphasis in original); originally appeared in *Vestnik Evropy* 159/160, no. 15 (1829). Dolinin quotes several other, similarly entertaining critiques authored, for instance, by Pogodin and Bestuzhev-Marlinskii. Ungurianu also amply documents these debates in *Plotting History*.

40. For a good overview of the size of the Russian reading public in the early nineteenth century, see Tosi, *Waiting for Pushkin: Russian Fiction in the Reign of Alexander I (1801–1825)*, 33–44; and also the valuable bibliography in Reitblat, *Chtenie v Rossii v XIX–nachale XX veka: annotirovannyi bibliograficheskii ukazatel'*.

41. "[T]he most interesting of the novelists who followed in [Scott's] footsteps were also the most critical of his accomplishment, or the best able to rethink it" (Maxwell, "The Historical Novel," 78). These words by Richard Maxwell, one of the scholars most enthusiastic about Scott's original achievement, suggest that even while the fashion for Scott still had its appeal, it was already becoming passé, and an uncritical emulation of his novels had become somewhat of an impossibility.

42. This appellation is cited from Dolinin, *Istoriia, odetaia v roman*, 234.

43. Lazhechnikov, *Sobranie sochinenii*, 4:5–6.

44. Ernst Johann von Biron (1690–1772), Anna Ioannovna's favorite and de facto ruler of Russia under her reign, and regent of the Russian Empire upon her death.

45. Ibid., 7.

46. Ryleev, *Polnoe sobranie sochinenii*, 611.

47. Ibid., 176–77.

48. In a letter to his friend and protégé Vissarion Belinskii, Lazhechnikov proudly notes readers' enthusiasm-bordering-on-mania for his novel, reminiscent of the sentimentalist-era reception of Karamzin's "Poor Liza": "I will tell you as someone who is fond of me . . . in Petersburg my *House of Ice* met with success unparalleled by that of any other novel in Russia: near the Sampsonievskii cemetery where Volynskii is buried was a constant assembly of carriages; Volynskii's tombstone is entirely covered in poems—fortunately, it is reported, nothing vulgar; and young people, who have shattered a marble vase (from that tombstone), are taking away pieces as relics." Lazhechnikov, *Sochineniia v dvukh tomakh*, 2:641.

49. Lazhechnikov, *Sobranie sochinenii*, 4:8.

50. Ibid.

51. See Modzalevskii, "Pushkin i Lazhechnikov."

52. Pushkin, *Polnoe sobranie sochinenii*, 10:554–55.

53. On the novel as participating in the "Petersburg text," see Ungurianu, "*Ledianoi dom* Lazhechnikova i peterburgskii kanon (K voprosu o genezise peterburgskogo teksta)." For an alternative interpretation, see Barskova's excursus on the connection between the topoi of winter and the Gothic genre in the "Petersburg text." Barskova, "Enchanted by the Spectacle of Death," 45–46.

54. In this regard it would indeed be worthwhile to develop a framework that combines the approaches inscribing Pushkin within his (largely eighteenth-century) philosophical readings—a very cogent entry in this category, for instance, would be Kahn's *Pushkin's Lyric Intelligence*—with those that emphasize his responding to literature, and crafting his own, in the context of Romantic fragmentary praxis. (The most compelling interpretation of this Romantic Pushkin is developed in Greenleaf's *Pushkin and Romantic Fashion*.) Neither of the studies mentioned considers Pushkin's historical fiction, but it is this writing that as a genre problematizes precisely such epistemological concerns as acquire very different treatments in the two epochs. Pushkin's approach to the integration of material from the historical sources at his disposal is amply documented in Blok, *Pushkin v rabote nad istoricheskimi istochnikami.*

55. Letter to Pushkin, November 22, 1835, *Russkii arkhiv* 3 (1880): 456. G. G. Ariel'-Zalesskaia was the first to conjecture ("K izucheniiu istorii biblioteki A. S. Pushkina," 341–42) that Pushkin had read archival materials on the Volynskii case while researching the Pugachev uprising. N. Petrunina seconds this hypothesis, showing that in 1836, months before his death, Pushkin was preparing documents from the Volynskii case for publication in his journal *The Contemporary*

(*Sovremennik*). Petrunina, "Dva zamysla Pushkina dlia 'Sovremennika' (K sporu mezhdu Pushkinym i Lazhechnikovym po povodu 'Ledianogo doma')."

56. Lazhechnikov, *Sobranie sochinenii*, 6:288–91.

57. In 1860, still during Lazhechnikov's lifetime, the historian I. I. Shishkin published in *Notes of the Fatherland* a revisionist historical account of the Volynskii affair based on the newly released archival files. This followed a previous blow from the periodical *Atenei*; see Afanas'ev, "Ob istoricheskoi vernosti v romanakh Lazhechnikova."

58. Several generations of Russian writers around the turn of the twentieth century had read *The House of Ice* as part of their childhood reading and revisited its themes in their adult lives. Most notably, in 1928 Viktor Shklovsky wrote a movie script based on the novel. For an intriguing interpretation of the twentieth-century fate of Lazhechnikov's novel, see Barskova, "Enchanted by the Spectacle of Death: Forms of the End in Leningrad Culture (1917–1934)," 41–43.

59. See Grigor'ev's influential "Vzgliad na russkuiu literaturu so smerti Pushkina" in Grigor'ev, *Sochineniia*, 2:48–124; Vinogradov, *Evoliutsiia russkogo naturalizma: Gogol' i Dostoevskii*, 162; and Vinogradov, *Etiudy o stile Gogolia*, 38–39. Grigor'ev concludes his laudatory review of *The House of Ice* thus: "Original as the creation of the Volynskii type is, the novel in its entirety is influenced by the Romantic movement of the young French literature." (Grigor'ev, *Sochineniia*, 2:114.) For an excellent overview of the Russian reception of freneticism, see also Busch, "N. A. Polevoj's *Moskovskij Telegraf* and the Critical Debate over 'Junaja Francija'"; and Busch, "Russian Freneticism."

60. Grigor'ev, *Sochineniia*, 2:113.

61. Ibid., 50.

62. See Busch, "N. A. Polevoj's *Moskovskij Telegraf* and the Critical Debate over 'Junaja Francija'"; and Lemke, *Nikolaevskie zhandarmy i literatura 1826–1855 gg.*

63. *Severnaia pchela*, no. 182 (1832).

64. Hugo, *Notre-Dame of Paris*, 410.

65. Lazhechnikov, *Sobranie sochinenii*, 4:155.

66. Pushkin, *Polnoe sobranie sochinenii v shestnadtsati tomakh*, 12:70.

67. The most famous Gothic text of this period to be inspired by Galvani's experiments was Mary Shelley's *Frankenstein*. For a fascinating reading of galvanism in the imagination of this time, one that, while focused particularly on Shelley, is illuminating for our analysis as well, see Mellor, "Frankenstein: A Feminist Critique."

68. Many scholars have analyzed Pushkin's borrowings and departures from Scott. Several of Scott's novels, including *Rob Roy* and *The Heart of Midlothian*, have been named as Pushkin's models. In addition to the bibliography cited previously on Scott in Russia, of which Iakubovich's and Altshuller's entries are the most relevant for an intertextual analysis of Pushkin's novel, see also Frazier, "*Kapitanskaia dochka* and the Creativity of Borrowing."

69. Pushkin, *Polnoe sobranie sochinenii v shestnadtsati tomakh*, 8/1:294–96; trans. Pushkin, *Complete Prose Fiction*, 281–83; subsequent quotations from *The Captain's Daughter* are cited from this translation by Paul Debreczeny.

70. Svetlana Evdokimova interprets these descriptions of the fortress as signs that the novel aims to explain historical events not as series of accidents, but as prepared by more general factors; the occupation of the fortress, in this view, is only a consequence of its rundown state. (Evdokimova, *Pushkin's Historical Imagination*, 79–80.) The strategies of historical explanation in the novel, an important question that remains beyond the scope of this chapter due to my focus on strategies of (un)spectacular representation, are compellingly discussed in Dolinin, "Historicism or Providentialism? Pushkin's *History of Pugachev* in the Context of French Romantic Historiography."

71. Pushkin, *Complete Prose Works*, 357.

72. On this historical episode, and on the multiple drafts of *The Captain's Daughter*, see Iulian Oksman's commentary in the *Literaturnye pamiatniki* edition of the novel: Pushkin, *Kapitanskaia dochka*.

73. Ibid., 103.

74. Tolstoi, *Polnoe sobranie sochinenii v 90 tomakh*, 46:187–88.

75. Commenting on this feature of the historical novel, which he dismisses as "filler," Franco Moretti notes that it has the effect of slowing down narrative pace. (Moretti, "Serious Century," 377.) Pushkin's "naked" novel is, by contrast, strikingly brisk and economical, thus departing significantly from the genre's conventions.

76. Gogol', *Polnoe sobranie sochinenii*, 8:384–85.

77. Iulian Oksman assembles a substantial sample of these early responses in the section titled "'Kapitanskaia dochka' v otklikakh ee pervykh chitatelei, kritikov i sovremennykh issledovatelei" in Pushkin, *Kapitanskaia dochka*, 209–44.

78. Lazhechnikov, *Sobranie sochinenii*, 4:121.

79. Scarry, *The Body in Pain: The Making and Unmaking of the World*, 4.

80. Pushkin, *Complete Prose Fiction*, 304–5.

81. Ospovat, "Istoricheskii material i istoricheskie alliuzii v 'Kapitanskoi dochke,'" 43. Ospovat emphasizes (ibid.) that Pushkin was thinking about the 1740s while working on *The Captain's Daughter*: "Pushkin engages in epistolary polemics with the author of *The House of Ice* literally on the eve or at the moment of returning to his work on *The Captain's Daughter* [. . .] and it is precisely at this time that he is introduced to Karamzin's *Memoir on Ancient and New Russia*."

82. For a fascinating account of the games writers played with the censorship in this period, see Vatsuro and Gillel'son, *Skvoz' "umstvennye plotiny": Ocherki o knigakh i presse pushkinskoi pory*.

83. For a particularly cogent reading of these echoes, see Groce, "Aleksandr Pushkin's 'The Captain's Daughter': A Poetics of Violence." Groce analyzes the image of the gallows, for instance, as a problematic "*locus* of a more contemporary violence" (67).

84. Pushkin, *Complete Prose Works*, 356. Alexander Zholkovsky observes that in *The Captain's Daughter*, as in many of Scott's novels, fictional and historical characters continually exchange glances of recognition, which moments provide additional glue for the fictional and historical plotlines. Zholkovsky finds a thematic explanation for such exchanges: "The paradigm of 'acquaintance/vision' is enriched by the motif of 'recognizing masks and roles.' Towards the latter gravitate both the socio-historical situations of 'imposture' and 'the theatricality of power,' and the motif of 'acting,' advantageous in terms of plot development and intrinsic to rulers as well as ordinary characters." (Zholkovskii, "Ochnye stavki s vlastitelem: iz istorii odnoi pushkinskoi paradigmy.") But in addition to such an immanent reading, acquaintance/vision/recognition can be seen also to bring the reader into the fold of the novel as an interpretive force, similar to the protagonists directly involved in the recognizing.

85. Pushkin, *Complete Prose Works*, 315, 317, 318.

86. Dolinin, "Eshche raz o khronologii 'Kapitanskoi dochki,'" 54.

Chapter 5. Mimetic Temporalities

1. The epigraph that opens this chapter is from *Vestnik Evropy* 70, no. 16 (August 31, 1813), 297. "Fashion of the olden days is a curious antique; changed fashion is a terrible skeleton; reigning fashion is a new and fresh flower." Because fashion was one of the most visible semiotic forms, which negotiated Russia's relationship with the West in the eighteenth century, the strikingly rich history of fashion discourse will of necessity be treated here only in a cursory manner. For a comprehensive history of fashion in Imperial Russia, see Kirsanova, *Kostium v russkoi kul'ture 18–pervoi poloviny 20 vekov*. For a sensitive and detailed treatment of the pre-Pushkinian discourse on fashion as well as its playful integration in *Eugene Onegin*, see the section titled "What was Hidden under the Pantaloons" in Proskurin, *Poeziia Pushkina, ili podvizhnyi palimpsest*, 301–47. For a study specifically devoted to the treatments of fashion in eighteenth-century Russian literature, see Ivleva, "Fashion and Sartorial Discourse in Eighteenth-Century Russian Literature and Culture."

2. In the introduction to *The Empire's New Clothes: A History of the Russian Fashion Industry, 1700–1917*, Christine Ruane stresses that the substitution of old social categories with new ones was one of the most glaring consequences of Peter's clothing reforms. The decrees discussed here are found in: Nos. 1741; 1887; 2015, *Polnoe sobranie zakonov Rossiiskoi imperii s 1649 goda, Sobranie pervoe*, 4:1, 182, 282. Peter issued a total of 17 decrees regulating appearance. For the effect Peter's reforms had specifically on women's fashion, see Hughes, "From Caftans into Corsets: The Sartorial Transformation of Women During the Reign of Peter the Great."

3. The philosopher and sociologist Gilles Lipovetsky has in fact advanced the argument for viewing fashion as essentially a democratizing phenomenon. Lipovetsky, *The Empire of Fashion: Dressing Modern Democracy*.

4. J. G. A. Pocock offers this relevant definition of history: "History [. . .] is public time. That is, it is time experienced by the individual as public being, conscious of a framework of public institutions in and through which events, processes and changes happened to the society of which he perceives himself to be part." ("Modes of Political and Historical Time in Early Eighteenth-Century England," 91.) This definition is useful for my study in that it helps clarify the complex departures from this understanding of history that I trace in the para-historical and para-public narratives of Russian history and the eighteenth century, such as those centered on fashion discussed in this chapter.

5. Kahan, *The Plow, the Hammer, and the Knout: An Economic History of Eighteenth-Century Russia*, 1.

6. This rich Russian tradition of satirical polemics over linguistic and sartorial fashion has received ample scholarly attention. Particularly interesting in the context of my study is Pavel Berkov's examination (*Lomonosov i literaturnaia polemika ego vremeni*, 117–36) of a 1750s polemic involving such prominent writers as Lomonosov, Sumarokov, and Elagin. Berkov uses this case study to illustrate a larger point about the complex reflections of socio-political life in eighteenth-century Russian literature.

7. Viazemskii, *Zapisnye knizhki*, 24.

8. For an array of perspectives on the European luxury debates, see Berg and Eger, *Luxury in the Eighteenth Century: Debates, Desires and Delectable Goods*; and Clery, *The Feminization Debate in Eighteenth-Century England: Literature, Commerce and Luxury*. In the early eighteenth century, fashion enters philosophical discourses in the debate on "luxury and necessity" linked to the Mandevillian notions of "private vices and public benefits," and in product-specific commercial pamphlets widely disseminated by Daniel Defoe and other Grub Street journalists. In the second half of the century, it becomes a crucial subject for the fledgling discipline of economics; thus, it is criticized in the treatises of French physiocrats who privileged agriculture over manufacture, and endorsed in the economic theory of Adam Smith and his followers, who associate consumer goods such as clothing with moral sentiment. Various aspects of this critical tradition are illuminated in Roche, *A History of Everyday Things: The Birth of Consumption in France, 1600–1800*; Goldsmith, *Private Vices, Public Benefits: Bernard Mandeville's Social and Political Thought*; Higgs, *The Physiocrats, Six Lectures on the French Économistes of the 18th Century*; and Rothschild, *Economic Sentiments: Adam Smith, Condorcet, and the Enlightenment*.

9. Roche, *The Culture of Clothing: Dress and Fashion in the "Ancien Regime,"* 49.

10. Iurii Lotman writes of the euphemistic convenience of fashion as a focus of critique: "The 'archaists' of the late eighteenth–early nineteenth centuries, in contrast to the Slavophiles, preferred to locate the beginning of 'degeneration' not in the Petrine reforms, but in the 'French contagion'—in the mid-eighteenth century—and condemn not the Europeanization of the political order, not Petersburg and not the German bureaucracy (as did the Slavophiles), but rather fashions, fops, and 'Kuznetskii

most.'" Lotman, "Ideia istoricheskogo razvitiia v russkoi kul'ture kontsa XVIII–nachala XIX stoletiia," 286. Kuznetskii most was the most fashionable Moscow street, sometimes compared to Parisian commercial thoroughfares.

11. For a brief and lively account of the clothing trends that arose in the wake of the French Revolution, see Steele, "The Revolution: Liberty, Equality and Antiquity."

12. Vigel, *Zapiski*, 1:133.

13. Quoted in Lotman, *Pushkin*, 574.

14. The ban on vests effected a noticeable change in the elite's appearance; after all, during Catherine's reign some nobles would don as many as seven vests at a time. Ibid.

15. In this sense, the Russian situation is similar to that of the Goethe-era German principalities as described in Purdy, *The Tyranny of Elegance: Consumer Cosmopolitanism in the Era of Goethe*. Purdy argues that "eighteenth-century German consumer culture began within the readerly imagination and [. . .] an elaborate and self-critical discourse on consumption existed in Germany well before any portion of that diverse Central European region approached industrialization on the scale of England or France" (2).

16. The English "fop" and "dandy" can (depending on context) be considered synonyms, but the Russian *shchegol'* and *dendi* are quite distinct concepts. The history of the former in "the gallant age" is recounted in a somewhat popularizing manner in Berdnikov, *Shchegoli i vertoprakhi: Geroi russkogo galantnogo veka*. The latter is the subject of Vainshtein, *Dendi: Moda, literatura, stil' zhizni*.

17. Flügel, *The Psychology of Clothes*, 111. As the main cause of this move toward a greater uniformity and dourness of male dress, Flügel enlists the French Revolution, which strove to deemphasize distinctions of wealth and rank manifested in the opulent costumes of the *ancien régime* elite. Daniel Roche describes the same phenomenon as "the political and moral rejection of the values of color." Roche, *The Culture of Clothing*, 61.

18. The most influential arguments for the social structuring of fashion and taste have been advanced in sociology; see Simmel, "The Philosophy of Fashion," in *Simmel on Culture: Selected Writings*, 187–205; and Bourdieu, *Distinction: A Social Critique of the Judgment of Taste*.

19. On the reception of Balzac in Russia, and particularly on his visit to the Russian Empire, see Grossman, "Bal'zak v Rossii."

20. Balzac, *Honoré de Balzac in Twenty-Five Volumes*, 1:21.

21. For Georg Lukács, the most prominent inheritor of the Scottian historical novel is indeed Balzac. Lukács, *The Historical Novel*, 34ff.

22. Balzac, *Honoré de Balzac in Twenty-Five Volumes*, 1:13.

23. For a recent treatment that draws upon a thorough bibliography, see Alex Woloch's chapter on the issue of typification in Balzac in *The One vs. the Many: Minor Characters and the Space of the Protagonist in the Novel*, 244–318.

24. Roche, *The Culture of Clothing*, 46.

25. Barthes, "The Reality Effect." Elizabeth Fay has recently argued (in *Fashioning Faces: The Portraitive Mode in British Romanticism*, 9–10) that already in the early Romantic period the self comes to identify with the objects and surface display that externalize it and mark the "conjunctions and disjunctions between the inner and outer," an account that ultimately points to a more complex motivation behind the insistence on material culture in the nineteenth-century novel than the one polemically offered by Barthes.

26. Intentionally archaicized, as noted in Cherniavsky, *Tsar and People: Studies in Russian Myths*, 130.

27. For a contextualization of Karamzin's and Glinka's journalism within contemporary Russian intellectual currents, see Martin, *Romantics, Reformers, Reactionaries: Russian Conservative Thought and Politics in the Reign of Alexander I*.

28. *Ruskoi vestnik*, no. 1 (January 1808): 6.

29. Lotman and Uspenskii, "Rol' dual'nykh modelei v dinamike russkoi kul'tury (do kontsa XVIII veka)."

30. Karamzin, *Letters of a Russian Traveler*, 261.

31. Quoted in Steele, "The Revolution: Liberty, Equality and Antiquity," 43. In later decades, many urban descriptions begin to draw on the sedimentation model. Cf., for example, this description of Petersburg in the 1830s by nineteenth-century cultural historian Mikhail Pyliaev: "On the main streets of Petersburg one would see people wearing entirely masquerade-like costumes. During the first years of Emperor Nicholas I's reign, it was still possible to come across people from the Catherinian age, alive and walking the streets wearing stars, cloaks, and golden camisoles [the *kamzol*, a specifically eighteenth-century men's jacket] with gilded keys on the back. One could see old brigadiers in white plumed hats; and not a few aristocrats appeared on Nevskii, following the custom of the mother-tsarina's court, with muffs in their hands and wearing red-heeled shoes." Pyliaev, *Zamechatel'nye chudaki i originaly*, 163. This vision of the city as something of a masquerade simultaneously inhabited by people of visibly different epochs is undoubtedly relevant for the next section's discussion of the encounter between Hermann and the Countess in Pushkin's "The Queen of Spades."

32. Quoted in Roche, *The Culture of Clothing*, 58.

33. N. M. Karamzin, "Zhenskie pariki," *Vestnik Evropy*, no. 1 (1802): 38–39.

34. Lynn Festa ponders the complex status of the wig in this period: "The wig's physical nature—the way it shuttles among different individuals, recomposing the body and its surfaces—erodes the boundaries that set the individual subject off from the world." Festa, "Personal Effects: Wigs and Possessive Individualism in the Long Eighteenth Century," 48. On wigs, see also the special *Eighteenth-Century Studies* issue devoted to hair (vol. 38, no. 1, Fall 2004), especially Rauser, "Hair, Authenticity, and Self-Made Macaroni."

35. Vigel, *Zapiski*, 1:51.

36. N. M. Karamzin, "Nechto o nyneshnem Parizhe," *Vestnik Evropy*, no. 1 (1802): 63.

37. Recall, for instance, the late-eighteenth–early-nineteenth century fascination with various technologies of magic: phantasmagoria, resurrection via galvanism, etc.

38. Sergei Glinka, "Dogadki," *Ruskoi vestnik*, no. 11 (November 1810): 100. Recall similar summations of Paul's distrust of French fashion by Vigel and Lieven in the previous section.

39. Ibid.

40. "Kuznetskii most, ili vladychestvo mody i roskoshi," *Ruskoi vestnik*, no. 9 (September 1808), 348.

41. Sergei Glinka, "Vkus i moda," *Ruskoi vestnik*, no. 10 (October 1809): 73.

42. Ibid.

43. This question might have been particularly difficult to pose, let alone disentangle at the dawn of the nineteenth century; neither in the eighteenth century nor in most of the nineteenth did historiography incorporate everyday life and material culture.

44. This section's title is the famous phrase "otvratitel'nye tainstva ee tualeta" (Pushkin, *Polnoe sobranie sochinenii v shestnadtsati tomakh*, 8/1:240), rendered thus in Pushkin, "The Queen of Spades," 218. All English quotations of "The Queen of Spades" will come from this edition.

45. Pogodin, "Pis'mo o russkikh romanakh," 139.

46. Kireevskii, *Kritika i estetika*, 81.

47. Ibid., 80. Kireevskii's journal *The European* (*Evropeets*) was closed after the publication of the second part of this article.

48. Pushkin, "The Queen of Spades," 205–6. Lauren Leighton reads this passage as anagrammatically containing the key to the card secret. Leighton, "Gematria in 'The Queen of Spades': A Decembrist Puzzle," 455–56.

49. Gershenzon, *Mudrost' Pushkina*, 85–86.

50. Benjamin theorizes new cinematic technologies in a way that might be surprisingly relevant here: "On the one hand, film furthers insight into the necessities governing our lives by its use of close-ups, by its accentuation of hidden details in familiar objects, and by its exploration of commonplace milieux through the ingenious guidance of the camera; on the other hand, it manages to assure us of a vast and unsuspected field of action [Spielraum]. [. . .] With the close-up, space expands; with slow motion, movement is extended." (Benjamin, *The Work of Art in the Age of Its Technological Reproducibility, and Other Writings on Media*, 37.) We may be dealing with a similar correspondence between perception and visual medium. It hardly seems accidental, that is, that Pushkin's novella pairs the techniques of close-up description of interior spaces with slow-motion yet economical reports of characters' gestures and movements; almost "ahead of its time," almost photograph-like, his still-life makes history swell and change its texture.

51. Delon, *L'invention du boudoir*, 12. Delon offers the boudoir's Begriffsge-schichte: "The boudoir seems linked to intimacy, caprice and mood swings. One has to wait until 1835 for the Academy to add two ideas: luxury and femininity."

52. Gender difference is clearly central to the novella's plot as well as to its meta-textual reading. I have touched upon the distinction between the feminine eigh-teenth century and masculine nineteenth century in my discussion of Russian odic poetry and its reception in chapter 1. But there is also evidence to suggest that this framing of the epochal divide is salient for Romantic literary culture in general. Thus, Gary Kelly writes, for example, of the "remasculinization" of Romantic liter-ary practice and the appropriation of female writing by mainstream masculine dis-course, an argument that also emerges in different forms in much of the Walter Scott scholarship addressed in the previous chapter. (Kelly, "Feminine Romanticism, Mas-culine History, and the Founding of the Modern Liberal State," 3.) At stake in the novella's alignment of femininity with the eighteenth-century past and masculinity with the nineteenth-century present is, in part, a gendering of history; but more important is the fact that unlike Turgenev (as we shall see in the book's last chap-ter), Pushkin is not content solely to marginalize the distaff epoch (here embodied in the Countess). He also exposes its lasting power, "refeminizing" (to follow Kelly's formulation) nineteenth-century social theater, if not literary practice.

53. Pushkin famously criticizes the descriptive clutter in the works of his French contemporaries (the very clutter Gershenzon imputes to Pushkin himself), "the near-sighted pettiness of French novelists these days" (*blizorukaia melochnost' nynesh-nikh frantsuzskikh romanistov*). Pushkin, *Polnoe sobranie sochinenii v shestnadtsati tomakh*, 12:9.

54. Orlando, *Obsolete Objects in the Literary Imagination*, 28.

55. The single most gripping first-person record of female life and power in the eighteenth century was the memoir of Catherine II, a text not intended for publi-cation, but read and copied by Pushkin in Odessa. In her erudite and thorough preface to the recent English translation, Hilde Hoogenboom emphasizes Cath-erine's reluctance to publicize her life-tale. Not only was the empress understand-ably unwilling to expose her son Paul's questionable parentage, she also adhered, according to Hoogenboom, to the Enlightenment dictum against exposing one's *histoire particulière* to contemporary judgment, a constraint relaxed (albeit to a lim-ited extent, by modern standards) precisely in the 1830s with the explosion in auto-biographical writing. (Catherine, *The Memoirs of Catherine the Great*, xlvii.) On the transformations in autobiographical writing from the eighteenth to the early nine-teenth century, see Tartakovskii, *Russkaia memuaristika XVIII–pervoi poloviny XIX veka: ot rukopisi k knige*. With these epochal distinctions in view, we begin to see parallels between Hermann the nineteenth-century adventurer and Pushkin the nineteenth-century historian. Both succeed in puncturing the feminine interiority of the Russian eighteenth century—Hermann in entering the boudoir and Pushkin in perusing the memoir—but are limited in their understanding and access.

56. Incidentally, among the many Russian courtiers painted by Lebrun, we find portraits of several women of the Golitsyn family, relatives of Princess N. P. Golitsyna, the recognized prototype of the Countess. For more on Lebrun's sojourn in Russia, see *The Memoirs of Elisabeth Vigée-Le Brun*; and Bischoff, "Madame Vigée Le Brun at the Court of Catherine the Great."

57. Even though other elements in the text suggest that Hermann conceives of his relationship to the Countess as essentially filial (as argued in Paul Debreczeny, *The Other Pushkin*, 232–33), the cultural and social gaps underscore not only the illegitimacy of that imagined bond, but also the illicit desire (for both erotic conquest and material advancement) as ultimately perverting the narrative of filiation between the two protagonists and, by implication, between the eighteenth and the nineteenth centuries.

58. Pushkin, "The Queen of Spades," 210.

59. Catherine II died at 67; the only other monarch in the dynasty to live beyond the age of sixty was Alexander II (assassinated at 63). In the 34 years of her reign, Catherine had 21 official favorites, a fact relevant when one considers Hermann's unoriginal fantasies about becoming the 87-year-old Countess's lover.

60. On Golitsyna as the Countess's prototype, see Rabkina, "Fakty, sobytiia, liudi. Istoricheskii prototip 'pikovoi damy.'" On Golitsyna's own autobiographical writing, see Mil'china, "Zapiski 'pikovoi damy.'"

61. In "The Posthumous Reputation of Catherine II," Simon Dixon assembles a corpus of writings by and about members of Catherine's intimate circle, featuring prominently the reminiscences of her ladies-in-waiting.

62. As Pushkin's close acquaintance, Vigel might have shared the story with him, but whether or not he did is immaterial. Such stories were not uncommon at the time, and the Catherinian lady-in-waiting was a figure so omnipresent as almost to stand as a type.

63. Note that even at the time of Pushkin's death in January 1837, both Golitsyna and Branitskaia were still alive.

64. Vigel, *Zapiski*, 1:42. Like Vigel, Pushkin might have encountered Countess N. P. Golitsyna as a child; his grandmother's estate, which he frequented, was close to the Golitsyns'. See Rabkina, "Fakty, sobytiia, liudi. Istoricheskii prototip 'pikovoi damy,'" 216.

65. Ibid.

66. Considered in tandem, the portraits of Branitskaia and Catherine [Figures 5 and 6] foreground the interlinking of allegory and mimesis in pre-Romantic portraiture—along with the subjects' aristocratic and royal identities. Catherine's image acquires meaning in standing illuminated against the background of its doubles, both historical (Peter I's profile, garlanded in laurels) and allegorical (Themis, embroidered on the cushion, and the statues of Prudence and Constancy occupying the architectural space behind her). In a similar vein, the portrait of Branitskaia is dominated by Catherine's bust, which is both bigger and higher than the

noblewoman who mimics and depends upon the empress. I am thankful to Erin McBurney for guidance in decoding Lampi's allegorical imagery.

67. "The Queen of Spades" has a reputation for being over-interpreted, perhaps precisely because of our sense that its abiding mysteries point in multiple directions and resist coherent readings. For an extensive bibliography of criticism on the novella that is, however, by now due for an update, see Cornwell, Pushkin's "The Queen of Spades," 79–86. Remarking upon the many detective-like investigations the novella has inspired, Caryl Emerson suggests that "in the story, [Pushkin] parodies our search for system [. . .]. In the seductive fragments of an explanation that are strewn around his story, we glimpse what might be the real logic of the tale: an allegory of interpretation itself." (Emerson, "'The Queen of Spades' and the Open End," 37.) In my own "search for a system," I propose framing the novella in the context of the historicist concerns of its time, rather than pressing this context to yield a definitive explanation of the work's mysticism. In drawing attention to the novella's epochal structuring, I especially dwell on the scenes preceding the Countess's death as those that stage a physical encounter between the two historical periods that my book as a whole brings into dialogue.

68. Pushkin, "The Queen of Spades," 219.

69. The Countess's Russian also abounds in colloquialisms, which English translations unfortunately tend to neutralize: *ia chai, batiushka* ("methinks, my dear fellow"); *Chto ty, mat' moia! glukha, chto li*? ("What, mother mine, are you deaf?"); *matushka* ("little mother"); *Chto s toboiu, mat' moia? s golosu spala, chto li*? ("What's with you, mother mine, have you lost your voice?"); *Chto s toboiu sdelalos', mat' moia! Stolbniak li na tebia nashel, chto li*? ("What's happened to you, mother mine! What, have you been hit with lockjaw?"); *Slava bogu, ia ne kartavliu i iz uma eshche ne vyzhila!* ("Thank God, I can still trill my r's, and my mind's not past its prime!").

70. Khanzhakhina, Vestnikova, and Chudikhina are the protagonists of Catherine's comedy *O Time!* (*O vremia!*, 1772).

71. In this portrait, Pushkin elaborates what Monika Greenleaf has identified in reference to Catherine's *Memoirs* as "the connection of visuality and corporeality with the Old Regime's world of feminized and personal power." Greenleaf, "Performing Autobiography: The Multiple Memoirs of Catherine the Great (1756–1796)," 424.

72. This moniker is not actually used in the novella, but is one by which N. P. Golitsyna was known in 1820s–'30s high society because of the mustache and beard she had grown as an old lady.

73. Pushkin, "The Queen of Spades," 205–6.

74. Quoted in Proskurina, "Krylov i Ekaterina II: stikhotvorenie 'Umiraiushchaia koketka' v kontekste russkogo libertinazha," 114. Proskurina persuasively demonstrates that many of Krylov's and his circle's satires targeted Catherine II as an aged libertine.

75. Greenleaf suggests quite a different purpose for distinguishing self from costume in Catherine's *Memoirs*: "[Catherine] treats what her body had been subjected

to as a domain of appearances, beneath which her purity of will and honor have survived intact. This is the way male lives are told: their spirit or character rise enriched above the body's vicissitudes, while a woman's bodily fate tends to be strictly correlated with the state of her soul." (Greenleaf, "Performing Autobiography," 413.) If underneath the female costume in Catherine's memoirs masculine virtue throbs, Krylov still finds there a disintegrating female body, as does Pushkin, albeit in far more complex fashion.

76. Wachtel, "Rereading 'The Queen of Spades,'" 16.

77. As Wortman discusses in *Scenarios of Power*, while Alexander I referenced his grandmother in his monarchic iconography, Nicholas I explicitly reoriented his own symbol-system away from Catherine II and toward the Petrine masculine model.

78. Pushkin, "The Queen of Spades," 212.

79. Ibid., 218.

80. A. D. P. Briggs connects the Countess's "negative eroticism" with her repeated undressing (*Alexander Pushkin: A Critical Study*, 221). The bedroom encounter of Hermann and the Countess is read as "both climax and caricature" in Gregg, "Germann the Confessor and the Stony, Seated Countess: The Moral Subtext of Pushkin's 'The Queen of Spades,'" 616.

81. On Pushkin's reading of Casanova in connection to this specific reference, see Reiser, "Pushkin i memuary Kazanovy." As I will argue, however, the presence of Casanova's memoirs in the novella far exceeds this one passing remark.

82. Roche, *The Culture of Clothing*, 416.

83. Ibid., 413. Roche further suggests that, in addition to old age, it was the Revolution, which we have seen muddling the relationship between fashion and social hierarchy in the previous section's discussion of Karamzin's Parisian impressions, that perturbed the late-career Casanova's lifestyle. For him, "to dress and undress women [. . .] was [. . .] to refuse the political roles of male, Roman, even Spartan, society" (419).

84. Cornwell discusses this archetypal triangle, but in relation to later writers rather than Casanova, Pushkin's acknowledged source. Cornwell, *Pushkin's "The Queen of Spades,"* 72–73.

85. Pushkin, "The Queen of Spades," 225.

86. Robin Aizlewood explores the doubling of characters in the novella in "The Alter Ego and the Stone Guest: Doubling and Redoubling Hermann in *The Queen of Spades*."

87. Vinogradov, "O 'Pikovoi dame.' Iz knigi 'Stil' Pushkina.'" 256.

Chapter 6. The Margins of History

1. The epigraph that opens this chapter is from Makogonenko and Serman, *Poety XVIII veka*, 2:305. "Old age comes to the lion: / He has grown feeble, his fury

cooled, / He has stopped tormenting other animals, / Is no longer fearsome. / No one is afraid of him; / He will not bite anymore. / Into a kennel the lion retired / And never comes out of it. / An ass / Comes to him; / But does not pay the lion respect, / Instead he strikes him with his hoof, / Repaying him for his former tyrannies. / The lion, / Aching in his soul, / Sensing such a disgrace to himself, / Said, moaning: / 'An ass dares push me now; / What a fate for a lion!'"

2. Pushkin, *Polnoe sobranie sochinenii v shestnadtsati tomakh*, 12:195.

3. The most succinct account of the nineteenth-century shift in the usage of the term "generation" is offered in Williams, *Keywords: A Vocabulary of Culture and Society*, 140–42.

4. In my reading, Arkadii Kirsanov emerges as the novel's protagonist precisely because it is he who continues the line from the fathers to the sons to the open-ended future intimated at the end of the novel, a continuity that is interrupted everywhere else in the book.

5. Earlier, as Pavel Petrovich is recovering from his minor duel wound, the narrator bluntly remarks: "He was indeed a dead man!" (*Da on i byl mertvets!*). Turgenev, *Polnoe sobranie sochinenii i pisem v 28 tomakh*, 8:363.

6. This understanding of Turgenev's character system might allow us to rethink superfluity as not only a social and psychological category, but also as a fundamentally historical one. The superfluous men are, like childless uncles, superfluous to a particular course of historical development.

7. Turgenev, *Fathers and Sons*, 65.

8. Ibid., 66. *Polnoe sobranie sochinenii i pisem v 28 tomakh*, 8:280. Here we might speculate that in a culture whose discourse is defined by the raznochinets rather than aristocratic ideology, genealogical conceptions of history generally become less relevant.

9. Here we might recall that in the course of Turgenev's career, Pushkin himself would cease to be felt as a living presence, with questions of his import, legacy, and progeny receiving a panoply of answers culminating in the speeches surrounding the 1880 celebrations. Ultimately, of course, Pushkin would be pronounced (including by Turgenev himself) the father of Russian language and letters; but some critics, particularly of the historicizing bent (e.g., Vasilii Kliuchevskii), did make attempts to consign him, however appreciatively, to a specific historical past.

10. On the centrality of portraiture to Turgenev's art, consider Henry James's early pronouncement, by now something of an axiom: "The germ of a story, with him, was never an affair of plot—that was the last thing he thought of: it was the representation of certain persons. The first form in which a tale appeared to him was as the figure of an individual, or a combination of individuals, whom he wished to see in action, being sure that such people must do something very special and interesting. They stood before him definite, vivid, and he wished to know, and to show, as much as possible of their nature." James, *Partial Portraits*, 314–15. Richard Freeborn (*Turgenev: The Novelist's Novelist*) describes Turgenev's style as "pictorial

realism" (49) and, moreover, advances an intriguing claim that the whole of the Russian novelistic tradition thrives more on portraiture than plot (35).

11. In considering Vasilii Trediakovskii's *Nachleben* in the nineteenth century, Irina Reyfman identifies him, echoing Radishchev, as the uncle (*diad'ka*) figure in Russian literary history, a sidekick to Lomonosov the father (*Vasilii Trediakovsky: The Fool of the "New" Russian Literature*, 19 et passim). While the meaning of "pseudofather" or "substitute" is not central to my conception of unclehood, Reyfman's reading of Russian self-mythologizaton and literary historiography as founded on rival origins—one, paternal-Lomonosovian, celebrated, and the other, avuncular-Trediakovskian, suppressed or discarded—describes a dynamic similar to the one I address in this book, whereby the eighteenth century as a legacy is alternately assessed as self or other.

12. Other scholars have remarked upon the eighteenth-century substratum of Turgenev's character networks. Calculating that of all the historical layers in Turgenev's narrators' or characters' pasts the Russian eighteenth century is the most developed and best represented, Natal'ia Khalfina reads this tendency as a function of Turgenev's palimpsestic representation of the present and of that end-goal of most histories of the novel, realism. (Khalfina, "Turgenevskie starichki: Zhivoi XVIII vek v proizvedeniiakh I. S. Turgeneva.") A shorter list than the one I've assembled here of Turgenev's eighteenth-century characters is given as background of the 1881 novella "Old Portraits" in Nazarova, "I. S. Turgenev v rabote nad 'Starymi portretami' (iz tvorcheskoi istorii)." Frank Seeley (*Turgenev: A Reading of His Fiction*) also notes the presence of eighteenth-century characters throughout Turgenev's oeuvre, claiming that they serve "to safeguard authorial perspective and balance by distancing his creation from his immediate circumstances" (184) and that they do not fall within any particular pattern: "[the] variety of types is noteworthy: they have generally as little in common as personages of Turgenev's own age or younger " (319), a reading that my interpretation of these characters seeks to problematize.

13. The narrator of *Smoke* (1867) repeatedly uses this term in his grotesque descriptions of an aged Catherine-era aristocrat.

14. Here it is important to note that neither the Slavophiles nor the Westernizers—their distinct views of the Russian Enlightenment notwithstanding—expended much praise for the eighteenth-century lifestyles or worldviews that the nineteenth century had consigned to the past.

15. Letter to K. D. Kavelin of December 17 (29), 1876, cited in the commentary to *Virgin Soil* in Turgenev, *Polnoe sobranie sochinenii*, 9:521.

16. Turgenev, *The Novels of Ivan Turgenev*, 2:46–47.

17. Ibid., 5:168–69. References to human "ruins" are interspersed throughout this section of *Smoke*. For example, "a repulsive old crone, with the odor of sanctity and evaporated sinfulness about her"; "the ancient ruin, who had long since ceased understanding anything—moreover she was completely deaf—only shook her head"; and "the ancient ruin with a mighty effort struck him with her fan on the arm; a

flake of plaster was shaken off her forehead by this rash action" (ibid., 170, 173, 178).

18. Ibid., 6:201–2.

19. Grigorii Bialyi interprets the ideological meaning of this episode similarly; see Bialyi, *Turgenev i russkii realizm*, 183–84.

20. Indeed, the palimpsestic and moribund quality of émigré life can be considered a topos in nineteenth-century Russian literature. With his characteristic poetic precision, Alexander Herzen similarly observes, "By the time Cannes and Grasse are reached, shades of time long past stray about, warming themselves in the sun; quietly huddled up, close to the sea, they wait for Charon and their turn." Herzen, *My Past and Thoughts*, 3:1439.

21. Turgenev, *Polnoe sobranie sochinenii i pisem*, 12:303.

22. Howe, "Turgenev: The Virtues of Hesitation." Victor Ripp (*Turgenev's Russia*) sees hesitation as a characteristic of the 1840s–'50s as an epoch and Turgenev's ambiguous posture (24) as a product of that formative period of his writerly career.

23. Richard Freeborn (*Turgenev: The Novelist's Novelist*) goes so far as to argue that in the case of Fimushka and Fomushka as well as more generally Turgenev's sympathies lie more with the eighteenth rather than the nineteenth century (xi, 174). In my view, such judgments are precluded by Turgenev's very approach to narrative, which imbues all characterization with a potential for eliciting sympathetic reactions, but ultimately also preserves—and asks the readers to preserve—an ambivalent distance.

24. While Howe praises this scene (ibid., 549), Frank O'Connor, among many other critics, believes it to be a flop (O'Connor, *The Mirror in the Roadway: A Study of the Modern Novel*).

25. Though Gogol's own historical writing typically recasts history as myth, effacing most markers of specific historical epochs, in the "old-world landowners'" parlor we nevertheless find a dusty portrait of Peter III; this idyll, too, is thus very clearly marked as belonging to the eighteenth century and going back specifically to the emperor who emancipated the gentry from obligatory state service, thereby enabling their pastoral lifestyle. Frank Seeley (*Turgenev: A Reading of His Fiction*, 85) sees Turgenev's early works as indebted to the Gogolian caricaturistic mode, but his later ones as overcoming it through "lyricism."

26. Turgenev, *The Novels of Ivan Turgenev*, 6:201–2.

27. Howe, "Turgenev: The Virtues of Hesitation," 549.

28. Turgenev, *The Novels of Ivan Turgenev*, 6:203–4.

29. Ibid., 217–18.

30. This metaphor is developed in Shklovskii, *Khod konia*.

31. For an alternative reading of "An Unfortunate Girl" that also attends to Koltovsky's eighteenth-century background, see Seeley, *Turgenev: A Reading of His Fiction*, 285–86.

32. Turgenev, *The Novels of Ivan Turgenev*, 15:84.

33. Ibid., 85–86.

34. Analyzing Dostoevsky's strategy for maintaining dynamic character systems in his novels, Alex Woloch pinpoints exactly this paradox inherent in minorness: "Dostoevsky focuses on that gap between what he calls 'motive' and 'action'—or between the interior thoughts of a human being (which are 'infinitely' complicated) and the finite, limited manifestation of this consciousness through external, social actions. If the narrative registers only action, it will elide the perspective of characters; if it attempts to register motive, it might lose the thread of narrative progression and have to devote too much 'space and attention' to minor characters." (Woloch, *The One vs. the Many: Minor Characters and the Space of the Protagonist in the Novel*, 13.) Woloch's argument as a whole, which theorizes narrative economies as a system of deliberate attention distribution, was instrumental to my conception of eighteenth-century minorness in Turgenev.

35. Tolstoy's acceptance of the eighteenth century as a formative period in Russian aristocratic genealogy is hardly surprising, considering his untroubled rootedness in Iasnaia Poliana, his familial estate, or his well-known affinity for Enlightenment philosophy and fiction. On the latter, see, for example, Eikhenbaum, *Lev Tolstoi. Kniga pervaia. 50-e gody*, 11 et passim; Kupreianova, *Estetika L. N. Tolstogo*; Lotman, "Russo i russkaia kul'tura"; Orwin, *Tolstoy's Art and Thought*; and Polosina, *Frantsuzskie knigi XVIII veka*.

36. Tolstoy, *Childhood, Boyhood, Youth*, 38.

37. On the work's narrative structure, see Wachtel, *The Battle for Childhood: Creation of a Russian Myth*, 7–57.

38. In *Eugene Onegin*, Tatiana's father, Dmitrii Larin, is also, as we find out from his epitaph, a brigadier. Here too this military rank marks him squarely as a man of the eighteenth century; in assigning the rank, Pushkin most likely also parodically associates the old Larin with Fonvizin's anti-hero. See Lotman, *Pushkin*, 610.

39. On Turgenev's eighteenth-century reading, see Schapiro, *Turgenev: His Life and Times*, 7.

40. Turgenev, *The Novels of Ivan Turgenev*, 14:220. Frank Seeley (*Turgenev: A Reading of His Fiction*, 273–74) presents an interesting case for seeing the brigadier Gus'kov as a Quixote type, but this reading does not attend to the melancholy framing of this character's senescence.

41. This type of attitude has also been described by Richard Freeborn as one of "sympathetic detachment" (*Turgenev: The Novelist's Novelist*). Elizabeth Allen (*Beyond Realism: Turgenev's Poetics of Secular Salvation*, 35–36) goes as far as to argue that the attitude of detachment and implicit disengagement from both characters and social issues renders highly problematic the characterization of Turgenev as a realist writer.

42. Tolstoy, *War and Peace*, 616.

43. The narrator's pathos-laden incomprehension in "The Brigadier" may stand as an extreme application of this strategy; but other Turgenev characters also have

difficulty coming to terms with the passage of time in their own lives. Recall, for instance, Nikolai Kirsanov, who senses his own slippage into pastness after confronting his son or Bazarov, but cannot grasp precisely when or why this slippage occurred.

44. The narrator's puzzlement in "The Brigadier" should recall a similar dynamic in Turgenev's "Three Portraits," discussed in this book's introduction.

45. Costlow, *Worlds within Worlds: The Novels of Ivan Turgenev*, 5.

46. Ibid., 7.

47. Crucially, Turgenev professed a dislike for Balzac's fiction precisely because of the clarity with which it mapped type onto a particular passion or vice that type was made to represent, engaging too much in reportage and ethnography, rather than committing itself to understanding and representing the ideals and fate of Balzac's society. Ladariia, *I. S. Turgenev i pisateli Frantsii XIX veka*, 99–100.

48. Sedgwick, "Tales of the Avunculate: Queer Tutelage in *The Importance of Being Earnest*," 63. I am thankful to Anastasia Kayiatos for bringing Sedgwick's framework to my attention.

49. Freeborn (*Turgenev: The Novelist's Novelist*, 54) compellingly focuses on what he characterizes as largely a theatrical chronotope of arrival in Turgenev's fiction, paying no heed, however, to the narrative space that lies outside these episodes of agitation produced by the arrival of Turgenev's protagonists.

50. Turgenev, *The Novels of Ivan Turgenev*, 8:51.

51. Two recent studies in Russian provincial *histoire des mentalités* have drawn attention specifically to the tensions endemic in this Russian pastoral and to its eventual undoing in the nineteenth century. See Newlin, *The Voice in the Garden: Andrei Bolotov and the Anxieties of Russian Pastoral*, and Randolph, *The House in the Garden: The Bakunin Family and the Romance of Russian Idealism*. On the content and implications of these eighteenth-century reforms, see Jones, *Emancipation of the Russian Nobility, 1762–1785*.

52. For an alternative treatment of the novella's eighteenth-century characters, see Seeley, *Turgenev: A Reading of His Fiction*, 319.

53. Turgenev, *The Novels of Ivan Turgenev*, 14:203.

54. In the opening section, the narrator offers the following conciliatory note regarding his relatives' involvement in Russia's peculiar institution: "It is needless to state that of the so-called 'serf question' no one even dreamed in those days; it could not disturb the peace of mind of Alexey Sergeitch: he was quite happy in the possession of his 'subjects'; but he was severe in his censure of bad masters, and used to call them the enemies of their order." Ibid., 189–90.

55. Turgenev, *Fathers and Sons*, 10.

56. While mentioning the estate culture's protracted death from 1861 to the Chekhovian world of the turn of the twentieth century, Priscilla Roosevelt ends her history of Russian estate culture precisely with the Emancipation Reform, evocatively suggesting that "since 1861 the country estate has survived almost as much

because of its hold on the Russian imagination as for any other reason." Roosevelt, *Life on the Russian Country Estate: A Social and Cultural History*, 318.

57. Belyi, *Sobranie stikhotvorenii 1914*, 53–55.

58. Khodasevich, *Sobranie sochinenii v 8 tomakh*, 1:64.

59. Turgenev, *The Novels of Ivan Turgenev*, 14:209.

60. It would be instructive to trace the revisions of this dynamic further into the twentieth century when both the eighteenth century and the Pushkin era are recovered by Soviet-era writers and scholars, often as surrogates for their unspeakable contemporaneity and recent past. Several scholars have examined the appropriation of Pushkin in the early Soviet era; fewer have dealt with rethinking the eighteenth century in this period; and to the best of my knowledge, no study has addressed both.

Epilogue

1. Tynianov, "Promezhutok," 176. Mikhail Vaiskopf (*Vo ves' logos*) has offered an expanded reading of Maiakovskii's eighteenth-centuryism, juxtaposing the two epochs' epic plots, heroic poetics, charismatic leaders, iconoclasm and icon-worship—in the case of the twentieth-century futurist, especially in his treatment of the figure of Lenin.

2. Tertz, *On Socialist Realism*, 71.

3. Toporov, *Peterburgskii tekst russkoi literatury*, 23.

Bibliography

Afanas'ev, A. N. "Ob istoricheskoi vernosti v romanakh Lazhechnikova." *Atenei* 32 (1858): 364–78.

Aizlewood, Robin. "The *Alter Ego* and the Stone Guest: Doubling and Redoubling Hermann in *The Queen of Spades*." In *Two Hundred Years of Pushkin. Alexander Pushkin: Myth and Monument*, vol. 2, edited by Robert Reid and Joe Andrew, 89–102. Amsterdam and New York: Rodopi, 2003.

Alekseev, M. P. "Val'ter Skott i ego russkie znakomstva." In *Literaturnoe nasledstvo*, vol. 91: *Russko-angliiskie literaturnye sviazi*, 247–393. Moscow: Nauka, 1982.

Alekseeva, N. Iu. *Russkaia oda: razvitie odicheskoi formy v XVII-XVIII vekakh*. St. Petersburg: Nauka, 2005.

Allen, Elizabeth Cheresh. *Beyond Realism: Turgenev's Poetics of Secular Salvation*. Stanford: Stanford University Press, 1992.

Al'tshuller, Mark. *Epokha Val'tera Skotta v Rossii: istoricheskii roman 1830-kh godov*. St. Petersburg: Akademicheskii proekt, 1996.

———. "Pushkin, Bulgarin, Nikolai I i Ser Val'ter Skott." In *Novye Bezdelki: Sbornik statei k 60-letiiu V. E. Vatsuro*, edited by S. I. Panov, 284–302. Moscow: Novoe literaturnoe obozreniie, 1995–96.

———. "Semen Bobrov and Edward Young." *Russian Literature Triquarterly* 21 (Spring 1988): 129–40.

———, and Iu. M. Lotman, eds. *Poety 1790–1810-kh godov*. Leningrad: Sovetskii pisatel', 1971.

Anisimov, E. V. *Rossiia v seredine XVIII veka: bor'ba za nasledie Petra*. Moscow: Mysl', 1986.

Arendt, Hannah. *On Revolution*. London, New York: Penguin, 1990.

Ariel'-Zalesskaia, G. G. "K izucheniu istorii biblioteki A. S. Pushkina." In *Pushkin: Issledovaniia i materialy*, 334–53. Moscow, Leningrad: Izdatel'stvo Akademii Nauk SSSR, 1958.

Averintsev, S. S. "Poeziia Derzhavina." In *Iz istorii russkoi kul'tury*, vol. 4, 763–79. Moscow: Shkola "Iazyki russkoi kul'tury," 1996.

Backvis, Claude. "Dans quelle mesure Derzhavin est-il un baroque?" In *Studies in Russian and Polish Literature: in Honour of Waclaw Lednicki*, edited by Zbigniew Folejewski et al., 72–104. 'S-Gravenhage: Mouton, 1962.

Baehr, Stephen Lessing. *The Paradise Myth in Eighteenth-Century Russia: Utopian Patterns in Early Secular Russian Literature and Culture*. Stanford: Stanford University Press, 1991.

Bakhtin, Mikhail. *Problemy poetiki Dostoevskogo*. Moscow: Khudozhestvennaia literatura, 1972.

Balzac, Honoré de. *Honoré de Balzac in Twenty-Five Volumes*. New York: P. F. Collier, 1900.

Bann, Stephen. *Romanticism and the Rise of History*. New York: Maxwell Macmillan International, 1995.

Baratynskii, E. A. *Stikhotvoreniia*. Moscow: Khudozhestvennaia literatura, 1986.

Barskova, Polina. "Enchanted by the Spectacle of Death: Forms of the End in Leningrad Culture (1917–1934)." PhD diss., University of California-Berkeley, 2006.

Barthes, Roland. "The Reality Effect." In *French Literary Theory Today: A Reader*, edited by Tzvetan Todorov, 11–18. Cambridge: Cambridge University Press, 1982.

Belinskii, V. G. *Polnoe sobranie sochinenii*. Moscow: Izdatel'stvo Akademii Nauk SSSR, 1955.

Belyi, Andrei. *Sobranie stikhotvorenii, 1914*. Edited by A. V. Lavrov. Moscow: Nauka, 1997.

Benjamin, Walter. *The Work of Art in the Age of Its Technological Reproducibility, and Other Writings on Media*. Edited by Michael W. Jennings et al. Cambridge, MA: Harvard University Press, 2008.

Berdiaev, Nikolai. *Smysl istorii*. Moscow: Mysl', 1990.

Berdnikov, Lev. *Shchegoli i vertoprakhi: Geroi russkogo galantnogo veka*. Moscow: Luch, 2008.

Berg, Maxine, and Elizabeth Eger. *Luxury in the Eighteenth Century: Debates, Desires and Delectable Goods*. Houndmills, Balsingstoke, Hampshire, New York: Palgrave, 2003.

Berkov, P. N. "Derzhavin i Karamzin v istorii russkoi literatury kontsa XVIII–nachala XIX veka." In *XVIII vek* 8, 5–15. Moscow, Leningrad: Izdatel'stvo Akademii Nauk SSSR, 1969.

———. *Lomonosov i literaturnaia polemika ego vremeni, 1750–1765*. Moscow, Leningrad: Izdatel'stvo Akademii Nauk SSSR, 1936.

Besserman, Lawrence L. *The Challenge of Periodization: Old Paradigms and New Perspectives*. New York: Garland Publishers, 1996.

Bestuzhev-Marlinskii, Aleksandr. *Sochineniia v dvukh tomakh*. Moscow: Khudozhestvennaia literatura, 1981.

Bethea, David M. *Realizing Metaphors: Alexander Pushkin and the Life of the Poet.* Madison: University of Wisconsin Press, 1998.

Bialyi, G. A. *Turgenev i russkii realizm.* Moscow, Leningrad: Sovetskii pisatel', 1962.

Bischoff, Ilse. "Madame Vigée Le Brun at the Court of Catherine the Great." *Russian Review* 24, no. 1 (1965): 30–45.

Blagoi, D. D. *Tvorcheskii put' Pushkina (1826–1830).* Moscow: Sovetskii pisatel', 1967.

Blok, G. *Pushkin v rabote nad istoricheskimi istochnikami.* Moscow, Leningrad: Izdatel'stvo Akademii Nauk SSSR, 1949.

Bolenko, K. G. "Poslanie A. S. Pushkina 'K vel'mozhe' kak instrument i ob"ekt polemiki: neskol'ko utochnenii." *Novoe literaturnoe obozrenie* 95 (2009): 127–45.

Briggs, A. D. P. *Alexander Pushkin: A Critical Study.* London and Canberra: Barnes and Noble Books, 1983.

Brown, Marshall. "Passion and Love: Anacreontic Song and the Roots of Romantic Lyric." *English Literary History* 66, no. 2 (Summer 1999): 373–404.

Buckler, Julie A. *Mapping St. Petersburg: Imperial Text and Cityshape.* Princeton: Princeton University Press, 2005.

Busch, Robert L. "N. A. Polevoj's *Moskovskij Telegraf* and the Critical Debate over 'Junaja Francija.'" *Canadian Review of Comparative Literature* 1, no. 2 (1974): 123–37.

———. "Russian Freneticism." *Canadian-American Slavic Studies* 14, no. 2 (1980): 269–83.

Catherine, Empress of Russia. *The Memoirs of Catherine the Great.* Translated by Mark Cruse and Hilde Hoogenboom. New York: Modern Library, 2005.

Chandler, James. *England in 1819: The Politics of Literary Culture and the Case of Romantic Historicism.* Chicago: University of Chicago Press, 1998.

Chekhov, A. P. *Sochineniia v 18 tomakh.* Moscow: Nauka, 1978.

Cherniavsky, Michael. *Tsar and People: Studies in Russian Myths.* New Haven: Yale University Press, 1961.

Chernov, S. N. "M. V. Lomonosov v odakh 1762 g." In *XVIII vek: Sbornik statei i materialov,* edited by A. S. Orlov, 155–80. Moscow, Leningrad: Izdatel'stvo Akademii Nauk SSSR, 1935.

Clark, J. C. D. *English Society, 1660–1832: Religion, Ideology and Politics during the Ancien Régime.* Cambridge: Cambridge University Press, 2000.

Clark, Timothy. "Enthusiasm and Enlightenment." In *The Theory of Inspiration: Composition as a Crisis of Subjectivity in Romantic and Post-Romantic Writing* by Timothy Clark, 61–91. Manchester: Manchester University Press, 1997.

Clery, E. J. *The Feminization Debate in Eighteenth-Century England: Literature, Commerce and Luxury.* New York: Palgrave Macmillan, 2004.

Clifford, Gay. *The Transformations of Allegory.* London, Boston: Routledge, 1974.

Clingham, Greg, ed. *Questioning History: The Postmodern Turn to the Eighteenth Century*. Lewisburg: Bucknell University Press, 1998.

Cornwell, Neil. *Pushkin's "The Queen of Spades."* Bristol: Bristol Classical Press, 1993.

Costlow, Jane. *Worlds within Worlds: The Novels of Ivan Turgenev*. Princeton: Princeton University Press, 1990.

Crary, Jonathan. *Techniques of the Observer: On Vision and Modernity in the Nineteenth Century*. Cambridge, MA: MIT Press, 1990.

Crone, Anna Lisa. *The Daring of Derzhavin: The Moral and Aesthetic Independence of the Poet in Russia*. Bloomington: Slavica Publishers, 2001.

———. "What Derzhavin Heard When Pushkin Read 'Vospominaniia v Tsarskom Sele' in 1815." *Pushkin Review* 2 (1999): 1–23.

Crotty, Kevin. *Song and Action: The Victory Odes of Pindar*. Baltimore: Johns Hopkins University Press, 1982.

Dan'ko, E. Ia. "Izobrazitel'noe iskusstvo v poezii Derzhavina." In *XVIII vek: Stat'i i materialy* 2, edited by G. A. Gukovskii, 166–247. Moscow, Leningrad: Izdatel'stvo Akademii Nauk SSSR, 1940.

Dashkova, E. R. et al. *Mon histoire: Mémoires d'une femme de lettres russe à l'époque des lumières*. Paris: L'Harmattan, 1999.

Davis, S. B. "From Scotland to Russia via France: Scott, Defauconpret, and Gogol." *Scottish Slavonic Review* 17 (Autumn 1991): 21–36.

Debreczeny, Paul. *The Other Pushkin*. Stanford: Stanford University Press, 1983.

Delon, Michel. *L'invention du boudoir*. Cadeilhan: Zulma, 1999.

De Man, Paul. "The Rhetoric of Temporality." In *Blindness and Insight: Essays in the Rhetoric of Contemporary Criticism* by Paul de Man, 187–228. Minneapolis: University of Minnesota Press, 1997.

Demoris, René. "Le corps royal et l'imaginaire au XVIIe siècle: Le Portrait du Roi par Félibien." *Révue des sciences humaines* 44, no. 172 (1978): 9–30.

Denby, David J. *Sentimental Narrative and the Social Order in France, 1760–1820*. Cambridge: Cambridge University Press, 1994.

Derzhavin, G. R. *Ob"iasneniia na sochineniia Derzhavina: im samim diktovannyia rodnoi ego plemiannitse, Elisavete Nikolaevne L'vovoi, v 1809 godu*. St. Petersburg: V tip. A. Smirdina, Izdannyia F. P. L'vovym, 1834.

———. *Sochineniia Derzhavina s ob"iasnitel'nymi primechaniiami Ia. Grota*. St. Petersburg: Izdatel'stvo Imperatorskoi Akademii nauk, 1864–83.

———. *Zapiski Gavriila Romanovicha Derzhavina, 1743–1812, s literaturnymi i istoricheskimi primechaniiami P. I. Barteneva*. Moscow: V tipografii Aleksandra Semena, 1860.

Dixon, Simon. "The Posthumous Reputation of Catherine II in Russia, 1797–1837." *The Slavonic and East European Review* 77, no. 4 (October 1999): 646–79.

Dmitriev, I. I. *Polnoe sobranie stikhotvorenii*. Leningrad: Sovetskii pisatel', 1967.

Dobuzhinskii, M. V. *Vospominaniia*. Moscow: Nauka, 1987.

Dolinin, A. A. "Eshche raz o khronologii 'Kapitanskoi dochki.'" In *Pushkin i drugie: sbornik statei k 60-letiu S. A. Fomicheva*, edited by V. A. Koshelev, 52–59. Novgorod: NovGu, 1997.

———. "Historicism or Providentialism? Pushkin's *History of Pugachev* in the Context of French Romantic Historiography." *The Slavic Review* 58, no. 2 (Summer 1999): 291–308.

———. *Istoriia, odetaia v roman: Val'ter Skott i ego chitateli, sud'by knig.* Moscow: Kniga, 1988.

———. "Val'ter-skottovskii istorizm v 'Kapitanskoi dochke.'" In *Pushkin i Angliia: tsikl statei* by A. A. Dolinin, 237–58 (Moscow: Novoe literaturnoe obozrenie, 2007).

Dostoevskii, F. M. *Polnoe sobranie sochinenii v tridtsati tomakh.* Leningrad: Nauka, 1980.

Duff, David. *Romanticism and the Uses of Genre.* Oxford: Oxford University Press, 2009.

Duncan, Ian. *Modern Romance and Transformations of the Novel: The Gothic, Scott, Dickens.* Cambridge: Cambridge University Press, 1992.

Edelstein, Dan. *The Enlightenment: A Genealogy.* Chicago: University of Chicago Press, 2010.

Eikhenbaum, Boris. *Lev Tolstoi. Kniga pervaia. 50-e gody.* Leningrad: Priboi, 1928.

———. *Skvoz' literaturu: Sbornik statei.* Leningrad: Academia, 1924.

Ekaterina II. *Sochineniia Imperatritsy Ekateriny II: proizvedeniia literaturnyia.* Edited by Ars. I. Vvedenskii. St. Petersburg: Izdatel'stvo A. F. Marksa, 1893.

Eliade, Mircea. *The Myth of the Eternal Return: Cosmos and History.* Translated by Willard R. Trask. Princeton: Princeton University Press, 2005.

Emerson, Caryl. "Grinev's Dream: *The Captain's Daughter* and a Father's Blessing." *The Slavic Review* 40, no. 1 (Spring, 1981): 60–76.

———. "'The Queen of Spades' and the Open End." In *Pushkin Today*, edited by David M. Bethea, 31–37. Bloomington and Indianapolis: Indiana University Press, 1993.

Evdokimova, Svetlana. *Pushkin's Historical Imagination.* New Haven: Yale University Press, 1999.

Fay, Elizabeth. *Fashioning Faces: The Portraitive Mode in British Romanticism.* Durham: University of New Hampshire Press, 2010.

Ferris, Ina. "'Before Our Eyes': Romantic Historical Fiction and the Apparitions of Reading." *Representations* 121, no. 1 (Winter 2013), 60–84.

Festa, Lynn. "Personal Effects: Wigs and Possessive Individualism in the Long Eighteenth Century." *Eighteenth-Century Life* 29, no. 2 (Spring 2005): 47–90.

Fletcher, Angus. *Allegory: The Theory of a Symbolic Mode.* Ithaca and London: Cornell University Press, 1964.

Flügel, J. C. *The Psychology of Clothes.* New York: International Universities Press, 1969.

Foucault, Michel. *The Order of Things: An Archaeology of the Human Sciences*. New York: Vintage Books, 1970.

Fradenburg, L. O. Aranye. "Group Time: Catastrophe, Survival, Periodicity." In *Time and the Literary*, edited by Karen Newman, Jay Clayton, and Marianne Hirsch, 211–38. New York: Routledge, 2002.

Fraiman, Tat'iana. "Derzhavin i Zhukovskii: K voprosu o tvorcheskom nasledovanii." In *Pushkinskie chteniia v Tartu, 3: Materialy mezhdunarodnoi nauchnoi konferentsii, posviashchennoi 220-letiiu V. A. Zhukovskogo i 200-letiiu F. I. Tiutcheva*, edited by L. Kiseleva, 9–29. Tartu: Tartu Ülikooli Kirjastus, 2004.

Frazier, Melissa. "*Kapitanskaia dochka* and the Creativity of Borrowing." *The Slavic and East European Journal* 37, no. 4 (Winter 1993): 472–89.

Freeborn, Richard. *Turgenev: The Novelist's Novelist, A Study*. London: Oxford University Press, 1960.

Gasparov, Boris. "Pushkin and Romanticism." In *The Pushkin Handbook*, edited by David Bethea, 537–67. Madison: University of Wisconsin Press, 2005.

Gershenzon, M. O. *Mudrost' Pushkina*. Tomsk: Vodolei, 1997.

Ginzburg, Lidiia. "Viazemskii i ego 'Zapisnaia knizhka.'" In *O starom i novom: Stat'i i ocherki* by Lidiia Ginzburg, 60–91. Leningrad: Sovetskii pisatel', 1982.

Gogol', Nikolai. *Polnoe sobranie sochinenii*. Moscow, Leningrad: Izdatel'stvo Akademii Nauk SSSR, 1937–52.

Golburt, Luba. "Derzhavin's Monuments: Sculpture, Poetry, and the Materiality of History." *Toronto Slavic Quarterly* 13 (Summer 2005). Available electronically: http://www.utoronto.ca/tsq/13/golburt13.shtml.

———. "Derzhavin's Ruins and the Birth of Historical Elegy." *Slavic Review* 65, no. 4 (2006): 670–93.

Goldsmith, M. M. *Private Vices, Public Benefits: Bernard Mandeville's Social and Political Thought*. Cambridge, New York: Cambridge University Press, 1985.

Golovina, V. N. *Memuary*. Moscow: Astrel' "Liuks," 2005.

Green, Martin Burgess. *Dreams of Adventure, Deeds of Empire*. New York: Basic Books, 1979.

Greenleaf, Monika. "Performing Autobiography: The Multiple Memoirs of Catherine the Great (1756–1796)." *The Russian Review* 63 (July 2004): 407–26.

———. *Pushkin and Romantic Fashion: Fragment, Elegy, Orient, Irony*. Stanford: Stanford University Press, 1994.

Gregg, Richard. "Germann the Confessor and the Stony, Seated Countess: The Moral Subtext of Pushkin's 'The Queen of Spades.'" *The Slavonic and East European Review* 78, no. 4 (October 2000): 612–24.

———. "Pushkin's Novelistic Prose: A Dead End?" *The Slavic Review* 57, no. 1 (Spring 1998): 1–27.

Greshishcheva, E. "Khvalebnaia oda v russkoi literature XVIII v." In *M. V. Lomonosov, 1711–1911*, edited by V. V. Sipovskii, 93–149. St. Petersburg: Izdatel'stvo Ia. Bashmakova, 1911.

Griboedov, A. S. *Gore ot uma*. Moscow: Nauka, 1969.

Grigor'ev, Apollon. *Sochineniia*. Moscow: Khudozhestvennaia literatura, 1990.

Groce, Alexander. "Aleksandr Pushkin's 'The Captain's Daughter': A Poetics of Violence." *Ulbandus Review* 13 (2010): 64–78.

Grossman, Leonid. "Bal'zak v Rossii." In *Literaturnoe nasledstvo* 31/32: *Russkaia kul'tura i Frantsiia*, 149–372. Moscow: Zhurnal'no-gazetnoe ob"iedinenie, 1937.

Grot, Ia. K. "Kharakteristika Derzhavina kak poeta." *Russkii vestnik* 61 (1866): 449–69.

———. *Zhizn' Derzhavina*. Moscow: Algoritm, 1997.

Gukovskii, G. A. *Pushkin i problemy realisticheskogo stilia*. Moscow: Goslitizdat, 1957.

———. "Russkaia poeziia XVIII veka." In *Rannie raboty po istorii russkoi poezii XVIII veka*, edited by V. M. Zhivov, 37–213. Moscow: Iazyki russkoi kul'tury, 2001.

———. "Vokrug Radishcheva." In *Ocherki po istorii russkoi literatury i obshchestvennoi mysli XVIII veka* by G. A. Gukovskii, 5–234. Leningrad: Gosudarstvennoe Izdatel'stvo "Khudozhestvennaia literatura," 1938.

Hamilton, Paul. *Metaromanticism: Aesthetics, Literature, Theory*. Chicago: University of Chicago Press, 2003.

Hamnett, Brian. *The Historical Novel in Nineteenth-Century Europe: Representations of Reality in History and Fiction*. Oxford: Oxford University Press, 2011.

Hayden, John O., ed. *Walter Scott: The Critical Heritage*. London: Routledge, 1970.

Herzen, Alexander. *My Past and Thoughts: The Memoirs of Alexander Herzen*. Translated by Constance Garnett. London: Chatto and Windus, 1968.

Higgs, Henry. *The Physiocrats. Six Lectures on the French Économistes of the 18th Century*. Hamden, CT: Archon Books, 1963.

Hixon, Jennifer J. "The Fall of Novgorod in Karamzin's Fiction and History." In *Russian Subjects: Empire, Nation, and the Culture of the Golden Age*, edited by Monika Greenleaf and Stephen Moeller-Sally, 193–210. Evanston: Northwestern University Press, 1998.

Hobson, Mary. *Aleksandr Griboedov's Woe From Wit: A Commentary and Translation*. Lewiston, NY: Edwin Mellen Press, 2005.

Horace. *The Complete Odes and Satires of Horace*. Translated by S. Alexander. Princeton: Princeton University Press, 1999.

Howe, Irving. "Turgenev: The Virtues of Hesitation." *The Hudson Review* 8, no. 4 (1956): 533–51.

Hughes, Lindsey. "From Caftans into Corsets: The Sartorial Transformation of Women During the Reign of Peter the Great." In *Gender and Sexuality in Russian Civilization*, edited by Peter Barta, 17–32. London: Routledge, 2001.

Hugo, Victor. *Notre-Dame of Paris*. Translated by John Sturrock. Harmondsworth, New York: Penguin, 1978.

Hunt, John Dixon. *The Figure in the Landscape: Poetry, Painting, and Gardening during the Eighteenth Century*. Baltimore: Johns Hopkins University Press, 1976.

Iakubovich, Dmitrii. "'Kapitanskaia dochka' i romany Val'ter Skotta." *Pushkin: Vremennik Pushkinskoi komissii*, no. 4/5 (1939): 165–97.

Ivleva, Viktoria. "Fashion and Sartorial Discourse in Eighteenth-Century Russian Literature and Culture." PhD diss., University of Wisconsin-Madison, 2009.

James, Henry. *Partial Portraits*. London and New York: Macmillan & Co., 1888.

Jay, Martin. *Downcast Eyes: The Denigration of Vision in Twentieth-Century French Thought*. Berkeley, Los Angeles: University of California Press, 1993.

Jefferson, Ann. *Reading Realism in Stendhal*. Cambridge: Cambridge University Press, 1988.

Jekutsch, Ulrike. "Das Lob Pauls I.: Herrscherpanegyrik in den letzten Jahren des 18. Jahrhunderts." *Deutsche Beiträge zum 14. Internationalen Slavistenkongress Ohrid 2008*, edited by Sebastian Kempgen et al., 461–73. Munich: Otto Sagner, 2008.

Jonas, Hans. "The Nobility of Sight." *Philosophy and Phenomenological Research* 14, no. 4 (June 1954): 507–19.

Jones, Robert E. *Emancipation of the Russian Nobility, 1762–1785*. Princeton: Princeton University Press, 1973.

Kagarlitskii, Iu. V. "Ritorika upodobleniia i ritorika sorevnovaniia: figury sblizheniia imen v russkom dukhovnom krasnorechii XVIII veka." In *Imenoslov. Zametki po istoricheskoi semantike imeni*, edited by F. B. Uspenskii, 209–30. Moscow: Indrik, 2003.

Kahan, Arcadius. *The Plow, the Hammer, and the Knout: An Economic History of Eighteenth-Century Russia*. Chicago: University of Chicago Press, 1985.

Kahn, Andrew. "Life-Writing in the 1830s: Viazemskii's *Fon-Vizin* and Pushkin's 'Table Talk.'" *Ulbandus Review* 12 (2009): 1–22.

———. *Pushkin's Lyric Intelligence*. Oxford: Oxford University Press, 2008.

Kapnist, Vasilii. *Sochineniia Kapnista*. St. Petersburg: V tipografii Imperatorskoi akademii nauk, 1849.

Karamzin, Nikolai. *Istoricheskoe pokhval'noe slovo Ekaterine II*. Moscow: V Universitetskoi tipografii u Liubiia, Gariia i Popova, 1802.

———. *Izbrannye sochineniia v dvukh tomakh*. Moscow; Leningrad: Khudozhestvennaia literatura, 1964.

———. *Letters of a Russian Traveler*. Translated by Andrew Kahn. Oxford: Voltaire Foundation, 2003.

———. *Pis'ma N. M. Karamzina k I. I. Dmitrievu*. St. Petersburg: V imperatorskoi akademii nauk, 1866.

———. *Polnoe sobranie stikhotvorenii*. Leningrad: Sovetskii pisatel', 1966.

———. *Zapiska o drevnei i novoi Rossii v ee politicheskom i grazhdanskom otnosheniiakh*. Moscow: Nauka, 1991.

Kelley, Donald R. "Ideas of Periodization in the West." In *The Many Faces of Clio: Cross-Cultural Approaches to Historiography*, edited by Q. Edward Wang and Franz L. Fillafer, 17–27. New York: Berghahn Books, 2007.

Kelly, Catriona. "Pushkin's Vicarious Grand Tour: A Neo-Sociological Interpretation of 'K vel'mozhe' (1830)." *The Slavonic and East European Review* 77, no. 1 (January 1999): 1–29.

Kelly, Gary. "Feminine Romanticism, Masculine History, and the Founding of the Modern Liberal State." *Essays and Studies* 51 (1998): 1–18.

Khalfina, Natal'ia. "Turgenevskie starichki: Zhivoi XVIII vek v proizvedeniiakh I. S. Turgeneva." *Literatura*, no. 21 (2006): 26–29.

Kheraskov, M. M. *Izbrannye proizvedeniia.* Leningrad: Sovetskii pisatel', 1961.

Khodasevich, Vladislav. *Derzhavin.* Moscow: Kniga, 1988.

———. "Gavrila Derzhavin: K stoletiiu so dnia smerti." In *Sobranie sochinenii* by Vladislav Khodasevich, vol. 2, edited by John Malmstad and Robert Hughes, 246–54. Ann Arbor: Ardis, 1990.

———. *Sobranie sochinenii v 8 tomakh.* Edited by John E. Malmstad and Robert P. Hughes. Moscow: Russkii put', 2009.

Kireevskii, I. V. *Kritika i estetika.* Moscow: Iskusstvo, 1979.

Kirsanova, R. M. *Kostium v russkoi kul'ture 18–pervoi poloviny 20 vekov: opyt entsiklopedii.* Moscow: Bol'shaia Rossiiskaia Entsiklopediia, 1995.

Klein, Ioakhim. "Poet-samokhval: 'Pamiatnik' Derzhavina i status poeta v Rossii XVIII veka." *Novoe literaturnoe obozrenie* 65 (2004): 148–69.

———. *Russkaia literatura v XVIII veke.* Moscow: Indrik, 2010.

Kochetkova, N. D. *Literatura russkogo sentimentalizma (Esteticheskie i khudozhestvennye iskaniia).* St. Petersburg: Nauka, 1994.

Kölle, Helmut. *Farbe, Licht und Klang in der malenden Poesie Derzhavins.* Munich: Wilhelm Fink Verlag, 1966.

Koselleck, Reinhart. "The Eighteenth Century as the Beginning of Modernity." In *The Practice of Conceptual History: Timing Histories, Spacing Concepts* by Reinhart Koselleck, 154–69. Translated by Todd Samuel Presner et al. Stanford: Stanford University Press, 2001.

———. *Futures Past: On the Semantics of Historical Time.* Translated by Keith Tribe. Cambridge, MA: MIT Press, 1985.

———. "Modernity and the Planes of Historicity." In *Futures Past: On the Semantics of Historical Time* by Reinhart Koselleck, 3–20. Translated by Keith Tribe. Cambridge, MA: MIT Press, 1985.

Kozlov, I. I. *Sobranie stikhotvorenii Ivana Kozlova.* Part II. St. Petersburg: V tipografii III Otdeleniia Sobstvennoi Ego Imperatorskogo Velichestva Kantseliarii, 1840.

Kozlov, V. P., and V. I. Buganov. *Kruzhok A. I. Musina-Pushkina i "Slovo o Polku Igoreve": novye stranitsy istorii drevnerusskoi poemy v XVIII v.* Moscow: Nauka, 1988.

Kupreianova, E. N. *Estetika L. N. Tolstogo.* Moscow, Leningrad: Nauka, 1966.

Kurke, Leslie. *The Traffic in Praise: Pindar and the Poetics of Social Economy.* Ithaca: Cornell University Press, 1991.

Ladariia, M. B. *I. S. Turgenev i pisateli Frantsii XIX veka.* Tbilisi: Izdatel'stvo Tbilisskogo universiteta, 1987.

Lappo-Danilevskii, K. Iu. "Literaturnoe nasledie N. A. L'vova." In *Izbrannye proizvedeniia* by N. A. L'vov, 7–22. St. Petersburg: Akropol', 1994.

Lazhechnikov, I. I. *Sobranie sochinenii.* Edited by S. A. Vengerov. Moscow: Mozhaisk-Terra, 1994.

———. *Sochineniia v dvukh tomakh.* Moscow: Khudozhestvennaia literatura, 1986.

Leighton, Lauren. "Gematria in 'The Queen of Spades': A Decembrist Puzzle." *Slavic and East European Journal* 21 (1977): 455–69.

———. *Russian Romantic Criticism: An Anthology.* New York: Greenwood Press, 1987.

Lemke, M. K. *Nikolaevskie zhandarmy i literatura 1826–1855 gg.* St. Petersburg: Izdatel'stvo S. V. Bunina, 1908.

Lermontov, Mikhail. *Polnoe sobranie stikhotvorenii v 2kh tomakh.* Leningrad: Sovetskii pisatel', 1989.

Levin, Iu. D. *Ossian v russkoi literature: konets XVIII–pervaia tret' XIX veka.* Leningrad: Nauka, 1980.

———. "Prizhiznennaia slava V. Skotta v Rossii." In *Epokha romantizma: iz istorii mezhdunarodnykh sviazei russkoi literatury,* edited by M. P. Alekseev, 5–67. Leningrad: Nauka, 1975.

Levitt, Marcus. *The Visual Dominant in Eighteenth-Century Russia.* DeKalb: Northern Illinois University Press, 2011.

Likhachev, D. S. *Poeziia sadov: k semantike sadovo-parkovykh stilei: sad kak tekst,* Izd. 2. St. Petersburg: Nauka, 1991.

Lipovetsky, Gilles. *The Empire of Fashion: Dressing Modern Democracy.* Princeton: Princeton University Press, 1994.

Loewen, Donald. "Questioning a Poet's Explanations: Politics and Self-Explanation in Derzhavin's 'Footnotes' and *Explanations.*" *Russian Review* 64, no. 3 (July 2005): 381–400.

Lomonosov, M. V. *Polnoe sobranie sochinenii.* Vol. 8, *Poeziia, oratorskaia proza, nadpisi, 1732–1764 gg.* Moscow, Leningrad: Izdatel'stvo Akademii Nauk SSSR, 1959.

Lopukhin, I. V. *Zapiski nekotorykh obstoiatel'stv zhizni i sluzhby deistvitel'nogo tainogo sovetnika, senatora I. V. Lopukhina, sochinennyia im samim.* Moscow: Universitetskaia tipografiia, 1860.

Loseff, Lev. "The Toy Town Ruined." In *A Sense of Place: Tsarskoe Selo and its Poets. Papers from the 1989 Dartmouth Conference Dedicated to the Centennial of Anna Akhmatova,* 35–50. Columbus: Slavica Publishers, 1993.

———, and Barry P. Scherr, eds. *A Sense of Place: Tsarskoe Selo and its Poets: Papers from the 1989 Dartmouth Conference Dedicated to the Centennial of Anna Akhmatova.* Columbus: Slavica Publishers, 1993.

Lotman, Iu. M. "Cherty real'noi politiki v pozitsii Karamzina 1790-kh gg. (k genezisu istoricheskoi kontseptsii Karamzina)." In *XVIII vek* 13, edited by G. P. Makogonenko and A. M. Panchenko, 102–31. Leningrad: Nauka, 1981.

———. "Ideia istoricheskogo razvitiia v russkoi kul'ture kontsa XVIII–nachala XIX stoletiia." In *O russkoi literature* by Iu. M. Lotman, 284–91. St. Petersburg: Iskusstvo, 1997.

———. *Pushkin*. St. Petersburg: Iskusstvo-SPb, 1995.

———. "Russo i russkaia kul'tura XVIII—nachala XIX veka." In Zh. Zh. Russo. *Traktaty*. Moscow: Nauka, 1969.

———, and Boris Uspenskii. "Rol' dual'nykh modelei v dinamike russkoi kul'tury (do kontsa XVIII veka)." In *Trudy po russkoi i slavianskoi filologii. XXVIII: k 50-letiiu professora B. F. Egorova*, edited by V. I. Bezzubov, 3–36. Tartu: Tartuskii Gosudarstvennyi Universitet, 1977.

Lukács, Georg. *The Historical Novel*. Lincoln: University of Nebraska Press, 1983.

Lyons, Martyn. "The Audience for Romanticism: Walter Scott in France, 1815–1851." *European History Quarterly* 14 (January 1984): 21–46.

Mah, Harold. *Enlightenment Phantasies: Cultural Identity in France and Germany, 1750–1914*. Ithaca: Cornell University Press, 2004.

Maigron, Louis. *Le roman historique à l'époque romantique: essai sur l'influence de Walter Scott*. Geneva: Slatkine, 1970.

Makogonenko, G. P. *Ot Fonvizina do Pushkina: iz istorii russkogo realizma*. Moscow: Khudozhestvennaia literatura, 1969.

———, ed. *Problemy istorizma v russkoi literature, konets XVIII–nachalo XIX v.* Leningrad: Nauka, 1981.

———, and I. Z. Serman, eds. *Poety XVIII veka*. Moscow: Sovetskii pisatel', 1972.

Marakuev, V. N. *Petr Simon Pallas, ego zhizn', uchenye trudy i puteshestviia*. Moscow: Tipografiia A. A. Torletskogo i Ko., 1877.

Marin, Louis. *Portrait of the King*. Minneapolis: University of Minnesota Press, 1988.

Marker, Gary. *Publishing, Printing, and the Origins of Intellectual Life in Russia, 1700–1800*. Princeton: Princeton University Press, 1985.

Marrese, Michelle Lamarche. *A Woman's Kingdom: Noblewomen and the Control of Property in Russia, 1700–1861*. Ithaca: Cornell University Press, 2002.

Martin, Alexander. *Romantics, Reformers, Reactionaries: Russian Conservative Thought and Politics in the Reign of Alexander I*. DeKalb: Northern Illinois University Press, 1997.

Mashinskii, S. "Na pozitsiiakh istorizma." In V. G. Belinskii, *Sobranie sochinenii v 9-ti tomakh*, vol. 5, edited by M. Ia. Poliakov, 514–33. Moscow: Khudozhestvennaia literatura, 1979.

Maxwell, Richard. *The Historical Novel in Europe, 1650–1950*. Cambridge, UK: Cambridge University Press, 2009.

McCalman, Iain. "Magic, Spectacle, and the Art of de Loutherbourg's Eidophusikon." In *Sensation & Sensibility: Viewing Gainsborough's Cottage Door*, edited by Ann Bermingham, 181–97. New Haven: Yale University Press, 2005.

Mee, Jon. *Romanticism, Enthusiasm, and Regulation: Poetics and the Policing of Culture in the Romantic Period*. Oxford: Oxford University Press, 2003.

348 Bibliography

Meehan-Waters, Brenda. "Catherine the Great and the Problem of Female Rule." *Russian Review* 34, no. 3 (July 1975): 293–307.

Meinecke, Friedrich. *Historism: The Rise of a New Historical Outlook*. Translated by J. E. Anderson and H. D. Schmidt. London: Routledge and Kegan Paul, 1972.

Mellor, Anne K. "Frankenstein: A Feminist Critique." In *One Culture: Essays on Science and Literature*, edited by George Levine, 287–312. Madison: University of Wisconsin Press, 1987.

Merzliakov, A. F. "Rassuzhdenie o rossiiskoi slovesnosti v nyneshnem ee sostoianii." *Trudy Obshchestva liubitelei rossiiskoi slovesnosti*. Part 1 (1812): 53–110.

Mikhailov, A. V. *Obratnyi perevod*. Moscow: Iazyki russkoi kul'tury, 2000.

Mil'china, V. A. "Zapiski 'pikovoi damy.'" In *Vremennik Pushkinskoi komissii*, Vyp. 22, 136–42. Leningrad: Nauka, 1988.

Modzalevskii, B. L. "Poslanie k vel'mozhe A. S. Pushkina." In *Pushkin* by B. L. Modzalevskii, 399–410. Leningrad: Priboi, 1929.

———. "Pushkin i Lazhechnikov." In *Pushkin i ego sovremenniki: izbrannye trudy (1898–1928)*, 523–41. St. Petersburg: Iskusstvo-SPb, 1999.

Moretti, Franco. "Serious Century." In *The Novel*. Vol. 1, *History, Geography, and Culture*, edited by Franco Moretti, 364–400. Princeton: Princeton University Press, 2006.

Nazarova, L. N. "I. S. Turgenev v rabote nad 'Starymi portretami' (iz tvorcheskoi istorii)." *XVIII vek*, vyp. 7, 373–79. Moscow, Leningrad: Nauka, 1966.

Nemirovskii, I. V. *Tvorchestvo Pushkina i problema publichnogo povedeniia poeta*. St. Petersburg: Giperion, 2003.

Newlin, Thomas. *The Voice in the Garden: Andrei Bolotov and the Anxieties of Russian Pastoral*. Evanston, IL: Northwestern University Press, 2001.

Nikolai Mikhailovich, Grand Duke of Russia, ed. *Russkie portrety XVIII i XIX stoletii*. St. Petersburg: Izdatel'stvo Velikago Kniazia Nikolaia Mikhailovicha, 1905.

O'Bell, Leslie. "The Spirit of Derzhavin's Anacreontic Verse." In *Die Welt der Slaven* 29, no. 1 (1984): 62–87.

O'Connor, Frank. *The Mirror in the Roadway: A Study of the Modern Novel*. Freeport: Books for Libraries Press, 1970.

Orlando, Francesco. *Obsolete Objects in the Literary Imagination: Ruins, Relics, Rarities, Rubbish, Uninhabited Places, and Hidden Treasures*. New Haven: Yale University Press, 2006.

Orwin, Donna Tussing. *Tolstoy's Art and Thought, 1847–1880*. Princeton: Princeton University Press, 1993.

Ospovat, A. L. "Istoricheskii material i istoricheskie alliuzii v 'Kapitanskoi dochke.'" *Tynianovskii sbornik*, no. 10 (1998): 40–67.

Oxford English Dictionary. Second edition, 1989; online version March 2012.

Petrunina, N. N. "Dva zamysla Pushkina dlia 'Sovremennika' (K sporu mezhdu Pushkinym i Lazhechnikovym po povodu 'Ledianogo doma.'" *Russkaia literatura*, no. 4 (1966): 153–60.

———. *Proza Pushkina*. Leningrad: Nauka, 1987.

Phillips, Mark Salber. "Macaulay, Scott, and the Literary Challenge to Historiography." *Journal of the History of Ideas* 50, No. 1 (Jan.–Mar., 1989): 117–33.

———. *Society and Sentiment: Genres of Historical Writing in Britain, 1740–1820*. Princeton: Princeton University Press, 2000.

Pittock, Murray, ed. *The Reception of Sir Walter Scott in Europe*. London: Continuum, 2007.

Platt, Kevin M. F. *Terror and Greatness: Ivan and Peter as Russian Myths*. Ithaca: Cornell University Press, 2011.

Pocock, J. G. A. "Modes of Political and Historical Time in Early Eighteenth-Century England." In *Virtue, Commerce, and History: Essays on Political Thought and History, Chiefly in the Eighteenth Century* by J. G. A. Pocock, 91–102. Cambridge: Cambridge University Press, 1985.

Pogodin, M. P. "Pis'mo o russkikh romanakh." In *Severnaia lira na 1827 god*, edited by T. M. Gol'ts and A. L. Grishunin, 133–40. Moscow: Nauka, 1984.

Pogosian, Elena. "Uroki imperatritsy: Ekaterina II i Derzhavin v 1783 godu." In *"Na mezhe mezh Golosom i Ekhom": Sbornik statei v chest' Tat'iany Vladimirovny TSiv'ian*, edited by L. O. Zaionts, 241–68. Moscow: Novoe izdatel'stvo, 2007.

———. *Vostorg russkoi ody i reshenie temy poeta v russkom panegirike 1730–1762 gg*. Tartu: Tartu Ülikooli Kirjastus, 1997.

Polevoi, N. A. "Sochineniia Derzhavina." In *Literaturnaia kritika. Stat'i i retsenzii 1825–1842* by N. A. Polevoi and Ks. A. Polevoi, 136–94. Leningrad: Khudozhestvennaia literatura, 1990.

———. "Utro v kabinete znatnogo barina." *Moskovskii telegraf*, no. 3 (1830): 160–80.

Polnoe sobranie zakonov Rossiiskoi imperii s 1649 goda, Sobranie pervoe. 45 vols. St. Petersburg: II otdelenie Sobstvennoi Ego Imperatorskago Velichestva kantseliarii, 1830.

Polosina, A. N. "Frantsuzskie knigi XVIII veka iasnopolianskoi biblioteki—kak istochnik tvorchestva L. N. Tolstogo." Kandidatskaia diss., IMLI RAN, Moscow, 2008.

Proskurin, Oleg. *Poeziia Pushkina, ili podvizhnyi palimpsest*. Moscow: Novoe literaturnoe obozrenie, 1999.

Proskurina, Vera. *Creating the Empress: Politics and Poetry in the Age of Catherine II*. Boston: Academic Studies Press, 2011.

———. "Krylov i Ekaterina II: stikhotvorenie 'Umiraiushchaia koketka' v kontekste russkogo libertinazha." *Novoe literaturnoe obozrenie*, no. 45 (2000): 104–21.

———. *Mify imperii: Literatura i vlast' v epokhu Ekateriny II*. Moscow: Novoe literaturnoe obozrenie, 2006.

———. "Peterburgskii mif i politika monumentov: Petr Pervyi Ekaterine Vtoroi." *Novoe literaturnoe obozrenie*, no. 72 (2005): 103–32.

Pumpianskii, L. V. *Klassicheskaia traditsiia: Sobranie trudov po istorii russkoi literatury*. Moscow: Iazyki russkoi kul'tury, 2000.

Purdy, Daniel L. *The Tyranny of Elegance: Consumer Cosmopolitanism in the Era of Goethe.* Baltimore and London: Johns Hopkins University Press, 1998.

Pushkin, Aleksandr. *Kapitanskaia dochka.* Edited by Iu. G. Oksman. Moscow: Nauka, 1964.

———. *Polnoe sobranie sochinenii v shestnadtsati tomakh.* Moscow, Leningrad: Izdatel'stvo Akademii Nauk SSSR, 1937–59.

Pushkin, Alexander. *Complete Prose Fiction.* Translated by Paul Debreczeny. Stanford: Stanford University Press, 1983.

———. *Eugene Onegin.* Translated by James E. Falen. Carbondale: Southern Illinois University Press, 1990.

———. "The Queen of Spades." In *The Complete Works of Alexander Pushkin,* 9:201–232. Norfolk: Milner and Co. Ltd., 2001.

Pyliaev, M. I. *Zamechatel'nye chudaki i originaly.* Moscow: Interbuk, 1990.

Quilligan, Maureen. *The Language of Allegory: Defining the Genre.* Ithaca: Cornell University Press, 1979.

Rabkina, N. A. "Fakty, sobytiia, liudi. Istoricheskii prototip 'pikovoi damy.'" *Voprosy istorii,* no. 1 (January 1968): 213–16.

Radishchev, A. N. *Polnoe sobranie sochinenii.* Moscow, Leningrad: Izdatel'stvo Akademii Nauk SSSR, 1938.

Raeff, Marc. *Origins of the Russian Intelligentsia: Eighteenth-Century Nobility.* New York: Harcourt, Brace and World, 1966.

———. "Seventeenth-century Europe in Eighteenth-century Russia? (Pour prendre congé du dix-huitième siècle russe)." *Slavic Review* 41, no. 4 (1982): 611–19.

Ram, Harsha. *The Imperial Sublime: A Russian Poetics of Empire.* Madison: University of Wisconsin Press, 2006.

Randolph, John. *The House in the Garden: The Bakunin Family and the Romance of Russian Idealism.* Ithaca: Cornell University Press, 2007.

Rauser, Amelia. "Hair, Authenticity, and Self-Made Macaroni." *Eighteenth-Century Studies* 38, no. 1 (Fall 2004): 101–18.

Reill, Peter Hanns, and Ellen Judy Wilson, eds. *Encyclopedia of the Enlightenment.* New York: Facts On File, 1996.

Reiser, S. A. "Pushkin i memuary Kazanovy." In *Vremennik Pushkinskoi komissii,* 125–30. Leningrad: Nauka, 1979.

———. "Russkii bog." *Izvestiia AN SSSR: Otdelenie Literatury i Iazyka* 20, no. 1 (1961): 64–69.

Reitblat, A. I. *Chtenie v Rossii v XIX–nachale XX veka: annotirovannyi bibliograficheskii ukazatel'.* Moscow: Gos. biblioteka SSSR im. V.I. Lenina, 1992.

Repcheck, Jack. *The Man who Found Time: James Hutton and the Discovery of the Earth's Antiquity.* New York: Basic Books, 2009.

Reyfman, Irina. "Imagery of Time and Eternity in Eighteenth-Century Russian Poetry: Mikhail Murav'ev and Semen Bobrov." *Indiana Slavic Studies* 8 (1996): 99–114.

———. *Vasilii Trediakovsky: The Fool of the "New" Russian Literature.* Stanford: Stanford University Press, 1990.

Riasanovsky, Nicholas. *A Parting of Ways: Government and the Educated Public in Russia, 1801–1855.* Oxford: Oxford University Press, 1976.

Rigney, Anne. *The Afterlives of Walter Scott: Memory on the Move.* Oxford: Oxford University Press, 2012.

Ripp, Victor. *Turgenev's Russia: From Notes of a Hunter to Fathers and Sons.* Ithaca: Cornell University Press, 1980.

Roche, Daniel. *The Culture of Clothing: Dress and Fashion in the "Ancien Regime."* Cambridge: Cambridge University Press, 1997.

———. *A History of Everyday Things: The Birth of Consumption in France, 1600–1800.* Cambridge, New York: Cambridge University Press, 2000.

Rogger, Hans. *National Consciousness in Eighteenth-Century Russia.* Cambridge, MA: Harvard University Press, 1960.

Roosevelt, Priscilla. *Life on the Russian Country Estate: A Social and Cultural History.* New Haven: Yale University Press, 1995.

Rothschild, Emma. *Economic Sentiments: Adam Smith, Condorcet, and the Enlightenment.* Cambridge, MA: Harvard University Press, 2001.

Ruane, Christine. *The Empire's New Clothes: A History of the Russian Fashion Industry, 1700–1917.* New Haven: Yale University Press, 2009.

Ryleev, K. F. *Polnoe sobranie sochinenii.* Edited by A. G. Tseitlin. Moscow: Academia, 1934.

Sacks, Peter M. *The English Elegy: Studies in the Genre from Spenser to Yeats.* Baltimore: Johns Hopkins Press, 1985.

Safiullin, Ia. "Derzhavin v otsenke romantikov." In *G. Derzhavin. Istoriia i sovremennost'*, edited by Ia. Safiullin, 113–24. Kazan': Izdatel'stvo Kazanskogo universiteta, 1993.

Samuels, Maurice. *The Spectacular Past: Popular History and the Novel in Nineteenth-Century France.* Ithaca: Cornell University Press, 2004.

Sandler, Stephanie. *Distant Pleasures: Alexander Pushkin and the Writing of Exile.* Stanford: Stanford University Press, 1989.

Scarry, Elaine. *The Body in Pain: The Making and Unmaking of the World.* New York: Oxford University Press, 1985.

Schamschula, Walter. *Der russische historische Roman vom Klassizismus bis zur Romantik.* Meisenheim am Glan: Anton Hain, 1961.

Schapiro, Leonard. *Turgenev: His Life and Times.* Cambridge, MA: Harvard University Press, 1982.

Schneiders, Werner. "Aufklärungsphilosophien." In *Europäische Aufklärung(en). Einheit und nationale Vielfalt*, edited by Siegfried Jüttner and Jochen Scholbach, 1–17. *Studien zum Achtzehnten Jahrhundert* 14. Hamburg: Felix Meiner, 1992.

———, ed. *Lexikon der Aufklärung. Deutschland und Europa.* Munich: C. H. Beck, 1995.

Schönle, Andreas. *Architecture of Oblivion: Ruins and Historical Consciousness in Modern Russia*. DeKalb: Northern Illinois University Press, 2011.

———. "Mezhdu 'drevnei' i 'novoi' Rossiei: ruiny u rannego Karamzina kak mesto modernity." *Novoe literaturnoe obozrenie* 59 (2003): 125–41.

———. "Prostranstvennaia poetika Tsarskogo Sela v ekaterininskoi prezentatsii imperii." *Tynianovskii sbornik* 11 (2002): 51–66.

———. "Ruins and History: Observations on Russian Approaches to Destruction and Decay." *Slavic Review* 65, no. 4 (2006): 649–69.

———. *The Ruler in the Garden: Politics and Landscape Design in Imperial Russia*. Oxford: Peter Lang, 2007.

———, and Julia Hell, eds. *Ruins of Modernity*. Durham: Duke University Press, 2010.

Scott, Walter. *Waverley, or, 'Tis Sixty Years Since*. Oxford: Oxford University Press, 1986.

Sedgwick, Eve Kosofsky. "Tales of the Avunculate: Queer Tutelage in *The Importance of Being Earnest*." In *Tendencies* by Eve Kosofsky Sedgwick, 52–72. Durham: Duke University Press, 1993.

Seeley, Frank Friedeberg. *Turgenev: A Reading of His Fiction*. Cambridge: Cambridge University Press, 1991.

Serman, I. Z. "Derzhavin v novom veke." *Novoe literaturnoe obozrenie* 27 (1997): 54–67.

———. "Govoriashchaia zhivopis' v poezii Derzhavina." In *Khudozhestvennaia kul'tura XVIII veka: Materialy nauchnoi konferentsii*, edited by I. E. Danilova, 334–55. Moscow: Sovetskii khudozhnik, 1974.

———. "Literaturnaia pozitsiia Derzhavina." In *XVIII vek. Sbornik 8*, edited by P. N. Berkov et al., 56–75. Leningrad: Nauka, 1969.

Shaw, Harry E. *The Forms of Historical Fiction: Sir Walter Scott and His Successors*. Ithaca and London: Cornell University Press, 1983.

Shcheglov, Iurii. "Iz illiustratsii poeticheskoi izobretatel'nosti Derzhavina. 3. Igrovaia ritorika 'Felitsy.'" In *Shipovnik: Istoriko-filologicheskii sbornik k 60-letiiu Romana Davidovicha Timenchika*, edited by Iu. Leving, A. Ospovat, and Iu. Tsivian, 525–46. Moscow: Vodolei Publishers, 2005.

Shcherbatov, M. M. *O povrezhdenii nravov v Rossii kniazia M. Shcherbatova i puteshestvie A. Radishcheva*. S predisl. Iskandera. London: Trübner, 1858.

Shklovskii, Viktor. *Khod konia*. Moscow: Gelikon, 1923.

Shvidkovskii, D. O. *The Empress & the Architect: British Architecture and Gardens at the Court of Catherine the Great*. New Haven: Yale University Press, 1996.

Simmel, Georg. *Simmel on Culture: Selected Writings*. Edited by David Frisby and Mike Featherstone. London, Thousand Oaks, New Delhi: Sage Publications, 1997.

Smoliarova, Tat'iana. *Parizh 1928. Oda vozvrashchaetsia v teatr*. Moscow: Rossiiskii gosudarstvennyi gumanitarnyi universitet, 1999.

———. *Zrimaia lirika: Derzhavin*. Moscow: Novoe literaturnoe obozrenie, 2011.

Steele, Valerie. "The Revolution: Liberty, Equality and Antiquity." In *Paris Fashion: A Cultural History* by Valerie Steele, 41–54. Oxford; New York: Berg, 1998.

Stennik, Iu. *Pushkin i russkaia literatura XVIII veka.* St. Peterburg: Nauka, 1995.

———. "Stikhotvorenie A. S. Pushkina 'Mordvinovu' (k istorii sozdaniia)." *Russkaia literatura*, no. 3 (1965): 172–81.

Stephen, Leslie. "Sir Walter Scott." In *Hours in a Library* by Leslie Stephen, vol. 1, 186–229. New York and London: Knickerbocker Press, 1907.

Struck, Peter T. "Allegory and Ascent in Neo-Platonism." In *The Cambridge Companion to Allegory*, edited by Rita Copeland and Peter T. Struck, 57–70. Cambridge: Cambridge University Press, 2010.

Tartakovskii, A. G. *Russkaia memuaristika XVIII–pervoi poloviny XIX veka: ot rukopisi k knige.* Moscow: Nauka, 1991.

Tertz, Abram. *On Socialist Realism.* New York: Pantheon Books, 1960.

Thaden, Edward C. *The Rise of Historicism in Russia.* New York: Peter Lang, 1999.

Thyret, Isolde. *Between God and Tsar: Religious Symbolism and the Royal Women of Muscovite Russia.* DeKalb: Northern Illinois University Press, 2001.

Tiutchev, F. I. *Polnoe sobranie stikhotvorenii.* Leningrad: Sovetskii pisatel', 1987.

Todd, William Mills, III. *Fiction and Society in the Age of Pushkin: Ideology, Institutions, and Narrative.* Cambridge, MA: Harvard University Press, 1986.

Tolstoi, Lev. *Polnoe sobranie sochinenii v 90 tomakh.* Edited by V. G. Chertkov: Moscow, Leningrad: Gosudarstvennoe izdatel'stvo khudozhestvennoi literatury, 1928–58.

Tolstoy, Leo. *Childhood, Boyhood, Youth.* Translated by Rosemary Edmonds. New York: Penguin, 1964.

———. *War and Peace.* Translated by Aylmer Maude. New York, London: Norton & Co. 1996.

Tomashevskii, B. V. *Pushkin.* Moscow, Leningrad: Izdatel'stvo Akademii Nauk SSSR, 1961.

Toporov, Vladimir. *Peterburgskii tekst russkoi literatury: izbrannye trudy.* St. Petersburg: Iskusstvo, 2003.

Tosi, Alessandra. *Waiting for Pushkin: Russian Fiction in the Reign of Alexander I (1801–1825).* Amsterdam, New York: Rodopi, 2006.

Trediakovskii, V. K. *Izbrannye proizvedeniia.* Edited by L. I. Timofeev. Moscow, Leningrad: Sovetskii pisatel', 1963.

Treip, Mindele Anne. *Allegorical Poetics and the Epic: The Renaissance Tradition to "Paradise Lost."* Lexington: University of Kentucky Press, 1994.

Tscherny, Nadia. "Likeness in Early Romantic Portraiture." *Art Journal* 46, no. 3 (1987): 193–99.

Turgenev, A. I. *Khronika russkogo; Dnevniki, 1825–1826 gg.* Edited by M. I. Gillel'son. Moscow: Nauka, 1964.

Turgenev, Ivan. *Fathers and Sons.* Translated by Michael Katz. New York: Norton, 1996.

———. *The Jew and Other Stories.* Translated by Constance Garnett. London: William Heinemann, 1899.

———. *The Novels of Ivan Turgenev.* London: William Heinemann, 1896; Reprint, New York: AMS Press, 1970.

———. *Polnoe sobranie sochinenii i pisem v 28 tomakh.* Moscow: Nauka, 1964.

Tynianov, Iu. N. "Oda kak oratorskii zhanr." In *Poetika. Istoriia literatury. Kino* by Iu. N. Tynianov, 227–52. Moscow: Nauka, 1977.

———. "Promezhutok." In *Poetika. Istoriia literatury. Kino* by Iu. N. Tynianov, 168–95. Moscow: Nauka, 1977.

———. "Vopros o Tiutcheve." In *Arkhaisty i novatory* by Iu. N. Tynianov, 367–85. Munich: Wilhelm Fink Verlag, 1967.

Ungurianu, Dan. "*Ledianoi dom* Lazhechnikova i peterburgskii kanon (K voprosu o genezise peterburgskogo teksta." *Russian Literature* 51 (2002): 471–81.

———. *Plotting History: The Russian Historical Novel in the Imperial Age.* Madison: University of Wisconsin Press, 2007.

Uspenskii, B. A. "'Russkii bog': k istorii frazeologizma." In *Filologicheskie razyskaniia v oblasti slavianskikh drevnostei: relikty iazychestva v vostochnoslavianskom kul'te Mikoly Mirlikiiskogo* by B. A. Uspenskii, 119–22. Moscow: Izdatel'stvo Moskovskogo universiteta, 1982.

———, and V. M. Zhivov. "Tsar' i Bog." In *Izbrannye trudy* by B. A. Uspenskii, 110–218. Moscow: Gnozis, 1994.

Vainshtein, Ol'ga. *Dendi: Moda, literatura, stil' zhizni.* Moscow: Novoe literaturnoe obozrenie, 2005.

Vaiskopf, Mikhail. *Vo ves' logos: religiia Maiakovskogo.* Moscow, Jerusalem: Salamandra, 1997.

Vatsuro, V. E. "I. I. Dmitriev: Kommentarii." In *Pis'ma russkikh pisatelei XVIII veka,* edited by G. P. Makogonenko, 437–45. Leningrad: Nauka, 1980.

———. "K vel'mozhe." In *Pushkinskaia pora: sbornik statei* by V. E. Vatsuro, 179–216. St. Petersburg: Akademicheskii proekt, 2000.

———. "Pushkin i problemy bytopisaniia v nachale 1830kh godov." In *Pushkin: Issledovaniia i materialy,* edited by V. E. Vatsuro and M. P. Alekseev, 150–70. Leningrad: Nauka, 1969.

———, and M. I. Gillel'son, *Skvoz' "umstvennye plotiny": Ocherki o knigakh i presse pushkinskoi pory.* Moscow: Kniga, 1986.

Veselovskii, A. N. *V. A. Zhukovskii: Poeziia chuvstva i "serdechnogo voobrazheniia."* Moscow: Intrada, 1999.

Viazemskii, P. A. *Fon-Vizin.* St. Petersburg. V tipografii departamenta vneshnei torgovli, 1848.

———. "O Derzhavine." In *Polnoe sobranie sochinenii* by Petr Viazemskii, 1:15–21.

———. *Ostaf'evskii arkhiv kniazei Viazemskikh,* St. Petersburg: Tipografiia M. M. Stasiulevicha, 1899.

————. *Zapisnye knizhki, 1813–1848*. Edited by V. S. Nechaeva. Moscow: Izdatel'stvo Akademii Nauk SSSR, 1963.

Vigée-Le Brun, Elisabeth. *The Memoirs of Elisabeth Vigée-Le Brun*. Translated by S. Evans. Bloomington: Indiana University Press, 1989.

Vigel, F. F. *Zapiski*. Moscow: Zakharov, 2003.

Vinitskii, Il'ia. *Dom tolkovatelia: Poeticheskaia semantika i istoricheskoe voobrazhenie V. A. Zhukovskogo*. Moscow: Novoe literaturnoe obozrenie, 2006.

Vinogradov, V. V. *Etiudy o stile Gogolia*. Leningrad: Academia, 1926.

————. *Evoliutsiia russkogo naturalizma: Gogol' i Dostoevskii*. Leningrad: Academia, 1929.

————. "O 'Pikovoi dame.' Iz knigi 'Stil'' Pushkina.'" In *Izbrannye trudy. O iazyke khudozhestvennoi prozy* by V. V. Vinogradov, 256–83. Moscow: Nauka, 1980.

Vol'pert, L. I. *Pushkin v roli Pushkina: tvorcheskaia igra po modeliam frantsuzskoi literatury; Pushkin i Stendal'*. Moscow: Iazyki russkoi kul'tury, 1998.

Voltaire, and Catherine. *Voltaire and Catherine the Great; Selected Correspondence*. Edited by A. Lentin. Cambridge: Oriental Research Partners, 1974.

Wachtel, Andrew. *The Battle for Childhood: Creation of a Russian Myth*. Stanford: Stanford University Press, 1990.

————. "A Historical Character in Search of a Genre: Vadim of Novgorod and the Prehistory of Intergeneric Dialogue in Russia." In *An Obsession with History: Russian Writers Confront the Past* by Andrew Wachtel, 19–45. Stanford: Stanford University Press, 1994.

————. *An Obsession with History: Russian Writers Confront the Past*. Stanford: Stanford University Press, 1994.

————. "Rereading 'The Queen of Spades.'" *Pushkin Review* 3 (2000): 13–21.

Wallace, Miriam L., ed. *Enlightening Romanticism, Romancing the Enlightenment: British Novels from 1750 to 1832*. Farnham, England; Burlington, VT: Ashgate, 2009.

Wellbery, David. "The Transformation of Rhetoric." In *The Cambridge History of Literary Criticism. Volume 5: Romanticism*, edited by Marshall Brown, 185–202. Cambridge: Cambridge University Press, 2010.

White, Hayden. *Metahistory: The Historical Imagination in Nineteenth-Century Europe*. Baltimore: Johns Hopkins University Press, 1973.

Whittaker, Cynthia Hyla. *Russian Monarchy: Eighteenth-Century Rulers and Writers in Political Dialogue*. DeKalb: Northern Illinois University Press, 2003.

Williams, Raymond. *Keywords: A Vocabulary of Culture and Society*. Oxford: Oxford University Press, 1985.

Woloch, Alex. *The One vs. the Many: Minor Characters and the Space of the Protagonist in the Novel*. Princeton: Princeton University Press, 2003.

Wortman, Richard S. Review of *A Parting of Ways: Government and the Educated Public in Russia, 1801–1855*, by Nicholas V. Riasanovsky. *The Journal of Modern History* 50, no. 1 (1978): 176–78.

————. *Scenarios of Power: Myth and Ceremony in Russian Monarchy*, vol. 1: *From Peter the Great to the Death of Nicholas I*. Princeton: Princeton University Press, 1995.

Zapadov, V. A. "Problema literaturnogo servilizma i diletantizma i poeticheskaia pozitsiia G. R. Derzhavina." In *XVIII vek. Sbornik 16*, edited by A. M. Panchenko, 56–75. Leningrad: Nauka, 1989.

Zhivov, V. M. "Gosudarstvennyi mif v epokhu prosveshcheniia i ego razrushenie v Rossii kontsa XVIII–nachala XIX veka." In *Iz istorii russkoi kul'tury*, vol. 4, 657–83. Moscow: Shkola "Iazyki russkoi kul'tury," 1996.

————. *Ocherki istoricheskoi semantiki russkogo iazyka rannego novogo vremeni.* Moscow: Iazyki slavianskikh kul'tur, 2009.

Zholkovskii, Aleksandr. "Ochnye stavki s vlastitelem: iz istorii odnoi pushkinskoi paradigmy." In *Pushkinskaia konferentsiia v Stenforde 1999: Materialy i issledovaniia*, edited by A. L. Ospovat, David Bethea, N. G. Okhotin, and L. S. Fleishman, 366–401. Moscow: OGI, 2001.

Zil'bershtein, I. S., and V. A. Samkov, eds. *Sergei Diagilev i russkoe iskusstvo: stat'i, otkrytye pis'ma, interv'iu. Perepiska. Sovremenniki o Diagileve.* Moscow: Izobrazitel'noe iskusstvo, 1982.

Ziolkowski, Theodore. *Clio the Romantic Muse: Historicizing the Faculties in Germany.* Ithaca: Cornell University Press, 2004.

Zorin, A. L., N. N. Zubkov, and A. S. Nemzer. *Svoi podvig svershiv.* Moscow: Kniga, 1987.

Index

Page references in italics refer to illustrations.

Benjamin, Walter, 227, 325n50
Berdiaev, Nikolai, 307n18
Bestuzhev-Marlinskii, Alexander, 173,
190, 246, 317n39; on history as
commodity, 164–66, 171, 175, 180,
313n1
Bibikov, A. I., 158
Biblical imagery. *See* Christian imagery
Biron, Ernst Johann von, 181, 182,
185–86, 192
Bloch, Ernst, 280n20
Bobrov, Semen, 114, 118; "Hundred-
Year Song," 130–32; "Prognosticating Response," 131–33. *See also
under* science
body: and censorship, 202; empress's,
34, 42, 58–71, 73, 110–11, 290n31,
295n89; in Eriksen's portrait, 59–62,
295n89; history embodied by, 199–
202, 212, 229–37; vs. ideal archetype, 62–64; mutilated, 198–202; and
pain, 199–200; in "Queen of Spades,"
224, 229–37, 328n75; and spirit of
the age, 224; in Turgenev, 256; and
wigs, 217–18, 324n34. *See also*
fashion; mutilated bodies; sexuality
bogatyrs, 120
Boileau-Despréaux, Nicolas, 44
book trade, 221, 229. *See also* literary
market
Borovikovskii, Vladimir, 100, *101*,
104
Bossuet, Jacques, 305n97
boudoirs, 225–27, 232–35, 326n51,
326n55
Bourdaloue, Louis, 305n97
Bova, 56
Branitskaia, Countess A. V., 228–29,
230, 327n66
brigadiers, 256–57, 333n38, 333n40
Brompton, Richard, *230*
Brown, Marshall, 305n94

Buckler, Julie, 302n70, 303n79
Buffon, Comte de (Georges-Louis
Leclerc), 220
Bulgarin, Faddei, 175, 183; *Dimitrii the
Pretender*, 169; on historical novel as
window, 170, 172; and Scott, 177–
78, 190
bylina, 308n20
Byron, George Gordon, 6th Baron
(Lord Byron), 139, 310n46, 311n74

Callimachus, 284n16
Cameron, Charles, 301n64
Cameron Gallery, 96, 300n61
Captain's Daughter (*Kapitanskaia
dochka*; Pushkin), 194–204; allusions
to *House of Ice* in, 201, 320n81; and
censorship/patronage, 201–2,
312n82; documentary research vs.
fiction in, 167, 189, 196–98, 203–4,
320n70; folkloric discourse in, 195,
198; gallows in, 202–3, 320n83;
Gogol on, 197–98; history rendered
familiar and ordinary in, 194–96;
as ironic comment on Scott and
historical fiction, 179, 203–4; length
of, 203–4; national character in,
197–98; and poetics of recognition,
176–77, 198, 201–4, 321n84;
simplicity and "naked" style of, 194,
196–97, 320n75; temporality in,
194–95, 204; Tolstoy on, 196–97,
198; and "To the Grandee," 143; and
Turgenev, 265; violence and pain in,
193, 195, 199–202, 320n83. *See also
under* frenetic school; historical fiction; *House of Ice*; "mediocre hero";
narrators; readers; Scott; visuality
caricatures, 162, 178, 196, 197; in
"Queen of Spades," 232, 329n80; in
Turgenev, 241–42, 245, 248–49,
332n25

250, 323n17; and memory, 217–19, 221; as metonym for society, 208; under Paul I, 74, 209; under Peter I, 205–6, 207, 321n2; Pogodin on, 222–23; and portraiture, 15–18, 225–27; and "Queen of Spades," 17–18, 212, 225–38; and Romanticism, 210–11; Russian periodicals on, 6, 15–17, 210, 214–22; in Scott, 211; and temporality/historical time, 6, 15–17, 205–8, 211–12, 217–23, 228–33, 236–38; in Turgenev, 18, 212, 243, 250; and urban life, 205–8, 210, 216–18, 222–24, 324n31. *See also* body; commercialism; femininity; France; hairstyles; historicism; mimesis; Paris; readers; Scott; sedimentation; temporality; westernization; wigs

favorites. *See under* Catherine II

Fay, Elizabeth, 324n25

Felitsa cycle (Derzhavin), 34, 47–59, 63–70, 93, 100, 115, 288n16, 290n26, 292n52, 292n58, 296n96; *byt*/everyday life embodied by, 55; Catherine's opinion of, 295n83, 295n87; as "continued" allegory, 47–49, 54; as dialogue with Catherine, 35, 47, 49–50, 291n44; and empress's body, 58–59, 63–70; ethical entanglement in, 291n47; grandees satirized in, 50–52; ideal/archetypal merged with human particularity in, 54–58, 63–64, 71, 294n79; lists of idle amusements in, 51–52; Murza mask in, 49–50, 144; narrative mode in, 47, 49–56, 63, 70–71, 99; negation in, 50–51, 64, 70, 291n48; painting/portraiture in, 65–70; as precursor of novel and realism, 55–56; as private and personalized, 35–36; and Raphael, 66–68, 295n87;

and "Ruins," 98, 106; in Slovtsov, 127; speaker's complex relation to addressee in, 64–65, 295n83; speaker's multiplicity in, 51–52, 54; and "Tsarevich Khlor," 47–50, 54, 70; undermines odic genre boundaries, 51–53, 56–57, 291n51; visuality in, 63, 65–70

female rule: as defining feature of eighteenth century, 30–32, 286n4, 293n71; panegyric ode evolves in response to, 30–34, 288n15; and Peter I's reforms, 30, 286n1; and royal lineages, 41, 286n2; and succession laws, 30–31, 286n5; as supplanted by Paul, 86–87; Turgenev alludes to, 251. *See also* Catherine II; Elizabeth; femininity

femininity: and boudoirs, 225–26, 326n51, 326n55; and Catherine II, 68, 104, 113, 286n4, 329n75; as defining trait of eighteenth century (in "Queen of Spades"), 225–26, 326n52, 326n55, 328n71; and epic heroism, 120; and fashion, 207–8, 211; and Lazhechnikov, 190; and Lomonosov's synthesis of soul and body, 42. *See also* interiority; masculinity

Ferris, Ina, 171, 315n20

Festa, Lynn, 324n34

fiction. See *Captain's Daughter*; frenetic school; historical fiction; *House of Ice*; Hugo; novel; "Queen of Spades"; readers; realism; Scott; Tolstoy; Turgenev

Flaubert, Gustave, 226, 283n42

Flügel, J. C., 211, 323n17

folklore and folkloric language: in L'vov, 120–21; in Pushkin, 195, 198; as recipe for historical fiction, 179; in Scott, 194

Moscow Citizens," 85–90, 91, 92, 298n29; "Poor Liza," 318n48
Kavelin, K. D., 250
Kelly, Gary, 326n52
Kheraskov, Mikhail, 108, 195
Khodasevich, Vladislav: on Derzhavin, 55–56, 292n61, 293nn62–63; "Prim ladies," 266, 268–69, 271
Kireevskii, Ivan, 238, 246, 325n47; "Nineteenth Century," 223; on spirit of the age, 7, 165, 168, 223–24
Klein, Joachim, 287n13
Kliuchevskii, Vasilii, 330n9
Kniazhnin, Iakov, 195, 300n57
Kock, Paul de, 190
Komarov, Matvei, 221
Koselleck, Reinhart, 130, 279n13, 280n14, 306n4; on modernity and time, 116–17, 278n8, 281n25
Kozlov, Ivan: "To Walter Scott," 174–75, 317n33
Krafft, Georg Wolfgang, 194
Krylov, Ivan, 303n78, 328n74, 328n75; "Nights," 233–34
Kutuzov, Mikhail, 165
Kuznetskii most, 220, 322n10

Lampi, Giovanni Battista (the Elder), 228, *231*
landscape. *See* country estates
language. *See* folklore
Last Judgment, 126, 129–30
Law of Succession: under Paul I (1797), 31, 286n5; under Peter I (1722), 30–31
layers. *See* historical layers; palimpsest; sedimentation
Lay of Igor's Campaign, 300n57, 308n20
Lazhechnikov, Ivan: "My Acquaintance with Pushkin," 188–89. See also *House of Ice*

Lebrun, Élisabeth. *See* Vigée-Lebrun
Leibniz, Gottfried Wilhelm, 10
Lermontov, Mikhail, 18; *Hero of Our Time*, 211; "Reflection," 159
LeRoy, Charles, 17, 225, 226
Levitt, Marcus, 281n22, 286n8, 294n77
libertinage, 233–37, 328n74
lichnost', 158–60, 163. *See also* selfhood
Lieven, Princess Dorothea, 209
Likhachev, D. S., 304n87
literary aristocracy debates, 141, 306n7
literary market: expansion of, 6, 117, 141; and historical fiction, 166, 176, 179. *See also* book trade; commercialism
local color, 191, 203, 211
Loewen, Donald, 292n55
Lomonosov, Mikhail, 35–47, 108, 132, 142, 289n23, 290n30, 297n12, 322n6; configuration of panegyric space in, 36, 287n13, 289n21; vs. Derzhavin, 21, 27, 35–36, 48–49, 52–57, 63–66, 71, 288n18; and empress's body, 42, 63–66; equivalence in, 36–45, 49, 56, 294n79; heredity motif in, 40–43; vs. Karamzin, 87; vs. L'vov, 120; merges past and present, 38–39; Merzliakov on, 52–53; and neo-Platonism, 63, 294n75; and Pushkin, 139, 141, 144; and rapture, 48, 53, 65, 288n18; repetition combined with uniqueness in, 41–42; rhetorical abundance and disorder in, 44–45, 115; as Russian Pindar, 57; sacralization in, 37, 42, 289n24, 294n79; and subservience vs. independence, 70; synthesis in, 37–38, 40–45; and *tishina*, 39; and Trediakovskii, 331n11; unity in, 27, 42. *See also under* allegory; Anna; Catherine I; Catherine II; Elizabeth; historicism; Olympian imagery;

ruins, 96–98, 300n56; "text of," 112, 302n70, 303n79; triumphal arches in, 103, 165, 302n75. *See also* Catherine II

Turgenev, Alexander, 174, 175

Turgenev, Ivan, 15, 22, 143, 226, 238, 334n47; anecdote of Fomushka/Fimushka in, 249–52, 261, 265, 332nn23–25; character system in, 240–48, 330n6, 331n12, 333n34; and chronotope of arrival/intermittence, 261, 334n49; and country estates, 261–66; and detachment, 333n41; diminutives in, 248–50; family genealogy/generational belonging in, 240–43, 252–60, 330n4; and fashion, 18, 212, 250; and hesitation, 249, 257, 332n22; historicism in, 18–19, 240–66, 269–70, 331n12, 332n25; narrator's identity in, 243, 257, 259, 262–64; novels vs. short fiction of compared, 248; and portraiture, 18–19, 242–43, 248–51, 330n10; and Pushkin, 18, 241–42, 245–46, 265, 269–70, 326n52, 330n9; repoussoir in, 250–52; and Scott, 240–41; shows limitations of mimesis/historicism, 259–60; table of eighteenth-century characters in, 244; and Tolstoy, 252–59. *See also under* caricatures; character types; historical layers; narrators; nobility; nostalgia; serfdom; temporality; uncles
—Works: "Brigadier," 244, 256–60, 261, 333n40, 333n43; *Fathers and Children*, 240–42, 244, 245, 252, 264–66, 330nn4–6, 334n43; *Nest of the Gentry*, 244, 245; "Old Portraits," 244, 263–64, 269, 334n54; "Peasant Proprietor Ovsiannikov," 244; "Phantoms," 244; "Quiet Spot," 244;

"Raspberry Spring," 244, 262–63; *Smoke*, 244, 245–46, 331n13, 331n17; *Sportsman's Sketches*, 244, 259, 261–63; "Three Portraits," 18–19, 244; "Unfortunate Girl," 244, 253–56; *Virgin Soil*, 244, 249–52, 261, 265, 332nn23–24

Turkish campaign. *See* Russo-Turkish Wars

turn of the century (1800): in Bobrov, 130–33; in L'vov, 118–21, 307n11; odes celebrate, 114–24, 306n3; in Radishchev, 121–24. *See also under* ode

Tynianov, Iurii, 273–74, 288n19, 292n61, 293n62

types. *See* character types

udal'stvo, 120, 307n17. *See also* heroism

uncles (in fiction), 239–45, 253, 260, 263, 312n1, 330n6, 331n11

urban life: and fashion, 205–8, 210, 216–18, 221–24, 261, 324n31; in frenetic school, 189, 191; in *House of Ice*, 180–81; in "Queen of Spades," 224–26. *See also* Paris; Saint Petersburg; street-fairs

Uspenskii, Boris, 215, 289n24, 307n11

Uvarov, Sergei, 214

Vaiskopf, Mikhail, 335n1

Valaam Monastery, 125

Vatsuro, Vadim, 142

Velázquez, Diego Rodriguez de Silva, 293n72

Venus, 34, 95, 98, 104, 303n78

verisimilitude: Barthes on, 168–69; in *Captain's Daughter*, 201; as central feature of historical fiction, 167–70, 314n9; defined, 167–68, 314n10; and *House of Ice*, 188–90, 192–93, 199; and *pravdopodobie*, 167–68; and